To: McKendree
From: Franklin
Date: 11-28-10

We pray your marriage will bring you great JOY... all because of Him!

Presented to

_____

From

_____

_____

date

COMPLETE GUIDE TO

The FIRST FIVE

YEARS *of* MARRIAGE

GENERAL EDITORS

PHILLIP J. SWIHART, Ph.D. & WILFORD WOOTEN, L.M.F.T.

TYNDALE HOUSE PUBLISHERS, INC., CAROL STREAM, ILLINOIS

Complete Guide to the First Five Years of Marriage

A Focus on the Family book published by
Tyndale House Publishers, Carol Stream, Illinois 60188

Focus on the Family and the accompanying logo and design are federally registered trademarks of Focus on the Family, Colorado Springs, CO 80995.

TYNDALE and Tyndale's quill logo are registered trademarks of Tyndale House Publishers, Inc.

All Scripture quotations, unless otherwise indicated, are taken from the *Holy Bible, New International Version®*. NIV®. Copyright © 1973, 1978, 1984 by International Bible Society. Used by permission of Zondervan Publishing House. All rights reserved.

Scripture quotations marked (AMP) are taken from *The Amplified Bible*, Copyright © 1954, 1958, 1962, 1964, 1965, 1987 by The Lockman Foundation. All rights reserved. Used by permission. (www.Lockman.org)

Some names and details of certain case studies in this book have been changed to protect the privacy of the individuals involved. The events and underlying principles, however, have been conveyed as accurately as possible.

Cover photograph copyright © by Michael A. Keller/Zefa/Corbis. Cover spine photographs of couple hugging and money © by Photos.com. Cover spine photograph of couple kissing © by Photodisc/Getty Images. Back cover photograph of rings on heart by Creative Studio Heinemann/Getty Images. Back cover photograph of couple © by Bananastock/Jupiter Images. All rights reserved.

Cover designed by Jennifer Ghionzoli

Interior photography
Jeff Lane: 7, 37, 71, 105, 153, 191, 223, 277, 307, 329, 389
Tracy Watkins and Jon Collins: xi

Library of Congress Cataloging-in-Publication Data
Complete guide to the first five years of marriage : launching a lifelong, successful relationship / by the counselors of Focus on the Family; Wilford Wooten, Phillip J. Swihart, general editors.
   p. cm.
  "A Focus on the Family book."
  ISBN-13: 978-1-58997-041-0
  ISBN-10: 1-58997-041-1
 1. Marriage. 2. Marriage—Religious aspects—Christianity. I. Wooten, Wilford, 1945- II. Swihart, Phillip J. III. Focus on the Family (Organization)
  HQ734.C643 2006
  248.8'44—dc22

                 2006009641

Printed in the United States of America
2 3 4 5 6 7 8 9 / 11 10 09 08 07

Contents

Introduction: Why Are the First Five Years So Important? 1

PART 1: GETTING TO KNOW EACH OTHER

How Well Do I Need to Know My Spouse? 9

How Honest Do We Have to Be? 14

How Can I Get Used to Being Two Instead of One? 17

Should I Tell My Spouse About My Past? 21

How Can I Get My Spouse to Open Up? 24

How Can I Understand My Spouse's Personality? 27

How Can I Adjust to My Spouse's Personality? 31

What Can I Do About My Spouse's Irritating Habits? 34

PART 2: EXPECTATIONS

Why Isn't Marriage the Way I Thought It Would Be? 39

Are Other People's Marriages Like This? 42

Why Isn't My Wife the Person I Thought She Was? 45

Why Isn't My Husband the Person I Thought He Was? 48

Why Isn't My Wife More Like Mom? 51

Why Isn't My Husband More Like Dad? 54

Why Isn't My "Blended" Marriage Blending? 57

Did I Marry the Wrong Person? 60

How Can I Change My Spouse? 63

Do I Have to Settle for Less? 66

PART 3: ROLES

What Does It Mean to Be a Wife? 73

What Does It Mean to Be a Husband? 77

How Should We Divide Up the Chores? 80

Who Should Take Care of the Kids? 83

Who Should Earn the Money? 87

What Does It Mean to Be the Spiritual Leader? 92

What If My Spouse Won't Take the "Right" Role? 96
What Roles Should We Have in a "Blended" Family? 100

PART 4: MONEY

Why Does My Spouse Spend So Much? 107
Do We Have to Have a Budget? 111
How Much Should We Spend? 114
How Much Should We Save? 117
How Much Should We Give? 120
How Can We Stay Out of Debt? 123
How Can We Get Out of Debt? 127
How Can We Cut Our Expenses? 131
How Can We Survive Unemployment? .136
Should We Buy a House? 140
What Investments Should We Make? 146
How Far Ahead Do We Need to Plan? 149

PART 5: SEX

What About Birth Control? 155
How Often Is Normal? 158
What If We Don't Like the Same Things? 161
Are We Doing It Right? 164
What Does He Want from Me? 168
What Does She Want from Me? 171
Where Did Our Sex Life Go? 174
What If My Spouse Is Using Pornography? 178
How Can We Have Sex When Kids Are in the House? 181
How Can We Put Our Sexual Pasts Behind Us? 184
What If We Need Help? 187

PART 6: COMMUNICATION

Why Won't My Spouse Talk to Me? 193
Why Won't My Spouse Leave Me Alone? 196
Why Don't We Speak the Same Language? 199
Why Does My Spouse Keep Hurting My Feelings? 202
How Can We Make Time to Talk? 206

How Can We Talk About Feelings? 209

How Should We Talk About Sensitive Issues? 212

How Can I Start a Conversation? 216

How Can We Communicate Without Talking? 219

PART 7: RESOLVING CONFLICT

Is It Okay to Fight? 225

How Do Other Couples Handle Conflict? 229

Why Does My Spouse Avoid Conflict? .233

Why Does My Spouse Overreact? 236

How Can We Work Out Disagreements? 239

How Can We Make Decisions Together? 244

How Can We Handle Racial and Cultural Differences? 247

How Should We Handle Friendships with Others? 252

When Should We Agree to Disagree? 255

What If We Have a Lot of Unresolved Conflicts? 258

What If an Argument Gets Out of Control? 260

Do I Have to Forgive My Spouse? 263

How Can I Get My Spouse to Forgive Me? 266

What If the Same Conflicts Keep Coming Up? 270

What If My Spouse Abuses Me? 273

PART 8: SPIRITUAL ISSUES

How Can Faith Keep Us Together?. 279

What If We Don't Like the Same Church? 282

Do We Have to Pray Together? 285

What Does a Christ-centered Home Look Like? 288

How Can I Help My Spouse Grow Spiritually? 292

How Can We Serve God Together? 296

What If My Spouse Seems to Be Losing His or Her Faith? 299

What If My Spouse Isn't a Christian? 304

PART 9: IN-LAWS

What Do I Owe My In-laws? 309

How Should We Handle the Holidays? .312

How Can I Cut My Spouse's Apron Strings? 315

What If the In-laws Aren't Christians? 320
What If an In-law Tries to Run Our Lives? 323
What If an In-law Doesn't Accept Me? 326

PART 10: CHILDREN

Do Children Really Change Everything? .331
When Should We Have Children, and How Many? 334
Is It Okay Not to Have Kids? 338
What If I Want Children, But My Spouse Doesn't? 342
Why Can't We Have Children? 345
How Can a Doctor Help Us Conceive? 348
What About Adoption? 351
How Will Pregnancy Affect Us? 355
What's Childbirth Really Like? 359
What Can We Do About Postpartum Depression? 362
What If Our Child Has Special Needs? 365
What If We Disagree over How to Raise the Kids? 370
How Can We Get a Break from the Kids? 374
How Can We Help Our Kids Grow Spiritually? 377
How Can We Make Sure Our Kids Succeed? 381
Should We Put Our Child in Day Care? .385

PART 11: STICKING WITH IT

Are We Falling Out of Love? 391
How Can We Keep Romance Alive? 394
How Can We Avoid Infidelity? 397
How Can We Keep from Drifting Apart? 400
How Can We Make It Through a Medical Crisis? 403
What If My Spouse Needs Psychological Help? 407
Is It Ever Too Late for a Marriage? 410
What About Marriage Counseling? 414
What Makes a Marriage Last? 417

Recommended Resources 421
Notes 423
Index 427

The Authors

Back row (left to right): Glenn Lutjens, James Groesbeck, Mitch Temple, Rob Jackson, James Vigorito

Middle row (left to right): Daniel Huerta, Amy Swierczek, Betty Jordan, Romie Hurley, Sheryl DeWitt, Sandra Lundberg

Front row (left to right): Phillip J. Swihart (General Editor), Gail Schra, Lon Adams, Sam Kennedy, Wilford Wooten (General Editor)

Not shown: Joann Condie

About the Authors

LON ADAMS, M.A., L.M.F.T.

Lon is the husband (for 45 years) of Linda, the dad of their three kids, and grandfather to 13. He's been counseling since 1978, when he began his internship at his church in Southern California. He's a graduate of Long Beach State College in social sciences, and Cal State, Northridge, where he received his master's degree in educational psychology. He has served as a men's group leader and mentor for the past 12 years, and also works with families who struggle with substance abuse addiction. He's been on the staff of the Focus on the Family Counseling Department since 1985.

JOANN CONDIE, R.N., M.S., L.P.C.

Joann is a licensed professional counselor and registered nurse who specializes in treating sexual addiction and sexual dysfunction. In addition to speaking and training professionals nationally, Joann is a counselor at Focus on the Family and maintains a private practice in Colorado Springs.

SHERYL DEWITT, L.M.F.T., L.M.F.C.C.

The late Sheryl DeWitt was the Senior Fellow for Family Life Studies at Focus on the Family Institute and a counselor for Focus on the Family. She was in private practice for over 17 years, working with individuals, couples, and families, and taught drug education programs in the public school system. She earned her master's degree in clinical-community psychology at California State University, Fullerton, and her bachelor's degree in psychology at Christian Heritage College. A licensed marriage and family therapist in the state of Colorado, she was also a licensed marriage, family, and child counselor in the state of California. She was married for 16 years and had two sons and one daughter.

JAMES GROESBECK, L.C.S.W., L.M.F.T.

James is a life coach, teacher, and counselor. He is the president of CoachMe International, Inc. and holds advanced degrees from the University of Michigan and the University of Colorado. His focus is marriage and relationship development and encouraging "twentysomethings" in their personal lives with Christ. James lives in Monument, Colorado, with his wife, Carol. They have two children and four grandchildren. James has been on the Focus counseling staff for three years.

DANIEL HUERTA, M.S.W., L.C.S.W.

Daniel is a bicultural and bilingual licensed clinical social worker. He has been married to his wife, Heather, for eight years; they have two children. Daniel has a bachelor's degree in psychology from the University of Colorado and a master's of social work degree from the University of Denver. He has been in the counseling field for 10 years as a volunteer counselor, school social worker, crisis counselor, mentor program coordinator, therapist, and mental health intern. Currently a therapist specializing in areas affecting children, adolescents, and young adults, he also provides counseling services over the telephone at Focus on the Family. In addition, he provides face-to-face counseling services for employees of Focus on the Family and serves on the Mental Health Association board.

ROMIE HURLEY, L.P.C., N.C.C.

Romie, a counselor for Focus on the Family, is a nationally certified licensed professional counselor. She has been in private practice in Texas and Colorado since 1988, specializing in marriage counseling, depression, communication, and women's issues.

ROB JACKSON, M.S., L.P.C., L.M.H.C., N.C.C.

Rob has provided professional counseling through his private practice since 1991. He offers workshops, seminars, and intensives for individuals, couples, and families. Having earned a master of science degree in clinical psychology in 1986, he is a licensed professional counselor in Colorado and Mississippi and a licensed mental health counselor in Washington. A national board certified counselor, he is a member of the American Association of Christian Counselors. In addition to serving as an adjunct professor for a seminary and an instructor at the university and high school levels, he is a licensed and ordained minister and deacon. Married in 1987, Rob and his wife, Renee, live with their two children in Colorado Springs.

BETTY JORDAN, R.N., M.A., L.P.C.

Betty graduated with a B.S. in nursing from Ball State University, completed two years at Lincoln Christian College, and received a master's degree in human development counseling from Sangamon State University. She is credentialed as a licensed professional counselor in Texas and Colorado, and as a registered nurse in Colorado. She has had supervisory, teaching, and intense psychotherapy experience in various settings including hospital, clinic, mental health center, and private practice. Her areas of expertise include individual, group, family, and marital therapy as well as conducting crisis evaluations. She is currently employed at Focus on the Family in the Counseling Department.

SAM KENNEDY, M.A., L.M.F.T.

Sam is a veteran of 16 years as a counselor at Focus on the Family. He also served for 11 years on the staff of a residential treatment center for troubled boys, and another 10 years as a pastor. He earned his bachelor's degree at Pasadena College and his master's degree at Azusa Pacific University. Married for 29 years to Jean Ann, also a family therapist, he has three grown children.

SANDRA LUNDBERG, PSY.D.

Sandra Lundberg received her doctorate in clinical psychology from Rosemead School of Psychology, Biola University in La Mirada, California. She is a licensed psychologist in Colorado, where she lives with her husband and two children. Having worked in a variety of inpatient and outpatient settings, she thoroughly enjoys helping couples and families. At the time this book was written, she was a staff psychologist for Focus on the Family as well as maintaining a private practice.

GLENN LUTJENS, M.A., L.M.F.T.

Glenn Lutjens is a licensed marriage and family therapist in the Focus on the Family Counseling Department and private practice. He has a master's degree in clinical psychology with a specialization in marriage, family, and child counseling from Rosemead School of Psychology. Glenn and his wife, Elizabeth, live with their three children in Colorado Springs.

GAIL SCHRA, M.S.W., L.C.S.W.

Gail is a telephone counselor in the Focus on the Family Counseling Department, where he has worked for three years. He has thirty years of experience as a clinician and administrator in community mental health and four years of experience as a U.S. Army social work officer in psychiatric and medical settings.

He received a bachelor's degree in psychology from Philips University and his master's degree in social work from Oklahoma University.

AMY SWIERCZEK

Amy, a former employee of the Focus on the Family Counseling Department, is the author of many inspirational articles. She is also the illustrator of the children's science book series Alphabet Science.

PHILLIP J. SWIHART, PH.D. (GENERAL EDITOR)

Phil is Director of Counseling Services and Community Relations for the Counseling Department at Focus on the Family. He holds a Ph.D. in clinical psychology from Purdue University and a master's degree from the University of California, Los Angeles. In addition to being in private practice as a clinical psychologist, he has served as an assistant professor at California State University, Northridge; Clinical Psychologist and Executive Director at the Center for Mental Health in Montrose, Colorado; Executive Director of the Ray Foundation, Denver; Executive Director of the Boulder County United Way, Boulder, Colorado; Division Director of the Pikes Peak Mental Health Center, Colorado Springs; and Psychologist at the Rocky Mountain Healthcare Brain Injury Program in Colorado Springs. He has been married for 36 years to Linda; they have three adult children.

MITCH TEMPLE, M.S., L.M.F.T.

Mitch serves as Lead Manager over Marriage Programs at Focus on the Family, where he is responsible for marriage-related programs, broadcasts, Web sites, magazine articles, and resource development. He also conducts three-day intensives nationwide for couples in crisis. He has served in churches as a singles, family, pulpit, and counseling minister for a total of 23 years. For over 10 years Mitch was an adjunct professor at a Christian university, specializing in crisis, business, and marriage and family-related issues. He also has clinical experience in working with statewide addiction programs. He served as an administrator, instructor, and co-founder for a ministry training school and seminary. A licensed marriage and family therapist, he has been in private practice and is a clinical Member of the American Association of Marriage and Family Therapists and the American Association of Christian Counselors. Mitch has been married to his wife, Rhonda, for 23 years. They have three children.

James Vigorito, Ph.D.

James has been licensed as a psychologist and listed on the National Register of Health Service Providers in Psychology for over 25 years. He is a sex offense-specific evaluator and treatment provider in the state of Colorado, and served on the Psychology Augmenting Panel of the Colorado Mental Health Grievance Board from 1995 to 1998. After receiving his doctorate in psychology from Yale University in 1978, he was Director of Crime Victim Assistance for the Hamden (Connecticut) Police Department. Before coming to the Counseling Department at Focus on the Family in 2000, he worked in the adolescent unit of South Florida State Hospital, at Christian Counseling Services of Fort Lauderdale, Florida, and at Christian Counseling Ministries of Buena Vista, Colorado. He has been married for 24 years to his wife, Patricia; they are the parents of two adult children.

Wilford Wooten, M.S.W., L.M.F.T., L.C.S.W.
(General Editor)

Wilford is Senior Director of the Counseling Department at Focus on the Family, where he has served for 13 years. Before coming to Focus he served in the army for 24 years as a social work officer. With over 35 years of experience working with individuals, couples, and families, he sees the first five years of marriage as critical. He has a master of social work degree and is licensed as a marriage and family therapist and clinical social worker. He has two sons and six grandchildren, and has been married to Joan for 39 years.

Acknowledgments

We appreciate the monumental editing needed for a volume encompassing the work of so many diverse authors, which was provided by John Duckworth, Senior Book Producer, Focus on the Family. We also wish to recognize our colleague Aarin Hovanec for her perceptive observations and comments. In addition, we're thankful for Sharon Manney's technical assistance in the preparation of this manuscript.

Introduction: Why Are the First Five Years So Important?

When it comes to the Indianapolis 500, it may be difficult to predict which lap will be most critical. But in a marriage, the first five years are central. That's when key adjustments are made and expectations are tested.

Take the experience of a young woman who "ran away from home" just two months after her wedding. She told Focus on the Family her story 10 years later.

"I've never thanked you for the way your ministry touched me 10 years ago. My husband and I had only been married two months when I panicked and felt that I just couldn't handle the change . . . so I packed my bags, called my pastor's wife to tell her I was leaving, and took off to 'escape my marriage.'

"As I was driving away from home in desperation and frustration, I turned on the radio. The *Focus on the Family* program was airing and you were interviewing a lady with a powerful testimony of how her own marriage had fallen apart . . . [and] how God had put it back together. At that precise moment, five miles out of town, I pulled over and broke down sobbing. The Lord dealt with me there in the car, and I turned around and went back home to my husband. Your ministry saved me from making a huge mistake. Thank you."

How you deal with the large and small crises of your marriage during the first five years sets important patterns for the future. That's true whether you're a woman or a man, and whether you tend to run in panic or stay and bury your feelings. Researchers have found consistently that those first years uniquely predict which marriages are likely to flourish and which may die an early death.

Researchers have found consistently that those first years uniquely predict which marriages are likely to flourish and which may die an early death.

Dr. Ted Huston, commenting on a 2001 study, stated that "couples' newlywed marriages and changes in their union foreshadow" the viability of their marriage—which will become evident after a few more years. "Disillusionment—as reflected in an abatement of love, a decline in overt affection, a lessening of the conviction that one's spouse is responsive, and an increase in ambivalence—distinguishes couples headed for divorce from those who establish a stable, marital bond."[1]

In other words, those first five years can be a time of rapid personal and relational growth—or a period of disappointment and deterioration.

BLISSED OUT OR STRESSED OUT?

Most marriages start with the delight of "being in love" and honeymoon excitement. The question is what happens next. Does bliss lead to adjustment, compromises, and learning to really love another person who may have very different needs and expectations? Or does it give way to poorly handled conflict, power struggles, and deepening frustration and resentment?

> Most marriages start with the delight of "being in love" and honeymoon excitement. The question is what happens next.

One young woman put it this way about the first year of her marriage: "I thought the first year would be wonderful. It was hell." She was just beginning to have a glimmer of hope that she and her husband would crawl out of that hole.

For many couples, those first years are a period of high expectations and severe disappointments. For the most mature, those years may be pleasant, even blissful. But none escape without challenges. Plastered-over differences begin to crack through. Contrasts that seemed so intriguing and attractive during a dating relationship can turn irritating and annoying when you live with them 24/7.

During those first few years, people "get naked" in more ways than one. And physical nakedness can be much less revealing than many other kinds.

Even in marriages that end up thriving, marital stressors may be—or at least seem to be—more intense during the first five years than later. Financial problems, for instance, challenge so many young couples in the first few years. So do schedules; a newly-married schoolteacher creating lesson plans for the first time may have a husband who sells insurance 50 to 60 hours a week. If they feel as if they never see each other, it's because they never do.

Trying to agree on priorities is stressful for new spouses, too. What purchases should they make? What should they forgo? Where should they live? Should they buy a house or rent an apartment? Just finding out what the other thinks is normal to spend on clothes or hunting trips can be enlightening—in a very negative way.

Other stressors include getting used to the in-laws. Discovering what your mate's family is really like can be a shock.

So is finding that neither of you seems to have any conflict management skills. As one comedian noted, "My wife and I never fight; we just have moments of intense fellowship." Instead of dealing constructively with the inevitable conflicts and disagreements found in any marriage, you may quickly devolve into blaming, yelling, and withdrawing—a toxic cocktail that can send a new marriage spiraling downward.

And then there's sex. Whatever happened to the glorious expectations you had in that wonder-world of dating? It may only take a few months of marital reality for the fantasies of "true love" and sexual excitement to clash with the disappointments of sharing a bed with another imperfect person who's sometimes tough to like, let alone love.

> During those first few years, people "get naked" in more ways than one.

For some, sexual boredom sets in during those first five years. The adventure and mystery are gone. As one wife put it, "As soon as the honeymoon was over, he went back to football games on TV and working on his 'classic' Chevy in the garage. He wasn't interested in talking. He just wanted sex—several times a week. That was it. There was no real intimacy at all. We just became roommates."

When that occurs, the question, "Whatever happened to foreplay?" becomes more insistent. Secret thoughts like, *He thinks he's turning me on by kissing my ears, but I hate having my ears kissed!* begin to multiply. Declarations such as, "What a wonderful lover I married!" disappear.

Another frequent stressor for many recently married couples is pregnancy— and the joys and strains of parenting. Trying to learn a whole new skill set is hard enough, but it's much harder when you're desperate for a few more hours of sleep. Even spouses with more than the usual maturity find themselves unusually irritable and hard to get along with.

The spiritual dimension of your relationship can be a point of contention early in your marriage, too. These years often form fertile ground for spiritual attack by an enemy who would love to destroy a relationship that God has blessed as holy.

For example, a husband may complain, "She sure isn't the woman of Proverbs 31!" A wife may say, "He's not even close to the 'spiritual leader' a husband ought to be!" Spiritual differences that were ignored or minimized during the idealism of courtship can become sources of serious conflict after a year or two of marriage.

So can the question of where and how to worship. What kind of church will you attend? If you have a child, will you raise him or her as a Presbyterian, Nazarene, Southern Baptist, Catholic, or something else? What about baptizing him or her? Many couples didn't discuss these questions when they were dating—resulting in early-marriage conflicts that may leave lasting scars in the relationship.

A GUIDE TO WORKING IT OUT

Many of the challenges of the first five years stem from distorted expectations. We live in a fast-food culture with a sense of entitlement to having everything happen on demand. But marriage doesn't work that way.

The apostle Paul advised Christians to "work out your salvation with fear and trembling" (Philippians 2:12). As radio Bible teacher Alistair Begg has noted, we need to do the same in our marriages. Many spouses are blindsided by the complexities of married life, having assumed they instantly and naturally know all they need to know about making a relationship work. Begg suggests that we should expect to work out the marriage relationship "with fear and trembling" rather than being cocky and deluded by the notion that it will all come easily.

> Many of the challenges of the first five years stem from distorted expectations. We live in a fast-food culture with a sense of entitlement to having everything happen on demand. But marriage doesn't work that way.

This is a book about working things out—trembling or otherwise. In the pages to follow you'll find answers to questions commonly asked by recently married couples. You'll probably find some issues you're struggling with. It's our hope and prayer that this book will be a rich source of help and encouragement on your journey through the partnership called marriage.

You can read this book from beginning to end, but you don't have to. You don't even have to read the answers in order. Take it down from your shelf when you're wrestling with a dilemma.

There's another distinctive to this volume, too. The many authors who've contributed have a working relationship with Focus on the Family. Most are professional staff members with Focus on the Family's counseling department. All are committed Christians and highly qualified, licensed mental health, marriage, and family therapists with many years of combined experience in working with thousands of couples and individuals across America.

The early years of marriage are a special adventure. As you explore your new partnership, explore this book, too. We believe you'll find it to be a thought-provoking source of creative solutions for meeting the challenges of your first five years together.

—Wilford Wooten and Phillip J. Swihart
General Editors

Part 1:
Getting to Know Each Other

How Well Do I Need to Know My Spouse?

When it comes to creating closeness in marriage, honesty is essential. But should you and your spouse know everything about each other?

What if you don't like what your spouse has to say about his or her past? And if there are secrets between you, will that lead to mistrust, doubt—even divorce?

When the two of you are vulnerable and transparent, it helps each of you understand where the other is coming from—which cultivates patience and compassion. But sometimes "letting it all hang out" can hurt a relationship. Where should you draw the line?

To help you know what kinds of information are really necessary, here are nine questions you *do* need to ask your spouse.

1. *"How were you raised?"*

There's no greater influence on your spouse than the way he or she grew up. Ask: "How did you get along with your mother and father? Were your growing-up years pleasant? Hurtful? What did you like about the way you were raised? What didn't you like? How do you think childhood may have shaped your views of the opposite sex, yourself, and intimacy (emotional and physical)? Have you dealt with any pain from the past? If so, how? If not, are you planning to do so?"

One wife discovered how valuable this kind of conversation can be. "Understanding that Brett and his mother didn't get along gave me some insight into our relationship," she said. "Brett's mother always criticized him and made him feel worthless. If he didn't please her, she would withdraw for days to punish him. Learning how his mom approached him and prefacing my confrontation by telling him I love him and I am not going anywhere but that I just want to resolve our issue, has helped a lot. Before I understood his fear of me abandoning him like his mom did, whenever I confronted him he would internalize everything so as not to upset me for fear I would leave. This never accomplished anything. Now he's willing to speak his mind with me."

> ॐ
> Sometimes "letting it all hang out" can hurt a relationship. Where should you draw the line?
> ॐ

Understanding your spouse in this way helps you not to take it personally when old patterns cause problems. It also helps you work together to overcome them.

2. *"How would you describe your relationship with God?"*

For Christians, marriage is a total commitment of two people to the Lord and to each other. It's a partnership intended to allow spouses to be themselves fully, to help refine each other, and to encourage each other to become the people God created them to be. For this union to be as successful as the Lord designed it to be, you need to understand how much you and your partner have in common when it comes to faith.

3. *"How do you deal with finances?"*

Tammy complained to her sister, "Larry grew up in a family where his mother took care of all the finances. She paid the bills and decided how the money was to be spent. I'm not good with finances and don't want that responsibility. I assumed that the man was responsible for the budget in the household."

> For this union to be as successful as the Lord designed it to be, you need to understand how much you and your partner have in common when it comes to faith.

Larry and Tammy needed to discuss how money was to be handled in their house. Both had come into marriage with different expectations but hadn't talked about them.

When they finally sat down and discussed finances, they decided Larry would be in charge of paying the bills because he seemed to have been gifted with financial wisdom. They mapped out a budget and pledged that before any big purchases were made, they'd agree on them together.

4. *"How do you see the roles of husband and wife?"*

"My mom was a stay-at-home mother," Quinn said. "She took care of the house and the kids. When Kathy went back to work, we would fight all the time because she didn't take care of the house like she should."

Kathy saw things differently: "Our finances were tight, so I wanted to go back to work. But he still expects that I cook, clean, and do all the caretaking of the house. He believes that's the woman's job. I think we should share the chores because we're both working. His view of our roles is much more traditional than how I feel is best for the both of us."

It's important to find out how your spouse thinks husband-wife roles should play out in your household, and how those roles might change during the seasons of your marriage. In the case of Quinn and Kathy, they decided that while she worked they would share chores—but when she was able to stay home, Quinn would be the breadwinner and Kathy would be in charge of household upkeep.

5. *"What roles should in-laws have?"*

What part does your spouse see both sets of parents playing in your life together?

"Susan always seeks her dad's advice before she seeks mine," Caleb says. "I love her dad, but feel it's my role as her husband to have her talk things over with me first." Having been pretty independent from an early age, Caleb feels betrayed and not trusted by Susan when she involves her parents in every decision.

Melina, on the other hand, grew up without a mom. She's come to love her husband, Spencer's, mother as if she were her own, and consults her mother-in-law on many decisions. Because Spencer is so close to his folks and trusts them implicitly, he enjoys the fact that Melina is willing to seek their counsel.

The way you deal with in-laws will depend on the depth and type of relationship you have with them. Make sure you understand your spouse's view of that relationship and what that means practically.

6. *"What do you expect regarding our sexual relationship?"*

Does your spouse believe sex is for procreation, relaxation, pleasure and fun, expressing intimacy, or all of the above?

Ask: "What kinds of things stimulate you? Who do you want to be the initiator? How would you like me to suggest having sex? How should I tell you I'm not in the mood? How often do you think we should have sex?"

Helping your partner pursue his or her passions is vital to your marriage's health. You won't know those dreams if you don't ask.

One wife, Mary Lee, said, "I always heard that the man was to be the initiator in sex. But when I asked Jim what he thought about that, he told me it would please him if I took initiative at times. It would make him feel like I desired him rather than just feeling like I was only accommodating his desires." The two of them discovered how freeing it was to talk about these things instead of having unspoken—and unmet—expectations.

7. *"What are your goals—for yourself and for us?"*

Ask your spouse what his or her dreams are. "Kevin is an incredible business-man," one wife said. "He's always been very diligent to work hard and provide well for our family. I thought he was happy until I asked him what he would do if he could do anything in the world. He said he would be in the ministry. He's now going to seminary. I'm so happy I asked him his dream; otherwise he may have stayed stuck in a job that supported us but wasn't fulfilling to him."

Helping your partner pursue his or her passions is vital to your marriage's health. You won't know those dreams if you don't ask.

> Inquire about your spouse's goal for your marriage, too. Is it closeness? Wealth? To have a family? Career success? To be used as a team in some ministry?

Inquire about your spouse's goal for your marriage, too. Is it closeness? Wealth? To have a family? Career success? To be used as a team in some ministry? Discuss these dreams and set realistic goals with time limits. For example: "In five years we want to be out of debt." "In one year we want to save enough money to go on a family mission trip."

8. *"How did you communicate and resolve conflict in your family?"*

In tears, Elizabeth told her mother, "Bobby yells at me when we talk to each other." Elizabeth didn't understand how her husband could think that was okay. She was an only child who'd rarely had conflicts with her family.

Bobby, on the other hand, was the youngest of five brothers. His was a fun-loving family that spoke loudly and often. He thought he was just talking passionately to Elizabeth; she heard it as yelling.

When the two of them finally discussed their families' communication styles, they began to understand the differences. Elizabeth no longer felt "run over," while Bobby saw that his wife's low-intensity way of talking didn't mean that she was indifferent.

9. *"Are there medical issues in your family?"*

Do heart disease, diabetes, or other medical problems run in your mate's family? Is your spouse dealing with a chronic condition? How is it treated? Have there been unusual deaths in the family?

It's important to know your spouse's medical history so that you can work together to prevent further problems, collaborate on diet and exercise, and consider possible implications for your children.

As you ask these nine questions, keep your spouse's temperament in mind. If he or she seems hesitant to talk, don't nag. Just explain why you're looking for information and how it can bring you closer.

Remember the importance of timing, too. For example, if your mate ignored your interest in sexual intimacy last night, try waiting until neither of you is upset to discuss sexual expectations. Likewise, a spouse who's tired, stressed, or sick won't be able to focus on the issues. As for a mate who's asked about family history, he or she may need time to gather information—or just think.

Be considerate of your spouse's feelings. But don't neglect to ask these questions. The only way to understand your mate is to know him or her.

—Sheryl DeWitt

How Honest Do We Have to Be?

1. Healthy relationships are built on trust.

    2. If you aren't totally honest, trust is impossible.

    3. Without trust, the relationship crumbles.

This sounds simple—too simple, as it turns out.

If you're a Christian, are you required to be "absolutely" honest with your spouse? After all, the Scriptures are clear that lying is a serious affront to God. Christians are to strive for honesty—and truth is absolute, not relative.

But what does that mean when your wife asks, "Does this dress make me look fat?" What does it mean when your husband was intimate with a girlfriend before he met you?

In other words, does perfect honesty exist in imperfect human relationships? And if you aren't completely candid with your spouse, will your marriage fall apart?

Are you required to be "absolutely" honest with your spouse? What does that mean when your wife asks, "Does this dress make me look fat?"

To answer those questions, we need to ask another: What does "honest" mean?

To be honest certainly is to tell the truth. But by "honest" do you mean simply that whatever you communicate is accurate? Or do you also mean that you're obligated to communicate all information you have on any and all topics, both from your present and past?

Being honest in the sense of telling the truth is not the same as imparting every thought and feeling you have. Joe and Suzie learned that the hard way.

They'd been married two years. Suzie often remembered that Joe had been "honest" in telling her during a premarital counseling session that he'd had sexual experiences with two other women before becoming a Christian five years ago. He'd also told her that no children had been the result of these liaisons, and that he'd never contracted any sexually transmitted diseases.

Suzie came into the marriage a virgin, but didn't think Joe's sexual history would be a problem for her. As time went by, however, she found herself thinking more and more about these "other women" and Joe's experiences with them. She decided to be "honest" and tell her husband that she was increasingly anxious about his past dalliances. If he would just answer a couple of questions, she said, she'd be able to forget the whole thing.

Wanting to put her concern to rest, Joe reluctantly agreed to talk briefly about these old girlfriends. Suzie wanted to know their names, how they looked, why Joe was attracted to them, how long he dated them, and whether he was in love with them at the time.

He was "honest" in describing one of them as a cute, sexy blonde and the other as an attractive, more intellectual redhead. He recalled being fascinated with the redhead, and "falling in love" or at least "in lust" with the blonde. Neither relationship lasted long after a brief sexual affair.

> Being honest in the sense of telling the truth is not the same as imparting every thought and feeling you have.

Much to Joe's disappointment, these "honest" answers did nothing to satisfy Suzie's increasing obsession with his history. She seemed even more anxious and began to demand detailed, intimate information about the two sexual relationships. Joe began to withdraw from Suzie's "interrogations" as he called them, and refused to talk with her about anything in his past.

Suzie, meanwhile, began to accuse Joe of hiding things from her. She said she could no longer trust him.

For Joe and Suzie, this effort to be "honest" turned into a painful, ugly series of interchanges that became toxic for their relationship, the dynamics of which remained unclear to both of them.

So is honesty the best policy?

Couples should be honest before making a lifelong commitment to marriage, disclosing information that could influence that decision. This includes medical and financial status, past marriages and children if any, spiritual journey and current walk in the faith, criminal history, and other "risk" factors.

In considering how honest to be in a marriage, though, it's important to examine the intent of the heart.

"Honesty" sounds pious, but can be a selfish excuse for meeting your own needs. In Suzie's case, one of her motives for demanding that Joe be "totally honest" was trying to relieve some insecurities. She was thinking, *How do I compare with my husband's past lovers? If I don't measure up, he'll be tempted again by another woman.* Her demand for even more intimate, detailed information became increasingly intense, resulting in a destructive process that had little to do with true honesty.

In the name of honesty, some people give their spouses too much information about past and present sinful actions and thoughts. To feel better about themselves, they dump their guilt feelings on their mates—unnecessarily hurting them.

Others have more sinister motives. Often the "honest" information being offered is carefully selected and intended to create anxiety in the spouse. For example, an insecure husband may try to create jealousy in his wife by describing how his female coworkers flirt with him.

Silence—choosing not to disclose all events of the day or all thoughts that cross your mind—isn't necessarily dishonest. In fact, sometimes the loving thing to do is to keep your mouth shut.

Giving a diplomatic answer in love rather than a cold, blunt "truth" is not the same as lying. In many instances, it's not particularly virtuous to "honestly" tell your husband that he's boring or not much of a lover.

And if your wife *does* ask, "Does this dress make me look fat?" the biblical admonition about "speaking the truth in love" (Ephesians 4:15) comes to mind. The flat truth is that the dress doesn't *make* her look fat. A more diplomatic and loving response than a simple "yes" is much advised. For example, you could tell her that although you think her blue dress looks better on her, she's very attractive no matter what dress she's wearing. "No, that dress doesn't make you look fat," you might say. "You look beautiful."

For Joe and Suzie, an effort to be "honest" turned into a painful, ugly series of interchanges that became toxic for their relationship.

Being truthful in marriage is vital. But before demanding or disclosing "all," first be honest with yourself about your motives. Is this for the benefit of your partner and the relationship? Or is it really an attempt to immaturely or selfishly meet some of your own needs? Can those needs be met in a more emotionally healthy and spiritually mature way?

If you can't answer those questions, you may need help seeing the issues more clearly. In that case, consider seeking the insight of a wise spiritual leader or professional Christian counselor.

—PHILLIP J. SWIHART

How Can I Get Used to Being Two Instead of One?

The sudden change that comes after the honeymoon can be one of life's most sobering moments. Some young couples describe this as "being hit in the face with cold water" or "being struck by lightning."

Others express it this way:

"I feel like I'm on another planet, and I want to go home!"

"I miss being able to do what I want to do, when I want to do it."

And here's a favorite that marriage therapists hear often: "If two becoming one means that I disappear as a person, forget it!"

> "I miss being able to do what I want to do, when I want to do it."

If you feel like this, don't think you're alone or that your situation is hopeless. The following quotations illustrate the fact that the adjustment period from aloneness to togetherness is often complex:

> I figure that the degree of difficulty in combining two lives ranks somewhere between rerouting a hurricane and finding a parking place in downtown Manhattan.
> —Claire Cloninger

> I love being married. It's so great to find that one special person you want to annoy for the rest of your life.
> —Rita Rudner

Many couples wonder how the blending of two personalities and sets of ambitions, desires, and dreams could ever be expected by a wise and all-knowing God! Trying to adjust from "freedom" to partnership can be difficult and exasperating—but it's a process, not just a destination.

Here are two principles to remember when moving from independence to interdependence in marriage.

1. *The feelings are normal.* When we shift from being single to being married,

we experience loss. Losing something leaves us feeling sad. But as we grow in our relationship with the person we committed to, the grief can turn to joy and contentment.

It's common for young couples to experience various levels of "buyer's remorse." That was the case with Nicole and Ted.

Nicole had waited for many years to find the right man to spend the rest of her life with. At age 33, she met Ted. Within 13 months they were married in her hometown of Atlanta.

Though she was certain Ted was the man God had chosen for her, Nicole missed her independence. Often she felt sad, conflicted, confused—wondering whether she'd made the wrong decision about marriage. She loved Ted and was thankful for him, realizing she couldn't have asked for a better man. But she struggled with having to give up her "alone time" and sense of freedom.

> ✌
> When we shift from being single to being married, we experience loss. Losing something leaves us feeling sad.
> ✍

After praying, studying the Bible, and getting direction from Christian friends, Nicole began to see that her feelings were normal and that most people experience them. She accepted the responsibility of honoring the relationship God had given her with Ted. Each day she made conscious efforts to enjoy her relationship with her new husband in the fullest sense.

Though she occasionally needed time alone, Nicole learned to think in terms of two instead of one. When tempted to do her own thing at Ted's expense, she resisted. When it would have been easy to plop down on the couch after a hard day's work, she spent time with her husband first. Ted responded in a similar way, and their marriage developed into a bond filled with joy and intimacy.

That's how closeness and biblical oneness develop in marriages in spite of selfish tendencies. Though challenging and often confusing, the transition from independence to interdependence is absolutely vital to your union.

2. *It takes work to grow in oneness.* On a torn envelope, Sarah finds the following note left on the kitchen table one morning: "Sarah, I know you said you would like to spend time with me. I agree that we've really grown apart lately. I think we need to spend more time together, and I know you were looking forward to relaxing for a couple of evenings. Well, you get your wish. The boss called and said I have to work tonight.

"By the way, would you mind ironing my golf shorts when you get home? I have a tournament tomorrow. Oh, before I forget, tomorrow night the guys are coming over to watch the game. You don't mind, do you? And something else—I'm leaving on business to San Diego Monday. I'll be gone the rest of the week."

If Sarah is like most wives, she's thinking, *How in the world does this goofball think we're going to get close if he's always gone or having someone over?*

She's right; healthy relationships don't just evolve, they're nurtured.

Suppose Jesus had taken the attitude that closeness would "just happen" with His disciples. "Okay," He might say. "I have called you guys to be apostles. You have left everything to follow Me. But I have a lot of stress on Me; I have to save the world! So My 'alone time' is very important. Your job is to take the gospel to the whole world, but I really think you can handle this without Me. I'll spend Saturdays with you, but the rest of the time you're on your own."

Is that how Jesus became "one" with His disciples? No. He understood the value of spending time with them, talking, teaching,

> Suppose Jesus had taken the attitude that closeness would "just happen" with His disciples. "Okay," He might say. "My 'alone time' is very important. I'll spend Saturdays with you, but the rest of the time you're on your own."

dining, and experiencing happy and challenging moments together. There were times when Jesus needed to be alone, but He understood the value of being with His followers, too. In the end, He gave His life for them and they gave theirs for Him—the ultimate testimony of oneness.

If you find yourself struggling with the challenges of togetherness, here are some simple suggestions.

1. *Remember who brought you together.* God has united the two of you for a reason. It's no accident. He calls you to become one (Genesis 2:24), to honor one another (Ephesians 5:22-33), to love one another (1 Corinthians 13), and to remain together until death separates you (Matthew 19:9).

2. *Change the way you think.* You're still an individual. But God has called you to leave your father and mother and unite with your spouse. That means making changes in your thinking (you belong to someone else now) as well as your behavior (you don't act like a single person anymore). Changing the way you think can change the way you feel. Start thinking like a married person, and you'll probably begin to feel like one.

3. *Educate yourself about God's desire for unity in your marriage.* Read Bible passages that emphasize the importance of oneness and unity (John 17; 1 Corinthians 7). Personalize them by inserting your name and the name of your spouse. Pray that God will show you any attitudes and actions that stand in the way of oneness. Stop focusing on your mate's mistakes, and start working on unity by changing yourself.

4. *Learn from others.* Ask couples you know who have strong marriages how they moved from independence to interdependence. What mind-sets and habits did they adopt that worked for them?

If you asked that of Bill and Ruth, here's what they might tell you.

Bill was independent. So was Ruth. For the first three years of their marriage things were so rocky that both felt they'd made a mistake in getting married. They developed separate interests and friendships, spent little time with each other, grew apart, and even considered divorce. But because of their church background, they felt they had to stay together.

Things changed on their third anniversary. They made a commitment to each other: No matter what, they would learn how to connect and develop intimacy. They began studying the Bible and praying together, and attended every marriage conference they could find. They made spending time together a hobby; where you saw one, you'd see the other. They took up golf and skiing. For the next 20 years they would have at least one date a week.

> *Start thinking like a married person, and you'll probably begin to feel like one.*

Recently Bill and Ruth went to another marriage retreat—where they were voted Most Dedicated Couple. Their switch from aloneness to togetherness hadn't just happened. They'd intentionally drawn closer and stuck with that commitment.

They'd probably tell you that intentional intimacy is an investment that always pays off—and they'd be right.

—MITCH TEMPLE

Should I Tell My Spouse About My Past?

If you've lived in a hot, humid climate, you probably know about cockroaches. They come out at night—and can be seen to scurry when a light is suddenly turned on.

The devil is a lot like a cockroach. He does his best work in dark places, thriving on secrets. Often when the light is turned on and the truth is revealed, he loses his power and runs.

Maybe you're harboring some secrets about your past. Does that mean you should shine the spotlight on them for your spouse? Will that make your marriage better—or worse?

There are good arguments to be made for turning on the light.

First, God's design for marriage is that couples become one spiritually, physically, and emotionally. There's a greater chance for this oneness when spouses are free from the guilt and shame that often goes with past moral failures—especially hidden ones.

Second, when two people come into a marriage with unresolved hurts or failures, it affects them as individuals. When those things are intentionally hidden, it can damage the relationship in a number of ways.

For example, let's say a wife hasn't told her husband that she was sexually abused as a child. Because of that past, she finds herself unable to be playful and relaxed in the bedroom. He begins to wonder, *Is it me?*

He starts to feel insecure about his ability to fulfill his wife sexually. *Is she comparing me to someone else?* he asks himself. He remembers her dropping a hint once that she had "a past," but refusing to share the details. His self-doubt grows.

Or the husband may have had a sexual relationship in the past. He may recall it as being more fulfilling or more exciting than what he has now with his wife. He finds himself longing for those days and that person. He begins to flirt with and fantasize about someone at work, trying to recapture the past. Not wanting his

> The devil is a lot like a cockroach. He does his best work in dark places, thriving on secrets.

wife to know about the old affair, he refuses to talk about his feelings—and the marriage continues to erode.

In cases like these, revealing secrets from the past—especially with the help of a counselor—might be constructive.

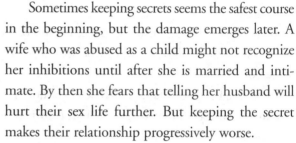

Sometimes keeping secrets seems the safest course in the beginning, but the damage emerges later.

Sometimes keeping secrets seems the safest course in the beginning, but the damage emerges later. A wife who was abused as a child might not recognize her inhibitions until after she is married and intimate. By then she fears that telling her husband will hurt their sex life further. But keeping the secret makes their relationship progressively worse.

Christian counselors differ on exactly how much of the past should be revealed to a spouse. Most would agree on the following principles, however:

1. *Honesty in a relationship is an important factor in building trust.*

2. *Detail and timing are important considerations.* For instance, a wife may benefit by knowing that her husband had sex before marriage. But knowing who, what, and where might make the information too visual and hurtful and feed the imagination in a negative way. As for timing, secrets tend to gain momentum and strength the longer you wait to reveal them. And the sting will be far less if the method and moment of telling are carefully and considerately planned rather than impulsive or offhanded.

3. *Some things are a must to share.* Examples:

- Having had a sexual partner, no matter how ashamed you may be about it, is something that should not be hidden from a mate. It should be disclosed before marriage, especially when there is a possibility of passing on a sexually transmitted disease.

- Experiencing an abortion, sexual abuse, having a baby out of wedlock, or giving up a child for adoption can cause problems in the relationship later if they haven't already—and should be discussed.

- Legal or financial "ghosts," such as lawsuits, bankruptcies, previous marriages, and criminal charges or convictions should be revealed.

4. *When in doubt about whether to share a particular secret, get help.* It's wise to seek counsel about the potential impact of turning on that spotlight. Revealing secrets of the past can strengthen a marriage—or cause insecurity and suspicion.

5. *Search your heart and know your motive.* Do you want to reveal a secret in order to hurt your spouse? To relieve yourself of guilt or shame? To just make yourself feel better? These aren't worthy motives, especially if the cost to your mate is pain and a breach in trust.

6. *Remember that you can always confess to God—and receive forgiveness.* "If we confess our sins, he is faithful and just and will forgive us our sins and purify us from all unrighteousness" (1 John 1:9).

Still not sure what to do? Here are four questions to ask yourself before sharing your past:

- Will this make my spouse feel more secure?
- Will this let my spouse know me better?
- Will this bring us closer?
- Will this prevent problems from coming up in the future?

If you're keeping a secret, be aware that it may indicate a larger problem. You may need help to deal with shame or a lack of freedom or a need for emotional healing. You may not sense enough trust in your relationship to ensure safety from judgment or rejection.

In that case, it may be time to explore those issues with a professional counselor who can give direction. It may be better to do this *before* marriage—but it's not too late to do it now.

—ROMIE HURLEY

Secrets tend to gain momentum and strength the longer you wait to reveal them.

How Can I Get My Spouse to Open Up?

Kim opened the pantry door as she began to make dinner. Her heart was heavy and her arms felt weak. Scanning the shelves for something to cook, she felt the familiar, hot sting of tears in her eyes.

She stared at a box of spaghetti. *Why won't Matt talk with me?* she thought. *Doesn't he care how I feel?*

She knew that when her husband came home he'd have an appetite for dinner. But what she hungered for was just a time to talk. *I can open a box of spaghetti, but I can't get Matt to open up,* she thought. *He never tells me what he's thinking or feeling.*

Sighing, she reached out for a jar of sauce. *How will we ever get to know each other at this rate? We've been married for almost two years, and I don't understand him any better than I did before our honeymoon.*

She took a heavy pot to the sink and began to fill it with cold water. *I've got to get a grip,* she thought, shaking her head. *It's not like our marriage is on the rocks. We're faithful to each other. He doesn't put me down or blame me when things get screwed up.*

Suddenly she had an idea. *Meatballs! I'll make Matt his favorite homemade garlic meatballs. He's sure to notice. And while we're eating dinner, maybe he'll finally open up.*

The strength in her arms started to return. She flew through the kitchen. Soon the atmosphere was inviting and warm. She even lit a candle for the table.

When Matt came home, he kissed Kim and they sat down to eat. Kim launched into an animated account of her day, assuming her excitement would show Matt what she wanted—conversation. But Matt was his usual quiet self. He didn't seem to notice the meatballs. He silently chewed and nodded.

Okay, she thought as they began to clear the table. *I shouldn't expect him to read my mind. I'll just come right out and tell him what I want.*

> "How will we ever get to know each other at this rate? We've been married for almost two years, and I don't understand him any better than I did before our honeymoon."

She started talking, explaining as clearly as she could how much she needed him to open up.

Unfortunately, all Matt heard was criticism. He shot back that he already did so much for her. He worked long hours and provided well for them. They even prayed together. What more could she expect?

The evening ended on a sour note. They both knew they had a problem, and needed help.

They called their pastor, who quickly referred them to a counselor in their church. As Kim and Matt told the counselor their stories, it became clear that Kim was having difficulty accepting the fact that Matt showed his love for her primarily through action—working hard—rather than by talking with her. As Matt listened to Kim, he began to realize that his actions weren't enough; they had to be accompanied by loving words that would speak to Kim's heart.

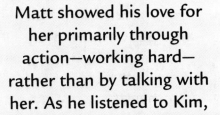

> Matt showed his love for her primarily through action—working hard—rather than by talking with her. As he listened to Kim, he began to realize that his actions weren't enough.

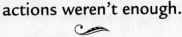

After considering the couple's situation, the counselor suggested a way to get conversation flowing between them. He called it "the Ten-Minute Plan."

Here's how it worked. The goal was to help Kim and Matt connect—in a way that fit their busy schedules. Three times a week, they were to spend four minutes reading a recommended marriage book together, four minutes having a positive discussion (no criticism), and two minutes praying. That was it—ten minutes of affirmation through reading, talking, listening, and praying, three times weekly.

It sounded easier than it turned out to be. But Kim and Matt didn't give up. They knew their marriage was at a turning point, and this crisis was an opportunity to enrich their lives together. They were determined that with God, good counseling, and a plan of action, they would make their good marriage great.

The Ten-Minute Plan worked so well that they soon wanted more interaction—and more minutes together. They set aside time each week to do a routine task, giving them a comfortable context in which to talk even more.

The task was to prepare one meal together. They'd plan the menu on Wednesdays, shop on Thursdays, and cook on Fridays. At first their meals were very American, but exploring cookbooks led them to discover international cuisine. That caused their interest in other countries to soar.

That interest, in turn, led to curiosity about missions and missionaries. As Kim and Matt prepared food from other cultures, they prayed for missionaries and discussed ways to support them.

By talking and listening, Kim and Matt found themselves more willing to open up to each other and adapt to each other's needs. They set aside even more time for loving talk and listening. Soon they knew each other better than ever.

As you try to get to know your spouse, is it hard for him or her to open up?

Here are five principles to remember:

> The Ten-Minute Plan worked so well that they soon wanted more interaction—and more minutes together.

1. Communicate your need for conversation in a clear, respectful, forthright way; don't assume your spouse knows what you're thinking.

2. Notice when your spouse *does* try to talk with you. Express your appreciation for that with sincerity and kindness.

3. Commit yourselves to the Ten-Minute Plan of reading, talking, listening, and praying together. Don't give up even though it may be difficult at first.

4. Turn a routine activity into a time of conversation. For Kim and Matt it was cooking; for you and your spouse it could be anything from shopping to hiking to visiting garage sales.

5. Maintain a sense of humor about unexpected challenges in your conversations. Be patient and persistent.

As Kim and Matt found, it *is* possible to help a spouse open up. If it doesn't happen for you as quickly as it happened for them, keep at it!

—James Groesbeck with Amy Swierczek

How Can I Understand My Spouse's Personality?

Jim and Donna have a problem.

If Jim were to write to an advice columnist, his letter might look something like this:

Dear Hazel:

My wife is totally opposite from me. I like to relax on the weekend. She wants me to work on the house the whole time and hates my watching TV.

Her need to talk is driving me crazy. I get annoyed when she asks me questions about work. She wants to go to a hot climate for vacations, and I enjoy winter sports. We're constantly at odds over the temperature in the house.

Our parenting styles are very different. She's really lenient with the kids. She constantly undermines my discipline, saying she has to "protect" the children from me.

I thought I knew her before we got married, but now I'm not sure. She has no interest in current events or sports, even though we used to watch basketball and tennis and talk about things going on in the world. Also, our choices in restaurants and movies don't come close to matching. I like barbecue and action films that she thinks are stupid. She likes Thai food and chick flicks that make me nauseous.

Since we're so different, I'm beginning to wonder if we should have gotten married at all.

Is there any hope for us, or will these differences destroy us? Please help me understand my wife and not let her weirdness tear us apart.

Signed,
Concerned in Colorado

If Donna were to write to the same advice columnist, her letter might read this way:

Dear Hazel:

My husband is totally opposite from me. I wait for the weekend with the hope that he'll help me do some of the things I've been unable to do alone. I look forward to spending quality time as a family, but all he wants to do is sit in front of the TV and vegetate.

He doesn't share much about his work, and seems annoyed when I ask him questions. He's so irritable with the children that they run to me for protection.

He wasn't this way when we were dating. He doesn't even seem like the same man I knew then.

He doesn't appear to enjoy spending time with me, either. Usually he seems really mad.

I shiver when he's home because he always feels too hot and wants to keep the thermostat low. We can't even agree on the same TV shows, movies, or restaurants. I like Thai food and romantic comedies that he thinks are stupid. He likes martial arts movies and charred turkey legs that make me nauseous.

Since we're so different, I'm beginning to wonder if we should have gotten married at all.

Is there any hope for us, or will these differences destroy us? Please help me understand my husband and not let his bizarre behavior tear us apart.

Signed,
Despondent in Denver

> "I like barbecue and action films that she thinks are stupid. She likes Thai food and chick flicks that make me nauseous."

Here's how that advice columnist might reply.

Dear Concerned and Despondent,

Start by remembering what drew you to one another in the first place. Did you once *like* the fact that your spouse was more outgoing than you were, or got you to try new foods or films, or was willing to complain about being overcharged when you weren't?

Did you really not notice the differences before you got married? Or did other qualities seem more important? If the latter was the case, are some of those qualities still there?

If you haven't already, take some personality tests such as the Myers-Briggs Type Indicator and the Taylor-Johnson Temperament Analysis. These are available from counselors. After taking the tests, discuss your individual qualities and how each of you brings balance and perspective to the relationship. This can actually be fun instead of dividing you.

It's time to have a heart-to-heart talk, preferably when both of you are relaxed and undisturbed by children, work, or phone. Pick a place that's conducive to talking. Consider this a brainstorming session, a time to let your spouse know that you intend to find ways for the two of you to get closer—and still be your unique selves.

Decide to help each other get what you want and need in life, and state that intention. Remember that the quality of a relationship is a function of how well it meets the needs of both parties.

Prepare for this meeting by thinking through what you want to say, so that you will share only what's true and comes from the heart. Plan to tell your spouse about the things you admire and appreciate in him or her. Discuss in a positive way the things you miss doing together. Ask what you can do to help get some of those things back.

> Did you once like the fact that your spouse was more outgoing than you were, or got you to try new foods or films, or was willing to complain about being overcharged when you weren't?

Apologize for the ways in which you haven't been there for each other. Ask what you can do to help one another relax.

Since your parenting styles are different, find a good childrearing book the two of you can read together; this can help you become more of a team. Read a "relationship book" like *The Five Love Languages* by Gary Chapman (Moody, 1996) or *His Needs, Her Needs* by Willard F. Harley, Jr. (Revell, 2001) to give you perspective on your differences. Pick a daily devotional you can read together or to each other, such as *Night Light* by Dr. James Dobson and Shirley Dobson (Multnomah, 2000).

Show an interest in really knowing one another. Intimacy has been defined as "into me see." It's important to "see into" each other in order to understand.

Lastly, don't allow or embrace any thoughts—spoken or unspo-ken—about giving up on the idea of being together. That road leads only to doubt and disaster. Stay committed to each other, and in time your spouse won't seem quite as mysterious.

Respectfully,

Hazel

—ROMIE HURLEY

How Can I Adjust to My Spouse's Personality?

"When she's stressed out, she talks all the time. If I get tired of talking to her after an hour or so, she gets a second wind and calls a friend!"

"He's so sensitive. I can't correct him without it making him angry. No matter what I say, he takes it wrong."

"After we leave a social event, I get so angry I can't see straight. She embarrasses me—not once, but throughout the evening."

If these statements hit home, you're not alone. Most of us have said—or at least thought—similar things about our spouses.

Couples often tell therapists that one of their toughest challenges is adjusting to a spouse's personality. Many of those people are ready to give up and resign themselves to a miserable state of existence. Others fear their situations will worsen to a point where the spouse's personality turns repulsive—and divorce will be inevitable.

So what do you do? Stay miserable? Get angry and resentful? Leave?

We suggest none of the above.

Instead, consider these facts about differences in personalities.

1. *God created us to be different.* He knew there would be a place in His plan for introverts and extroverts, for thinkers and feelers, for those who are planners and those who are spontaneous. He created some people to be dreamers and some to be content with things as they are. "Different" doesn't automatically equal "wrong."

Proverbs 22:6 can be translated to recommend training a child "according to his bent." In other words, it's good to discover a child's distinctive personality and bring her up in a way that complements her personality instead of tearing it down. Why not apply this idea to marriages, too? Are you willing to allow your spouse the same freedom to be unique—and not the same as you?

When we realize that God planned for people to be different, it's often easier to accept and adjust to a spouse's personality. It may even become possible to cele-

> Many people are ready to give up and resign themselves to a miserable state of existence. Others fear their situations will worsen to a point where the spouse's personality turns repulsive.

brate those differences. Otherwise, why would God create us in such variety—only to tell us to pair up and remain together for life? He's a God of compassion, not cruelty!

2. *It's easier to spot a flaw than to see a strength.* Jesus put it in terms of spying a speck in another's eye, versus seeing a log in our own (Matthew 7:3-5).

When you were dating, you probably found it easy to focus on the admirable traits of your future mate. You seemed to like the same things, enjoyed the same conversational topics, and tended to overlook each other's quirks.

Bennett, for instance, married Deb because she was such a "great communicator." Now he's annoyed because she's such a "great agitator." Dana married Marcus because he was such a "confident, strong manager." Now he's an "overconfident jerk." Juan married Paula because she was "so sweet and kind." Now he doesn't respect her because "she lets people run over her."

God created us to be different. He knew there would be a place in His plan for introverts and extroverts, for thinkers and feelers, for those who are planners and those who are spontaneous.

What changed? Why do the same personality traits we once celebrated suddenly become "logs" in our mate's eye?

During the dating process, the goal is often to conceal the "real" you and present your best side. After the wedding, the masks are dropped and unsightly reality rises to the surface. Stress, crises, pain, and disappointment also have a way of exposing what we formerly attempted to hide.

That's why it's a good idea for dating couples to go through the seasons of a year together. This allows you to see one another's imperfections. It's a test of whether you're committed enough to stay together for the rest of your lives.

"But it's too late for that," you may be saying. "We're already married!"

Then it's time to recognize the next fact.

3. *Your ability to tolerate your mate's personality changes with time.* Most of us can stand negative behavior for a while. But everyone has a limit!

Belinda, for example, could put up with Jeff's ability to make a joke out of everything—for about a year. After she became the brunt of his jokes, her level of tolerance changed. She reached a point where she despised his voice, especially his laughter.

Is that the case with you? Maybe it's not that your spouse's personality has become more of a problem; it may be that your ability to value or overlook some attributes has diminished.

Reaching your limit is no excuse for giving up on a marriage, though. Sometimes it's enough to realize that the change is in your "irritation threshold" and adjust that gauge accordingly. At other times, you may need help from a counselor to express your frustration and find a healthy tolerance level.

4. *Sometimes it's not really about personality.* Could it be that your mate has done something that deeply hurt you—and his personality has become the contention point?

That was the case with Barry. He'd always liked the fact that his wife, Wendy, was sociable and outgoing. But then he discovered that she'd been flirting with a coworker. Now Barry viewed her personality as a threat.

When your spouse hurts you, it tends to change the way you think and feel toward him or her. You suddenly see that person through tinted lenses, not clear ones.

>
> **Why would God create us in such variety—only to tell us to pair up and remain together for life?**

If this is the case with you, healing has to occur before everyday personality issues can be objectively dealt with. Identify the real issue. Work on it—with the help of a counselor if needed. Commit to overcoming your tendency to focus on the negative aspects of your spouse's personality.

First Corinthians 12–14 urges us to appreciate individual differences. The apostle Paul explains that every member of the "body" is valuable. Just because a part is different doesn't give us the right to despise it and set it apart from the others.

The same is true with your mate's personality. It may be different and sometimes difficult to manage. But God doesn't want this to allow division in your marriage.

One of Paul's points to the Corinthians might be summarized this way: "Learn to accept and adjust to each other, no matter what people look like or act like." That applies to husbands and wives, too.

—MITCH TEMPLE

What Can I Do About My Spouse's Irritating Habits?

When you got engaged, you probably thought you were marrying the person of your dreams. After the wedding day, though, you realized your spouse had some annoying habits.

Suddenly the person who could do no wrong was in need of a makeover.

Maybe you started a reforming program, only to discover that you don't have enough resources or power to change your spouse. Now your refrain sounds something like this:

"Cathy is always late for everything. Last week I decided to go on to church without her, and then for some reason she gets mad at me!"

"Jeremy always leaves the toilet seat up, and it annoys me in the middle of the night when I fall in. I have begged him to be more thoughtful of me."

"Cindy never listens to me. She always interrupts me and never lets me talk. I've learned to just shut up and keep quiet."

"Bob thinks it's funny to start burping contests at the table with our boys. It is *very* embarrassing."

Chances are that you married your spouse not just because you had similarities, but also for the differences. You may have been attracted to these differences because of your need to feel completed by another person. These traits may be endearing before marriage, but can disrupt the relationship afterward.

Do you have to live with these habits? Should loving this person be enough to enable you to overlook them? And if you can't, should you feel guilty?

Being annoyed by your spouse's habits is normal. The key is to learn to work together to change the habits that can be changed and learn to accept those that can't.

First, ask yourself why you want your spouse to change. Is it for your own good only? Might the change make you feel better, but cause your mate to feel imprisoned? Or is the change to help eliminate behaviors that keep your spouse

> ❧
>
> **"Jeremy always leaves the toilet seat up, and it annoys me in the middle of the night when I fall in. I have begged him to be more thoughtful of me."**
>
> ❧

from growing emotionally and spiritually? In other words, are you helping to set your partner free or just restricting his or her freedom?

If changing the habit would truly benefit both of you, change may be worth trying. But keep these guidelines in mind:

1. *Address the problem honestly.* "Honey, it bothers me when you burp at the table. It teaches the children a bad habit, and it's rude and offensive to guests."

2. *Explain the benefit of change.* "Eating at the table will be more pleasant for all of us. The boys will also respect your table manners and you'll be a good testimony to our guests."

3. *Don't command change.* "You're such a slob at the table. Stop being so messy." Instead, *request* change. Your spouse will respond more favorably.

4. *Don't attack your mate.* "You are a horrible listener. It's no wonder no one talks to you." When you attack your spouse, you crush his or her spirit—and don't get much cooperation. Confront the problem; don't attack the person.

5. *Discuss ways to bring about change.* Change is hard. Let your spouse know that you're on his or her side. Help him or her find ways to change those habit patterns. If the problem is overeating, for instance, go with your spouse to the gym, cook healthy meals, and go out to eat less often. Be your mate's advocate.

Being annoyed by your spouse's habits is normal. The key is to learn to work together to change the habits that can be changed and learn to accept those that can't.

6. *Encourage your spouse's growth.* "You're doing a great job. I'm really proud of the effort I see. Thank you for your dedication to making this change."

7. *Recognize that change takes time.* Be patient with your spouse. Praise little steps that you see. Everyone wants to feel successful. So don't discourage your mate with comments like, "This is taking forever. How many more times do we have to deal with this?" Discouragement stunts growth, but encouragement goes a long way in motivating change. Let your spouse know you're in this together for the long haul.

8. *Focus on your spouse's good habits, not just the irritating ones.* "John makes me mad," one wife said. "I have asked him to clean the tub after each use. He never does.

"Last week when I was getting ready for work, I received a call from the hospital. John was in an accident. As I quickly dressed to go to the hospital, I noticed the dirt ring in the bathtub. I began to sob. The Lord brought to mind all the wonderful qualities of my husband, and I felt so petty for complaining about the ring in the tub. When John came home several days later, I found myself sitting in the bathroom and thanking the Lord that I would have more time with John and more rings in the tub. I was reminded of Philippians 4:8: 'Whatever is honorable, pure, just, lovely . . . think on these things.'

"When I see the ring now, I turn my thoughts to the wonderful qualities of my husband and the annoyance of that ring in the tub disappears."

9. *Pray for your spouse.* God is ultimately the one who makes change possible in any of us. So pray for your mate's efforts. And since some behaviors may never change, ask God to give you grace to accept the differences between you and your spouse.

10. *Seek to change the habit, not the person.* It's possible to help your spouse drop an irritating habit—as long as it's the habit you're trying to change. If you're trying to alter your spouse's personality or temperament, you'll be fighting a losing battle that will end in frustration for both of you.

Take Susan and Lee, for example. Susan, an extremely social person, loves to stay after church to talk, is the last to leave a party, and likes to be the center of attention. In contrast, her husband, Lee, is reserved, prefers to be in the background, and is exhausted by socializing. Lee has learned to go to parties with Susan out of love for her. But she can't expect him to become a fan of social gatherings. She needs to appreciate his willingness to go with her and not try to make him the extrovert she is.

If you follow the aforementioned guidelines and don't meet with success, it's time to ask yourself whether the battle is worth it. Some habits are so ingrained that if they don't involve moral issues or character flaws, it may be best to live with them. Bringing them up repeatedly may lead only to more bitterness and conflict.

Keep praying for your spouse. And when you think of him or her, focus on his or her positive traits—instead of that irritating habit.

—SHERYL DEWITT

Part 2: Expectations

Why Isn't Marriage the Way I Thought It Would Be?

On their honeymoon, Ed and Renee spent hours gazing into each other's eyes—contemplating how they'd spend their next 50 years. They decided to write those plans down as a road map for the future.

But before long, those plans hit several speed bumps.

Ed lost his job.

Renee was diagnosed with diabetes.

Habits that seemed cute at first became annoying.

When they had a son, Renee decided to stay home—which tightened the family purse strings. Ed worked more to compensate, further reducing their time together. When she voiced concern, it only seemed to irritate him.

They still loved each other. But this wasn't how either of them had written the script on their honeymoon.

You might find yourself wondering if *your* early dreams of marital bliss were more illusion than reality. Why isn't marriage turning out the way you planned?

In premarital counseling, couples often explore their expectations of marriage. But what does that mean? Are expectations the way you think your marriage *will* look, or the way you *want* it to look? The two can be very different!

People draw their marital expectations from two wells. One is courtship. If dating was wonderful and starry-eyed, why would you expect marriage to be otherwise? *If spending 20 hours a week brings us such joy,* you might think, *more time together as husband and wife could only be better!*

But think back to your courtship. Wasn't it largely a mirage?

What did you do when you didn't want to be alone? You got dressed up and did fun things together. What did you do when you were tired of talking? You went home. How did you deal with financial decisions? You made them on your own.

When you were dating, there were some built-in escape valves in your

> They still loved each other. But this wasn't how either of them had written the script on their honeymoon.

relationship. Now that you're married, there's no other home to go to. Your spouse's finances are yours, and vice versa.

By its nature, courtship allows a couple to live in denial. Marriage makes that posture much more difficult to maintain.

The other well of marital expectations is the marriage you saw firsthand when you were growing up.

That relationship provided one of two images for you to view. Either the marriage didn't seem worth duplicating, or it did.

Even if the marriage you saw was conflicted and unhappy, you may have believed things would be different for you. Without that hope, the decision to remain single would have seemed pretty appealing. But simply raising your expectations won't make your marriage better than that of your parents. You need to face past hurts and disappointments, perhaps with the help of a counselor or pastor. That may not have the same thrill that romance does, but it makes it more likely that you'll experience a fulfilling and romantic marriage.

On the other hand, you may have been fortunate enough to see a model of marriage worth replicating. For that you can rejoice! But there's a pitfall there, too. You may be locked into thinking that the way you saw Mom and Dad relate is the only healthy way for a marriage to function.

For example, let's say that your parents were both even-tempered; decisions came easily for them. You or your spouse might be more opinionated and need to discuss matters longer. That's okay, even though it's different. There are many styles in marriage that can be healthy.

> By its nature, courtship allows a couple to live in denial. Marriage makes that posture much more difficult to maintain.

Parents can affect your marital expectations in other ways, too. That was true with Tom and Jill.

Tom's expectations about marriage weren't being met. Through reading and counseling he finally recognized that those expectations were an effort to cope with a painful childhood. Growing up, he'd often been under his mother's controlling thumb. He'd brought into marriage a vow that he'd never get close enough to his wife to let her control him as Mom had. As a result, he'd never gotten close enough to truly connect with Jill.

Tom had to work through his hurts before he could begin to relate to Jill in a more meaningful way. The two of them met periodically over coffee with a seasoned couple in their church, learning what they might expect in each new stage of marriage.

They still have struggles. But Tom is learning more about God's expectations for their marriage. Unless he depends on God for the ability to love Jill, he doesn't have a prayer to make it happen. He's also learning that by staying true to his marriage, he's growing in ways he never thought possible.

Tom brought his own expectations to marriage, but God had a better idea.

> Tom brought his own expectations to marriage, but God had a better idea.

If your expectations about marriage have been unrealistic, it's time to challenge them. But if you do, and still have concerns, consider the possibility that the problem might not be your expectations. You might have a problem in your marriage.

Harboring unrealistic expectations doesn't mean that everything else in a marriage is on track. Your qualms might be slightly off target, but they could be early warning signs about issues that will cause more trouble if you don't resolve them. Talk about them with your spouse in a respectful way; see whether the two of you can address them. If that fails, look to a pastor or counselor for help.

—GLENN LUTJENS

Are Other People's Marriages Like This?

Do you wish you could look "behind closed doors" and know just how "normal" or "average" or "abnormal" your marriage is, compared to those of other couples?

Maybe you're not very happy with your marriage right now. Perhaps it seems so far from the romantic ideal you began with—and assumed was true for most other husbands and wives. Or you've been comparing your marriage with those of friends, relatives, and coworkers who seem much happier with their relationships than you do with yours.

What *are* other people's marriages really like?

The answer begins with the fact that there is no such thing as a perfect marriage. Marriage consists of two imperfect human beings, two sinners, trying to live in total bliss and harmony. Thus the phrase "the perfect marriage" is really an oxymoron. It can't happen.

All marriages are less than the union of two infallible people, both of whom are totally happy with it at all times. So other people's marriages are indeed "like this."

Your marriage may be imperfect—but "normally imperfect." Every spouse must put up with all kinds of irritating behaviors, habits, and traditions, preferences that seem quite odd, and choices that lack logic—precisely because you aren't clones of each other and have brought a whole history with you into the marriage.

For example, the two of you may have very different sexual expectations. One wants sex "all the time" (maybe three times a week). The other is satisfied with twice a month, and anything beyond that seems like a chore. Or one of you is very neat and the other thinks nothing of discarding clothing here, there, and everywhere. Or one of you gets irritated over "every little thing" (no sense of humor at all) while the other is totally laid-back, seemingly troubled by nothing.

> Your marriage may be imperfect—but "normally imperfect." Every spouse must put up with all kinds of irritating behaviors, habits, and traditions, preferences that seem quite odd, and choices that lack logic.

These kinds of differences are to be expected. If you could peek behind the doors of others' marriages, you'd find that "normal" permits rather wide variances in most areas.

There are, however, limits to "normal" or "average." All marriages are not equally troubled or dysfunctional.

That's because everyone brings his or her unique personality to the relationship. How those personalities interact creates a dynamic like no other, for good or ill.

Both spouses also bring the experiences that have shaped their personalities. They bring healthy patterns of behavior—and toxic ways of coping that can be extremely destructive to a marriage.

They bring expectations that they may or may not be able to put into words. They bring old wounds that may never have healed, as well as new hurts that have been piling up during the first few years of marriage.

> If you could peek behind the doors of others' marriages, you'd find that "normal" permits rather wide variances in most areas. Still, all marriages are not equally troubled or dysfunctional.

Each relationship, then, is a complex mixture of ingredients that can come together to make a rich and rewarding sharing of lives—or, at the other extreme, create dynamite, always on the edge of blowing apart.

Michael and Sherri were an example of the latter.

They met one May at a church singles' group. Suddenly they found themselves madly in love. During their short courtship they ignored the possible implications of some very striking differences. They felt that since they had such strong feelings for one another, wanted to be with each other every waking hour, and found each other endlessly fascinating, nothing could prevent them from marrying by July. They saw no point in premarital counseling, beyond one short visit with the pastor.

July arrived, and the wedding. By October, they began to discover some very annoying points of contention.

Michael was shocked that Sherri had no desire to have Sunday lunch, almost every week, with his parents and other relatives. It had been a long tradition in his large and close-knit family. Sherri had dreamed of long walks in the park with a picnic basket and a blanket on Saturday afternoons. Michael was much more interested in watching football games with his old college buddies.

Sherri had hurt feelings about this, but said nothing. In her family, feelings were usually left unspoken, especially by her mother.

Sherri found herself uninterested in Michael's sexual advances, not feeling romantic at all. He had no clue about why she was cold and distant in bed, and responded angrily to her rejections. Michael's display of hostility scared Sherri. When her father lost his temper when she was growing up, he'd often abused her mother and sometimes Sherri herself.

Sherri withdrew even more. She and Michael barely talked to each other, much less shared intimate thoughts or prayed together about their problems.

Sherri wondered whether other people's marriages were like hers. Eventually she began to think about what it might be like to be married to some other man.

If your marriage seems in the doldrums, or even in danger of exploding, don't give up hope as Sherri did. All marriages require hard work to survive and succeed. Even when you compare your marriage with what you *think* is going on in others' relationships and feel yours doesn't measure up, maintain your commitment and your vows to each other and to God.

> Sherri wondered whether other people's marriages were like hers. Eventually she began to think about what it might be like to be married to some other man.

Avoid casting yourself in the role of victim, telling yourself things like, *I bet that woman would never put up with my husband,* or *If that guy's wife was giving him sex only once a month, he would have been out of there a long time ago.* Those kinds of comparisons only serve as excuses for an easy exit out of your marriage—which would violate your vows to your spouse and to God.

If you could see what other people's marriages are really like, here's one truth you'd observe at work in all of them: You can't force your husband or wife to change, but you can change your own attitudes and behaviors. In so doing, you can improve the dynamic in your relationship, and the marriage will change—usually for the better.

—PHILLIP J. SWIHART

Why Isn't My Wife the Person I Thought She Was?

Was your wife someone different before you got married? Has she changed for the worse over time?

It's much more likely that you saw her through rose-colored glasses while you were dating, and now the glasses are off. And guess what? You're probably not the person she thought *you* were, either.

Before the wedding, differences tend to seem intriguing, interesting, and attractive. A few months or years into the marriage, however, what seemed so inviting in the semi-fantasy world of dating now seems considerably less than idyllic.

That beautiful angel you married turns out to be a real woman. She has flaws that weren't previously apparent. She may handle things in ways that you find inefficient, and isn't interested in your suggestions about how to do them differently—even though, from your viewpoint, your ways are obviously superior.

> Guess what? You're probably not the person she thought you were, either.

You discover to your shock that she has the capacity to express a range of emotions not plumbed in your dating days. You hadn't felt that hot edge of her temper nor the cold, steely glare she now feels free to display.

Perhaps your wife has expectations you never guessed were there. You assumed hers would match yours—and they don't.

How do these "mistakes" occur?

Barbie and Carl were so in love. They wanted to be with each other constantly. Unable to endure the thought of a long, drawn-out courtship, they married within three months of their first meeting.

Barbie was a life-of-the-party sort of girl—a social butterfly. A former high school cheerleader, she was bubbly and happy-go-lucky.

Carl was an A student in college. He had serious career plans in accounting and business. He liked books and challenging discussions about theology and politics. Not having dated many girls, he was in a daze when Barbie was willing to go out with him.

Barbie saw Carl as a responsible, mature man who'd provide stability and security in her life. Carl saw Barbie as the perfect complement to his otherwise rather pedestrian life.

They quickly decided they were perfect for each other. Surely they'd have no problems that couldn't easily be resolved.

Two years into their marriage, though, there was a deep rift in their relationship. Carl was coming home from the office just wanting to read a book or have some quiet space. He didn't want to talk to Barbie about her day or her shopping plans for the next. At bedtime he didn't feel very amorous.

Barbie seemed frustrated and angry when Carl had no interest in dinner parties or going out dancing with her old friends. Going to church on Sunday mornings was more than enough social life for him.

> The girl who appeared to be such a wonderful, bouncy, free spirit now looks like an irresponsible, immature twit with no depth at all.

Carl was angry and frustrated, too. Barbie was chronically late and seemed not to care how annoying this was to him. She was running up bills on the credit card and was irresponsible about paying them. She visited the hair salon frequently, apparently wanting to look very sexy when going out. In his view she was a terrible housekeeper, leaving the place in a mess most of the time.

What had gone so terribly wrong with this relationship? Had Barbie really changed?

Carl and Barbie were opposites—and always had been. "Opposites attract" may be a common phenomenon but doesn't necessarily lead to a strong marriage. Far too often what seemed irresistible in the swirl of hormones and emotional highs during a fast courtship turns out to be irritating in the 24/7, "up close and personal" daily life of husband and wife.

The mature and responsible guy seems to become a stiff, nit-picking perfectionist, boring and sexually uninteresting. The girl who appeared to be such a wonderful, bouncy, free spirit now looks like an irresponsible, immature twit with no depth at all.

Is that what's happened with your wife? The truth is that she's the same woman you fell so much in love with. But *you* have changed—stripped of your illusions about her. You're disappointed.

So what should you do?

You might find it helpful to sit down and list the reasons why you chose this particular woman to be your wife. Think of all her attributes that you enjoy and value. Think of yourself as the author of the Song of Solomon, writing about your bride. Shift your focus from the negative and critical to the positive and appreciative.

Then make a date to share these thoughts with her.

If this seems impossible, consider the very real possibility that your marriage is at a crossroads. Disappointment may be making you vulnerable to the attentions of others, who you might imagine would better meet your needs and expectations. Or you may just be resigning yourself to years of regret about your choice of a spouse, bitter that you're obligated to stay in a marriage without any hope of realizing your dreams.

> The truth is that she's the same woman you fell so much in love with. But you have changed—stripped of your illusions about her.

If this describes you, it's past time for you and your wife to seek marriage counseling. Find a Christian professional who won't reinforce the lie that happiness lies just around the corner if only you escape from this mistake and move on to something new.

Your situation is not at all hopeless. But it does require a fresh perspective and some tools to employ in developing a more mature relationship.

—Phillip J. Swihart

Why Isn't My Husband the Person I Thought He Was?

When she entered counseling with her husband, Erica had one purpose: getting Jim "fixed."

Jim had fallen into patterns that might work for a single guy, but certainly wouldn't do for a married man. He sometimes worked four extra hours without calling to inform Erica, for instance.

He'd changed so much, she thought. When they'd been dating, she'd figured Jim knew how to handle his finances; at least his car was never repossessed. Now they received monthly surprises from MasterCard, detailing Jim's "toy" purchases. Likewise, his apartment had always seemed neat when Erica visited during their courtship. But now his underwear rarely made it the two yards from the foot of their bed to the hamper.

It's easy to understand why Erica hoped the counselor would take on the challenge of setting her husband straight. She wanted the "old" Jim back.

You might be asking yourself these days, "What happened to the guy *I* used to know? Did he change, or was I just seeing him differently then?"

The answer is probably, "Yes." That's because both reflect the truth.

Maybe he *does* act differently now. Your husband probably wanted to seal the deal; he wanted to win your heart. Do you think he would jeopardize losing you by sharing all of his idiosyncrasies with you? Would you do that with him?

Was it deception? It's more like "selective expression." He behaved in a way that he figured would increase your likelihood of saying, "I do." He put his best foot and shiniest shoe forward.

Some of his behavior during those days probably wasn't so deliberate. Thinking of you thrilled his heart during courtship. That type of romantic fire shapes one's actions; loving deeds come easily to one so smitten by romance. You probably felt the same excitement, with your reactions being affected as well.

> Jim's apartment had always seemed neat when Erica visited during their courtship. But now his underwear rarely made it the two yards from the foot of their bed to the hamper.

In Luke 6:32, Jesus conveys this principle with the question, "If you love those who love you, what credit is that to you?" Reciprocating romantic love comes naturally to most people. Over time, it's common for the romance—and therefore some of the motivation for "good behavior"—to fade somewhat.

It's also true that in many ways your husband hasn't changed, but you now view him differently. There are three reasons for that.

What happened to the guy you used to know? Did he change, or were you just seeing him differently then? The answer is probably, "Yes."

1. *Time.* The longer you're married, the more time you have to observe your spouse's behavior. You see things that weren't as noticeable back then.

2. *Distance.* You now see him up close. There's no end to the date, no "See you next week." The artificial nature of dating keeps many behaviors concealed. You currently see him when he's hungry and tired. Women may have their "time of month," but men have their "time of day." When his stomach is empty you may see a whole new side of your man you never knew existed.

3. *Desire.* You viewed your husband during courtship as you wanted to see him. We tend to construct a person in our minds to match the excitement we want to feel. We mentally create that person in a way that will make us happiest.

So the question becomes, "What do I do now that I've found out he's different from the way I thought he was?"

Debating whether he misrepresented himself or you misread him won't solve anything. Here are three actions you can take.

1. *Choose to love him.* We're told in Ephesians 5:32 that marriage reflects the relationship between Christ and the church. There are inadequacies in the church, yet Christ still loves her.

2. *Look at how you may have changed as well.* Jesus warns in Matthew 7:1-2 that the yardstick we use to judge others will be used to measure us, too.

3. *Realize that you may have legitimate concerns.* Voice them to your husband in a constructive way with the hope that he'll be willing to work toward change—or at least understand your concerns.

Remember Erica? She was surprised when the counselor wasn't willing to "fix" Jim. It wasn't that he didn't recognize the need for changes in Jim's working and spending habits. But the counselor also saw that Erica was mostly trying to control her man.

Debating whether he misrepresented himself or you misread him won't solve anything. But there are actions you can take.

As Erica worked with the therapist, she saw how she had become less expressive and more withdrawn over time. She began learning ways to communicate her frustrations to Jim in a manner that didn't leave him feeling disrespected.

Erica found that as she and Jim showed more kindness and care toward each other, her feelings toward him deepened. She didn't necessarily feel the same romance as when they courted, but she sensed her love was more mature than it had been before.

—GLENN LUTJENS

Why Isn't My Wife More Like Mom?

Kevin had it all—a good education, a successful career, and a brand-new, beautiful bride named Terri. He was a smart guy. But, like many men, Kevin made a very common mistake.

It was all quite innocent. But he asked Terri one of the most potentially controversial questions any man could ask his new wife (other than, "Can we have sex again?").

"Terri," he said, "why aren't you more like Mom?"

As you can imagine, Kevin didn't have time to explain himself. As soon as the words escaped his lips, Terri broke down in tears and ran out of the room, devastated.

Through the double-bolted door and between Terri's sobs, Kevin tried to explain what he really meant to say. He hadn't intended to hurt his wife. But he couldn't vindicate himself.

Often when young husbands ask a question like that, they're attempting to make a suggestion, "just something to consider." But young wives, who are often very self-conscious in their new roles, usually don't see it that way. They view it as a comparison with the woman their husbands have idealized since birth. They see themselves placed side by side with a person who has at least 20 or 30 years of successful domestic experience under her belt. They conclude, "How can I compare to that?"

By the time sons marry, many mothers have mastered the art of preparing flawless meals and cleaning the house to spotless status in record time. Or at least their sons remember them that way. It's easy to forget that Mom made her share of domestic blunders and was once inexperienced herself. Sons tend to recall Mom as the queen of the world who could prepare an exquisite Italian dinner while simultaneously rewiring the house.

It's easy for a husband to assume that his new bride knows how to prepare common dishes—but she may not. He may think she'll clean and cook at the

> Kevin didn't have time to explain himself. As soon as the words escaped his lips, Terri broke down in tears and ran out of the room, devastated.

same level as his mother. But a young wife simply hasn't had the opportunity to master those skills—and may not have the inclination.

Many new husbands have made the "comparing wife to mother statement" or implied the same nonverbally. A wise man is one who can learn from and grow through his mistakes—or at least the mistakes of others. So, based on the experiences of fellow husbands who have said the wrong thing, here are a few principles to remember.

1. *Comparing your spouse with others illuminates her flaws.* It's like painting a mole on her face bright red; everybody will notice it.

Comparing your wife to your mother puts your spouse in a position where she'll fall short no matter what. After all, most of us tend to compare the "model" person's best assets to apparent weaknesses in the other.

Consider how unfair it would be for a wife to compare her new husband to her father. The latter might make twice the money the son-in-law did at his age, act as CEO of his own company, spend all his free time with his family, and serve as an elder in his church. No man could measure up to that kind of example. It would be like comparing Homer Simpson to Abraham.

Instead of comparing, try accepting and encouraging your wife. These biblical instructions apply to spouses, too:

"Accept one another, then, just as Christ accepted you, in order to bring praise to God" (Romans 15:7).

"Therefore encourage one another and build each other up, just as in fact you are doing" (1 Thessalonians 5:11).

2. *Learn to see your spouse through God's eyes.* God created David with distinctive strengths, yet David had obvious failings. In some ways he wouldn't have compared favorably with many ancient Israelites. Though a great king, he was a failure as a father. Though strong in battle, he was a poor warrior against lust. Yet, with all his flaws, God said David was a man after His own heart.

We can be glad that God doesn't judge or place value on us by comparing our weakness to others' strengths. You can follow His example by valuing your wife as the unique individual God created her to be—not as a faint echo of your mom.

> ❧
>
> It's easy to forget that Mom made her share of domestic blunders. Sons tend to recall Mom as the queen of the world who could prepare an exquisite Italian dinner while simultaneously rewiring the house.
>
> ❧

3. *List and thank God for your wife's good qualities.* Sit down and compile a list of positive characteristics you see in your wife. If you've let yourself become nearsighted when it comes to seeing her good qualities, ask a mature Christian who knows both of you well to help you in this process.

After you identify these qualities, talk to God about them. Thank Him for each attribute. Ask Him to help you recognize and value this quality daily. If you do this consistently, you'll tend to compare less.

4. *Sing your wife's praises.* A "wife of noble character" is described in Proverbs 31. The author, King Lemuel, must have known the value of recognizing and extolling a spouse's good attributes. He saw and praised this bride as trustworthy, conscientious, and industrious. He touted her as a woman who managed her money well and who deserved the highest level of honor from her children and her husband. Note his final observation in verse 29: "Many women do noble things, but you surpass them all."

> Consider how unfair it would be for a wife to compare her new husband to her father. It would be like comparing Homer Simpson to Abraham.

What a wise and compassionate man! If you insist on comparing your spouse to others, remember King Lemuel's example—and make sure you compare your wife in a positive way.

Focusing on your mate's strengths and beauty has a way of diminishing the tendency to spotlight her weaknesses. Isn't that what true love is all about?

—MITCH TEMPLE

Why Isn't My Husband More Like Dad?

Three little girls were playing in the backyard on the swing. One said, "My dad is the strongest and fastest man in the world."

"No," said the second girl. "My daddy is strongest and fastest!"

"Yeah? Prove it!" the first girl demanded.

"Well, he's faster than a bullet!" the second one boasted.

"That's nothing," the third little girl said. "My daddy can run faster than a car!"

After a short silence, the first girl declared, "My dad is the fastest and I can prove it! He gets off work at five o'clock and is home by four!"

> No wonder so many wives compare their husbands unfavorably with their dads. But the reality is— and this is big—your husband is not your father.

Daughters tend to see their dads as superhuman—or at least special. Research has shown repeatedly that fathers have a huge impact on their girls. For example, close father-daughter relationships foster a sense of competence in girls' mathematical ability. Daughters who live in the same home with and are close to their dads are likely to start dating and having sex at a later age.

Dad is the first man with whom a daughter builds a relationship. That connection forms a framework for the way she views male-female relationships. Dad often teaches her how to make decisions, to work, and to care for others. For better or worse, he teaches her how a husband acts.

No wonder so many wives compare their husbands unfavorably with their dads. But the reality is—and this is big—*your husband is not your father*.

Here are three principles to remember in that regard:

1. *Your husband doesn't have your dad's experience.* When it comes to earning wisdom through practice, your dad has at least 20 years on your husband. Along the way, your father made mistakes and learned from them. So can your husband.

2. *Your dad wasn't perfect.* It's easy to forget someone's imperfections after you've moved away. But there were times when your father let you down, wasn't affectionate, wasn't communicative, wasn't as caring as he needed to be.

3. *Your father and your husband aren't supposed to be the same.* They have two distinct personalities, sets of experiences, families of origin, cultures, and environments in which they were raised. It's impossible for them to be alike. To think otherwise is unfair and unreasonable.

So what do you do? Secretly reprogram your husband to become your dad's twin? Send him to the same company that cloned Dolly the sheep?

No. You have to stop comparing your husband to your father.

Along the way, your father made mistakes and learned from them. So can your husband.

If your spouse displays behaviors or attitudes that disturb or hurt you, talk with him about them. Comparisons won't help.

Here are four more suggestions for breaking the comparison habit.

1. *Accent the positives and devalue the negatives.* Parents who harp on the negatives destroy their children's ability to value themselves. Wives who see in their husbands only the negatives and fail to appreciate the positives destroy their own ability to trust and respect their spouses.

2. *Commit yourself unconditionally to your husband.* "Above all, love each other deeply, because love covers over a multitude of sins" (1 Peter 4:8). Love, respect, and honor your mate in spite of his shortcomings. Allow your commitment to him to inspire you to change the way you see him and his faults.

This doesn't apply, of course, if your husband is abusive or needs help with psychological problems. These conditions need professional assessment and treatment. But annoying habits, mannerisms, and frustrations can be tolerated and dealt with by changes in his behavior or your own attitude.

3. *Honor both your husband and your father.* Your dad deserves honor and appreciation for his strengths. If you feel he fell short of being a great father, honoring him doesn't mean you approve of his neglect or bad habits. You're not ignoring his failures; you're choosing to honor him for who he is, your father. Taking that attitude, you're likely to work at improving your relationship with him.

The same attitude and approach should be taken with your husband—despite his weaknesses.

4. *Put your husband's faults in perspective.* Mary Andrews, an older lady, was teaching a church class of young, married women. They were discussing problems in marriage when one of the class members raised her hand.

"I realize this appears trivial," the woman said, "but my mom always said that a man who is too lazy to pick up his socks isn't worth a nickel! Well, I married a nickel. My husband never picks up his socks no matter how many times I ask him! He will do it for a day or two; then he goes back to his old habit. It is driving me crazy. I am beginning to lose respect for him."

Other ladies in the class affirmed that they had the same problem with their husbands.

Mary allowed the ladies to vent for a few minutes. Then she said softly, "You know, I had the same problem with my husband." Then she simply looked down and began turning pages in her Bible.

"Well," said a member of the group, "tell us what you did to get him to stop!"

"Actually, I was not successful in getting him to stop throwing his socks on the floor," Mary replied. "We have been married 43 years, and he still does it."

She continued, "I simply decided that this was not the worst habit he could have. My father drank all the time and came home night after night and kept us in constant fear and upheaval. Compared to my father, I came to realize that throwing socks on the floor was a minor battle that I chose not to fight.

"Besides," Mary concluded, "I decided a long time ago: I would rather my husband throw his socks at the foot of my bed than someone else's."

It's okay that your husband is not like your father. Celebrate the differences.

Commitment in marriage means that you've promised your utmost devotion, affection, and unwavering love to an imperfect person. Even if he's nothing like your dad.

—Mitch Temple

> If your spouse displays behaviors or attitudes that disturb or hurt you, talk with him about them. Comparisons won't help.

Why Isn't My "Blended" Marriage Blending?

When you remarried, others may have warned you about hazards ahead. Perhaps you thought love and respect would overcome any obstacles.

Now you wonder: How did things get out of control?

The "blended" family is more complex than the biological family—partly because there are parent-child relationships that predate this marriage. Biological families and stepfamilies are similar in that parents need to function as a team. If either parent places his or her child's need above the need to be a team, there's a crack in the wall. Children will spot the crack and fear that their needs won't be met. That may lead to anger and rebellion.

Children want the security of a functioning family that loves and accepts them. How can you and your spouse create a team that does that?

1. *Let Dad lead.* Every team needs a leader. One of a husband's leadership responsibilities is to honor his wife, as revealed in 1 Peter 3:7: "Husbands, in the same way be considerate as you live with your wives, and treat them with respect as the weaker partner and as heirs with you of the gracious gift of life, so that nothing will hinder your prayers."

Want all the members of your "blended" family to respect both parents? When you and your mate follow the directions of 1 Peter 3:7 consistently, your children are likely to follow your example.

Want all the members of your "blended" family to respect both parents? When you and your mate follow the directions of 1 Peter 3:7 consistently, your children are likely to follow your example.

2. *Honor the children.* This requires a lot of listening. Try scheduled family meetings. These enhance communication, allow input for decision making, and promote family identity. They're also good times for each family member to express feelings.

Forming a strong family identity usually takes extra work in a "blended" family. But when a child has that sense of identity, peer pressure has less influence on him or her.

3. *Make a plan.* Your parental team needs a proactive strategy. One approach is to write—under parental leadership and with children's input—a behavioral contract that outlines the expectations of each child and parent. It also identifies the consequences children or parents will be choosing if they decide not to comply.

Such an agreement gives each family member the freedom to make choices and to be affirmed. If you like, include a point system to reinforce appropriate choices.

Will these three steps guarantee that your family "blends"? No. To deal further with this challenge, you may need to carefully observe the family dynamics in your home and consider the following three suggestions.

1. *Is a family member being disruptive?* Sometimes a non-custodial parent or other family member causes chaos, deliberately or not. If that's happening to you, the idea of being honored is the furthest thing from your mind; you'd settle for an end to the hostilities.

> If you thought in the beginning that love and respect were keys to the success of your remarriage, you were right. But did you begin to doubt that when the first conflict arose?

When someone becomes disruptive, every person in the family system is pressed to dance around the needs of the one acting out. Each person loses the opportunity to get his or her own needs met—but the needs don't go away.

In that situation, brief, intensive family therapy is a good idea. It can help each person feel validated, develop a plan for safe behavioral change, and reduce stress. Even if all family members won't agree to counseling, the willing ones are encouraged to participate.

2. *Are you expecting too much too quickly?* Remarrying brings tremendous change. So does combining families. And change can bring tremendous pain, even under the best circumstances.

Research reveals that it takes an average of four to seven years for a stepfamily to reach a satisfactory comfort zone.[1] Each child needs time to get acquainted with the stepparent, to no longer feel a need to take care of any of the adults in the family system, to no longer feel bound by loyalty to either parent, to freely express emotions and needs to any parent, to be mentored on a one-to-one basis, to experience trials together, to enjoy activities as a family, and to learn to forgive.

3. *Are you fighting a spiritual battle?* If you thought in the beginning that

love and respect were keys to the success of your remarriage, you were right. But did you begin to doubt that when the first conflict arose?

Your real enemy may be the author of self-doubt, guilt, and condemnation (Revelation 12:9-10). Try lining up together as a family against Satan, not against each other. When you think your family is hopelessly fragmented, remember this: "Therefore, there is now no condemnation for those who are in Christ Jesus" (Romans 8:1).

Do things seem out of control in your stepfamily? The good news is that you aren't the One in control. You're in charge of submitting to Him, and can do in His strength what needs to be done (Philippians 4:13).

—BETTY JORDAN

Research reveals that it takes an average of four to seven years for a stepfamily to reach a satisfactory comfort zone.

Did I Marry the Wrong Person?

Movie star Mickey Rooney said, "Marriage is like batting in baseball; when the right one comes along, you don't want to let it go by." It sounds good, until you realize that Mickey was married eight times. He must have had a lot of "good pitches" to swing at!

Not to be outdone, Glynn DeMoss Wolfe, the world record holder of 26 marriages at the time, made a similar comparison. "Marriage is like stamp collecting," he said. "You keep looking to find that rare one."

Both men held what might be called the "needle in a haystack" view of picking a mate. According to this perspective, there's only one spouse with whom you could be happy. That person needs to be found even if it means discarding a spouse who no longer looks right for you.

Significant emotional pain lies in the wake of such a view. You won't find a "wrong needle" clause in the Bible that gives you an "out" if you conclude that your spouse isn't right for you. Instead you'll find in Malachi 2:15, "Do not break faith with the wife of your youth."

Marriage is not primarily about finding the right spouse. It's about being the right person.

When you're single, you experience a range of contentment from low to high. When you marry, that range has the potential to become even wider in both directions. Greater contentment—or discontentment—can take place than in your single years.

If you and your loved one were unhappy as singles and expected marriage to fulfill your lives, you probably were greatly disappointed as your level of contentment dropped even lower. But if you sensed meaning and purpose in your lives individually and wanted to share them in a lifetime commitment, you likely experienced an increase in contentment. You might call this the Mine Theory of Mate Selection. You either find the "land mine" or the "gold mine" in marriage.

If you entered marriage hoping to finally find happiness in your mate, you

> Some hold what might be called the "needle in a haystack" view of picking a mate. According to this perspective, there's only one spouse with whom you could be happy.

probably didn't find it. Like a carpenter who may first have to remove the floor-boards in order to shore up the joists underneath, you may first need to find contentment individually.

During courtship, people are often sure they've found the "gold mine." Both spouses-to-be tend to get excited about this wonderful, new relationship. The fireworks of romance help them act kinder, more selflessly, and more empathetically than they might when the fire fades.

We tend to fill in the gaps regarding the person we love. We assume during courtship that since he's willing to sit and listen to our feelings about life, he'll show the same concern after marriage when we want to talk about our frustrations. When he doesn't, we assume we married the wrong person.

In reality, he probably was not as wonderful as you thought he was before you married. On the other hand, he's probably not as terrible as you might now be thinking.

In his classic work, *The Art of Loving*, Erich Fromm declares, "To love somebody is not just a strong feeling—it is a decision, it is a judgment, it is a promise. If love were just a feeling, there would be no basis for the promise to love each other forever."[1]

> Marriage is not primarily about finding the right spouse. It's about being the right person.

Dr. James Dobson conveys a similar message in his book *Romantic Love*: "You see, [a couple's] love is not defined by the highs and lows, but is dependent *on a commitment of their will.* Stability comes from this irrepressible determination to make a success of marriage and to keep the flame aglow *regardless of the circumstances.*"[2]

When the two of you walked down the aisle, each of you became the right person for the other. Yes, you may look back and second-guess your reasons. But you entered an arena in which learning to truly love someone takes a lifetime.

Is your spouse perfect? Not a chance. Welcome to the human race.

That's what Larry and Linda learned.

Larry no longer felt the excitement he had when he and Linda were dating. She didn't speak to him as sweetly as in the old days. And if her spending habits continued, the two of them would end up in the poorhouse. Larry concluded that he'd made a mistake by marrying Linda.

When they entered counseling, Larry assumed Linda was not the woman for him. But he came to understand that even though Linda wasn't perfect, learning to love her was helping him grow as a spouse and become more lovable.

Larry might not have married Linda, knowing what he now knows about her. Yet he recognizes that beyond human decisions, God somehow works His purposes into the equation.

Larry no longer views marriage with a "needle in a haystack" mentality. He considers Linda as the one he's promised to love both in sickness and in health.

—Glenn Lutjens

When the two of you walked down the aisle, each of you became the right person for the other. You entered an arena in which learning to truly love someone takes a lifetime.

How Can I Change My Spouse?

A psychologist named Dr. Negri once decided his fiancée needed to change. Figuring he'd get an early start, he set out to remake the woman before they married. In therapy sessions he attempted to mold his patient, 30 years younger, into the perfect spouse.

After treatment was completed, they married. But the therapy seemed to fail as soon as he got the wedding ring on her finger.

She didn't want to wash the dishes or vacuum. Dr. Negri often had to watch their baby because his wife refused. The couple ended up in divorce court.

The psychologist said that he made one mistake when he took on the transformation. He forgot to do therapy on himself.

By now you may have noticed certain "flaws" in your spouse. Before you married, you saw shadows of irritating behaviors, but figured you'd get used to them over time—or you'd get your spouse to change.

Well, you haven't.

There are primarily two reasons why you might want to change your spouse.

1. *You want to see your spouse replicate your actions.* If you squeeze the toothpaste from the bottom of the tube, or put the toilet seat cover down, you probably want your spouse to do so, too. It's easy to approach differences with the attitude that your way is the right way.

2. *You want your spouse to meet your needs.* The more needy you are, the more likely you have a detailed agenda of what you want those changes to look like.

Which of these reasons applies to you?

Maybe you want your spouse to be like you. But consider the truth that many factors account for the differences between mates—family background, gender, cultural variations, temperament. God could have created clones if He wanted spouses to be carbon copies of each other. Instead, He wants you and your unique qualities to work with your spouse's unique characteristics.

Before you married, you saw shadows of irritating behaviors, but figured you'd get used to them over time—or you'd get your spouse to change. Well, you haven't.

It's a bit like vision. Close one eye; what happens? You lose depth perception cues. That's because you're viewing things from only one angle. When you look with two eyes, the slightly different vantage points of each eye turn your vision into a 3-D experience.

Instead of trying to make your mate "see things your way," you can benefit from having different perspectives. If you and your spouse view a situation from slightly different vantage points, you can blend those views and see things more accurately than either of you could individually.

Do you want your spouse to change in order to meet your needs? It's not unreasonable to want your needs met. But it *is* unreasonable to see your spouse as your private genie.

If you squeeze the toothpaste from the bottom of the tube, you probably want your spouse to do so, too. It's easy to approach differences with the attitude that your way is the right way.

In Philippians 2:4 Paul says, "Each of you should look not only to your own interests, but also to the interests of others." Are you as concerned about responding to your spouse's interests as you are with how your interests can be served?

There's nothing wrong with wanting to see your spouse change and grow. People are like trees; if we're not growing, we're probably dead. But you can only change you!

That doesn't mean there are no limits to what's appropriate in a marriage. You don't need to accept abusive behavior. Physical aggression toward a spouse is never right. Name-calling and belittling words also violate the God-given value to be reflected toward a mate.

What if you want change for reasons that aren't selfish?

In an effort to coax constructive change in a spouse, many resort to manipulation. They leave pamphlets or books around in the hope that the spouse will get the hint. Don't take that route.

If you have a concern, take ownership of your feelings. Voice them honestly and respectfully. Sometimes expressing them in a note can reduce defensiveness and cut through communication difficulties.

Consider the case of Bill and Sue.

For the first few years of their marriage, Bill saw their differences as a threat to his "headship." He tried unsuccessfully to "get her in line."

Finally Bill realized that his job was not to change Sue. He tried voicing his concerns constructively to her: "I know that there's been a lot going on for you lately, but I feel frustrated when clothes are left lying around the apartment. Is it something I can help you with?"

When Bill gave Sue the freedom to see issues from her viewpoint, he found that in the areas that mattered most she was willing to make adjustments. He also realized that many changes he'd thought necessary were not.

—GLENN LUTJENS

There's nothing wrong with wanting to see your spouse change and grow. But you can only change you!

Do I Have to Settle for Less?

Martha's dad was a real "fix-it" guy. He was frequently in the garage, repairing kitchen appliances or doing home improvement projects. But when Martha married her husband, Chuck, she was shocked to discover that Chuck was nothing like her dad. He had no problem ignoring an ever-growing list of things around their house that needed tightening, replacement, or repair.

Chuck had never been handy with home repairs, since he and his single mother lived in an apartment. Chuck's mom usually just notified the landlord when something needed attention.

At first Martha was perplexed when Chuck failed to notice items that needed repair. Then she was frustrated. In time she felt hurt, as though his failure to tackle home maintenance projects was intentional. Finally she went to her dad, embarrassed, and asked for his handyman help.

When it came to fixing things, Martha had to settle for less.

Should a spouse have to do that?

To figure out the answer to that question, we have to ask ourselves, "Less than what?"

Frequently marital disappointments are based on our expectations—what we thought life would be like after marrying. What we usually mean when we ask, "Do I have to settle for less?" is "Do I have to settle for less than I expected?"

> When it came to fixing things, Martha had to settle for less. Should a spouse have to do that?

Let's rethink the whole issue by asking, "Now that I'm really getting to know my spouse, with his or her capabilities and limitations, how am I reacting? Does my disappointment have to do with something he or she could change? Did I know about it and choose to overlook it? Was I not aware of it?"

Another question to ask yourself: "Is my dissatisfaction based on comparison? Am I looking at another person, wishing my spouse had his or her qualities?"

And still another: "How does all of this square with my wedding vows? Didn't I say something like, 'forsaking all others' and 'for better or worse'?"

Let's look at three ways *not* to deal with the question of settling for less.

1. *The self-centered approach.* "It's not fair that I don't get to be happy," you might say. Try replacing that with, "Is there anything my spouse can do to improve this situation? Does he or she understand how important it is to me? Have we talked and prayed about it?"

"And my God will meet all your needs according to his glorious riches in Christ Jesus" (Philippians 4:19). This may be an excellent verse to think about when you're feeling cheated. Your job may be to love and accept the one you've chosen, and trust God to motivate change according to His plan.

2. *The cynical approach.* Your spouse hasn't changed as you want him or her to. Maybe you'll have to put up with that for the rest of your life. You can choose to be cynical about that. Or you can choose to focus on what you love and cherish in your spouse.

> "It's not fair that I don't get to be happy," you might say. Try replacing that with, "Is there anything my spouse can do to improve this situation? Does he or she understand how important it is to me?"

In Martha's case, she finally realized she loved Chuck for all the positive things he represented—not for what he couldn't (or hadn't yet learned to) do in the way of home repair. It was a tough lesson, but accepting Chuck's limitations was part of Martha's maturation process.

You can also choose to defuse cynicism by maintaining a sense of humor. Martha may shrug and say, "Boy, is my dad going to be glad about all the stuff he gets to fix at our house."

3. *The vengeful approach.* One newlywed was overheard saying, "If I have to settle for less, so does he!"

Most of us may not have been so deliberate in our "get even" response, but it's something we've all thought about. That approach is a far cry from this one: "Finally, all of you, live in harmony with one another; be sympathetic, love as brothers, be compassionate and humble. Do not repay evil with evil or insult with insult, but with blessing, because to this you were called so that you may inherit a blessing" (1 Peter 3:8-9).

Anger and bitterness will eat away at your relationship. If you aren't able to make progress alone in dealing with these feelings, get help. Bring them to a pastor's or counselor's office for discussion and prayer.

Jerry struggled with settling for less—until he got help from a military chaplain and a pastor. Jerry had always wanted to marry a woman who'd "saved herself" for him. But then he'd met Lucy, a divorced single mom, at a church picnic. He'd been struck with Lucy's strong spiritual character, and was immediately accepted by Lucy's daughter, Heather.

When Jerry allowed himself to think about the idea of marrying Lucy, he found himself in conflict. If he married her, he'd have to accept that she'd been another man's wife—and that she'd be the sexually experienced one in their bedroom.

Jerry talked with his chaplain about this inner battle. The more Jerry grappled with his feelings about Lucy's past, the more he realized that Lucy couldn't change it. He'd either have to accept and forgive it, or move on without her.

In a very emotional discussion, Jerry revealed his struggle to Lucy. He admitted that a part of him wanted her to be changed, but he knew that

Anger and bitterness will eat away at your relationship. If you aren't able to make progress alone in dealing with these feelings, get help.

couldn't be. She seemed to understand. After praying together, they sought the counsel of her pastor, who was in charge of premarital counseling.

The pastor asked some hard questions: Could Jerry accept Lucy's past? Could he modify his expectations? Would Lucy and Heather be able to accept the frequent moves of a military family?

Jerry, Lucy, and Heather thought things over. Jerry decided that having Lucy and Heather in his life was more important than the feeling that he'd have to settle for less. His disappointment was finally resolved when he and Lucy made a commitment to each other.

Are you struggling with "settling" where your spouse is concerned? Here are five things to remember.

1. You aren't alone. God, who loves you, knows about your situation. He wants more for you than you could ever imagine (see Ephesians 3:20).

2. Accepting your mate as he or she really is demonstrates your growth in maturity and love. That goes hand in hand with forgiving his or her shortcomings.

3. If you respectfully discuss your unmet expectations with your spouse, change may be possible. If it isn't, forgiveness is the salve that comforts those unfulfilled hopes.

4. This is a two-way street. Consider whether your spouse is already accepting and forgiving some trait of yours that he or she would prefer to see changed.

5. Discussing these issues in the presence of a third party, such as a pastor or therapist, can help.

—LON ADAMS

> You can choose to be cynical. Or you can choose to focus on what you love and cherish in your spouse.

Part 3:
Roles

What Does It Mean to Be a Wife?

Valerie threw her coat to the floor and screamed, "Robert, this is it! I am tired of being treated like a child. You will not allow me to be an adult. You force me to act like a child by the way you treat me. I can't express my opinion or offer any advice. It always has to be your decision—and if I question that decision, you try to argue me back down. I don't know what God intended for a wife to be, but I don't think it was to be like this!"

What *does* it mean to be a wife?

It's a question that's been asked since the beginning of time. Surely every young wife and wife-to-be has at least *thought* about it.

Much of the confusion about what it means to be a wife stems from our culture's messages on the subject. Hollywood often portrays women as independent, strong, superior, and answerable to no one. But is that what a wife should look like? What are her roles? What should a husband expect of her?

> Hollywood often portrays women as independent, strong, superior, and answerable to no one. Is that what a wife should look like?

If you're struggling with your role (or your spouse's), you're not alone. When these issues are unresolved, it often leads to a sense of hopelessness going into the wedding and a sense of contention afterward.

Let's answer the question by looking at its opposite: What does it *not* mean to be wife? Here are three principles to think about.

1. *A wife is not a maid.* Some husbands expect their wives to take care of all domestic chores. Some wives are content with this arrangement, especially when the husband assumes a handyman role. But both partners should negotiate this and feel comfortable with the result.

Mandy and Maury simplified the division of labor by agreeing that everything inside the home would be her responsibility—and everything outside the door would be his. That worked well until Mandy decided that taking the garbage out, a job she'd been doing, wasn't "inside" work. She voiced her concern to Maury, but it fell on deaf ears. The next day, Maury pulled into the driveway to discover the trash can sitting outside the front door!

Nowhere in Scripture does God command wives, "Thou shalt perform every household task alone, no matter how sick or tired thou mayest become or how many sleepless nights thou hast experienced." God didn't intend a wife to be the family butler, cook, and domestic engineer without support from her husband.

Just as wives are not exempt from helping out with yard work, husbands aren't excused from mutually agreed upon duties inside the home. Was Eve expected to perform every domestic chore by herself? When she became pregnant with Cain, who do you think she depended on? Since no one else was around to help out, we can safely assume that Adam took up the slack.

> ❧
>
> **Nowhere in Scripture does God command wives, "Thou shalt perform every household task alone, no matter how sick or tired thou mayest become or how many sleepless nights thou hast experienced."**
>
> ❦

Adam's view of Eve was reflected in his statement of appreciation when God first presented her to him: "The man said, 'This is now bone of my bones and flesh of my flesh; she shall be called "woman," for she was taken out of man.' For this reason a man will leave his father and mother and be united to his wife, and they will become one flesh" (Genesis 2:23-24). Couples need to adopt the same team approach, recalling that God has brought them together in a partnership.

2. *A wife is not a doormat.* The Bible does say that the husband is the "head" of the wife, and that wives are to be in submission to their husbands. But nowhere does it grant "dictator" status to husbands, or require that wives must fulfill a husband's every wish and command, no matter how unreasonable or uncaring.

Submission is an attitude, a spirit of being under someone's leadership in the domain of marriage. Paul says in Ephesians 5:22, "Wives, submit yourselves to your husbands as to the Lord." But he also says, "Submit to one another out of reverence for Christ" (Ephesians 5:21). Submission doesn't mean that a woman can be mistreated or harmed by her husband simply because he's the leader of the home.

Submission doesn't necessarily mean agreement, either. Just because a wife is under her husband's leadership, she doesn't necessarily agree with everything he does or every decision he makes.

How does that work in real life? Think about what happens when you accept a job. You agree to submit to someone else's authority. You don't give up your freedom and rights as a human being. You're still supposed to be treated with respect and kindness.

Submitting at work is critical to career development. The employee who willingly submits to the job's requirements will get something in return—job satisfaction and the security of regular income. We give, but we also receive.

The same is true of roles in marriage. A wife voluntarily places herself in a position of submission to God and to her husband's leadership. She doesn't give up her individuality. She gives her heart, body, and soul to a relationship of mutuality and service.

If you follow God's commands on how to treat your mate, you'll love, respect, honor, and cherish each other. You'll find no human doormats in your home.

3. *A wife is not to be the downfall of her husband.* God designed women to be husband builders, not husband wreckers. As the Bible puts it, "The LORD God said, 'It is not good for the man to be alone. I will make a helper suitable for him'" (Genesis 2:18).

Adam was engineered to work hard, lead his family, and overcome challenges. God gave Eve the ability, power, and free choice to either build up her husband or tear him down.

Proverbs 14:1 says, "The wise woman builds her house, but with her own hands the foolish one tears hers down." Most wives don't set out to destroy their mates. But they often allow stress, frustration, and resentment to motivate them to treat their husbands in ways that dishonor them. Constant nagging and criticism, for instance, can wear a man down more quickly than a 60-hour week of hard labor! This kind of behavior destroys a man's ability to be what he should be—a confident leader.

When a man feels disrespected and demoralized, he often reacts by withdrawing from the relationship. His ability to be truly close to his wife has a lot to do with how she treats him. As Ephesians 5:33 (AMP) says, "Let the wife see that she respects and reverences her husband—that she notices him, regards him, honors him, prefers him, venerates, and esteems him; and that she defers to him, praises him, and loves and admires him exceedingly."

So what does it mean to be a wife?

> Submission doesn't mean that a woman can be mistreated or harmed by her husband simply because he's the leader of the home. It doesn't necessarily mean agreement, either.

There are many ways to answer that question. But here's one summary you might keep in mind. The apostle Paul urged older women to teach younger women, "so that they will wisely train the young women to be sane and sober-minded—temperate, disciplined—and to love their husbands and their children; to be self-controlled, chaste, homemakers, good-natured (kindhearted), adapting and subordinating themselves to their husbands, that the word of God may not be exposed to reproach—blasphemed or discredited" (Titus 2:4-5, AMP).

—MITCH TEMPLE

> If you follow God's commands on how to treat your mate, you'll love, respect, honor, and cherish each other. You'll find no human doormats in your home.

What Does It Mean to Be a Husband?

"A man is not where he lives, but where he loves."
—Latin Proverb

John was working long hours at his office, providing financially for his family. That, he believed, was his duty as a husband. Seldom at home, he didn't realize what his schedule was doing to the foundation of the family he was trying to establish.

Before he knew it, he was living by himself.

Stunned, he asked himself why his wife had suddenly left him.

The warning signs had been there, but John had been too busy to recognize them. The fact was that he'd developed a skewed perspective of his role as a man and husband several years before marrying Susan. As a young man he'd watched his father work long hours, and came to believe that his identity and level of success depended on how others saw his accomplishments. Compliments drove his work ethic.

John was struggling with loving and accepting himself. He worked long and hard to gain the praise of others—but neglected his family because building a strong marriage usually doesn't earn many accolades.

What does it mean to be a husband? John thought he knew, but discovered otherwise.

You don't have to make the same mistake. Here are some qualities found in Ephesians 5:19-33 that help define what a husband is and does.

1. *Love shown in sacrifice and commitment.* A husband's love needs to be unselfish. It's not always tied to sexual desire, which by its nature is self-seeking.

How might things have been different for John if, when awakening every morning, he'd started the

A husband's love needs to be unselfish. It's not always tied to sexual desire, which by its nature is self-seeking.

day by figuring out how to make it a special one for Susan? That act of sacrificial, committed, unselfish love could have revolutionized their relationship.

Love from a husband also needs to be natural, not dutiful. Making sacrifices out of mere duty isn't an expression of love; it may just be an effort to avoid failure and pain. That's not to say that loving deeds will always be accompanied by warm feelings; sometimes the actions come first and the feelings are a step behind.

2. *Leadership and courage.* Leaders need to first learn how to serve (see Matthew 20:26). Then they can lead through example. In John's case, he could have helped his family by showing how to express unconditional love, set boundaries, provide guidance, exercise self-control, and manage money.

Husbands need courage, too. But that quality isn't just about driving through thunderstorms and stopping burglars. A husband also needs the courage to admit his mistakes, and to participate in his own growing and maturing process.

3. *Sound priorities.* A husband must learn about his wife's needs, put them above his own, and respond to them—physically and emotionally. John needed to say no to his competitive drive sometimes. He needed to learn that the most rewarding thing—above applause, recognition, money, success, and attention—is being able to love another person to the point that you would give your life for her.

That's not to say that a husband must erase his boundaries and individuality. It's important to maintain friendships, dreams, goals, vision, and "healthy space." But a "me first" attitude is the opposite of the one commanded in Scripture (see Philippians 2:3-4).

> Husbands need courage. But that quality isn't just about driving through thunderstorms and stopping burglars.

4. *Communication and thanksgiving.* A husband needs to keep learning more about his wife and to communicate verbally and nonverbally. It's not healthy to trust only in yourself.

Just as a man can't read a woman's mind, a woman can't read a man's. Take time to share your thoughts. Let your spouse into your life.

5. *Unity.* The marriage covenant represents the greatest unity a man will ever have. It's a closeness that's above that between parents and children and among friends.

Both Old and New Testaments (Genesis 2:24; Ephesians 5:31) affirm that husband and wife "will become one flesh." There's a unity that goes beyond the physical.

Joan and Bill are examples of what happens when these principles are applied in a marriage.

Recently married, Bill was getting involved in as many things as possible at work in an attempt to "move up" in his career. He was trying to establish what he called "a good name."

Joan was also working full-time, but was home in the evenings. As a result, she spent many lonely nights and weekends waiting for Bill to come home. The couple's romance and intimacy were becoming nonexistent.

Joan asked Bill to begin saying no to work requests that weren't essential. He listened to her need to connect and began to set limits on his job commitments.

This was difficult for him initially, but the relationship began to thrive. He began to feel better about himself. He noticed that things were even improving at work, too.

It was clear that God was honoring Bill's commitment to listen and respond to his wife. If only John had made that commitment while he still had the opportunity.

What does it mean to be a husband? There are many steps a man takes in his marital journey, but the first—and perhaps most important—is committing himself to fulfilling his God-ordained purpose of meeting his wife's needs.

—DANIEL HUERTA

A husband must learn about his wife's needs, put them above his own, and respond to them—physically and emotionally.

How Should We Divide Up the Chores?

When you fell in love, was the question of how to divide up the chores on your radar screen? Probably not.

But now that you're married, chores are one thing you can't escape. The daily routine for all but the very wealthy consists of activities like cooking meals, doing the dishes, washing clothes, maintaining household appliances, repairing the car(s), handling the finances, parenting the kids (if any), feeding the animals (if any), choosing insurance, and cleaning the house or apartment. Some chores pop up right after the honeymoon; others emerge over time.

It's common to think in terms of "male" and "female" chores. But should a wife automatically be in charge of shower curtains, while her husband specializes in replacing shower heads?

Christian couples may tend to think such male/female distinctions are biblical rather than traditional. But the Bible doesn't specifically support the notion that, for example, only women must cook and only men must calculate the budget and finances. After all, Jacob prepared the stew that Esau ate (Genesis 25); the "wife of noble character" in Proverbs 31 dealt with business concerns.

> It's common to think in terms of "male" and "female" chores. But should a wife automatically be in charge of shower curtains, while her husband specializes in replacing shower heads?

How you feel about dividing up chores has a lot to do with the way your parents handled this question.

Steve assumes the husband is supposed to handle all the chores outside the home and the wife handles those inside. That's the way his parents did things.

His wife, Abby, on the other hand, had a father who masterminded the family finances, vacuumed the floors, and did the gardening. She expects Steve to do the same.

Down the street, Greg recalls how his mother balanced the checkbook and painted the walls. He thinks his wife, Tyra, should follow that pattern.

Tyra, meanwhile, had a father who loved to cook. Why, she wonders, won't Greg follow in his footsteps?

Differences like these lead one spouse to feel the other isn't "pulling his or her weight" when it comes to household duties.

One young husband and wife, married only six months, came to a counselor because they'd been arguing constantly over chores. The husband was upset because his wife "wasted time" and didn't get as much done as he expected. The wife was resentful because her husband didn't feel he should have to help at home after putting in a hard day at the office.

That couple wasn't unusual. Anger and arguments over sharing responsibilities often bring spouses into counseling for resolution.

So is there a right answer to the question of dividing up chores?

A quick response might be to suggest adopting the Fox News motto, "Fair and Balanced." But what does that mean?

Here are more specific guidelines that may help prevent or bridge areas of conflict when it comes to chores.

1. *Think positively.* Most husbands and wives enter marriage expecting to share the load to some degree. Figuring out how to make the sharing balanced and appropriate is not only desirable, but possible.

2. *Consider the rewards.* When husband and wife work outside the home, tackling chores together lifts the load. It gives you more time for individual activities. It gives you more time together.

> **How you feel about dividing up chores has a lot to do with the way your parents handled this question.**

3. *Concentrate on giftedness, not gender.* Rather than emphasizing "male" and "female" chores, talk about which jobs you enjoy or don't mind doing. Which do you have a knack for? Which would you prefer not to do?

4. *Allow for exceptions.* Helping each other out with chores during times of stress, busyness, or illness is very much appreciated by a spouse. It also tends to be reciprocated.

5. *Write it down.* Making a list of what needs to be done is essential. It's too easy to forget who's supposed to do what.

6. *Stay flexible.* No matter how fair and equal things seem at the start, you may have to make adjustments along the way. One spouse who was at home may begin a full-time job. Another may endure serious illness or injury.

7. *Don't go strictly by the numbers.* Fair and equal doesn't necessarily mean "one for you, one for me." Remember that some chores are more difficult and time-consuming than others.

8. *Chart yours, mine, and ours.* A busy, young husband and wife struggled to balance their desire for fun with the reality of day-to-day duties. They developed a simple chart that made the "to do" list look less intimidating—and more equally distributed.

MATT'S CHORES
1. Painting the house
2. Repairs on vehicles
3. Developing a budget
OUR CHORES
1. Care for the garden
2. Cleaning the house
3. Planning vacations
MARY'S CHORES
1. Buying groceries, fixing meals
2. Balancing checkbook
3. Home decorating

Dividing up chores is an opportunity for cooperation rather than conflict. A key to the challenge of marriage is striving to understand each other and seeking to meet each other's needs—and this is a great area in which to practice.

Even the act of discussing and dividing up what needs to be accomplished can lessen conflict. If you find yourself stuck in these issues, though, don't hesitate to seek assistance from a more experienced couple or a counselor.

—WILFORD WOOTEN

> When husband and wife work outside the home, tackling chores together lifts the load. It gives you more time together.

Who Should Take Care of the Kids?

Craig and Amy have a three-month-old boy, Joshua. Amy is staying home with him; Craig is working.

Amy had always looked forward to being a stay-at-home mom, and she loves it. Still, the days get long. Sometimes she feels uncertain about the best way to care for her baby.

She's growing frustrated with Craig, too. He goes off to work each day, comes home, and expects dinner to be ready and the house to be spotless.

Doesn't he realize how hard it is to do work at home all day? she thinks. *He never offers to change the baby's diapers. When I ask him, he just complains and looks at me like it's putting him out.*

Today, when her husband comes home, she tries one more time. "Craig, Joshua is crying. Could you please go change his diaper?"

Craig rolls his eyes, but reluctantly picks up Joshua and takes him to the nursery to change him.

Amy doesn't know it, but Craig is thinking, *I have no idea what I'm doing. She has so much more practice at this. She babysat when she was young and she's with him every day, all day. Why does she want me to do this? Oh, man! Look at that mess!*

In walks Amy.

"Craig, you're doing it wrong! You know you need to . . ."

Craig thinks Amy should take care of the baby. Amy thinks Craig isn't doing enough.

Who's right? Is caring for the kids Mom's job, or Dad's?

Like many parents, Craig and Amy haven't told each other their expectations in this area. They aren't telling each other about their struggles with being parents, either. Both feel insecure; both are trying to do the best they can.

Women often say they want their husbands to help with parenting tasks like diapering and feeding the baby. When Dad starts to help, though, Mom jumps

"He never offers to change the baby's diapers. When I ask him, he just complains and looks at me like it's putting him out."

in to correct everything he's doing. As a result, both spouses get more irritated—and the husband shrinks from trying to help next time, fearing his attempts will be criticized.

So, how can the two of you avoid such conflict and answer this question for yourselves? Here are four suggestions.

1. *Talk it out.* Begin by clearly discussing your expectations for your child-rearing roles. Try questions like the following.

- Do you share the traditional belief that the woman is the nurturer and stays home with the child, while the husband is the provider and goes out to earn the income?
- If so, how does that play out on a daily basis? Is the woman not employed outside the home? Does she run a home-based business in addition to caring for the children?
- Do you expect the wife to tend to the children all day and all night?
- Is the wife also supposed to have the home spotless, dinner prepared, and breakfast and lunch made for her husband each day?
- Do you have a view that's less traditional, with husband and wife sharing responsibilities for income-providing and parenting?
- If so, how are the responsibilities shared? For example, if one spouse is a part-time stay-at-home parent and the other is a full-time employee, do you share household and child-rearing tasks in the evening?

These can be difficult things to think through, much less talk through. But such discussions are vital, and it's best to start having them before your children arrive if possible. The point of these talks is not to set your arrangements in stone, but to start talking about expectations and work toward compromises in areas of disagreement.

> "I have no idea what I'm doing. She babysat when she was young and she's with him every day, all day. Why does she want me to do this? Oh, man! Look at that mess!"

Once kids are on the scene, keep talking. You may find your minds, hearts, and plans changing.

2. *Question the assumption that both parents must be employed.* These days it's common for spouses in our culture to share child-rearing tasks to some degree. The biggest struggle is over whether both husband and wife should keep working outside the home.

Before having a baby, many women believe they'll want to continue their employment. When the baby arrives, though, they often change their minds. What happens then depends on a couple's financial situation—real or imagined.

Many couples believe it would be impossible to live on one income. When a baby arrives, though, some find they can cut back on expenses and make income stretch so that Mom can stay home with the child.

Not everyone can do this, of course. As the two of you consider the possibilities, though, be sure to get the facts on the financial and emotional costs and benefits of returning to work versus staying home.

3. *Be a team.* God designed babies to benefit from the love and care of both parents. You and your spouse were designed to fall in love with your child. All of this can happen only when you spend time together.

Some parents, especially some dads, avoid spending that time with their little ones. These parents protest that they're not familiar with

> Each of you is a necessary member of the team. A father's rough-and-tumble playing goes a long way toward developing a child's equilibrium, while a mom's snuggling and singing cultivate attachment and emotional and verbal skills.

changing diapers, warming bottles, giving baths, and the like. But your baby needs you; child-care skills can be learned. Don't use inexperience as an excuse for abdicating your responsibility.

Each of you is a necessary member of the team. Moms and dads offer different experiences to their children; a father's rough-and-tumble playing goes a long way toward developing a child's equilibrium, while a mom's snuggling and singing cultivate attachment and emotional and verbal skills.

4. *Cut each other some slack.* It's normal to be inexperienced and uncertain when taking care of infants. This is an area in which to give each other grace, not to criticize. If you're more experienced than your spouse in being with small children, be patient. Let your mate find his or her own way and comfort zone with the baby.

Fathers, for example, are often more comfortable with babies when the latter are a little older and more developed—especially as the baby's neck strength increases and she can hold her own head steady. Fear of holding the baby earlier tends to lessen with practice.

This doesn't mean, of course, that dads shouldn't be expected to invest time in their kids before the children can play catch or watch a football game. If you're an uncertain parent, ask your spouse to help you find your own way to care for your little one. If you're the more confident parent, be merciful. Grace is a key to developing a strong bond with your child and to strengthening the bond with your mate.

Remember Craig and Amy? After talking with a girlfriend, Amy decided she needed to back off and let Craig relate to Joshua in his own way. The most important thing, she realized, was that Craig was spending time with the baby and loving him. If Joshua's diaper was backwards, that wasn't a make-or-break issue.

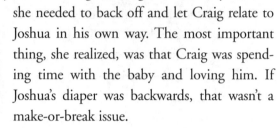

If you're an uncertain parent, ask your spouse to help you find your own way to care for your little one. If you're the more confident parent, be merciful.

So tonight Amy has dinner waiting for Craig when he gets home from work. Joshua, in the baby swing next to the table, coos as the spouses talk.

Finally Amy says, "Craig, if you could please watch Joshua for me for an hour this evening, I need to take a shower and wash my hair and shave my legs. I really just need some time to myself."

Craig looks a little concerned. "Honey," he says, "a whole hour?"

"Yeah," Amy replies. "You'll be fine. And if you need me, I'll just be in the next room."

Craig smiles and agrees to give it a go.

An hour later, Amy emerges from her mini-vacation. As for Craig, it seems his fears were unfounded. Father and son are asleep on the couch, and it's Amy's turn to smile.

—SANDRA LUNDBERG

Who Should Earn the Money?

Is "bringing home the bacon" always the husband's responsibility?

Should the task of providing income be split 50-50?

What if the wife earns more than the husband?

If you're struggling with issues like these, maybe it's because you think there's only one right answer to the question of who the breadwinner(s) should be—and your marriage doesn't fit that model.

But is there only one acceptable arrangement? And what if you designate a breadwinner, only to have pregnancy, unemployment, or disability upend your plans?

Consider the stories of these three couples.

1. *Mack and Claudine.* They'd graduated from college with honors. He headed for seminary; she was accepted at a prestigious business school, where she got her MBA. Mack made no secret of how strongly he felt God's call to full-time ministry; Claudine was equally attracted to the business world, where she felt she could let her faith shine while making a good living.

After graduate school, while they were still engaged, Mack accepted a position at a church near the seminary. Claudine found a great entry-level job—but it meant a 60-mile commute on weekends to see Mack and attend his church.

Finally they married. Now they had to decide where to live. Mack ended up making the bigger compromise, moving about 40 miles so that Claudine wouldn't have a one-hour commute to her demanding job.

Mack's mother had worked part-time when he was in high school, so a working wife wasn't an unfamiliar concept. But the difference between his pay and Claudine's took some getting used to. Claudine's job provided incremental raises and other benefits; Mack felt fortunate that the church gave him a small cost-of-living pay increase after his first year.

When Claudine became pregnant, she and Mack had some tough issues to decide. Who would keep working, and who would be home with the baby?

> If you're struggling with issues like these, maybe it's because you think there's only one right answer to the question of who the breadwinner(s) should be—and your marriage doesn't fit that model.

They based their decision on what seemed like financial necessity. It required compromise and sacrifice, especially for Mack. He'd never considered it possible for someone called to full-time ministry to become Mr. Mom—but that's exactly what happened. For the time being, at least, he would stay home with their new baby. Claudine, after her maternity leave, would continue in her career and provide for their family.

2. *Jim and Carol.* They seemed perfectly matched. She'd always wanted the security of being a stay-at-home wife and eventually mother, as her mom had been. Jim's parents had followed a similar pattern, and he'd always thought their way was best.

Jim remembered his dad saying, "If I'm not the breadwinner, I'd feel like a failure." That arrangement was compatible with Carol's ambitions, who didn't consider herself a potential career woman—and who'd never pursued much more than part-time jobs during college summers.

When this couple bought a new home with fairly stiff mortgage payments, Jim said something Carol wasn't prepared to hear: "We may need you to get a job and help out, if my raise doesn't come through."

It didn't come through. Worse, the company went through a round of lay-offs. Jim felt fortunate not to be one of them.

They sat down to talk about their bills. Monthly commitments, combined with a credit card they'd used on a summer trip, had strained their resources to the limit. Jim felt that asking Carol to help out by getting a job was perfectly reasonable. After all, she wasn't pregnant yet.

Jim and Carol assumed they understood each other's attitudes about who should make the money. But when finances got tight, it was clear they'd assumed too much.

But Carol thought, *Frankly, I shouldn't have to work. That's why I married Jim.* Since their courtship she'd thought Jim wanted his wife to be home full-time—even before children came along. "Why should we change plans now?" she asked.

As they talked, Jim seemed more than worried. He was angry. About the only thing they agreed on was that Carol should start managing the checkbook. Jim wanted her to see how carefully they had to conserve their income.

Carol began to budget carefully, including what she spent on groceries. It was an eye-opening experience.

At last report, Carol was still under pressure to get a job. Jim was yearning for more leisure activities and spending options. He thought an annual fishing trip and vacation were only reasonable—and only affordable if Carol went to work.

3. *Bill and Carmen.* They'd married during their first year of college, but had promised to finish school. But by the second semester of their junior year, Carmen was working 20 or 30 hours a week in a campus office, taking only two classes.

She was weary, but agreed that Bill needed to get his degree as soon as possible. He carried extra units and was pressed to maintain high grades in order to keep scholarship money coming in.

Bill applied to graduate schools. Carmen could see that her role was changing. She would be the breadwinner while her husband pursued academic achievement.

Her parents weren't thrilled that she'd lost sight of her goals. Soon she was enrolled in just one class and still had only junior status.

When Bill graduated with honors and was accepted into the school of his choice, there were lots of cheers and applause for him. Carmen forced a smile and said all the "right" things about taking a backseat to launching Bill's career.

At the office, Carmen envied the other women. They didn't have to put their husbands through school. They could have babies, and take maternity leave or quit their jobs altogether.

Carmen sank into depression. She could see the concern on Bill's face. But she couldn't tell whether it was concern for her—or just worry about his studies.

What can we learn from these stories about who should earn the money in your marriage?

1. *Be clear in the beginning about what you want.* Who should provide the income is a subject that requires discussion and agreement as a couple enters marriage.

Jim and Carol assumed they understood each other's attitudes about who should make the money. But when finances got tight, it was clear they'd assumed too much. Bill and Carmen hadn't addressed the question of whether one spouse should put the other through school. The result was resentment.

Have you discussed how each of you would feel about one spouse earning much more than the other, or what would happen if one of you couldn't work? Now's the time to put your thoughts and feelings into words.

Have you and your spouse talked about who should earn the money in your household? Have you discussed how each of you would feel about one spouse earning much more than the other, or what would happen if one of you couldn't work, or whether one spouse's employment could require both of you to move to a different part of the country?

Now's the time to put your thoughts and feelings into words. If doing so generates more heat than light, you may need the help of a pastor or counselor to communicate and negotiate.

2. *Realize that things change.* Life didn't go as planned for any of the couples in these stories. Compromise and self-sacrifice became the order of the day, even for those who thought they had everything worked out.

Unexpected pregnancy, illness, loss of a job, or other unforeseen circumstances require flexibility. That usually means a willingness to adjust one's personal ambition or goals.

Sit "loose in the saddle" as you launch your marriage and family. Believe that our loving heavenly Father allows challenges to our plans, sometimes to stretch us and develop our characters and affirm our faith in Him.

> Is it worth damaging your relationship with your spouse in order to preserve a certain kind of money-earning arrangement? Bringing home income is a challenge, but the greater challenge is learning how to work together as a couple.

3. *Be open to new patterns.* Jim and Carol assumed their parents' approach to earning a living was the right one, and tried to copy it. But family tradition may not always work for you. Whether it's the goal of having only the husband working, or how soon a spouse must complete formal education, keep in mind that careers and modes of moneymaking aren't necessarily hereditary.

4. *Maintain hope for the future.* When Mack had to set aside his plans for full-time ministry, he was no doubt discouraged. But if God was indeed calling him, God would provide a way to answer that call.

Don't give up if you have to delay or modify your goals in order to support your family. The same God who gives us big dreams also keeps our feet on the ground with instructions like, "If anyone does not provide for his relatives, and especially for his immediate family, he has denied the faith and is worse than an unbeliever" (1 Timothy 5:8).

5. *Remember that you're committed to each other, not just to an economic model.* What is it really costing Jim and Carol to fight over the question of whether she should work? Will Bill and Carmen's marriage survive their effort to get Bill through school?

In other words, is it worth damaging your relationship with your spouse in order to preserve a certain kind of money-earning arrangement?

Bringing home income is a challenge, but the greater challenge is learning how to work together as a couple. Financial security is a worthy goal, but a greater one is to fulfill our responsibility as spouses committed to marriage, come what may.

—Lon Adams

What Does It Mean to Be the Spiritual Leader?

Kim and Trevor were highly involved at their church. They enjoyed serving in various roles, while trying to make sure they didn't spend so much time on church work that they couldn't nurture their new marriage.

When Kim was asked to take charge of a preschool choir, she hesitated. She'd need time to pray and discuss the opportunity with Trevor, she said. After all, her husband was the spiritual leader of their home.

When you hear that story, how do you react? Is Kim right in thinking of her husband as the spiritual leader? Or does she sound like a throwback to the days of pilgrim hats and porridge?

Many people these days would pick the latter. At the very least, they'd have questions about the idea of husbands exercising spiritual leadership.

Some husbands wonder, "What am I supposed to do, act like a preacher?"

Some wives ask, "Why is *he* supposed to be the only spiritual leader? Why can't we both do it?"

Others say, "My husband's not interested in leading. What am I supposed to do?"

> Is Kim right in thinking of her husband as the spiritual leader? Or does she sound like a throwback to the days of pilgrim hats and porridge?

These questions have at least two things in common. First is an acknowledgment that families need leaders. Second is the issue of control: Who's really in charge, and why?

While the Bible clearly affirms the equality of men and women (see Galatians 3:28), God assigned the responsibility of spiritual leadership to husbands: "Wives, submit to your husbands, as is fitting in the Lord. Husbands, love your wives and do not be harsh with them" (Colossians 3:18-19).

Differing roles don't mean, however, that God considers wives inadequate, less important, or less responsible as "suitable helpers" (see Genesis 2:18). Only an unwise man would reject his wife's opinions and assistance, since God created her to be his best earthly resource.

Where does this leave the Christian woman whose husband is an unbeliever—or uninterested in spiritual leadership? Like the single Christian woman, she still has a Husband who nurtures and equips her. Like all Christian women (and men), she answers first to God.

The wife whose husband can't or won't be the spiritual leader is to be an example to him and a representative of Christ. She resists participating in anything—pornography, for example—that would bring him spiritual harm. If he causes physical, mental, or spiritual hurt to her or their children, she carries out her duty to leave with them immediately, lest she endanger him by enabling him to sin.

But what about husbands and wives who share an active faith in Christ? What is a spiritual leader supposed to *do*?

Christians have varying opinions on the mechanics of this question. In fact, this may be one of the most divisive issues in the church today.

Generally speaking, if a Christian husband and wife have a healthy relationship, they make decisions together as equals—agreeing that Christ is the ultimate Head of their home. They compare their individual aptitudes and assume tasks based on their strengths. In some areas of service they share tasks. But they both recognize that the husband carries the greater responsibility for leadership.

A spiritual servant-leader is ready to protect, help, and defend. For instance, if his wife is being treated badly by a parent, in-law, or boss, a man following Christ's example will sacrifice relational comfort when necessary to come to her defense.

A true spiritual leader imitates Christ. He's attuned to his family's needs, providing physical support, grace, and encouragement. He's concerned for the spiritual welfare of family members and takes initiative to help them grow in their relationship with God.

> Some husbands wonder, "What am I supposed to do, act like a preacher?"

Even in hard times, he doesn't regard this role as boring or overly difficult. It's what he was made for. Not just willing to die for the members of his family, he's ready to live for them, too.

Since spiritual leadership grows from a man's relationship with Christ, it defies a simple description. But here are a few ideas to help you get a better picture of the qualities needed.

1. *Connection to God.* He seeks his happiness in Christ first, realizing he can lead effectively only if he has an intimate relationship with God. Understanding he has nothing to give if he doesn't first receive from God, he looks for spiritual sustenance so he'll be able to feed his family's heart.

2. *Balance.* He pursues this for the good of his faith and family. He has the freedom to enjoy his own interests, knowing it's okay to spend an occasional Saturday morning on the golf course as long as it doesn't usurp important family time. He discusses things with his wife rather than handing down unilateral decisions, finding safety in the give-and-take of their partnership.

3. *Nurture.* He attends to his family's physical health and sustenance, and considers the mental and emotional needs of each person. He seeks to superintend his family's spiritual development individually and corporately. He knows his goal is a whole, functional family, not just a bunch of polished individuals.

4. *Action.* As problems emerge, he looks for proven resources that will help. He's proactive, spotting potential challenges and solutions. Instead of waiting until things get worse, he remains on the offense, delighting in applying solutions to his loved ones' needs.

5. *Integrity.* He seeks to be the safest, most respected man known by his family. He deals with each person carefully, but with resolve, recognizing that he's a steward of what God has given him. His servant leadership inspires other family members to go beyond their duties and be imitators of Christ—and of him.

A spiritual servant-leader is ready to protect, help, and defend. A true spiritual leader imitates Christ.

That's the kind of person Trevor was trying to be when Kim came to him about the request to oversee the children's choir. He could tell Kim was torn between her desire to please the music committee director and her concern about the added responsibility.

"What do *you* want to do?" he asked.

"I . . . really don't want to let them down," she said anxiously. "All the parents said I'd be just right for this job."

He smiled, shaking his head. This was so typical of her—wanting to please, but regretting it later. He knew the ending wouldn't be happy if she took the job out of a sense of duty.

"I'll respect whatever you decide, Kim," he said. "But I can't say it sounds like a wise investment. Sunday afternoons are always a nice time for us to be together before another busy week. I'd miss that. And I'd be concerned you might be more stressed going into your week, too."

She frowned. "I hadn't thought of it that way," she said. "You're right. I almost gave away our favorite time of the week! Do you think it would be selfish of me to turn them down?"

"Not at all," Trevor assured her. "I just appreciate your willingness to consider my advice."

"What would I do without your level head?" she said with a laugh.

"For one thing," he teased, "you'd be a lot busier."

Spiritual leadership shouldn't be a grim prospect. It should enhance a couple's relationship, and flow from each spouse's growing relationship with God.

—ROB JACKSON

A spiritual leader seeks his happiness in Christ first, realizing he can lead effectively only if he has an intimate relationship with God.

What If My Spouse Won't Take the "Right" Role?

Many husbands and wives would like to "recast" their spouses in the "right" roles, as if their marriages were stage plays. These adjustments, they think, are the gateway to happiness.

"If only he would be the spiritual leader, things would be better in the house."

"If only she would cook and clean, there would be less stress around here."

The reality is that no one can force another to take on the "right" role. But the good news is that many spouses, if given the opportunity, will shoulder the necessary roles to make a marriage successful.

Two people who are truly committed to one another will do what's necessary to "fill in the gaps" in their relationship. If one is forced or nagged into assuming a needed role, though, the tendency for him or her is to lose interest in taking on the "right" part.

When Barb married Philip, she assumed that he was handy. She expected him to fix whatever needed fixing around the house or on the cars. Little did she know that Philip wasn't skilled in these areas. He'd never been shown how to do simple home or auto repairs.

Which of you should keep track of relatives' birthdays? Which of you should take kids to the doctor, hang pictures on the walls, or ask the neighbor to turn down his music?

She began to criticize him, which made him even more disinterested in helping. In fact, it began to disconnect him from her altogether.

Philip needed to be encouraged by his wife. He needed the time and opportunity to learn what he hadn't been taught. Instead, he felt ridiculed and hurt.

You and your spouse can avoid that pitfall by listening to each other's views on what "right" and "wrong" roles are. You'll need to do it patiently and respectfully.

Which of you should keep track of relatives' birthdays? Who should research where to send charitable donations? Which of you should take kids to the doctor, hang pictures on the walls, or ask the neighbor to turn down his music?

Only the two of you can answer those questions. But the following principles can help guide your discussion of which roles are right for you.

1. *The right role brings you together instead of driving you apart.* Remember that you're dividing responsibilities, not your relationship. It's usually not helpful to assign roles "because you're the man" or "because that's women's work," for instance. If your "one flesh" (Genesis 2:24) team is to work, you need to work together.

> The right role brings you together instead of driving you apart. Remember that you're dividing responsibilities, not your relationship.

2. *The right role takes your strengths and weaknesses into account.* Look at each other's assets and liabilities; try to base roles on the use of strengths. For example, if one of you is more interested and more effective in maintaining a checkbook, that person should assume the responsibility.

3. *The right role allows for flexibility.* The flexibility starts during the discussion process. Try to negotiate without "hardheadedness." Think of this as an exercise in togetherness, a way to cooperate in accomplishing vital tasks. Flexibility should continue as you carry out your responsibilities; for instance, if one spouse has handled all cooking and cleaning but takes a job outside the home, it's unrealistic to expect him or her to keep up with all the old duties as well as the new ones.

4. *The right role may be sacrificial.* There are some jobs nobody wants—but they need to be done anyway. Few of us aspire to clean the toilets, keep raccoons out of the garbage cans, or take the baby's temperature in the middle of the night. Review each other's strengths to determine which spouse comes closer to being the "expert" in an area, but don't expect an exact match. This will take humility and cooperation from both parties; if only one person (or neither) is willing to sacrifice, resentment and division will most likely make their way into the relationship. If this is the case for you, enlist a pastor or counselor to help break the stalemate.

When it comes to getting your spouse to take on a needed role, encouragement can go a long way. Cheer with your words as well as with hugs and smiles. Noticing your mate's efforts creates an atmosphere of support and teamwork.

Husbands especially need to feel appreciated, and thrive when complimented on their efforts to take on the "right" role. Wives also enjoy compliments, of course, but tend to get the most satisfaction from seeing their husbands help around the house without expecting anything in return and on their own initiative.

It's common in Christian counseling for a wife to ask, "What should I do when my husband won't assume the role of spiritual leader?" Christian husbands who avoid that role may do so because they feel anxious, self-conscious, unworthy, or overwhelmed by the prospect.

The counselor may respond with questions like these:

"How are you being a part of the solution?"

"Are you encouraging your husband, or are you nagging and putting him down because he won't assume the role?"

"When he reads Scripture, do you frequently correct him while he's trying?"

"What will happen if your husband never assumes the role?"

The answers to these questions are very important. They help the wife to focus on what can be controlled and changed.

Look for each other's spiritual strengths. Build a healthy spiritual life together. If your spouse isn't interested in that, you may need to assume a leadership role. Seek guidance from your pastor as you do so. Look for a mentor whose spiritual life you admire. Make it a point to renew yourself spiritually on a daily basis, and to find new and exciting ways to bring the Bible to life for your children if you have any. Keep praying for your spouse's spiritual growth, too.

You can't *make* your spouse take on the "right" role. But you can work on the kind of relationship that makes it easier to assume the roles that are best for both of you.

That was the case with Greg and Laura, who'd just married. Both had managed their money wisely as singles; Greg liked learning about the subject, and Laura had a bachelor's degree in mathematics. She also seemed more organized about maintaining her checkbook and paid close attention to deadlines.

>
> There are some jobs nobody wants—but they need to be done anyway. Few of us aspire to clean the toilets, keep raccoons out of the garbage cans, or take the baby's temperature in the middle of the night.

At first Greg wanted to be the family financial expert. Soon, though, he realized Laura was the best one for the job.

Laura, meanwhile, realized that she didn't know—or care to know—much about investing. So Greg assumed that responsibility.

This arrangement worked because Greg and Laura admitted their weaknesses and acknowledged their spouse's strengths. Their relationship allowed them to work together in the "right" roles.

Finding the "right" roles in a marriage takes honest self-assessment, time, experimentation, and a willingness to adjust. It also takes a dedication to each other that's bigger than the logistics of who does what.

—Daniel Huerta

> You can't make your spouse take on the "right" role. But you can work on the kind of relationship that makes it easier to assume the roles that are best for both of you.

What Roles Should We Have in a "Blended" Family?

When you marry, you bring your whole history with you. This is true in remarriages, too—and is likely to be a lot more complicated.

Even if a first marriage ended in divorce, husbands and wives may find themselves nostalgic for aspects of those "good old days." A spouse may be compared with an ex-spouse in a way that leaves him feeling as if he's living with a ghost.

> A husband may forget how he used to complain about his "compulsive neat freak" ex-wife. Now he expects Wife Number Two to keep house in the style of Number One.

Depending on the length of the prior marriage and the positive experiences therein, a new spouse may find herself competing with and unable to live up to the memories. This can be very subtle and even unconscious on the part of the spouse who recalls "better times." She might remember how her ex-husband used to bring flowers monthly, marking the day they met. Even if this was only a cynical gesture meant to mask the fact that he was cheating, the wife may subconsciously long for the ritual in the new marriage.

A husband may forget how he used to complain about his "compulsive neat freak" ex-wife. Now he expects Wife Number Two to cook, keep house, and iron his shirts in the style of Number One.

Remarriage is especially challenging when there are children involved. The longevity rates for second marriages are already poor, and look almost dismal when children are being "blended." But the good news is that with patience, education, love, and understanding, stepparents can form strong, enriching relationships with their stepchildren.

Understanding and assuming healthy roles in a "blended" family can't be reduced to a simple formula, and it can't be accomplished overnight. But the following suggestions can get you started down the road to harmony.

1. *Consider family counseling before problems arise.* Even couples who are sensitive to their children's needs hardly ever include the kids in premarital counseling. Children need help to prepare them for what lies ahead.

It's a good idea to get family counseling before patterns get too set in a remarriage. This allows kids to learn healthy ways to communicate and express feelings. Seeking help early also sends the message that counseling is not punishment, and can even be a fun way to learn about each other.

2. *Make the relationship priority one.* The first goal of stepparenting is to build a relationship with the stepchildren. This takes a lot of patience, but mustn't be neglected. Until that relationship is developed, efforts to discipline stepchildren are likely to lead to rebellion.

3. *Administer discipline carefully.* Your approaches to discipline should be discussed in premarital or family counseling. But the real challenges often don't come until after a few weeks or months of marriage.

Discipline is best administered by the biological parent, with the stepparent's support. This is especially true in the beginning of a remarriage. With time, as the parent-child relationship develops, the stepparent can initiate more.

4. *Stand united.* Use the "we" word as much as possible so the children know that you and your spouse are a united front. Kids are good at "triangulating"—aligning themselves with one parent against another. Stepparents are especially vulnerable to this because they often want so badly to connect with the stepchildren.

Let's say your stepchild comes to you and says, "Mom doesn't understand that I need to have new skates. Can you convince her that it's really important for me to get them?"

Your response might be, "Let's talk to your mom together and hear why she doesn't think that's a good idea. Then she and I will let you know what we decide."

5. *Don't push.* It's easy to try too hard to be liked and to befriend the stepchild. Don't put undue pressure on the child to engage, or to try to make him open up. Just be interested, available, and accepting, and look for opportunities to connect in a fun (or at least nonthreatening) way.

6. *Model a healthy marriage.* One of your roles is to teach your child to respect your new spouse by demonstrating that respect. Show appreciation for your spouse verbally and physically. Be affectionate, but not so demonstrative that it makes the kids uncomfortable.

7. *Show affection appropriately to the kids.* As you do, keep each child's personality and age in mind. Some children love hugs; others are more comfortable with a little nudge or an impromptu wrestling match.

The longevity rates for second marriages are already poor, and look almost dismal when children are being "blended." But there's good news, too.

8. *Remember the romance.* Take care of yourself and nurture your marriage. Watching parents who love and respect each other gives children a sense of security.

9. *Be real with your feelings.* Self-control and an even temper promote peace and trust in children. You don't have to be perfect, though. If you and your spouse don't agree on some issues, learn and model positive ways to resolve conflict.

10. *Don't compete with a child's biological parent.* Even if the child is angry or disappointed at her birth parent, be a positive influence. Help the child believe that she's loved by that parent.

11. *Allow a grace period.* Just as there's a honeymoon for the parents, there's a time when children should be given extra space to adjust to new situations, rules, and privileges. How long should it be? Some experts believe it can take seven years for a family to "blend," so avoid rushing the initial stage.

12. *Spend one-to-one time.* Pick a date night or special event to enjoy with each child. Use the time to get acquainted, but avoid turning it into an interrogation or lecture.

13. *Spend all-together time.* Encourage family nights. If your kids are old enough, take turns planning them. For ideas, look at the Focus on Your Child Web site at www.focusonyourchild.org.

Consider family counseling before problems arise. Children need help to prepare them for what lies ahead.

14. *Read encouraging books.* Two to start with could be *The Smart Step-Family* by Ron L. Deal (Bethany House, 2002) and *Daily Reflections for Stepparents* by Margaret Broersma (Kregel, 2003).

15. *Let them claim your name.* Wish your stepchildren would call you Mom or Dad? Try to put your expectations aside. If there's no pressure, they'll probably come up with a form of address that both of you can live with.

16. *Cultivate their confidence.* Find ways to help all your children feel good about themselves. Avoid comparing them to each other or pitting them against each other.

17. *Don't play favorites.* Look for the good and the strengths in all the children, and highlight them.

18. *Put away the yardstick.* Avoid comparing your new spouse with your ex-

spouse. Whether the comparisons are negative or positive, it's unfair to expect one person to measure up to another.

19. *Say what you want.* What are you hoping for from your spouse and your kids? They can't read your mind. Identify and explain your expectations in a positive way.

20. *Build on where you've been.* If your first marriage failed, your role now can be constructive. Instead of majoring in anxiety and guilt, use the failure as a springboard for learning and improving.

—ROMIE HURLEY

Wish your stepchildren would call you Mom or Dad? If there's no pressure, they'll probably come up with a form of address that both of you can live with.

**Part 4:
Money**

Why Does My Spouse Spend So Much?

Making no effort to be quiet, Graham comes to bed. It's about 1:00 A.M. Anna has been asleep for three hours, but she's wide awake now.

"Anna," says Graham, "we're never going to make it if you keep spending so much money."

Stress squeezes Anna's stomach. She knows Graham has been working on their finances. She'd like to pretend she didn't hear him, but figures she can't.

She turns toward him. "Honey, what can I do? I try not to spend too much. There are things that we need."

Graham sighs. "We *need* $50 worth of makeup from Dillard's? We *need* $120 worth of groceries a week? We *need* to buy new furniture for the living room and put up new curtains? These are *not* needs, Hon."

Anna stares at the ceiling. "Okay, the furniture and the curtains may not be needs, but my makeup and—"

Graham interrupts, "Honey, you're beautiful. You don't need to spend that kind of money on makeup."

"But that's what it costs. And I don't buy it that often." She tries to snuggle next to Graham, but he pulls away.

You can start by agreeing that you both want the same things concerning money—a certain amount of security and a certain amount of freedom.

"Are you kidding?" he says. "I'm so stressed out, and you think you can just cuddle up and be cute and it'll all be okay. You've got to take some responsibility here, Anna. Things are not okay."

As Graham and Anna have found, it can be a huge problem between husband and wife when one of them spends—or seems to spend—too much. But it's a problem the two of you can face and conquer together, especially if you keep the following principles in mind.

1. *Understand that you're on the same team when it comes to finances.* Chances are that neither of you wants to be told by your spouse exactly how much you can spend or where you can spend it. This doesn't communicate respect or trust for one another.

You can start by agreeing that you both want the same things concerning money—a certain amount of security and a certain amount of freedom. Those amounts may not be the same, but the general goals are. More importantly, you both want to emphasize the health of your relationship over the details of accounting.

When you're on the same team, it's easier to come up with creative solutions to spending disagreements. For instance, Graham and Anna might decide that each spouse will have a certain number of dollars set aside for grooming supplies each month or each quarter—rather than spending "as needed" on a "need" that hasn't been agreed upon.

2. *Understand the underlying reasons why your spouse overspends.* Let's say a husband and wife go to the mall. The wife buys face powder and the man buys a computer program. Neither accuses the other of overspending.

But what if these people feel compelled to go back to the mall the next day or week? What if the wife buys the newest trend in eye makeup and lipstick? What if the man buys another piece of software he doesn't really require and a memory expansion card that allows him to use it? They may be trying to meet needs that purchases can't satisfy.

You've probably heard a variety of reasons for overspending: deprived childhood, privileged childhood, depression, anxiety, the thrill of the hunt. All of these have one thing in common: a search for security. Consciously or not, the spender thinks something like, "If I have this, I'll be in style." Or, "I'll be accepted." Or, "I'll be safe." Or, "I'll be okay."

> Consciously or not, the spender thinks something like, "If I have this, I'll be in style." Or, "I'll be accepted." Or, "I'll be safe." Or, "I'll be okay."

Buying things doesn't provide real security. It does nothing to change God's love for us. Due to the consumerism so prevalent in our culture, it's an ongoing battle for many people to let go of the fleeting gratification of things for the long-term security of a relationship with God through Christ.

Before making a purchase, husbands and wives need to ask themselves, "What am I trying to do?" If the answer has anything to do with finding fulfillment or escaping stress or pain, don't buy the item. It will never meet that need. Instead, take your quest for security to your heavenly Father and find it in Him.

If your spouse struggles in this area, support him or her in seeking security from God instead of goods. A pastor or counselor can help.

3. Understand what things cost and how often they must be purchased. People often enter marriage with very different experiences of spending, saving, and tithing—and preconceived ideas about what things should cost.

Take that husband and wife at the mall, for example. He buys a piece of computer software; she buys makeup from a department store. Each experiences "sticker shock" over the other's purchase.

"How can you spend that much for a little eyebrow pencil?" the husband protests. "You can get a whole box of Magic Markers for the same price!"

"Look who's talking," says the wife. "You just spent more on that computer tax program than it cost to hire that guy to do our taxes last year."

Both partners end up on the defensive.

Marriage counselors sometimes have couples go through lists of purchases, mark down what they think the prices of those items would be, and compare notes. Something like this may be worthwhile if the two of you struggle with the costs of each other's purchases. You may also want to divide the same list into wants and needs, indicate how often you think each item should be purchased, and compare results.

Knowing a certain computer program is purchased once, with upgrades bought every year, for example, will help spouses agree on the real cost. So will learning that $20 worth of powder could last three months for some women and six months for others.

4. Understand that you must live on less than you earn. Living from one paycheck to the next isn't comfortable for anyone. It can lead each of you to feel taken for granted, used, and insecure about the future of your marriage and finances. That insecurity is heightened when you ask the question, "What if I lost my job?"

The real problem may not be your spouse's spending or earning, but a failure to budget. That was true of Graham and Anna.

Let's look in on them three months later.

They've been working on their finances, reviewing their spending and goals once a week. They've disciplined themselves to take from one area to cover another so that they don't bust their new budget.

Over a cup of coffee Graham says, "Okay, Anna. I've finished looking at our finances for this month."

> "How can you spend that much for a little eyebrow pencil?" the husband protests. "You can get a whole box of Magic Markers for the same price!"

"I think we did better," Anna says. "I spent more on groceries than we planned, though. Like detergent and fabric softener and stuff."

"So," Graham replies, "that explains the $150 bill at Sam's instead of the usual $100."

Emphasize the health
of your relationship
over the details
of accounting.

"Yeah," Anna says.

"How long do fabric softener and detergent usually last us?"

"At least six months."

"So it's not something we have to buy every 30 days," says Graham.

Anna shakes her head. "No, no."

Graham sighs, relieved.

—SANDRA LUNDBERG

Do We Have to Have a Budget?

For many couples, "budget" is a scary word.

What bothers you about the idea of having a budget? Is it fear that there won't be enough money? Is it not liking to be told what to do, even by a list of numbers? Does budgeting sound too complicated?

Jennifer and Josh have been told that they ought to have a budget. They're not sure they like the idea. Here are some benefits they need to consider.

1. *A budget establishes a spending plan.* When Josh and Jennifer decide to go to a movie, it will come out of their entertainment fund—with no "guilt trip" attached. When they choose to buy a toaster, they can take money from the discretionary fund or the personal spending fund. That's because they'll have decided in advance what to do. Having a plan gives you options, and having options means freedom.

2. *A budget encourages saving.* If they follow their budget, at the end of the month Jennifer and Josh will have put $100 in savings. Without a budget, that fund may not accumulate.

3. *A budget reduces stress.* With a budget, both Jennifer and Josh will understand how much money is available each month. When they respect the system, finance won't be a primary focus of conflict—which it often is early in marriage. As 1 Timothy 6:10 puts it, "For the love of money is a root of all kinds of evil." You and your spouse want to love each other, not money—and not allow money to cause division.

What bothers you about the idea of having a budget? Is it not liking to be told what to do, even by a list of numbers?

4. *A budget allows for the unexpected.* Emergency expenses can be overwhelming, especially in a new marriage. Setting aside funds for surprise expenditures can help reduce pressure on both Josh and Jennifer. Emergencies are traumatic enough without the chaos that can result from not having a "rainy day" account.

5. *A budget encourages giving.* Having a budget can help Josh and Jennifer to honor God with what's already His. Jesus said, "Do not store up for yourselves

treasures on earth, where moth and rust destroy, and where thieves break in and steal. But store up for yourselves treasures in heaven, where moth and rust do not destroy, and where thieves do not break in and steal. For where your treasure is, there your heart will be also" (Matthew 6:19-21).

Budgeting that allows for generosity will help Josh and Jennifer discover how giving to God's work promotes peace and joy and enhances their closeness to Him.

6. *A budget discourages debt.* Having a plan and sticking to it will keep Josh and Jennifer from overcommitting themselves financially. Debt is a burden on any marriage. If you're in debt, formulating a plan to eliminate it could be a gift to your relationship. Crown Financial Ministries (www.crown.org) is one organization that provides advice on debt reduction as well as budgeting.

7. *A budget can be flexible.* Josh and Jennifer, like many couples, fear a budget will be a straitjacket. But financial freedom can be expanded by constantly evaluating the budget. Maybe there's a better car insurance plan. Perhaps refinancing the mortgage to save interest is an option. Or Josh and Jennifer may want to take half the money from the "dining out" budget for the next year and put it into a "save up for vacation" account.

8. *A budget can encourage spouses to submit to the same authority—God.* To set up a budget, you have to set priorities. Discussing those and seeking God's direction in the process can go a long way toward financial harmony. If Josh and Jennifer look to God and His Word for guidance, they won't be competing to be in charge of each other's spending habits.

> A budget reduces stress. When you respect the system, finance won't be a primary focus of conflict— which it often is early in marriage.

When you get right down to it, a budget is simply a financial plan. The budget Jennifer and Josh design will have a chance to work only if they respect each other and are willing to give up "entitlement issues." In other words, Josh can't insist on going on a hunting trip using part of the rent money. Jennifer can't buy on impulse and then accuse Josh of not making enough money.

Let's say Jennifer and Josh decide to try a budget based on their annual gross income of $46,000. Here's how they might divide their monthly expenses.

Mortgage or rent	$900
Utilities	$100
Transportation	$140
Insurance (home)	$100
Insurance (cars)	$200
Insurance (health)	$150
Insurance (life)	$ 50
Phone	$100
Cable	$ 30
Food	$300
Discretionary (entertainment)	$200
Personal spending	$100
Giving	$300
Savings	$100
Emergency fund (e.g., auto repair)	$300
Taxes (income)	$763
TOTAL	**$3,833**

Your categories and amounts may vary. But if you want the freedom of planned spending, freedom from financial chaos in emergencies, freedom from debt, and joy in giving, a budget probably is for you.

Living on a budget means learning to live on less than your income. It may involve discipline, planning, and sacrifice. But it could be one way to experience genuine freedom on the "Monday mornings" of your marriage.

—BETTY JORDAN

How Much Should
We Spend?

When Teri and Phil came into the counselor's office, they were in crisis.

They'd brought debt into their marriage, but had never had a handle on how to reduce it. Now they were spending several hundred dollars a month more than they made. Not having a budget, they didn't even know where their money was going. They didn't have enough cash to do anything for themselves or their three children.

As a result, their marriage was in trouble. They barely spoke to each other.

Knowing how much you can spend is vital to the health of your relationship as well as your bank account. But deciding how much that is may not be a simple matter.

For one thing, people enter marriage with different patterns of spending, saving, and giving. Trying to merge two systems often leads to conflict. Here are examples:

- Angie is perfectly comfortable charging large amounts of money—and letting charges accrue for months or years at a time. Garth prefers not to charge anything—or at least to pay off the entire account at the end of each month.
- Karl and Trina grew up in families that took different positions on whether it's okay for Christians to borrow money. Karl believes it's fine to take out a loan for a car. Trina doesn't agree; she thinks cars should be paid for with cash.

You and your spouse need to agree on your spending habits, which means coming up with a plan of compromise that you're both comfortable with.

How can you do that?

Some couples simply look around at their friends and neighbors, then base their outgo on what they think other people are spending. But in our materialistic culture,

> Teri and Phil were spending several hundred dollars a month more than they made. They didn't even know where their money was going.

keeping up with the Joneses is a great way to get yourself in trouble financially. Instead, take a look at these five guidelines to consider when deciding how much to spend.

1. *Always spend less than you make.* This could be 80 percent of your take-home pay. Or, if you really want to be cautious, try 70 percent.

What happens to the remaining money? If you're spending 80 percent, put 10 percent into your tithe and 10 percent into savings and retirement. If you decide to spend 70 percent, put 10 percent into tithe, 10 percent into savings, and 10 percent into retirement.

Why not spend it all? Psalm 24:1 says, "The earth is the LORD's, and everything in it." When we recognize this, we understand that none of "our" money is really ours. God entrusts it to us to use as stewards. Being good guardians of those funds includes giving a portion back to God and using a portion to prepare for the future.

2. *Establish a budget.* This will help you consistently spend less than you make. Try basing it on a three-month average of your expenses.

Knowing how much you can spend is vital to the health of your relationship as well as your bank account. But deciding how much that is may not be a simple matter.

To begin, find out exactly what you're spending and where. Many couples have found it works for each spouse to keep a notepad or extra checking account register handy so that each transaction can be written down. At the end of the week or month, compare your two records. Use the average of what you're spending in each area.

Don't be surprised if this is an eye-opening—even unsettling—experience. You may find that you're spending far more in a particular area than you thought.

The two of you may need to reconsider your priorities. Spending $1.50 a day on a cup of coffee and $6 on lunch, for instance, really adds up over the long haul. You might agree to reallocate this money to another category.

3. *Set limits and stick to them.* Once you've established your budget, it's time to implement it.

Let's say you're overspending in one category by $50. That money has to come from somewhere. Look in your other categories and get the money from there.

The goal is to stay within your total budget. You may want to build in a

"Miscellaneous" category or a cushion to cover overspending or unforeseen expenses.

4. *Be creative.* If an idea helps you stick with your budget, try it. You may want to set up a bill-paying method that fits your paydays, for instance. If you're paid twice a month, you might be able to satisfy part of a bill with the first paycheck and the rest with the second.

A variation on this plan would be to pay bills in certain categories with the first paycheck and other categories with the second. For example, rent or mortgage might be paid with your first paycheck; groceries and utilities might come from the second.

5. *Be open to change.* Review your spending monthly, or even weekly if necessary. Modify your budget as needed. After all, your account balance today will be different from what it was yesterday—and different from what it will be tomorrow. Knowing what and when to change takes constant monitoring.

In the case of Phil and Teri, change was a necessity. With the help of a counselor, they set up a plan.

First, they realized they had to forgive each other for all the pain they'd caused with their spending habits and poor communication about finances.

Second, they prayed together for a new beginning.

Third, they established a budget and a plan to get out of debt.

Taking these steps gave Phil and Teri more freedom to decide where their money would go, rather than being enslaved by bills. Being able to direct their funds instead of just finding them mysteriously gone at the end of the month helped the couple feel more capable of making informed spending decisions.

> To begin, find out exactly what you're spending and where. Don't be surprised if this is an eye-opening—even unsettling—experience.

Eventually Phil and Teri were able to earmark money for their children's extracurricular activities and to pay off Phil's college loans. They took a vacation without incurring debt. They also gained a bright outlook on the future—and a revitalized sense of working together, rather than being at odds with each other.

As Phil and Teri found, time spent bickering over spending habits is time wasted. Marriage is more satisfying—and glorifying to God—if you're working as a team.

—SANDRA LUNDBERG

How Much Should We Save?

Paul and Amanda were full of complaints when they came to their first counseling appointment.

"Paul bought a new motorcycle and he didn't even ask me about it," Amanda said. "I was planning on saving the money that Paul spent toward the down payment on our new house."

"She never wants me to spend anything," Paul countered. "She always wants to save our money toward some bigger goal. I earn the money in this family, and I think I should be able to spend it how I want to."

After the sparks died down, the counselor asked Paul and Amanda about their backgrounds. The two families had very different patterns of spending and saving.

As a result, the two spouses had very different views on saving money. Amanda was concerned about the security and stability of their household; her fear was falling behind on house payments and not having a roof over her head. Paul felt confident about providing for his family and didn't want Amanda to worry.

> "She always wants to save our money toward some bigger goal. I earn the money in this family, and I think I should be able to spend it how I want to."

When it comes to saving, are you more like Paul or more like Amanda? And if you and your spouse don't see eye to eye on saving, how can you work things out?

The first thing to realize about saving is that it's necessary—even if those around you don't agree. You may have friends who aren't saving any money at all, or who are spending more than they earn. The fact is that two spouses who suddenly lose their income could, in today's financial climate, run through their savings in six months—and even become homeless. Saving is important!

So how much money should you save? That depends partly on how you earn it.

If your income is consistent, it's a good idea to save at least three to four months' worth of expenses as an emergency fund. If it takes $1,500 to keep your home running for a month, you should save $4,500 to $6,000.

If your income fluctuates—perhaps because you work on commission or are self-employed—you should save at least six months' worth of expenses as an emergency fund. Set this aside before you save toward a car, a down payment on a house, college tuition, or retirement. Don't dip into this fund to cover monthly budget overruns. This cushion is for crises like unemployment or major medical expenses.

"But I don't make enough money to save any of it," you may be saying to yourself. Start small! Even $25 a month is significant. The goal is to start establishing that cushion.

The Bible advises saving money, even if it's a little at a time. "Dishonest money dwindles away, but he who gathers money little by little makes it grow" (Proverbs 13:11).

It's wise to put away a portion of your income in case of crisis or to meet goals. Don't let your fear of never having "enough" money saved stand in the way of saving at all.

Two spouses who suddenly lose their income could, in today's financial climate, run through their savings in six months—and even become homeless.

The amount you save also depends on your needs. These can be broken down into three categories: short-term, intermediate, and long-term.

Short-term needs are those you anticipate in the next one to two years, and an emergency fund to provide the three-to-six-month reserve mentioned earlier. These resources are best kept in accounts that are easy to access without penalty—for example, cash or money market accounts.

Intermediate needs are those you expect to encounter in two to five years—replacing a car or finishing a basement, for instance. You might use certificates of deposit or short-term investments with little volatility to meet this savings goal.

Long-term needs might include a child's college fund or saving for retirement. For this fund you'll want investments that stay ahead of the inflation rate—typically equity-type investments or stock market investments with a diversified portfolio.

Here's another good idea: a "save to spend" strategy. If your car is paid off, make a car payment to yourself in a separate account each month. Drive your car until you've saved enough to buy a replacement. Once you've paid cash for this car, begin making payments to a car fund account again. You'll be earning interest on the money for the car rather than paying it to someone else.

You can apply this idea to housing costs, too. Let's say you're renting an apartment for $700 a month. If you can budget $1,000 a month, you'll be setting aside $300 toward the purchase of a home. This helps to establish the habit of spending less than you earn—an uncommon practice in our society, but one that puts you in a good position to face unforeseen events.

Is it easy to agree on how much you should save as a couple?

Not always. Paul and Amanda found it difficult at the start to talk about the subject. Over time, though, they learned that talking more about their finances helped them become more comfortable.

As they talked, Paul realized that Amanda didn't really want to control all his spending. She needed to be assured of the savings they did have, to know that Paul had prepared for crises. Paul, on the other hand, needed Amanda to trust him and to respect his decisions.

> If your income is consistent, it's a good idea to save at least three to four months' worth of expenses as an emergency fund. If your income fluctuates, make it at least six months' worth.

When they agreed on how much to spend and save each month, they both felt more comfortable and confident in each other. They came up with a new rule: When one spouse wanted to spend over $400 on a particular item, he or she would consult the other first and not spend that money without reaching agreement.

Some couples may decide to set that limit at $50. No matter what amount you choose to spend or save, agreeing helps bring you together.

Planning how much to save, though it may be difficult, builds freedom into your life. You may have to negotiate as a couple your savings goals, and it may sometimes be hard to stick to them. But when the two of you work together toward those goals, you can find great satisfaction in achieving them.

Talk with your spouse about how much you'd like to save. Failure to plan can create tension in a marriage—the kind that's difficult to work through.

—SANDRA LUNDBERG

How Much Should We Give?

Tom and Latisha took different approaches to tithing—the practice of giving 10 percent of one's income to the church.

Tom believed they should tithe from their gross income. He backed up this idea with Bible verses on giving from the "firstfruits" (Proverbs 3:9).

Latisha didn't think believers were called to tithe in the New Testament era. She was comfortable giving when she felt like it, and thought Tom was being legalistic.

The two of them often disagreed over how to use money for tithing and other purposes. They decided to see a counselor.

The counselor started out by observing that all we have belongs to the Lord. As Psalm 24:1 puts it, "The earth is the LORD's, and everything in it."

When Tom and Latisha acknowledged that, it helped them put into perspective the importance of giving back to God. Other Scriptures they read with the counselor included 2 Corinthians 9:7: "Each man should give what he has decided in his heart to give, not reluctantly or under compulsion, for God loves a cheerful giver." This led to a discussion of giving as a reflection of the heart—not just a division of "God's portion" and "our portion."

> Tom believed they should tithe from their gross income. Latisha thought he was being legalistic.

Giving is a very personal thing. Many couples struggle to decide how much money, or what portion of their income, they should give back to God. As you decide, these two principles may be helpful:

1. We are simply stewards of what God entrusts to us. When people refuse to acknowledge that, they tend to be selfish with the things God has entrusted to them.

2. The point of giving is to aid other believers, the poor, and widows and orphans, and to assist in evangelism around the world (see 1 Corinthians 16:1-2; Galatians 2:10; James 1:27).

This doesn't mean tithing is universally practiced among Christians, of course. Sadly enough, Barna Research found that even though evangelicals are the most generous givers, only 6 percent of those who call themselves "born again" gave their churches 10 percent in 2002.[1]

What about the question of whether you should tithe before or after taxes? Not everyone agrees on the answer. But applying the concept of firstfruits (Proverbs 3:9) would seem to recommend giving from one's total income. Following this principle would mean tithing gross income, not after taxes and Social Security and other deductions have been taken.

You may be thinking, *But we don't make enough money to give like that.* Here are some questions you may need to ask yourself.

1. What does it mean for you to be a wise steward? If you have an income, God is entrusting you with it. How does He want you to use it?

2. How have your attitudes about giving been shaped by the society around you? We live in a consumer culture, but Matthew 6 talks about storing up treasures in heaven and not on earth. Are you caught up in a spending mentality that leaves you unable to give?

3. How might giving help you to grow spiritually? Could the discipline of having less available to spend teach you something about materialism?

Even when you and your spouse have thought and talked about these questions, giving may not come easily. If it hasn't been your habit, getting started can be difficult. After all, it's contrary to the idea that possessions will give you pleasure.

So how can the two of you find joy in giving? Strangely enough, you'll find out when you begin to give. Once you see how God continues to provide for you, and how He uses what you've given, you'll probably wonder why you ever held back.

That's where Tom and Latisha ended up, though it took awhile to get there. When they started tithing from their gross income and sometimes giving additional offerings, they saw that they were still able to meet their other financial responsibilities.

Latisha found herself respecting Tom's leadership in this area and beginning to share his belief in tithing from their "firstfruits." She felt more grateful for all the things God had blessed them with. When finances became tight occasionally, she even began to question whether they'd been giving faithfully.

> Giving is a very personal thing. Many couples struggle to decide how much money they should give back to God.

In time, both Tom and Latisha stopped trying to blame tight finances on "imperfect" tithing. They realized that they simply needed to be good stewards in spending, saving, *and* giving.

—SANDRA LUNDBERG

How Can We Stay Out of Debt?

When Chris and Parker got married, they had very different ways of using their credit cards.

Parker tended not to use his card at all, but kept it for emergencies. When he used it, he paid it off in full at the end of the month.

Chris, on the other hand, saw credit cards as "free money." She used hers frequently, and usually didn't pay more than the minimum due.

Not surprisingly, this caused a problem. Parker feared Chris would sink them in debt. Chris thought Parker was just being a miser and making her life difficult. Debating whether they should maintain separate credit cards or joint accounts, they finally went to a financial planner—hoping he would help them work through their differences.

Staying out of debt isn't just a concern for "misers" like Parker. More and more couples are finding themselves "in over their heads," even bankrupt. Credit card misuse is one factor—but not the only one.

How can the two of you stay out of debt? By avoiding the following four common pitfalls.

Pitfall #1: No budget. Many couples never establish a budget, but it's an excellent way to stay out of debt. Prepare your budget based on three months' expenses. Allow for savings for short-term and long-term needs. Take those savings out of your paycheck at the start of the month, not at the end of the month after spending has been done.

Once your budget reveals where you're spending your money, you can look for places to cut back as needed—making it less likely that you'll sink into red ink.

Pitfall #2: Careless credit card use. Too many couples have adopted Chris's view—that "plastic" is "free money." The result: crushing credit card debt that only gets heavier as interest is added.

When you make a credit card purchase, note in your checkbook register the amount of money for that transaction. Write "CC" for credit card where you'd typically put

> Parker feared Chris would sink them in debt. Chris thought Parker was just being a miser and making her life difficult.

the check number. When the credit card bill comes, pay it off using that money.

This helps to ensure that you won't spend more than what's available in your checkbook. But remember: Just because there are more checks in the checkbook, that doesn't mean more money is available!

Should you get rid of your credit cards altogether? You don't have to—if the two of you discipline yourselves not to spend what isn't in your checking account. Pay off your purchase in 30 days. Make sure credit card spending is for needs, not wants. If you've budgeted, you'll have allotted funds for needs—while wants may be beyond your means.

Get rid of *extra* credit cards. You need only one or two. Avoid carrying gas cards, store credit cards, and the like. If a salesperson urges you to sign up for such a card in order to save a percentage on your purchase, ask yourself whether it's worth it. Will you be paying it off at the end of the month? Is this a need or a want? Is it in the budget?

If you do sign up for a store credit card, consider destroying it when it comes in the mail. If you take this approach, contact the company to close the account. Note that a pattern of opening and closing accounts like this may hurt your credit rating, so it may be best not to open them in the first place.

Pitfall #3: Unnecessary or risky loans. Remember Proverbs 22:7: "The borrower is servant to the lender."

More and more couples are finding themselves "in over their heads," even bankrupt. Credit card misuse is one factor—but not the only one.

Whenever possible, use the "save to spend" purchasing plan instead of borrowing. Budget for larger purchases, and don't buy them until you've saved the cash to pay for them. Example: If you've just paid off your car, continue to drive it and make car payments to a designated savings account. You may be able to save enough to pay for your next vehicle without the burden of ongoing debt.

Is it possible to live without loans? Yes, though it requires self-discipline.

Cars, for instance, are purchases for which many people go into debt. But cars are depreciating assets; the instant you drive off the lot, you've lost money. Instead of buying the new car of your dreams, it may be best as a wise steward to buy a used car for which you can afford to pay cash. The same is true of other purchases that decrease in value—snowmobiles, computers, sofas, TVs.

What about home loans? Most people have to finance a home purchase. Assuming you can afford the payments, home purchases are generally considered "safe" debt because houses historically have increased in value (though this is not guaranteed). Shop carefully for a home loan, however; terms that seem attractive in the short run may end up costing you dearly.

One risky loan to avoid is a consolidation loan—the kind that promises to merge your debts and reduce your monthly payments. Before considering this type of loan, ask yourself: How did I get into debt in the first place? Was it a crisis, like a huge medical bill after an accident, or a pattern of buying things I couldn't afford?

> If you've just paid off your car, continue to drive it and make car payments to a designated savings account. You may be able to save enough to pay for your next vehicle without the burden of ongoing debt.

People with unwise spending habits often end up worse off with a consolidation loan; they think the lower monthly payment justifies spending more, and spend themselves further into debt. And since these loans are typically secured using your car or home, you could lose either if you fall behind in your payments.

What about one other kind of loan that many young couples consider—borrowing from parents?

This is a complicated decision. If the choice is between an 18 percent interest rate on a bank loan or only needing to pay back the principal or a low interest rate to your parents, it may be worth it to accept their help. If you choose to do this, put in writing a clear agreement about how repayment will take place. Then honor it. Don't take advantage of your parents' goodwill by paying late or not at all.

Borrowing from parents can be emotionally risky. There should be no relational strings attached to the loan; this is where it typically gets most complicated. When you borrow from family or friends, they often feel justified in telling you how you should spend your money. If you don't follow their directions, they may get frustrated—which can create tension.

Whatever your choice, you and your spouse need to agree on money borrowed from parents—not to mention your other spending and borrowing habits.

Pitfall #4: Ever-rising standard of living. When you get a raise, consider saving that money instead of using it to increase your standard of living. You'll have more of a "cushion" in the event of a medical crisis, layoff, or job change.

One man lived on less than half of what he made. When he lost his job, he was able to access the money he'd saved from previous raises to cover his costs while building an income in a new career. This takes great discipline, and discipline takes practice.

> Borrowing from parents can be emotionally risky. There should be no relational strings attached to the loan; this is where it typically gets most complicated.

In the case of Chris and Parker, staying out of debt began with seeing a financial planner before it was too late. They avoided increased conflict and stopped the downward spiral of debt that Chris's approach threatened to put them in.

Chris learned to pay attention to her credit card balances. She also realized she was being selfish and risking their plans for financial stability. She and Parker set goals for spending and saving.

Like many people who fall into debt, Chris had felt deprived when she couldn't spend on a whim. Unlike many, however, she came to realize she'd rather wait for fewer, more durable possessions than impulsively buying a truckload of clothing and appliances that weren't worth having in the first place.

—SANDRA LUNDBERG

How Can We Get Out of Debt?

When Denise married Toby, she brought something unique to the relationship: a huge debt.

Ten thousand dollars, to be exact.

Denise had racked up the bills by spending on wants that she thought were needs before she met Toby.

The problem was that Denise wouldn't deny herself anything. As a single woman in an apartment, she'd bought a dining table, chairs, and buffet because she "needed" them. She'd bought each season's most fashionable dress, purse, and shoes, and all the trendiest makeup.

Toby had been attracted by her style and impressed by her home décor. But he and Denise hadn't had any detailed discussions of finances before they married. He didn't know she was outspending her income.

Denise, meanwhile, didn't seem to realize how out-of-control her spending had become. She expected Toby's income to cover her debt and enable her to spend even more.

> Denise didn't seem to realize how out-of-control her spending had become. She expected Toby's income to cover her debt and enable her to spend even more.

After they married, Toby felt taken for granted. Sure, he made a good salary; but what if things changed? And why should he have to pay for things he didn't see as priorities—things he thought were paid for? Their marriage was beginning with debt, and with the obligation to pay it off.

As Denise and Toby found, debt puts huge stress on a marriage. Each spouse is forced to wrestle with matters of security and priorities—as well as frustration with himself and his mate.

What can you do if you and your spouse are in debt? Here are some keys to unlocking that "debtor's prison."

1. *Talk about it.* Denise and Toby could have used some nice, long conversations about money before they married. Once they were wed, they discovered that the need to talk wasn't going to go away.

Effective communication and compromise are crucial to surviving debt.

The "saver" spouse may want to deprive the "spender" of any new purchases, no questions asked—but that approach will just lead to more tension and reproach.

If you're in debt, you and your mate will have to agree on a plan to pay it off—while continuing to live and enjoy each other. None of that can happen without honest communication. If either of you feels left out, it will be like a diet that you can't stand to stay on. With mutual goals and greater understanding, you can work things out.

> Debt puts huge stress on a marriage. Each spouse is forced to wrestle with matters of security and priorities— as well as frustration.

2. *Make a list.* Sit down together and list all your debts—credit cards, school loans, car payments. Note the amount owed on each debt, the interest rate of each, the minimum payment due, and any payments made above the minimum.

3. *Create a strategy.* Come up with a plan to pay off each debt.

Let's say you have three credit cards, each with a balance of several thousand dollars. The cards' interest rates are 19.9 percent, 12 percent, and 1.9 percent. Regardless of the amount owed on the cards, the best practice is to take all money paid above the minimum on the two cards with the lower interest rates and apply it to the card with the highest interest rate. Continue to pay the minimum on the other two cards.

For example, if the card with the 19.9 percent rate has a $1,200 balance, the card with the 12 percent rate has an $1,800 balance, and the card with the 1.9 percent rate has a $1,000 balance, you'll still begin by paying off the $1,200 on the 19.9 percent rate card.

After paying off the card with the highest interest rate, apply the money you were paying on that card to the one with the next highest interest rate. Following this method, you avoid paying unnecessary interest.

School loans may be part of your debt. Usually these have a lower interest rate because they're subsidized. If possible, include them in your debt payoff plan *after* the credit cards while meeting minimum payments on the student loans.

If you're making payments on a car, increase those payments after paying off the credit cards. Once you pay off the car, practice the "save to spend" method; each month, set aside money toward a new car as if you were still making car payments.

4. *Avoid "easy outs."* They're seldom as simple as they seem.

Consolidation loans, combining your obligations in one "easy" payment, aren't recommended if your debts were caused by unbridled spending. Unless you change your spending habits, you may find a false sense of security in the "low" monthly payment and spend even more. And since these loans usually are secured on your car or home, defaulting could mean losing either.

What about bankruptcy? Every effort should be made to repay a debt; you're responsible to pay for what you've purchased. If the debt is from a catastrophic event—say, a million-dollar heart transplant for which you can never pay—there are bankruptcy laws in place to give you relief. But you should not use bankruptcy, which in itself can threaten your financial future, to relieve a spending problem.

5. *Keep enjoying each other—more inexpensively.* It takes frugality to free up money to pay debts. But that doesn't mean you should stop nurturing your relationship.

It doesn't take much money to enjoy one another. Have a picnic in the park or the family room. Play board games. Read aloud to each other instead of watching TV shows that bombard you with messages about buying more things you can't afford. Consider dropping cable or satellite channels in favor of checking out classic DVDs or tapes from the public library. Think of creative ways to surprise your spouse without spending a dime.

6. *Get help if you need it.* You may want to work with a financial planner or debt counselor. A good advisor will work with you toward your goals, be available to answer your questions, be easy to understand, and help you craft a plan to remedy debt and prepare for the future. A Christian financial planner can be of extra help when you hold similar worldviews and values.

The "saver" spouse may want to deprive the "spender" of any new purchases, no questions asked—but that approach will just lead to more tension.

Avoid advisors who offer a one-size-fits-all approach, or who want to put your money in risky investments you're not comfortable with. Know for sure what you're paying for; you may be able to get the same advice for free from a library book, Web site, or Christian organization.

7. *Don't fall in the trap again.* When Denise realized how impulsive spending had trapped her in debt, she took action. She put her credit cards in a jar of water in the freezer. Whenever she was tempted to purchase something on a whim, she had to wait for the cards to thaw.

She ended up getting that jar out of the freezer several times. But each time the wait helped her to evaluate the importance of the purchase.

Denise and Toby came to agree that *her* debt before marriage was now *their* debt. Paying it off would require sacrifice from both of them. They committed $200 a month from her paycheck and $700 from his to pay this debt off before making any other major purchases. They also started using the "save to spend" strategy.

> If either of you feels left out, it will be like a diet that you can't stand to stay on. With mutual goals and greater understanding, you can work things out.

Things were rough for them at first. But the team approach paid big dividends, helping them develop skills in communication and problem solving that would come in handy throughout their marriage.

There were deeper changes, too. Instead of trying to find security in possessions, Denise began to find it in her relationships with God and with Toby. Toby came to realize that God was in control, and would honor his diligence at work and in giving by providing all that Denise and Toby really needed.

—Sandra Lundberg

How Can We Cut Our Expenses?

"You say, 'If I had a little more, I should be very satisfied.' You make a mistake. If you are not content with what you have, you will not be satisfied if it were doubled."

—Charles Spurgeon

A lot of people are working harder than ever so that they'll have more to spend—hoping that will give them pleasure and satisfaction. Too often all they end up with is a rented storage facility to hold their new belongings.

Gene and Sally were headed in that direction. Recently married, they were living beyond their means. They had a choice: Cut expenses or face financial disaster.

When they listed their expenses, they discovered that both of them had been making unnecessary purchases. Gene had developed a habit of rewarding himself for his work, and Sally tended to be impulsive in her buying.

Neither Gene nor Sally used coupons or paid attention to whether or not things were on sale. They believed "more and newer is better." In fact, they dreaded the very idea of having to find creative ways to spend less.

When bills arrived, Gene and Sally would feel depressed, frustrated, and angry. Both were driven by pleasure and avoided conflict and pain.

Maybe you feel like that. Many couples have psychological barriers to cutting expenses. Here are a few of the things that may be running through your mind:

- "I've worked hard for this money and need a reward."
- "My kids may not think I love them if I don't spend more money on them."
- "My husband needs to spend money on me to show that he cares."
- "If I buy this, others may like me or respect me more."
- "I grew up poor, but now I have the money to spend."
- "Others may see me as stingy if I never buy anything."
- "Life's too short to be saving all the time; money's for spending and having fun."

It doesn't help when advertisers work so hard to identify and use those psychological barriers. Marketers know that people are pleasure driven, and that many of them will spend themselves into debt in the hope of feeling loved, safe, or worthy—or to show love to others. Marketers don't dwell on the painful side of spending, which is paying bills.

Gene and Sally had their own set of psychological barriers to cutting costs. Gene told Sally they needed to spend as much money as possible before they had children, because the buying and fun would end when kids arrived. Gene also liked owning the latest gadgets that would help him feel important in the eyes of friends and coworkers.

Sally, on the other hand, felt a need to buy extravagant things for her family and friends. She also liked elaborate vacations.

> They decided to turn frugality into a contest. They began competing to see who could save more money.

When bills arrived, Gene and Sally would feel depressed, frustrated, and angry. Both were driven by pleasure and avoided conflict and pain.

With the help of a counselor, Gene and Sally learned the following steps to dismantling psychological barriers that keep couples from cutting expenses.

1. *Separate self-worth from possessions, including money.* Gene needed to develop a realistic, appropriate sense of his value. Self-worth is knowing you're loved regardless of what you have or do, knowing you're valuable just because you exist. Gene believed his worth depended on what he owned and how he looked in the eyes of others. He came to see that this would require an endless pursuit with emptiness and disappointment waiting at the end.

Do you fear that you won't be accepted if you don't have certain things? The fact is that you can't control how anyone thinks of you. Gene will never know whether others value him on the basis of his financial situation. Sally will never be sure whether her family really felt more loved when she bought them expensive gifts. But once she realized she was valuable in her family's eyes regardless of what she gave them, she experienced much-needed emotional freedom.

2. *View money as a tool and necessity, not as a joy producer.* Gene and Sally decided to make money something that would enhance their marriage rather than tear it apart. After reading some books, they developed their own budget-

ing system. Their beliefs about money changed; they began to see it not as a source of happiness but as a resource entrusted to them by God.

This belief caused them to change the order of their spending, which became as follows:

a. Tithe

b. Pay debt (mortgage, credit cards, school loans)

c. Budgeted necessities (food, gas, auto, electricity)

d. Invest and save (mutual funds, retirement plans)

e. Have fun with what's left over or plan ahead for larger purchases.

3. *Recognize that cutting expenses can be adventurous, even fun.* Gene and Sally decided to turn frugality into a contest. They began competing to see who could save more money.

Each month, each spouse got an envelope with cash to spend on personal items. At the end of the month, whoever had the most money left in his or her envelope would get a no-cost request met (a chore needing to be done, a back rub, a walk, an evening of uninterrupted sports or movie viewing, video game night with the guys, etc.).

4. *Expect to grow in the process of cutting expenses.* Sally and Gene began to realize that conflict and lean times could bring significant personal and marital growth. This caused both of them to *seek* growth each time they encountered disagreement or difficulty. They knew the ultimate result would be maturity.

> List all necessary expenses. Make separate lists for purchases driven by emotion, things you "like," convenience, or a desire to be noticed.

As Paul taught in Romans 5:3-4, "We also rejoice in our sufferings, because we know that suffering produces perseverance; perseverance, character; and character, hope."

5. *Forgive the failures and develop trust.* When Gene and Sally were first married, Gene bought a mountain bike that cost a lot more than they could afford. His friends had been comparing bikes, and he'd felt driven to "top" them.

After that incident, Sally had a hard time trusting Gene's money management. She also kept bringing it up when she wanted to buy something for her family.

Without trust and a sense that both spouses are making sacrifices, it's difficult to undertake cost-cutting. Once Gene and Sally let go of the past and committed to joint beliefs about spending, their trust began to grow.

Once you've dealt with the psychological hurdles, how should you go about cutting expenses? The process doesn't have to be as painful as Gene and Sally first assumed. Here are just a few ideas to get you started on reducing expenditures—without having to turn off the electricity or limit your diet to crackers and ketchup.

1. List all *necessary* expenses. Make separate lists for purchases driven by emotion, things you "like," convenience, or a desire to be noticed. Then focus on the necessary list and develop a joint strategy for reducing the rest.

2. Look at the grocery ads and plan your menu for the next month. If you schedule a few days for dining out, agree on the number of outings and on sharing dishes; restaurants can quickly empty a wallet or checking account.

3. Avoid shopping without purpose, unless you're firmly committed not to buy while you're browsing. Shopping can be entertaining for the whole family, but can also create a pattern of impulsive, temptation-driven expenditures.

4. Use the Internet to comparison-shop and find the lowest prices. When shopping in brick-and-mortar stores, do what Gene and Sally did: Avoid buying anything that isn't on sale.

5. Plan errands so that gas isn't wasted by backtracking. Make a list of this week's destinations and decide when you'll be in the vicinity. If the errands can wait, group them for maximum efficiency and minimum travel expense.

> Use the Internet to comparison-shop and find the lowest prices. Plan errands so that gas isn't wasted by backtracking.

6. Buy a used car instead of a new car. Unless they're part of a collector's series, automobiles depreciate—some more quickly than others. Check consumer guides to find out which are expected to keep the most resale value.

7. If you'll only watch a DVD once, rent it instead of buying. If you'll only read a book once, check it out of the public library if possible. Purchasing favorite books, those given as gifts, and those you'll use as references makes sense, but you may be able to convince your local library to stock a title you'd rather not buy.

How did things work out for Gene and Sally? They reduced their spending by carefully planning how to spend the money entrusted to them. Sally prioritized shopping trips; Gene decided his "rewards" would be at Christmas and his birthday. If there were others, they would be random surprises from his wife with a limit to the spending.

When Sally and Gene went out to eat, they shared a salad and main dish—which was plenty for them. Most importantly, they separated their self-worth from their spending and decided to find pleasure in *managing* rather than *spending* their money. Their flexibility and hard work resulted in less stress, tension, frustration, anger, and disappointment. It increased their level of trust and love, and both reported more satisfaction with marriage and life in general.

—DANIEL HUERTA

How Can We Survive Unemployment?

Coming home from work, Paul wondered how he was going to face Susan. *How on earth can I tell her I lost my job?*

Susan had pledged to love him for better or worse, but they'd never planned on this. *Will she really still love me? What if I can't find another job? What are we going to do?*

Driving into the garage, he sighed. *I just feel so worthless. The economy isn't good around here right now. I don't know how I'm going to find another job.*

He opened the door from the garage into the kitchen. There was Susan at the stove, making dinner.

She turned and smiled. "Hi, Honey! How was your day at work?"

"It was okay."

She looked at him curiously. "You don't sound okay."

He swallowed. "Well, I won't be going back to work tomorrow."

Her eyes widening, Susan set down the spoon she'd been using. Her voice seemed faint as she asked him to tell her what happened.

Three minutes later he'd explained everything.

"Oh, Honey, I am so sorry," Susan said. She took a deep breath. "We'll get through this, and we'll figure it out."

Paul felt himself relax, but only a little. What would the next few days and weeks and months hold? Would Susan continue to stand by him? Would she get frustrated with him and lose respect for him as a man? How would this affect their marriage?

As it did for Paul and Susan, losing a job often comes as a shock. Nobody likes to think about being unemployed. But it's a state that's more and more common. Whether due to corporate "right-sizing," termination, or career change, it's always an uneasy time.

What causes the stress? First, the spouse

> The spouse who's lost his or her job may have suffered a serious blow to the identity. This is especially true for husbands, since most men largely define themselves by their work.

who's lost his or her job may have suffered a serious blow to the identity. This is especially true for husbands, since most men largely define themselves by their work. They also tend to believe that the husband's earnings are the family's primary income, whether that belief is stated or not.

Second, many couples haven't saved enough money to get them through a prolonged period of unemployment. Running out of money is a real possibility, depending on how long joblessness lasts. So is going into debt with credit cards or losing a house if you default on a mortgage. All this weighs heavily on both partners, especially the one who feels most responsible to "win the bread."

So what should you do when unemployment hits your marriage?

Try to find a position you can be enthusiastic about—but if that's unavailable, take a job simply because it will earn a living wage for your family.

1. *If you've been providing for your family but have lost your job, get right back into the job market.* Try to find a position you can be enthusiastic about—but if that's unavailable, take a job simply because it will earn a living wage for your family. You can work on longer-term career goals at the same time.

This is especially important for men; male self-esteem seems to require making a contribution. Many men become increasingly depressed and anxious if they're at home when the family needs their income.

2. *Don't rule out relocating.* While this may seem to be the end of the world if it means moving away from your support system, you can choose to look at it as a fresh start. If a new position calls you to a new city, you can develop roots and a support network there. This also may be a time when the two of you can nurture your relationship as you're "cocooned" from the demands of family and friends.

3. *Be flexible about the "breadwinner" role.* Sometimes a wife may have greater earning potential than her husband does. If she's taken a part-time job in order to care for her children, for example, that may need to be re-evaluated. If her husband is likely to be out of work for an extended period, perhaps he could provide childcare while the wife earns more in a full-time position.

4. *Cut expenses.* Look for activities and plans you can put on hold. Can you and your spouse do without restaurant lunches for awhile, even if they're only

trips to McDonald's after church? Can you avoid buying new clothes for six months? Can you turn down the heat in the winter and put on more sweaters?

On the other hand, it's not good to make small children shiver in their rooms or require older kids to give up all extracurricular activities because the price of baseball bats has gone up. Are you eligible for low-income heating fuel assistance? Can you find that sports equipment at a garage sale or secondhand store?

5. *Maintain the marriage.* Depression and money-related stress are no strangers to the unemployed, and both can grind away at your relationship. If your spouse has lost his or her job, do what Susan did. Avoid the temptation to ask a million questions when the "pink slip" arrives. Don't lecture your spouse about his responsibility to the family. Support your mate in his crisis, even though it's a crisis for you, too.

Help your spouse in his job search. State clearly that you're ready to cut unnecessary expenses. Spend time together—enjoying one another instead of letting all your conversations focus on work and money. Reduce anxiety by writing out a plan for your finances, including opportunities to earn cash, barter services, and carry on family activities in less costly ways.

You and your spouse need each other more than usual during this season of your lives. It may be a long season, but you can guard your relationship despite the stress—if you make that relationship a priority.

> Help your spouse in his job search. State clearly that you're ready to cut unnecessary expenses.

That's what Paul and Susan are finding.

Today Susan comes home from the grocery store and finds Paul at the kitchen table. Paul says, "Honey, God is really answering our prayers."

"How so?" she asks, setting two plastic bags on the counter.

"Well, you know that company I interviewed with last week? They just called and they want a second interview."

"That's wonderful," Susan says. "When is it?"

"Actually, it's tomorrow."

"Is there anything I can do to help you get ready tonight?"

"Just pray for me."

"Oh, Honey, I am! And I will be."

Paul says, "I just have to get this job. I just want to be working again."

Susan reaches down and rubs his neck. The muscles feel tense, so she keeps rubbing. "I know," she says softly. "I know."

—SANDRA LUNDBERG

Should We Buy a House?

If you buy a house, it will be one of the largest and most important purchases you'll ever make. You may also consider it one of your biggest investments.

Some would say it doesn't make sense *not* to buy a house. What other investment tends to grow in value while it's being used? There's no guarantee that a home's worth will increase, but that's been the general trend over the years.

A first house usually isn't the one a couple lives in for a long time. So there's no need to insist that it be a "dream" house. It's enough if it builds equity toward a down payment on the next home.

Real estate agent Donald Stull says the process of buying a home can have financial and social benefits. Financially, it gets a husband and wife to do what they may not ordinarily do—invest a large amount of money. Socially, it creates an opportunity for them to compromise and communicate their dreams.

Buying a home has the potential to be a moneymaker and a memory producer for couples. It can be exciting, but stressful. The two of you, should you decide to buy, need to communicate openly throughout the process.

Should you seek wisdom from your parents on the question of purchasing a home? If they've been poor financial stewards, asking their advice on this subject might not be the best choice. But if they've displayed sound, consistent stewardship of their money, it would be helpful to seek their perspective.

A few parents have saved money to assist their children with the purchase of a first home. It's not wrong to accept their gift if it's an unconditional one. But if there are "strings" attached to the funds, it would be wise to say, "Thank you, but no thanks." There are potential dangers in loans from family members because of the entitlement often felt by the lender. Wisdom doesn't have to be paid back, but money does.

So should you buy a house? Here are four factors to consider.

1. *Your ability to pay for it.* You'll need the down payment, of course. But then there are the monthly mortgage payments.

If you don't have a budget already, develop one to see how much money is available each month to put toward those payments (including taxes and insurance). If those payments don't require you to cut out essentials like food, utilities, clothing, giving, and saving, then you may be ready to purchase a home. Realtors and lenders often advise couples to make sure they aren't "getting in over their heads" by using the following formula:

- Divide your fixed debt (the mortgage you're considering, credit cards, student loans, car payment—anything that requires long-term payback) by your gross income (before taxes and deductions).
- Turn the result into a percentage by moving the decimal two places to the right. To pass muster with most lenders, the percentage generally should be under 36 percent, preferably under 30 percent, and as close to 20 percent as possible. Still, some lenders will allow up to 45 percent, depending on the applicant's credit score.

2. *Timing.* There are times when renting may be the wisest choice, even if you've saved up a down payment. Here are a few examples:

- It's likely that you'll be moving soon.
- Your income probably will take a dive in the near future.
- One or both spouses are completing schooling, making for a very tight budget.
- You don't have an emergency fund—usually at least three months' salary.

At other times, however, it's good to remember that by renting you're building someone else's equity and assets—not your own.

3. *"Forgotten" costs.* Couples don't always remember that the costs of home ownership don't end with the mortgage payment. Here are some to keep in mind:

> There are times when renting may be the wisest choice, even if you've saved up a down payment. At other times, however, it's good to remember that by renting you're building someone else's equity and assets—not your own.

- Fees associated with loan processing and purchase of the home.
- Upkeep (everything from water heaters to roofs to painting).
- Property taxes and mortgage insurance, both of which tend to increase.

4. *Government benefits.* Mortgage interest is tax deductible, which is important since the first seven or so years of a mortgage are mainly interest payments. Real estate taxes are deductible, too. For specifics, consult an accountant or attorney who specializes in this area.

Another benefit is the opportunity to participate in government programs that assist first-time home buyers. This help usually comes in the form of mortgage credit certificates or mortgage revenue bonds, generally offering a lower interest rate—and sometimes even the down payment as well.

5. *The value of ownership.* When you own a house, you have more control of your living environment than when you rent. You can decorate the house or remodel it without having to ask a landlord—though you may need a building permit if you're attempting a major makeover. You can put nail holes in the wall, paint murals on the ceiling, and plant a garden. How much is that worth to you?

Your decision about home-buying is important, but so is the *way* you and your spouse make that decision. The process you go through can be a barometer of how healthy and mature your relationship is.

> Your decision about home-buying is important, but so is the way you and your spouse make that decision. The process you go through can be a barometer of how healthy and mature your relationship is.

As you consider whether to buy a house, each spouse needs to be listened to and understood. The two of you need to pray about it, focusing on what God might want you to do. Sometimes God chooses to speak through the wise counsel of others; in the words of Proverbs 18:15, "The heart of the discerning acquires knowledge; the ears of the wise seek it out." Wisdom isn't knowing everything; it's being able to listen.

Here are three principles to follow when making a big financial decision like this.

1. *Be willing to grow through the experience.* Buying a house is stressful. But stress can either dampen discernment or spur growth.

For example, Greg and Sara were planning to buy a house. Sara had grown up in an upper-middle-class neighborhood, dreaming of owning a home. Greg, on the other hand, grew up in family that sometimes had trouble paying its bills. Now, as Sara stood on the verge of realizing her dream, Greg focused on the financial burdens that home ownership could bring.

They prayed about their decision. But instead of seeking God's guidance, each of them seemed to be telling Him what to do. It wasn't until they concentrated on finding out what God might have in store for them that they began to receive answers. When they stopped trying to dictate their future based on their pasts, they learned valuable lessons about humility, faith, and sound judgment.

2. *Communicate and prioritize together.* You might start by making a "pros and cons" list about buying a house. This will give the two of you something to look at, discuss, and pray about.

Listen carefully to each other's desires and concerns. You can't both listen at the same time, so decide who'll speak first.

3. *Seek counsel.* A trusted real estate agent can be your best ally. Don't hesitate to ask questions, including the question of which mortgage lender the agent trusts most.

> There are potential dangers in loans from family members because of the entitlement often felt by the lender. Wisdom doesn't have to be paid back, but money does.

Another potential resource: people who've recently gone through the home-buying process. Ask them plenty of questions, too.

What if you decide that you *should* buy a home but really can't afford it? Begin to develop a financial plan that lets you reduce or even eliminate fixed debt. Freeing up money for a down payment and then building equity in a small home usually is a good long-term plan. Dreams can come true, but they require patience, perseverance, and time.

They also require agreement between the two of you. If one spouse dreams and the other prefers only "reality," resentment and division may enter the relationship. Try to look together toward a reality that's based on a long-term perspective.

Unfortunately, some recently married couples make mistakes when they buy a home—mistakes that take several years to correct financially and emotionally.

Here are seven common home-buying mistakes couples make during the early years of marriage.

1. *Assuming property values will always go up.* The housing market isn't always favorable. Just as there are increases, there can be decreases in the worth of a home. There have been times when houses actually lost value and times when their value rose at a rate lower than inflation.

2. *Being blinded by emotion.* Some couples rush into buying, driven by the

need to be noticed and admired. They want to "show off" whether or not they can afford the house. Purchases driven by emotion tend not to be the wisest; those driven by careful thinking tend to have positive results.

3. *Too much window-shopping.* "We're just going to look and dream," some spouses tell each other. But this can be dangerous, especially for those who make decisions impulsively. It's also a way for hard feelings and disconnection to develop in a relationship when "browsing" leads nowhere—or to a decision to buy more than a couple can afford.

4. *Trying to "win."* Some couples turn the decision-making process into a battlefield. Each spouse becomes so focused on what he or she wants that hurtful statements or "silent treatments" result. Major resentments can begin to take root during the process of deciding whether or not to buy a house.

A first house usually isn't the one a couple lives in for a long time. So there's no need to insist that it be a "dream" house.

5. *Counting on raises.* It's easy to predict that you'll be making more money in five years or to count on a career you don't have yet. That happened to Luke and Brenda, who went house-hunting while Luke was still in graduate school. They were enticed by a house beyond the scope of their budget—thinking they'd be able to afford it when Luke got a better job. "Don't count your chickens before they're hatched" may be an old saying, but it still applies.

6. *Overspending.* When many young couples begin earning "real paychecks," they want to start buying things—even if they've committed themselves to a mortgage. They see ads for big-screen TVs that offer no-interest financing for a year and sign up—only to see car repairs and emergency doctor visits eat up the money they'd meant to put toward repaying the debt. They find themselves with fixed debt higher than the maximum 36 percent mentioned earlier—and a risk of losing their home to foreclosure. To exceed that percentage and maintain financial stability, a couple must be very disciplined in its spending. The answer to overspending: Stick with a budget.

7. *Getting the wrong loan.* Too many couples consider only which loan would be most convenient—not which would be wisest. Some lenders, for example, offer a low interest rate for the first three or five years—but it soars after that. As a result, a couple might find itself refinancing, which could cost

$2,500 to $5,000. There are many kinds of loans, which makes it important to consult a trusted mortgage lender and real estate agent.

With all these challenges, buying a house may appear to be a daunting task. But it can be a wonderful experience if the two of you seek wisdom, have patience, communicate, and plan ahead. And remember: Money will buy a house, but it's up to you to establish what goes on inside.

—Daniel Huerta

What Investments Should We Make?

"Sure," you may be thinking. "Investing is a good idea. We'll put a little money aside for when we're old, and the rest will take care of itself."

Unfortunately, it's not quite that simple.

Bill and Mary managed to save $150,000 by the time they retired. Assuming their investment would be safe, they put it into government bonds that paid 12 percent interest. The annual income they received from that was $18,000.

But they ran into a problem 20 years later when the bonds matured and they had to renew—at a much lower rate of 5.1 percent. Their income dropped to $7,650 a year—which didn't buy nearly what it had when they'd retired. What they thought was a safe investment turned out to be anything but.

After reading about Bill and Mary, you may be thinking, "Investing sounds too complicated. Maybe we should just deal with it later." But procrastination isn't the answer—especially when failing to invest wisely could have a huge effect on how you and your spouse spend your future together.

An old saying goes, "People don't plan to fail; they fail to plan." When it comes to investing, you need three kinds of plans: *short-term*, *intermediate*, and *long-term*.

Short-term plans are to meet needs that might occur in the next one or two years, including emergencies. With short-term investments, the primary goal is liquidity—making sure the money is quickly available to you. Money markets, savings accounts, and certificates of deposit will be among the most likely places to invest this money.

Intermediate needs are those you're likely to face two to five years from now—down payment on a home or car, for instance. You may be able to earn a little more interest toward these expenses by taking a little more risk. Sample investment options in this category include government bonds, corporate bonds, and equity income investments. The longer you can hold the investment

> If you understand the power of compound interest, you're destined to earn it; if you don't, you're destined to pay it. The earlier you start planning for retirement, the better off you'll be.

and the more risk you're willing to take, the more you *may* earn (though it's not guaranteed).

The typical *long-term* investment is for retirement. That's where compound interest comes in.

It's been said that if you understand the power of compound interest, you're destined to earn it; if you don't, you're destined to pay it. In other words, the earlier you start planning for retirement, the better off you'll be.

Let's say you're 25 years old, and that you plan to retire when you're 67. You have 42 years to save toward your retirement. If you invest $4,000 a year in an Individual Retirement Account (IRA), you'll have invested $168,000 in 42 years. But because of compound interest, if you've gotten an 8 percent rate of return, you'll have about $1,216,974! If you've gotten a 10 percent rate of return, it would be $2,150,547!

> Investment is selfish if you're investing only in your own comfort. But it's also a matter of stewardship.

On the other hand, if you wait 10 years to start investing, you'll end up with about $536,854 at an 8 percent rate of return. Waiting 10 years will have cost you $680,120.

As you can see, you can't afford to wait! Get started now, even if you have to start small.

Despite the numbers, some couples wonder whether investing is selfish—a form of hoarding. Certainly it's selfish if you're investing only in your own comfort (Matthew 6:19-24; 25:31-46). But investing is a matter of stewardship. Look at Matthew 25:14-28, the parable of the talents. The only person reprimanded was the servant who buried the money and didn't invest it.

Then there's 1 Timothy 5:8: "If anyone does not provide for his relatives, and especially for his immediate family, he has denied the faith and is worse than an unbeliever." Investing can be a way to accomplish that, and to provide for yourself when you're no longer able to work or when God calls you to some other endeavor.

If you have children, investing provides a good model for them, too. It can teach them stewardship, self-discipline, and the value of delayed gratification. It can also enable you to help your child "get on his feet" as a young adult or provide financial aid to an aging and ailing parent.

To make the best use of the funds God has entrusted to you, find a financial planner who shares your beliefs. This is especially helpful when you and your spouse disagree over which investments are wise.

If, after consulting a financial planner, you still disagree, pray about it—separately and together. It's important to wait until you agree—or at least are willing to compromise—before investing. An investment that doesn't work out can become a source of resentment between spouses if only one supported it.

Procrastination isn't the answer—especially when failing to invest wisely could have a huge effect on how you and your spouse spend your future together.

Remember the story of Bill and Mary? Here's a happier one about a couple who got better advice.

Nick and Andrea invested $150,000 over the years in a balanced equity portfolio that paid dividends and was structured to keep up with inflation.

At the beginning of their retirement they took 6 percent of their original investment as income, which was $9,000 a year. After 20 years, that $150,000 is worth roughly $598,000—and they're receiving an income from the account value, which is $35,880 a year.

Getting good counsel is part of being a good steward. For a plan that meets your needs and your "risk tolerance," talk with a professional investment advisor.

—SANDRA LUNDBERG

How Far Ahead Do We Need to Plan?

Here come Carly and Andrew into the financial planner's office.

Carly is 46. So is Andrew. They haven't saved anything for retirement yet. They've been getting kids through school, paying the mortgage, and doing all the other things they've chosen to do.

The financial planner has bad news for Carly and Andrew. To meet their goal of retiring at age 65, they need to save $2,500 a month.

The problem is that they make $2,500 a month—total.

Carly and Andrew will have to work longer or retire on an income that's a lot less than what they'd assumed. Why? Because they didn't plan early and take the steps necessary to achieve their goals.

When you're young, you may wonder, "Can't we wait until we're older to start all that financial planning?"

Sure, you can. The downside is that the longer you wait, the harder it is. You limit your options for investment. And you lose the benefit of compound interest (see "What Investments Should We Make?").

The further you travel down the road of marriage, the more demands there are on your income. For instance, if you have children you'll find yourself having to pay for school clothes, uniforms for extracurricular activities, maybe braces. If your parents are living, they'll be getting older, too—and may need your help. Pressures like these can make it more difficult to form the investing habit.

> The further you travel down the road of marriage, the more demands there are on your income. That can make it more difficult to form the investing habit.

If you live in the U.S. and are relying on Social Security to take care of you, think again. The best-case scenario, some experts say, is that the program will provide only a third of your living expenses when you retire. Already many people who thought they could rely largely on Social Security are having to keep working—just to afford a lower standard of living than they expected.

When should you start your financial planning? Now.

When should you start investing? As soon as possible.

Even if you can't set aside $4,000 a year in an Individual Retirement Account (IRA), perhaps you can begin by investing $25 each pay period. When it comes to long-term planning and compounding interest, every little bit counts. So the sooner it's put away, the better.

The urgency to plan applies to more than retirement, too. If you have or anticipate having children, you may want to help provide for their college education. The first thing to do is establish a plan for saving and investing toward that goal.

By starting early, you can put away less money on a monthly basis to help cover the growing cost of tuition. The longer you wait, the more money you'll need to set aside each month. A financial planner can tell you about specialized programs to help fund a child's college education.

Some couples realize the need to start planning financially, but put it off because they don't know their way through the maze of stocks, bonds, certificates, and annuities. What they need is a financial planner.

Even if you know a thing or two about money, a financial planner is a specialist who can help. That's what Dave, a structural engineer, learned in a conversation with Bob, a financial planner. The two of them were talking about Dave's investments; Dave said that when it came to financial planning, he wanted to do everything himself.

"Why?" Bob asked.

"Well, I don't want to pay for the advice. I don't need that help."

> Some couples put this off because they don't know their way through the maze of stocks, bonds, certificates, and annuities. What they need is a financial planner.

"You know," said Bob, "there are plenty of books out on how to build a bridge. So do you think that if I went out and read every book there is on how to build a bridge that I could build one as good as you?"

"No," Dave said. "Absolutely not."

"Why not?"

"Well, I've been trained in civil engineering," Dave replied. "I have an understanding of how bridges are built, and I've built many bridges and know how they work."

"Isn't that the same thing we're doing here?" Bob asked. "I'm trained as a financial professional, and I know things that you may or may not have picked up off the Internet or by reading books."

Dave saw Bob's point—and Bob helped him make some decisions that will positively affect Dave's retirement.

Another planning expert who can guide you is an attorney. Have you and your spouse prepared your wills? If you have children, have you chosen—and named in legal documents—guardians who'll care for them in the event of your death?

Few people like to think about those subjects. Many couples avoid them, claiming they'll deal with wills and guardianships "someday." But as James 4:14 says, "Why, you do not even know what will happen tomorrow. What is your life? You are a mist that appears for a little while and then vanishes."

A will determines where your assets will be directed; a medical power of attorney can outline a plan for your care if you're incapacitated and unable to tell a physician or family members what you want. Wills and guardianships are keys to a child's future; without a legal plan, children are placed under the guardianship that a court decides is best. You wouldn't want this if you were alive; why let it happen in the event of your death?

"Make plans by seeking advice," says Proverbs 20:18. And when it comes to preparing for the future, there's no time like the present.

—SANDRA LUNDBERG

**Part 5:
Sex**

What About Birth Control?

It's a week after the honeymoon.

Ken is in the bedroom, rummaging through the top drawer of his dresser. He calls to Paula, who's brushing her hair in the bathroom. "Babe, we're going to be out of condoms soon. What do you want to do about birth control?"

Paula chuckles. "I thought we'd just let nature take its course."

Ken turns a little pale.

After a dramatic pause, Paula walks into the bedroom. "Actually, I have an appointment scheduled with the doctor next week to talk about our options."

Ken sighs, relieved. "Well, let me know what you decide."

"Okay."

"Hey," Ken adds. "You weren't thinking about any of those hormone implant things, were you? Those sort of scare me."

"No, I'm pretty much planning on the pill."

"Sounds good."

Is birth control something you and your spouse talk about as easily as Ken and Paula do? Are the two of you in agreement about the rightness or wrongness of the pill, intrauterine devices (IUDs), and whether the husband or wife is more responsible for contraception?

Are the two of you in agreement about the rightness or wrongness of the pill, intrauterine devices (IUDs), and whether the husband or wife is more responsible for contraception?

The subject of birth control isn't without controversy. The following thoughts may help you and your spouse sort out some of the moral, medical, and relational issues surrounding it.

Focus on the Family holds that all human life is sacred, and that life begins with fertilization—the union of sperm and egg. We believe preventing fertilization is not morally wrong, but oppose any method of birth control that acts after fertilization and ends a human life by preventing implantation in the womb. Since an intrauterine device (IUD) is thought to interfere at least on occasion with implantation of a fertilized egg, possibly ending a life, we would oppose it.

Birth control pills—oral contraceptives—have become controversial because some of them are believed to occasionally end life after fertilization. This is a complex matter, partly because there are many different formulations of oral contraceptives. At present it appears that birth control pills which contain only progesterone do not reliably prevent ovulation. This is also true of the contraceptive Norplant, which is no longer on the market in the U.S. and Canada, but which some women might still have implanted.

What does this mean for you? It means that using progesterone-only pills or Norplant may allow fertilization to occur, with a greater chance that the pregnancy will be ectopic (outside the uterus). This may be evidence that these contraceptives disrupt normal implantation of a fertilized egg. Thus Norplant and the progesterone-only pill are a problem for those who believe life begins at conception.

The most commonly prescribed oral contraceptives are pills that contain both estrogen and progesterone. These, and Depo-Provera injections, seem to work primarily by suppressing ovulation. If they work only through this mechanism, they're true contraceptives—preventing sperm and egg from uniting. But if they increase the likelihood of losing a fertilized egg—sometimes referred to as the "abortifacient" effect—they would present the same problem as Norplant and the progesterone-only medications.

> Birth control pills—oral contraceptives—have become controversial because they're believed to occasionally end life after fertilization.

The majority of physicians we consult with believe that Depo-Provera and the estrogen/progesterone pills do not have an abortifacient effect. The minority feel that when conception occurs on these medications, there is enough of a possibility for an abortifacient effect to warrant informing women about it.

People with strong pro-life convictions may hold differing opinions about using oral contraceptives. And scientific reasoning isn't the only factor that influences a couple's attitudes on birth control. You and your spouse should examine the facts and prayerfully consider your approach to family planning.

Some couples, wanting to avoid any concerns about the abortifacient nature of certain contraceptives, choose to use a barrier method (like condoms) or a timing method of birth control. Either of these may require a bit more planning and preparation.

Whatever birth control method you choose, it should be a joint decision.

And whatever you decide, it may change over time along with changes in the wife's biochemistry and in your lifestyle.

The two of you also need to agree on when you'd like to have children and how you'll try to accomplish that goal. If you're looking for the "perfect time" to have a child, it's unlikely that you'll find it. For most couples, there's never a moment when life is stress-free or readiness for parenting is at 100 percent. For some couples, infertility is a problem—something you usually can't know when you start trying to conceive.

Birth control can be a contentious subject in a marriage. Take Trent and Tracy, a couple considering a timing-based form of family planning popularly referred to as "the rhythm method." They've heard it's been highly effective for couples who are trained in the method and who follow through on the detailed charting and delayed gratification required. Tracy is enthused; Trent has doubts. If Trent isn't fully convinced and just "goes along" to please Tracy, the chances are good that there will be stress between them. They need good communication and clarity before committing to this program.

> Whatever birth control method you choose, it should be a joint decision. And whatever you decide, it may change over time.

Some husbands want to place responsibility for birth control solely on their wives. That's a recipe for trouble; if the wife denies him sex for a time in order to avoid conception, the husband may feel rejected or assume she's doing this for selfish reasons. If the wife becomes pregnant, the husband may blame her instead of owning his share of the responsibility. Make sure that in your marriage, both spouses understand birth control as a his-*and*-hers issue.

Birth control need not strain your relationship. It can even help the two of you grow closer. As in all areas of marriage, the key is not to make assumptions about the whos, whats, and whens, but to talk through your concerns, desires, and expectations—and come up with a plan that works for both of you.

—SANDRA LUNDBERG

How Often Is Normal?

Shifting uncomfortably at one end of the living room couch, Brady avoided the gaze of his wife, Deanna, who sat at the other end.

"I don't think I'm . . . *abnormal* to want sex several times a week," he said, keeping his voice down. "But the way you act, you'd think I was some kind of pervert."

"No, I don't think that, Brady." Deanna couldn't keep the tears from spilling down her cheeks now. "It's just that with the baby and everything, I don't have anything left to give at the end of the day."

Brady got up and started pacing in front of the fireplace, his arms extended in exasperation. "We waited to get married—and you know how hard that was. I thought once it was 'legal' we'd want to do it all the time!"

> "We waited to get married—and you know how hard that was. I thought once it was 'legal' we'd want to do it all the time!"

Brady and Deanna aren't the only couple clashing over the question of how often they "should" have sex. The issue usually comes up when spouses' expectations about the frequency of intercourse don't match—a common complaint.

Researchers don't all agree on how often the average couple has sex. According to *Understanding Human Sexuality* by Janet Shibley Hyde and John D. DeLamater (McGraw-Hill, 1997), the largest percentage of married couples reporting in a study said they had intercourse three times a week. But as an article on the MayoClinic.com Web site points out, "Statistics on sexual behavior can be quite misleading. For example, a couple might read that the average married couple has intercourse three times a week. They may not be aware, however, that this average includes a wide range. The frequency of intercourse might range from zero for some to 15 or 20 times a week for others. Therefore, even if their frequency of intercourse is more or less than three times a week, their behavior is within the range of normal human experience."

Oversimplified averages can create anxious reactions. If you have sex more than twice a week, does that make you abnormal? If you have sex twice a month, is your marriage less healthy than most?

Here are five things to remember when you and your spouse aren't sure whether the frequency of your sexual activity is "normal."

1. *Every couple is different.* Frequency of sexual activity can be a measure of the general health of a marriage. But there's no numerical standard that applies to every couple.

Factors like gender, individual expectations, developmental maturity as a couple, and cultural differences all affect the numbers. In early marriage these variables are especially evident, as the honeymoon effect wanes and we find out where our own "normal" will land on the scale.

During the first years of marriage, it's especially important to discern which sources of information about sexuality can be trusted. You can't gauge what's normal from the impressions given by many TV shows and movies, for instance. Sex also deserves the honor of privacy, which discourages comparing notes with friends on what works for them. In addition to seeking wise, godly counsel from a mentor, you might find helpful several books by Christians. You'll find some listed among the resources at the end of this guide.

If you have sex more than twice a week, does that make you abnormal? If you have sex twice a month, is your marriage less healthy than most?

2. *Quality precedes quantity.* The parenting myth of "quality time" over "quantity time" happily is being debunked. When it comes to sex, though, quality really is more important than quantity. This doesn't mean either spouse has an excuse to cop out of marital responsibilities in the bedroom. It's a call to excellence.

If you're dissatisfied with your sex life, instead of first complaining about the frequency, examine the quality. Ask yourself, "Would *I* want to be married to me?" Consider how well you meet your spouse's sexual needs; find out what changes might be in order. Once communication increases and needs are satisfied, increased frequency usually isn't far behind.

3. *There's a time to serve.* Sadly, a lot of factors in our broken world can leave one or both spouses needing special consideration. Sexual trauma, addiction, abortion, and disease affect our sexuality in profound ways. Recovery is often slow, requiring patience and understanding from both partners.

A woman's reproductive cycle also requires understanding from her husband. Premenstrual syndrome (PMS), menstruation, and pregnancy—not to mention breastfeeding and caring for infants and young children—can leave a wife drained physically and emotionally. At these times, a husband will do well to keep the "big picture" in mind, remembering that sexual intimacy may suffer temporarily—but his sacrificial service will yield fruit for the relationship in the future.

4. *Be intentional.* Impulsive, spontaneous sex can be great, but it tends to fall by the wayside as jobs, mortgages, and children enter the picture. It's certainly possible (and preferable) to keep a fun-loving chemistry going throughout marriage, but depending on that alone is often not enough.

> Frequency of sexual activity can be a measure of the general health of a marriage. But there's no numerical standard that applies to every couple.

If you give your spouse only the leftovers of your time and energy, neither of you will be sexually satisfied. Planning a time and place for intimacy seems anything but intimate, but the lack of negotiation can lead to lack of fulfillment—or worse, to looking elsewhere for it.

5. *Sex is a picture.* Scripture paints a beautiful portrait of Christ's return for His beloved Bride, the church. Our spiritual union with Him is echoed in every aspect of our earthly marriages, including sexuality. For example, a healthy husband and wife will want to focus on the quality of their sexual relationship, not just how often they have sex. It's about the relationship—not the numbers.

It can be easy to forget that, as Brady did during that confrontation with Deanna. He remembered it later, when the two of them dropped the baby off at her mother's on the way to their weekly date.

At their favorite Italian restaurant they drifted into small talk, both regretting the earlier conflict.

"Hon, I'm sorry I raised my voice to you earlier," Brady finally blurted, then glanced around to make sure other diners weren't looking his way. "I think I've just been feeling like you don't want me like you used to. I mean, I know in my head there are other reasons. My heart just doesn't always pay attention."

Deanna fished in her purse for more tissues. "I do want to show you how much I love you," she whispered, hoping the people around her didn't notice her tears. "I get caught up in the diapers and the feedings and everything else. I'm glad we've at least got our date night to remind us to focus on us, too."

—ROB JACKSON

What If We Don't Like the Same Things?

Jill didn't know what to say when she opened Mark's gift. The pretty package had been a total surprise. "It just made me think of you," he'd told her.

Judging by the size of the box, she'd thought it might be a new scarf or a sampler of chocolates. The last thing she'd expected was this lace teddy.

Didn't Mark know she wasn't the lingerie type? She could imagine how big her thighs would look in this thing.

Sometimes she thought they'd never see eye to eye when it came to sex. They'd been married only a year, and already their differences were clear. What would things be like five years from now—if they made it that far?

Jill and Mark are learning to their chagrin that sexual arousal is a very individual matter. One spouse wants the lights on; the other wants it dark. Each partner prefers a certain touch, a certain time, even a certain temperature.

When you and your mate like "different strokes," what should you do? Here are five suggestions.

1. *Discover your comfort zone.* You probably would expect to negotiate which colors to paint the rooms of your new house, or whether to serve tofu for dinner. Why be surprised if you encounter some differences in your sexual desires? As you discover your "comfort zone" as a couple, keep in mind that this process is a normal developmental task for every marriage.

Some argue that this process could be helped along by living together before the wedding. But statistics prove otherwise. Studies reveal that, instead of increasing sexual compatibility, premarital cohabitation actually boosts the likelihood of sexually transmitted disease, sexual dysfunction, codependency, divorce, and loss of trust. Clearly, becoming one flesh is sacred for a reason.

> Didn't Mark know she wasn't the lingerie type? She could imagine how big her thighs would look in this thing.

2. *Be a servant.* Your approach to sex should mirror your approach to marriage in general: "Serve one another in love" (Galatians 5:13).

Solomon referred to his wife as "my sister, my bride" (Song of Solomon

4:10). Can you keep the perspective of being brother and sister in Christ as well as being spouses? A servant's attitude can guard against letting differences in bed become a power struggle or cause for resentment.

Basic issues of preference, such as whether to have the lights on or which positions are more pleasurable, are good opportunities to listen and learn what pleases your spouse. If something causes one partner embarrassment or discomfort, he or she should never feel pressured to participate. It's also important that both partners express preferences without criticism and without judging each other.

3. *Discern moral issues.* Each of us enters marriage with an "arousal template" or set of stimuli that triggers sexual interest. If you've had prior sexual relationships or exposure to pornography, for example, unhealthy appetites may have been added to your template.

Even between consenting spouses, certain sexual behaviors are still wrong. For example, a husband may claim that pornography helps his sex life—but its use actually constitutes an act of adultery (Matthew 5:27-28). Any sexual practices that are demeaning or physically harmful will damage true intimacy as well as violate biblical guidelines. Work together to find *what's* right instead of fighting over *who's* right.

4. *Address trauma or addiction.* If conflict over sex escalates beyond simply choosing a "menu" you both like, it's possible there's a history of sexual trauma for one or both spouses. Associating shame or fear with sexuality is a powerful dynamic to overcome. Severe trauma can produce a condition known as Sexual Aversion Disorder. Survivors of childhood sexual abuse often need the help of a professional Christian counselor to restore a healthy sex life.

> Sometimes she thought they'd never see eye to eye when it came to sex. What would things be like five years from now—if they made it that far?

Addiction to pornography, fantasy, and masturbation can put another big roadblock in a couple's path. Seeing sex as forbidden, dirty, or provocative leads to unhealthy fixations. A spouse may feel the addict is "not really there" during sex or that he or she is being used as a sexual object rather than loved intimately. Childhood sexual trauma is a frequent precursor to pornography addiction, and professional therapy is a critical tool for recovery.

5. *Talk about sex.* No matter what your sexual differences are, the first step to connecting well sexually is to do so verbally. Sometimes discussing these issues during intimacy can evoke feelings of shame or embarrassment. So it's often a good idea to wait and discuss it later, outside the bedroom.

Once you've established a healthy pattern of communication, conversation can even contribute to the sexual experience. You and your spouse can connect physically and at deeper levels as well. Talking about your love and desire for your spouse will build a safe, satisfying experience for both partners before, during, and after sexual intercourse.

As you discover your "comfort zone" as a couple, keep in mind that this process is a normal developmental task for every marriage.

Let's get back to Jill and Mark. Jill's still standing there with the gift of lingerie. What should she do?

Mark hesitates, seeing her expression. "I—I hope I didn't shock you with the present," he stammers. "I know it's not your usual style, but I really thought you'd look beautiful in it."

Jill smooths the gold ribbon on the box. She starts thinking about how Mark has shown her in so many ways that she is God's gift to him.

A shy smile plays across her lips. She even quits worrying about how her thighs would look in this outfit.

Okay, she thinks. *As long as he treasures me like this, I'll wrap his gift any way he likes.*

—Rob Jackson

Are We Doing It Right?

Lisa and Tom had been married two and a half years when Lisa set up an appointment for them to see a counselor.

"Tell me what you'd like to work on in therapy," the counselor said.

"Our sex life," Lisa answered.

"Yeah," Tom added. "She never wants to do it, and I'm getting tired of waiting. My friends are doing it three to five times a week. And, man, I'm lucky if I get it once!"

"Okay," the therapist says. "Let me get a little more information here. You guys have been married two and a half years." They both nodded. "How was your sex life when you first got married?"

"Well, at least it was more often," Tom grumbled.

Lisa looked down at the carpet, tears forming in her eyes.

"Lisa," the therapist said, "tell me what's going on from your perspective."

"Well, it's not like I thought it would be."

The therapist nodded. "Can you tell me more about what you mean by that?"

"Well, I just thought it would be a lot more fun."

"She just does it because she has to," Tom declared. "Not because she wants to. And I don't know why she doesn't want to."

Lisa looked up, suddenly finding her voice. "You are so careless and selfish!" she cried. "We used to talk. We used to kiss. Now whenever you reach for me I know there's just one thing on your mind—sex."

> "She just does it because she has to. Not because she wants to. And I don't know why she doesn't want to."

"Okay," the therapist said, intervening. "How much time do you guys spend when you make love?"

"Oh, about 10 minutes," said Tom.

Lisa agreed. "Yeah, about 10 minutes."

"Well, that could be a big part of the problem," said the therapist. "Let's begin by looking at the arousal cycle for men and women, you guys. Women are just barely getting going at 10 minutes. But if you're expecting it's going to be over by then, your body doesn't even know what to do."

When it comes to sex, many recently married couples wonder whether they're "doing it right"—especially if, like Lisa and Tom, they find themselves dissatisfied with the way things are going.

There are a number of factors that contribute to whether your sexual intimacy is satisfying. "Doing it right" is just one of them.

For example, a good sexual relationship has a lot to do with how the two of you are doing *outside* the bedroom. If you're having problems with sexual intimacy, you're probably having trouble in other areas as well. This can be an indicator that you need to work on your relationship.

Another factor in sexual difficulties may be the "gender gap." You've probably heard the many analogies about differences between males and females: "Women are like teapots, slow to boil. Men are like waffles, able to compartmentalize everything." Husbands and wives *are* different, in sexual behavior as in many other ways.

For instance, a woman's arousal cycle is closer to 30-45 minutes than it is to 10. If, like Tom and Lisa, you find that an entire sexual act usually takes 10 or 15 minutes, the two of you may have problems with communication, respect, and understanding. This is also a common reason why sex is painful for some women.

On the other hand, if you're taking a generous amount of time to pleasure each other without the pressure of reaching orgasm and find that intercourse is still painful, it may be time to speak with your physician and a therapist who specializes in working with sexual dysfunction.

A good sexual relationship has a lot to do with how the two of you are doing *outside* the bedroom. If you're having problems with sexual intimacy, you're probably having trouble in other areas as well.

Establishing a solid sexual relationship in your marriage should be a goal the two of you share. To attain that goal, your sexual experiences need to be satisfying for both of you. Here are a few keys to finding that satisfaction—keys that show "doing it right" is about more than technique.

1. *Take care of your body.* Regular exercise, good nutrition, and good hygiene are just as important now that you're married as they were when you were single. During your dating days you most likely presented your best self to each other—showered, shaved, powdered, and perfumed. Married couples often get lazy about these things. But if you don't want to be taken for granted—much

less avoided—maintain those good grooming habits that contributed to your attraction to one another.

2. *Be upfront.* Each of you needs to take responsibility for whether or not your sex life is satisfying. Tell your spouse what feels good to you and what you need; don't assume he or she will "just know." Your spouse can't read your mind. As for faking satisfaction—that will only hurt both of you, damaging mutual trust and guaranteeing that you won't get your needs met. So figure out what you need and go for it.

3. *Plan ahead.* Make your sexual relationship a priority. You may need to schedule blocks of time to be physical together, times when you won't let other things interrupt—including the demands of work or get-togethers with friends.

Scheduling sex may at first seem contrived and unnatural. Yet you may find that it leads to better sexual experiences for the two of you, thereby improving the quality of your marriage.

> If you find that an entire sexual act usually takes 10 or 15 minutes, the two of you may have problems with communication, respect, and understanding.

4. *Take the time.* Plan special days and moments together. Make them romantic, even experimental. For some couples this comes naturally; for others sex has become repetitive and boring, and kicking stale habits takes extra effort. Make time to talk about your sexual relationship—preferably when you're not in the middle of a sexual encounter. Take time with sexual activity itself, remembering the hugging, kissing, and caressing the two of you probably enjoyed before marriage. If you've dropped that because now you have the opportunity for intercourse, bring it back. Foreplay has value on its own, and is part of the buildup to intercourse. For the wife in particular, these preliminary steps are very important.

5. *Give yourselves a break.* Your sexual times together need to be free of the demand for having an orgasm, and from any anxiety associated with that. Replace those stressors with closeness, warmth, pleasure, and fun. You'll be more likely to "lose yourself" in your spouse and the feelings you're enjoying together.

6. *Deal with scars and habits.* Real intimacy can be difficult to achieve if you're carrying around the baggage of sexual abuse, premarital sexual relations, or pornography use. These can inhibit sexual arousal, trust, and the ability to enjoy and complete intercourse. If one of these is an issue for either of you, it's

an issue for both of you. Don't wait to get help. There are trained Christian therapists who can assist you.

How can you find the right therapist? Ask your pastor or physician for a referral. Or call Focus on the Family at (719) 531-3400 (ask for the counseling department), which maintains a national referral network. When you find a therapist, interview him or her over the phone. Ask about the person's Christian commitment and how much experience he or she has working with couples' sexual problems. Inquire about fees. It's your right to get satisfying answers to these questions.

After their first appointment with the therapist, Lisa and Tom had a lot to talk about.

"I didn't know my going fast was making you feel so bad," Tom said. "I thought it would take the pressure off you if I just got it over with."

Lisa shook her head. "I don't want to just get it over with! Well, sometimes I do. But mostly that makes me feel used. I just want it to be like it used to be, when we'd spend hours just hanging out, talking, laughing. I never thought it would be like this."

"So you think we need to go see the therapist again?" Tom asked.

"Absolutely."

In terms of rebuilding a fulfilling sexual relationship, Lisa and Tom were finally doing it right.

—SANDRA LUNDBERG

Take responsibility for whether or not your sex life is satisfying. Tell your spouse what feels good to you and what you need; don't assume he or she will "just know."

What Does He Want from Me?

Julie watched the attractive, career-oriented women at her husband's office party and felt an unfamiliar pang of worry.

Derek was naturally outgoing, and that ability to connect with others had been a big factor in his success in sales. A devoted Christian, he'd never given her reason to doubt his fidelity. But it was obvious women noticed him.

What was it the expert on that talk show had said? "If you don't romance your husband, someone else will."

Julie shivered. Their sex life had been declining since their honeymoon three years earlier. She'd never really understood what had gone wrong.

What does he want from me? she thought.

Do you ever wonder the same thing about your husband? Magazine articles at the supermarket checkout counter may feature articles about "Twelve Secret Ways to Please Your Man," but does your spouse really want you to show up at the front door in Saran Wrap?

> Magazine articles at the supermarket checkout counter may feature articles about "Twelve Secret Ways to Please Your Man," but does your spouse really want you to show up at the front door in Saran Wrap?

Like most other aspects of marriage, it's not that simple.

Women are often characterized as mysterious and men as more basic and straightforward. But one-dimensional stereotypes about sports cars versus pickup trucks only take us so far. Men can be inscrutable, too—and a wife who wants to be a good sexual partner looks for keys to unlock his mysteries as well.

Here are five steps toward being the partner your husband wants.

1. *Be secure in your own sexuality.* Be proactive. Instead of maintaining a passive role, invest in the growth and development of your sex life. Rather than leaving him to guess your needs and preferences, speak candidly and without criticizing. Especially if your husband was sexually pure before marriage, there are things that only you can teach him about what you want.

Many husbands wish their wives would more often initiate sex. In the safety of this God-ordained arena, they want to be pursued. The feeling that he's desirable meets a deep need in every man. Find out how he likes to be approached and add that to the menu occasionally.

2. *Affirm his masculinity.* There are nonsexual ways to affirm your husband, too. In private, you either build or diminish his confidence in the way you regard his interests, hobbies, parenting skills, and friendships. Showing respect for the things that are important to him directly affects your whole relationship.

There are opportunities to affirm your husband in public as well. Consider how you talk to others about him, especially in his presence. Criticism or barbed jests quickly shoot down intimacy on every level, physical or otherwise. And even though nonsexual touch is often described as a woman's need, your hand on his hand or shoulder tells him and others, "This man is mine, and I'm glad."

Women are often characterized as mysterious and men as more basic and straightforward. But one-dimensional stereotypes about sports cars versus pickup trucks only take us so far.

3. *Give him freedom of access.* It's a thorny subject, but a husband's feeling of having to "beg" for sex is too common a complaint to omit. While you aren't supposed to be some kind of 24-hour convenience mart, do examine your attitude of availability. If you find yourself frequently making excuses, figure out what's behind that pattern. Do your part to identify and eliminate the barriers that keep you from enjoying sex, so you can be a receptive, enthusiastic partner.

Part of receptivity includes keeping him informed of your menstrual period, ovulation, premenstrual syndrome (PMS), and other physical needs or limitations. The intricate, delicate nature of a woman's body bewilders and intimidates many husbands. Take the time to demystify your gynecological or obstetric issues. This will allow him to be a more confident partner while building intimacy in your marriage.

When physical or other issues prohibit intercourse, explain why—assuring your husband that you aren't just putting him off indefinitely. Be aware that even when your libido is low, his may be as strong as ever. Use creativity and teamwork to find a menu of sexual touch that will satisfy both partners' needs until intercourse is possible again.

4. *Understand his sexual needs.* Men need sex in order to feel intimate; women need intimacy in order to feel sexual. While this is a broad generalization, it

describes a basic contrast in our creation. Testosterone causes your husband to desire and think about sex more than you do. Most men desire sex at least three times a week and think of it more often than that.

While you shouldn't blindly force yourself to serve him sexually whether you feel like it or not, at least start by asking him what his needs are. Your discussion should assure him that you don't see your differences as an issue of bad versus good. It's important for him to know you understand his needs and that you care about meeting them.

> Many husbands wish their wives would more often initiate sex. In the safety of this God-ordained arena, they want to be pursued.

5. *Help him stay faithful.* A man's visually-oriented arousal mechanism is part of God's purposeful design. The fact that your husband delights in how you look, feel, and smell can be a source of enjoyment for you both. Neither of you should obsess over appearance or compare yourself to Hollywood icons, but general attention to how you keep yourself is an important part of his sensory experience.

Be especially mindful of how our culture affects men. Pray for your husband's spiritual, emotional, and physical protection. Provide a safe environment in which he can admit his inevitable struggles and temptations. Don't enable him with a "boys will be boys" attitude, but don't judge him for being tempted, either. Rather, consider his vulnerability a sacred trust that can bond you closer as you serve each other in Christ.

Driving home from the office party, Julie took a deep breath. "Derek," she said finally, "I want to make sure I'm meeting your needs as a wife."

Derek's eyes widened. "You mean . . . um . . . sexually?"

"Well, yeah. Those women obviously noticed you. I just want to make sure you feel . . . satisfied."

Derek looked thoughtful. After a long moment he reached over and gently squeezed her hand. "That's really nice of you to say. I know we have some things to work on, but I'm very satisfied with you. I thought you knew that."

Julie sighed. "Sometimes I don't understand what I should do. I want to be the kind of wife you can talk to. I mean, to tell me if there are things you wish were different or better. We need to talk more."

Derek nodded slowly.

We might not be there yet, Julie thought. *But it's a start.*

—ROB JACKSON

What Does She Want from Me?

"Do you want to talk about it?" Evan's voice was flat, his eyes unable to meet Anna's.

"Yeah, I guess," she said, and shrugged.

Looks like she's given up, he thought.

Last night had been hard for both of them. After two and a half years of marriage, they seemed to have reached a dead end, sexually speaking. They'd tried new things, but it was a hit-or-miss process. Even when he tried to pleasure her the way she suggested, he never seemed to get it right. They both just ended up frustrated.

What do women want? he thought. *I mean, what does* she *want?*

Understanding what your wife wants starts with recognizing that your sexual appetites and responses aren't quite like hers. Some differences are obvious; others are more subtle. Here are some examples:

- The male body can be ready for intercourse more quickly than the female.
- A man's physical response is often "hot linked" with visual stimulation; a woman's sexual response usually takes more time and is tied to emotion.
- Some women can achieve another orgasm soon after the first, while the man's "turnaround" time is much longer.

Gender differences make things complicated enough. Beyond that, each individual's sexual response is unique.

What does your wife want from her sexual relationship with you? Here are four things most women need from their husbands.

1. *Romance.* A woman's need for emotional intimacy to precede physical intimacy is at the heart of what we call romance. But being romantic involves more than buying her roses—though they're usually a good idea. Almost any action or setting can be romantic when it holds special meaning for the participants.

Romance can mean something different to each individual, but the common

> Understanding what your wife wants starts with recognizing that your sexual appetites and responses aren't quite like hers.

factor for most women involves a feeling of being valued. Become a student of your wife at the physical, emotional, mental, and spiritual levels. Ask her what turns her on sexually. Find out what makes her feel cherished. Strive to be the world's greatest expert on her. While you learn the mechanics of pleasing her, you'll be showing her you think she's worth studying.

2. *Nonsexual touch.* A husband can easily make the mistake of thinking that "doing unto others" (see Matthew 7:12) includes approaching his wife sexually in the way he'd like her to approach him. But the application of Jesus' teaching here is to woo her as *she* desires and needs to be approached.

Men often like overtly sexual advances, but most women say they prefer a more relational approach. Your nonsexual touch throughout the day tells your wife you value her as being much more than just an object of desire. If the only time you touch her is when you want sex, the inadvertent message you send is that you want to use her body rather than love her whole person.

3. *Intimacy.* For most wives, emotional intimacy must precede physical intimacy. Respect, safety, and friendship are essential to unlocking her heart. If you habitually criticize or make barbed jokes about her, you'll find she's not responsive sexually when she feels unsafe emotionally.

If both of you are Christians, intimacy—the connection of minds and hearts—can be a natural extension of your shared faith. It may seem strange to think in terms of being brother and sister in Christ, but it's actually the key to your deepest bond. Sharing your thoughts, goals, needs, and hurts is a way of renewing your minds together in Christ (see Romans 12:2).

>
> **Being romantic involves more than buying her roses—though they're usually a good idea.**

4. *Purity.* A wife's sense of emotional safety depends on how much she can trust you. This isn't limited to sexual fidelity. She needs to see you being voluntarily accountable for your time, your money, your eyes, and every other aspect of your life. In other words, show her she can entrust herself to you.

A second part of her need for your purity is your role in her spiritual nurture. Servant leadership in the home carries out God's intended role for the husband to be a picture of Christ. Just as Christ laid down His life for His bride, the church, take every opportunity to pour out your life for her sake (see Ephesians 5:25-31). When your wife sees you growing, serving, and leading spiritually, it frees her to give herself to you in every way, including sexually.

Those four principles apply to most wives. But what about yours?

When you get right down to it, there's only one way to find out what your wife really wants. Ask her.

That means honest conversation, even if it's a little uncomfortable at first. Here are Evan and Anna again, trying to get that conversation going.

Evan sets two cups of coffee on the kitchen table and sits across from his wife. She's the first to speak, and the frustration tumbles out.

Find out what makes her feel cherished. Strive to be the world's greatest expert on her.

"I just felt so awkward last night. I always imagined sex would be easy, like a romantic movie. You know, where the characters just fall into each other's arms and automatically know what to do without any words."

Evan nods, relieved that they're finally getting things into the open. "Me, too. Those movies leave you thinking there isn't anything confusing or messy." He pauses, watching the coffee steam in his cup. "Look . . . I think we just need to say what we're thinking and wanting. If something doesn't work, we can figure it out together."

Anna shrugs again, but this time with a smile. "I guess. We're a good team on everything else. Why not this, too?"

—ROB JACKSON

Where Did Our Sex Life Go?

Eric came into the counselor's office looking troubled. He and Sylvia had just celebrated their third wedding anniversary, and he wasn't feeling good about it.

Sylvia was thrilled in her role as mother of their nine-month-old son, Steven. Eric, on the other hand, wondered whether Sylvia would ever be interested in a sex life again.

Their dating life, engagement, and first two years of marriage had been great. Eric was a successful teacher and coach; Sylvia had left her teaching job just two months before Steven was born, to be home full-time.

> "She treats me like I'm not important to her anymore. Sex is the last thing on her mind."

"Frankly," Eric confided to the counselor, "she treats me like I'm not important to her anymore. Since she's had the baby and been home, I'm pretty much the guy who just comes and goes with a hello and good-bye kiss, and nothing else. To me, it seems like since she started breastfeeding our son, sex is the last thing on her mind."

Eric had concluded that taking care of their baby had left Sylvia feeling fulfilled and satisfied, and she simply didn't need Eric in that way. He admitted that even though he loved Sylvia and wanted to be understanding, something had to change.

————

When Karla and Stan were dating, she was finishing up her formal training to be a registered nurse. Stan had just been promoted after seven years on the fire department's emergency medical response team. They had a lot in common, it seemed.

Stan was everything Karla wanted in a man, and was thrilled when he asked to marry her. She got a job with a cancer research team at the nearby university's medical training center. At first it seemed like the perfect job, but soon it conflicted with the rotating shifts of Stan's employment.

Eventually it was hard to find any time together. Having abstained sexually before marriage, they'd been happy since the wedding to express their love physically. But now their schedules seemed to make that next to impossible.

———

Jennifer and Phil had very different backgrounds. She was a longtime Christian; he'd become a believer shortly before they met at a singles' convention. Having led a somewhat promiscuous lifestyle in the "old days," Phil was fascinated with Jennifer's purity as well as her beauty. When they got involved in premarital counseling, they took the personality profiles. They weren't surprised when the tests showed that the two of them were of contrasting types.

> Quirks like frequent throat-clearing and occasional but irritating belches gave her reason to be disinterested in lovemaking—especially if they'd already had sex once or twice that week.

The differences didn't keep them from getting married. A few months after the wedding, though, problems became apparent. Jennifer found that Phil expected her to be sexually available most of the time—almost on demand. He couldn't seem to understand why she wasn't as interested as he was.

Other things bothered her, too—especially habits and quirks like frequent throat-clearing and occasional but irritating belches. These gave her reason to be disinterested in lovemaking—especially if they'd already had sex once or twice that week.

Soon they hardly had sex at all. Phil felt his wife was boycotting their love life with no valid reason.

———

All these stories have two things in common. First, they're about disappearing sex lives. Second, they sound pretty serious.

It's true that issues like these can significantly disrupt a couple's sexual expression—and a marriage, if not dealt with properly. But there's no need for Sylvia, Eric, Karla, Stan, Jennifer, and Phil to panic. You don't have to, either, if you're facing a similar plight.

Here's how each of these couples dealt with their situations.

———

Sylvia spoke to Eric's counselor about her sexual apathy. As it turned out, fear of another pregnancy was behind her disinterest. She soon recognized that she wasn't treating Eric fairly by asking him to be "understanding" indefinitely.

Guilt feelings and "shoulds" are by no means the best motivation for meeting your mate's needs in the bedroom. But, like Sylvia, you may have to begin there, and work on bettering your attitude. It helped Sylvia immensely just to talk to someone about her concerns. It also helped that she readily admitted Eric's needs were very important to her.

If fear of a potential pregnancy is keeping you from a healthy sexual relationship with your spouse, it's a reason for frank discussion about family planning and precautions—not for total abstinence.

———

What about Karla and Stan? There was no mystery about the cause of their dwindling lovemaking. They were enthusiastic about being a sexual couple, but didn't find it easy to demonstrate that due to their work schedules.

Their solution: carefully planning relaxed, intimate times together. They arranged "dates" to have sex and put them on their calendars.

If busyness is doing the same thing to your sex life, you may have to get out your DayTimer, too. Time pressures will always trump relaxed time and leisure activities—especially marital sexual intimacy—if you let them.

———

The conflicts that Jennifer and Phil had over "small irritations" had a lot to do with differing expectations about their sexual relationship. Boycotting that relationship, as Jennifer had been doing, was not the answer.

> It's true that issues like these can significantly disrupt a couple's sexual expression—and a marriage, if not dealt with properly. But there's no need to panic.

In cases like these, seeking advice from a pastor or counselor is a good idea. So is getting prayer support. And remembering this biblical admonition is always sound policy for the marriage bed: "The husband should fulfill his marital duty to his wife, and likewise the wife to her husband. The wife's body does not belong to her alone but also to her husband. In the same way, the husband's body does not belong to him alone but also to his wife. Do not deprive each other except by mutual consent and for a time, so that you may devote yourselves to prayer. Then come together again so that Satan will not tempt you because of your lack of self-control" (1 Corinthians 7:3-5).

When Phil began to sit and listen to Jennifer's concerns and hurts, it made a great deal of difference in her attitude. She became more willing to be attentive to his sexual needs, even as he became more sensitive to hers.

———

Not every couple struggling with sexual apathy needs to seek specialized sex therapy. Frequently having a respected pastor or Christian counselor listen and offer objective advice and support makes the difference. Often a couple realizes what has caused the apathy, but needs encouragement to face it and deal with it.

> Not every couple struggling with sexual apathy needs to seek specialized sex therapy. Often a couple realizes what has caused the apathy, but needs encouragement to face it and deal with it.

That's certainly true of husbands who are having to abstain from sex because their wives are pregnant. If you're in that situation, be careful not to turn to substitutes like Internet pornography. Develop strong accountability relationships and prayer support. Be intentional about continuing to love and pursue your wife in appropriate ways; love notes and flowers are always a good idea. Seek to keep your sexual interest focused on your wife, even as you trust God for the ability to keep your thoughts under control. And remember that abstinence from intercourse doesn't totally preclude demonstrating sexual love for each other.

Whatever the cause of your "disappearing" sex life, don't let the situation drag on forever. Expecting a spouse to simply understand and respect the other's lack of interest isn't a long-term solution. Facing the real issues—and, if necessary, getting help—is.

—LON ADAMS

What If My Spouse Is Using Pornography?

If you're like most spouses who discover a mate's pornography habit, the experience evokes strong emotions. Fears, anger, and insecurities often erupt—along with a deep sense of betrayal.

Such was the case with Michelle. During courtship she first discovered pornographic magazines in Jeremy's apartment. He laughingly dismissed her puzzled stare by shifting the blame to his roommate.

Later she uncovered a stash of porn in Jeremy's truck. Quickly he apologized and promised, "Once we're married, I won't need this phony stuff." He appeared sincere, and she believed him.

Sometime after the wedding, however, Jeremy began staying up long after Michelle went to bed. She would get up and catch him watching pornographic videos. He always promised to quit—and he did, for a while.

Finally she discovered a receipt with charges for phone sex. She began to wonder if their whole relationship was nothing but lies.

Husbands aren't the only ones who succumb to sexual temptation, of course. Sean was looking for information on the Internet when he stumbled across evidence of his wife's online sexual chats. Gripped with shock and rage, he frantically searched for more proof. How could his sweet wife, Heather, act like a faithful Christian—while she was secretly corresponding in graphic sexual language with a total stranger?

> He always promised to quit—and he did, for a while. She began to wonder if their whole relationship was nothing but lies.

If you're a wounded spouse like Michelle or Sean, it's normal to be overwhelmed with feelings of hurt, self-doubt, and anger. Fear may be attempting to ambush you, to push you into the mistaken response of under- or overreacting.

Remember to guard your heart and resist the temptation toward fear (see Philippians 4:6-7). Instead, use the power of healthy emotions to motivate you into appropriate action.

The first step is to become informed on the problems of pornography and other intimacy disorders. Here are three misconceptions many couples believe, and the truths that can set you free of them.

Misconception #1: "This problem is entirely my fault. If I were thinner, better in bed, stopped nagging, earned more money, or helped more around the house, this never would have happened."

Truth: You are not to blame for your spouse's decision to get involved in pornography, phone sex, sexual chat rooms, strip clubs, etc. You might be a wonderful wife or husband, and your spouse still could choose to be unfaithful in some manner. Your spouse made these bad choices for a variety of reasons, many of which predate your marriage.

Misconception #2: "If my unfaithful spouse said he stopped acting out sexually, my job is to forgive, forget, and simply believe all is well. My spouse is not willing to get help for his or her addictive sexual struggle, so I'm helpless to do anything but wait until he or she is ready."

Truth: Blindly ignoring the issue or naively believing "all is well" is not biblical. God knows everything that went on behind closed doors and in the secret places of your spouse's heart. He wants to provide His healing help and discernment. He even goes further and instructs us to ask for His wisdom (James 1:5-8).

It's normal to be overwhelmed with feelings of hurt, self-doubt, and anger. Fear may be attempting to ambush you, to push you into under- or overreacting.

Tolerating your mate's disrespect and inappropriate behavior isn't wise. The longer you postpone setting limits, the more difficulty you'll have in repairing the damage done to you, to the marriage—and, yes, even to your mate. Sin injures the doer *and* the receiver in this type of violation.

If you aren't sure whether confrontation is biblical and appropriate, read Dr. James Dobson's book *Love Must Be Tough* (Multnomah, 2004).

Misconception #3: "Since my husband (or wife) betrayed me, I will never be able to trust him or her again. The damage to the marriage is irreparable."

Truth: Nothing injures a marriage quite like sexual indiscretions. Wayward spouses need to understand it is *their* responsibility to rebuild lost trust. But rather than trying to figure out *who* or *what* to blame, seek professional help together. If your spouse refuses to go, it's important to go by yourself. The challenge will be greater, but much can be done to empower you for the next steps.

What are those steps? You might think of them in terms of the acronym FAITH:

F=Fear not

A=Assess your support system

I=Insist your spouse decide

T=Talk to a trained Christian counselor

H=Heed biblical principles

Now is the time to plant your feet firmly in the bedrock of God's love and His provision for you and your family, even when it appears your world has been blown apart. It's also time to enlist the support and prayer partnership of two or three trusted Christian friends, rather than trying to hide your "secret" from everyone. It's time to be clear with your spouse: He or she must decide to have you *alone* as a marriage partner, not you plus pornography or prostitutes or online lovers. It's time to talk with a professional, a Christian therapist who specializes in sex addiction. And it's time to test the advice you get against the principles of Scripture.

> You are not to blame for your spouse's decision to get involved in pornography. Your spouse made these bad choices for a variety of reasons, many of which predate your marriage.

That acronym and those steps are taken from the Focus on the Family booklet *Nothing to Hide: Hope for Marriages Hurt by Pornography and Infidelity* by Joann Condie. For more information on how to approach this problem, request a copy of the booklet from Focus on the Family at 1-800-A-FAMILY.

Another helpful resource is Pureintimacy.org, a Focus on the Family Web site. This site offers articles dealing with sexual brokenness, addictions, and intimacy disorder.

Your marriage can be repaired through prayer and God's guidance as you and your spouse diligently work with a trained Christian counselor to resolve intimacy disorder—the underlying factor in pornography addiction. You can receive healing for the wounds of the past, and tools for facing the future. Together you can develop a healthy intimacy of mind, spirit, and body.

Remember, God is for you. With His help, you can do it.

—JOANN CONDIE

How Can We Have Sex When Kids Are in the House?

Monica was upset. She'd turned down her husband Jerry's sexual advances at bedtime tonight—again. Jerry had taken it personally.

Why can't he understand? she thought. Didn't he know she was exhausted after getting the children to bed for the night?

That wasn't the only reason, though. She was also afraid she'd wake the kids if she "let herself go" in lovemaking.

What if they heard what was going on? Worse, what if they walked in? She didn't know how to answer the questions they'd have about what was happening in the bedroom.

Monica and Jerry have a very common problem. Most couples find their sexual dynamics disrupted when there are children in the home. Lack of privacy and fatigue from the hectic demands of family life eas-

> "What if they heard what was going on? Worse, what if they walked in?"

ily lead to communication breakdowns. Because a healthy sex life gives strength and protection to the marital relationship, though, it's important to be intentional in nurturing the sexual relationship.

What should you do if having kids in the house is putting a damper on your sex life? Five suggestions follow.

1. *Clarify the issue.* Take the initiative to meet with your spouse to discuss the situation. Find a time and setting that lends itself to uninterrupted conversation.

Put your thoughts on paper before the meeting. These notes can serve as a script or be given to your spouse to read. Men tend to process visually, so seeing things in black and white leads to quicker understanding.

Remember that even though the immediate problem is maintaining your sex life with kids in the house, your goal is to nurture your relationship. So begin the meeting by assuring your mate of your continued, loving commitment. Make it clear that you appreciate your spouse's efforts to contribute to a good family life.

As you talk, keep in mind these general principles for marital problem solving:

- A woman's greatest need is to be loved, while a man's is to be respected.
- With God's help, any challenge can be overcome together.
- Communication succeeds when the desire to understand your spouse overrides the desire to defend yourself.
- Each partner brings a unique perspective to the table; solutions are reached when you're willing to better understand and serve each other.

2. *Describe the factors leading to your present outlook.* Because each person lives in a different world, understanding one another is no easy task. Our bodies function differently, homes have distinct rules and customs, and daily routines vary greatly. Your spouse may not share your fear of being heard during lovemaking, for example. As you reveal your feelings and opinions, discover the factors that shape your spouse's unique perspective, too.

To do this, use the reflective listening technique. The wife makes a single point in a sentence or two; the husband summarizes what he heard her say. No judgment or criticism is allowed. The wife either acknowledges the accuracy of the husband's summary or clarifies her original statement. The husband then makes a single point, and the wife listens and summarizes. Additional points are made in the same way.

3. *Frankly discuss sexual expectations and desires.* If you thought having children wouldn't affect your sex life, say so. If you assumed you'd never have intercourse again after the kids arrived, let your spouse know.

> Even though the immediate problem is maintaining your sex life with kids in the house, your goal is to nurture your relationship.

The two of you probably differ in your expectations about things like sexual frequency and technique. Your objective is to seek common ground, a place where each spouse is comfortable.

4. *Be open to novel solutions.* Brainstorming often results in unexpected solutions. For example, many wives are concerned about privacy and a buffer against being overheard. Husbands can install locks, or rig music or white noise to muffle sounds emanating from the bedroom. Baby monitors can be used to alert parents in the event of an emergency.

Once you've come up with a strategy, stay flexible. Sometimes a plan will be tried, evaluated, and modified by the end of the week. Regular dates with your spouse provide good opportunities to touch base on this and other topics of concern.

5. *Prepare a response to your children's questions.* Despite efforts to maintain the privacy of the sex act between parents, unanticipated interruptions may occur. Protecting innocence takes precedence over completion of intercourse, so be ready to offer answers as needed.

Children's curiosity is best addressed with a confident response, in mutually agreed upon terminology like this: "After all these years, we still love each other and sometimes get excited to spend time together." If your kids have seen the two of you holding hands, kissing, and going out on dates, they're probably comfortable with the idea of parental closeness.

Take those five steps, and you'll likely find yourself well down the road to resolving the "But the kids might hear" dilemma. That's what Monica and Jerry did.

Monica hired a sitter and took Jerry out for a dessert date. She handed Jerry the thoughts she'd written down. To her surprise, Jerry smiled and thanked her. He was visibly relieved by the assurance that she remained sexually interested in him.

Jerry offered to put the children in bed two nights a week. He and Monica agreed on a better time for intimacy. He also decided to put a lock on their bedroom door and to play background music that would muffle their interaction. They agreed on how they would address the concerns of the children, too.

When the conversation was over, Monica and Jerry left the restaurant pleased with their plan—and with their success in conflict resolution.

—James Vigorito

> You can install locks, or rig music or white noise to muffle sounds emanating from the bedroom. Baby monitors can be used to alert parents in the event of an emergency.

How Can We Put Our Sexual Pasts Behind Us?

Julie thought sex was something dirty that had ruined her life. She took no pleasure in intimacy with her husband.

Her plight had its roots in her childhood. That was when her father had forced her to perform sexual acts. The experience had repulsed her, but at the same time proved she had something men desired. When she got to college, she was sexually promiscuous.

Later, after becoming a Christian, Julie continued to go too far. She once let a man from church feel her breasts, and she and her husband had sex before they were married.

When a dysfunctional sexual past haunts you, it usually haunts your spouse—and your whole relationship.

It's not supposed to be that way, of course. Sex is a beautiful gift from God, intended to mirror the spiritual union between His people and Himself. No wonder Satan, God's enemy, attacks the physical symbol of this deep spiritual truth.

>
> **When a dysfunctional sexual past haunts you, it usually haunts your spouse—and your whole relationship.**
>

Many struggle with guilt from wrong sexual choices they've made. Others are bitter over wrong choices made by an abuser. Still others wrestle with anger over wrong choices a spouse has made in having an affair.

How does that affect a marriage? A husband who won't take personal responsibility for his actions may unfairly accuse his wife of wrongdoing. A wife who was abused as a child may be too inhibited to be intimate. Spouses who had sexual relations with each other before marriage while publicly professing a commitment to wait may blame each other for the shame they feel.

If you're suffering from the fallout of your sexual past, here are some things you need to know.

1. *Unresolved hurt from your sexual past disrupts healthy sexual functioning.* Surveys indicate that many people have been pressured into a sexual act at some

point. The intense emotions accompanying that event are often too much for a child or adolescent to process. Hurt and confusion may be mixed with pleasure and excitement. The violated person may sense that something isn't quite right, but dismisses the feeling because the perpetrator showed interest in him or her.

Many caught in this bind are also sworn to secrecy, often threatened with harm. Others fear that they will be blamed. Most carry the false burden of guilt that they were somehow responsible for the offense.

Consensual sex prior to, or outside of, marriage may also influence your sexual functioning now. Pregnancy, abortion, venereal diseases, and the bonds formed through sexual relationships can trigger emotional distress for years.

2. *Problems are opportunities to draw closer to God.* A troubled sexual past may look insurmountable, but it's not—if you run toward God instead of away from Him.

God designed life to be more than we can manage on our own. More than anything else, He wants us to come to Him to be made whole again. Only a relationship with Him through Christ can set us free from guilt and anger.

3. *God wants to heal the deep hurts of the sexual past.* As ointment is applied to heal an injury, the power of God must be personally applied to each wounding of the human spirit.

The first step in sexual healing is gaining the courage to face your pain. This process may be time consuming, and may require the help of others. Because broken trust is always involved at some level, you must deal simultaneously with two things you most fear: recalling the trauma and being vulnerable to be hurt again.

A husband who won't take personal responsibility for his actions may unfairly accuse his wife of wrongdoing. A wife who was abused as a child may be too inhibited to be intimate.

4. *Core beliefs, thoughts, and feelings affect present sexual behavior.* Outward behavior is really the tip of an iceberg dominated by underlying emotions, thoughts, and core beliefs. Great freedom comes from understanding these factors and the deeper assumptions that drive them.

5. *Professional help is often needed to resolve past sexual hurts.* Under the guidance of the Holy Spirit and with the help of qualified therapists, many come to experience profound emotional healing. This includes breaking long-standing, destructive behavior patterns.

That was the case with Julie. She told her husband that problems from her sexual past were keeping her from enjoying intimacy with him. She'd prayed about the situation, but the emotions were too overwhelming to deal with on her own.

Her husband thanked her for sharing her burden. He prayed with her, adding that he would continue to fast and pray.

> A troubled sexual past may look insurmountable, but it's not—if you run toward God instead of away from Him.

The two of them were referred to a Christian counselor who specialized in healing of sexual hurts. Over several sessions, Julie learned how to correct the underlying beliefs and thought patterns that triggered her painful emotions, much to the benefit of her marriage.

—James Vigorito

What If We Need Help?

Justin and Jill couldn't have been more frustrated. Everyone saw them as the perfect Christian couple, but they weren't satisfying each other sexually.

It wasn't for lack of trying. They loved each other very much, and had been careful not to engage in sex until marriage. They prayed about it and studied the Bible together, but couldn't find a solution.

What bothered them most was not knowing where to turn for help. They didn't want to involve family members in this private area of their marriage. They were too embarrassed to speak to their pastor or their friends from church. Fear of getting unbiblical advice kept them from consulting a trained professional.

Many couples balk at the idea of getting help when they have sexual difficulties. If you're in that category, please consider the following.

Many couples balk at the idea of getting help when they have sexual difficulties. But Christians are not immune to problems in a fallen world.

1. *Christians are not immune to problems in a fallen world.* The consequences of sin—our own and that of others—affect everyone. While some may be miraculously spared from persecution and even returned to life after death, Hebrews 11:35 tells of others who've been tortured and killed. Why assume that our relationships, including our sex lives, can't be damaged in such a world?

Scripture is clear about the fact that God loves people and is concerned about their welfare. Whether or not we're aware of it, He is present and active in the midst of a trial—even a sexual problem in a marriage—working to bring good from it.

2. *Love alone may not correct all of life's problems.* Justin and Jill's sexual difficulty didn't stem from a lack of love. If you're having trouble in your sexual relationship, it doesn't necessarily mean that you won't need help if you just love each other more.

That's partly because some people have been more deeply wounded by life than others have. Love is powerful, but it might not single-handedly overcome the hurt experienced by one who's been sexually abused. It might not dismantle the self-centered fantasy pattern of a husband who's formed a habit of self-gratification. It might not erase the despair of a wife who feels physical pain every time she has intercourse.

Assurances of love, sincere as they may be, don't always lead to resolution. Healing may involve opening yourselves to the wisdom and care of others.

3. *It's wise—not a lack of faith—to seek godly counsel.* Trusted, God-honoring individuals and organizations offer resources and referrals that identify possible solutions for spouses with sexual problems. Why not use those resources?

It's usually easier to offer advice than to humble yourself and accept it from others. But sometimes that's the kind of help you need. And finding that others care enough to listen can deepen your appreciation for the interconnectedness of those who follow Christ.

4. *Specialists shed light on situations that most of us haven't personally encountered.* Some counselors and pastors have spent a lifetime prayerfully researching the factors that contribute to healthy relationships and satisfying sexual experiences. Why not benefit from this information?

Many pastors and therapists have seen enough couples to observe not just behavior, but *patterns* of behavior. That can lead to quicker resolution of the difficulties in your sexual relationship.

5. *Consult those with the highest level of expertise in your area of concern.* It's tempting to settle for the nearest or least expensive counseling alternative. But pastors and therapists tend to specialize in areas of treatment where they've achieved the greatest success. Ask your prospective counselor how others who've sought similar assistance from him or her have fared. Reputable professionals should give an honest reply when asked how much experience they have in tackling a particular issue.

> If you're having trouble in your sexual relationship, it doesn't necessarily mean that you won't need help if you just love each other more.

Because treatment involves opening the deepest areas of concern to another, seek assurance in advance that the practitioner adheres to professional standards—and a spiritual outlook compatible with your own. If you have trouble finding the right person, call Focus on the Family at (719) 531-3400, asking for the counseling department, which maintains a national referral network.

Justin and Jill finally took steps to get help. They decided that Justin would ask their pastor for resources and referrals related to their sex life.

They began reading books on sex that were written by Christian authors. It was reassuring to discover that other couples had overcome similar difficulties. Justin and Jill also appreciated the fact that the books discussed the subject tastefully and backed up advice with Scripture.

They didn't stop with reading, though. Soon they were meeting with a counselor who offered pointers that significantly improved their level of sexual satisfaction.

—James Vigorito

It's usually easier to offer advice than to humble yourself and accept it from others. But sometimes that's the kind of help you need.

Part 6: Communication

Why Won't My Spouse Talk to Me?

A *Non Sequitur* cartoon by Wiley Miller pictures a couple in bed. The wife has put down the book she's been reading and said something to her husband. Here's what he heard: "Time for the annual review of how you make my life a living nightmare."

All she actually said, though, is, "Sweetie, let's talk about us."

Why do some spouses—especially some husbands—seem to view communication as a form of torture?

Betsy is wondering about that. She's hurt that her husband, Carl, seems to have lost interest in her. She interprets his lack of communication as evidence that he doesn't love her. This puts her in a panic; she becomes needy and controlling, trying to force Carl to "talk about the problem." This creates more pressure for Carl, who retreats further.

Carl is overwhelmed by Betsy's need for conversation. It feels like a void that could never be filled. This is decreasing his desire to be intimate with her; he's finding excuses to avoid even spending time together. He'd rather hang out with friends who are less demanding.

When the person you married seems to change into someone else—as Betsy thinks Carl has—it's normal to feel disappointed and even hurt. She knows that part of this change is to be expected after settling into the day-to-day of married life, but she longs for that other guy—the before-marriage one who couldn't seem to stop talking nor get enough of her. She was so excited back then, and believed it would go on forever. Now she feels duped.

Maybe you do, too. Maybe you fear your uncommunicative spouse isn't interested in you, isn't excited about you, or doesn't love you anymore. You might doubt that you married the right person—or feel inadequate, insecure, and desperate for attention.

When that happened to Betsy, she changed, too. Now Carl finds himself wondering what happened to the self-assured, strong woman he first fell in love with. He misses her.

> Why do some spouses—especially some husbands—seem to view communication as a form of torture?

Carl doesn't realize it, but Betsy has always had an unusual need for attention and communication. That's because she had a very stoic father whom she was never able to please. It's good to examine whether your need to talk is reasonable or the result of a troubled upbringing.

Even if the latter is the case, though, most couples need help to discuss their needs in a productive way. Having different attitudes toward talking doesn't mean there is something wrong with either spouse, that anyone was deceived, or that the marriage is hopeless.

Relating to each other is not a technique we're born with. It's like a muscle that needs to be developed over time—and massaged when it hurts.

If you have a spouse who doesn't want to talk as much as you do, the following suggestions may help.

Having different attitudes toward talking doesn't mean there is something wrong with either spouse, that anyone was deceived, or that the marriage is hopeless.

1. *Read about the differences between men and women, especially as they relate to communication.* These differences are a mystery to almost everyone except God, but they may help to explain why your spouse tends to be the silent type. You could start by reading "Why Don't We Speak the Same Language?" in this book.

2. *Learn to not take things too personally.* In Betsy's case, her need to talk was influenced by her relationship with her father, not just her relationship with Carl.

3. *Don't overanalyze your partner.* Betsy assumed Carl's "lockjaw" was proof that he didn't love her anymore. You may think you know what's behind your spouse's unwillingness to talk, but you can't read his or her mind.

4. *Talk about your feelings in a non-accusatory, non-blaming way.* To do otherwise will only drive a reluctant talker further away, especially when it comes to discussing emotions.

5. *Ask your spouse what would make him feel less overwhelmed when it comes to communication.* Would it help if you set aside a regular time for talking? If you waited until he decompressed after work?

6. *Ask your spouse for a specific, short commitment of time.* Most reluctant talkers can handle a conversation if they know it won't last forever. Let your mate set the limit. You may find that it increases as he or she grows more comfortable.

7. Learn each other's personality type, and how it shapes communication style. See "How Can I Understand My Spouse's Personality?" in this book. Make the process fun—a discovery of your uniqueness, not an opportunity to stereotype each other.

For more insights on the subject of tight-lipped mates, see "How Can I Get My Spouse to Open Up?" in this book.

One of the hardest things for couples to learn is to lay down their lives for each other (see John 15:13) in the mundane world of daily living (see Romans 12:1). Learning to understand the needs of a spouse who talks less or more than you do requires sacrifice. It means not demanding your rights, and loving another as you love yourself. But these are things we can do because God promises to help us by His Holy Spirit if we ask.

> Don't overanalyze your partner. You may think you know what's behind your spouse's unwillingness to talk, but you can't read his or her mind.

It's easy to get discouraged when all you hear from your spouse is silence. It may seem that things are hopeless, but you can gain new perspective through prayer, reading the Bible, or seeking counsel from a pastor or therapist.

Here's what Betsy and Carl did.

Betsy wanted to confess her feelings of hopelessness to Carl about their situation. But she knew she had to do it in a loving and safe environment. One evening she served his favorite meal, then later tucked the children into bed. Then she talked.

His reaction encouraged her. He expressed his support for their marriage and his love for her, which helped her understand that his silence wasn't caused by a lack of caring. Carl revealed how the demands for conversation affected him, and the ways in which he may have been withdrawing for self-protection.

Carl promised to start using a short daily devotional book with Betsy, one she'd bought several months before and was excited about. The two of them set up a plan for a biweekly date night. They also decided to learn more about healthy communication.

Betsy and Carl recommitted themselves to their marriage. They promised each other that, instead of giving up, they would get help if they needed it.

—ROMIE HURLEY

Why Won't My Spouse Leave Me Alone?

Bill is avoiding his wife, Carol.

He knows he's doing it, too. And he feels guilty about it.

But he thinks it's the only way to deal with his predicament.

He can't seem to handle her frequent demands for conversation. He feels that she nags him continually. When he just wants to relax, she has another emotional outburst about how he never talks to her.

Bill hasn't told Carol exactly how he feels about all this. He doesn't want her to get angry or hurt.

But Carol is already both of those things. She can't believe Bill chose once again to spend Saturday golfing with his buddies. She was looking forward to spending the day with him, hoping they could find some of the closeness they once shared.

> If you're feeling nagged to talk, you're probably feeling overwhelmed, too. Avoidance may seem like the only solution for relief.

She feels rejected. The more he avoids talking with her, the more insecure she feels and the harder she tries to get him to "open up."

If you're feeling nagged to talk, you're probably feeling overwhelmed, too. Avoidance may seem like the only solution for relief. This relief is only temporary, though, because it leaves your spouse without resolution—and often determined to try harder.

You may begin to feel like a trapped victim, at the mercy of your spouse's "need to talk." Worse yet, you may anticipate another session of having your shortcomings pointed out.

Avoidance doesn't work. But here are some suggestions if you're feeling cornered by a spouse who always seems to be asking, "Can we talk?"

1. Take the initiative to spend time doing things together *other* than talking.

2. Go to a Christian bookstore and buy a book about communication in marriage. Read from it aloud to your spouse and ask her questions about her reactions.

3. Share a chore, like doing the dishes. You may find yourself communicating during the dull moments.

4. When she's not expecting it, ask her what she really needs. Say, "How can I show you I love you?" or, "What would make your day easier?"

5. Put the newspaper away, neglect a hobby, or shut the TV off in order to spend time with your spouse.

6. Keep a sense of humor. Find cartoons about how different men and women are, and how they communicate. Make more fun of your own gender than the other person's.

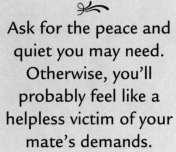

Ask for the peace and quiet you may need. Otherwise, you'll probably feel like a helpless victim of your mate's demands.

These are all good things to do, but it's also important for you to ask for the peace and quiet you may need. Otherwise, you'll probably feel like a helpless victim of your mate's demands.

One way to do this is to set a specific time to talk. This should thrill your spouse, since it represents a commitment to communicate. The limits need to be spelled out, though, in order to avoid false expectations. Your spouse may be thinking of a marathon conversation, while you may dread anything longer than a TV sitcom.

Try 20 or 30 minutes to start. That's probably the most you'd want for a serious discussion. Pray at the beginning and the end if you like. Get a kitchen timer and stick to the limit. Promise not to run, but allow for a time-out if things get too intense.

What should you do during that time? Here are some ideas.

• Explore and discuss your needs for communication.

• Explore and discuss your needs for quiet or alone time.

• Explore and discuss your needs for outside friendships and recreation.

• Use "I" statements to convey feelings of being pressured, overwhelmed, or discouraged. This will help keep your spouse from feeling attacked. For example: "I feel hopeless when I hear 'We need to talk,' because it reminds me of my mom. She always used that phrase when I was in trouble." This is better than, "You're just like my mom!" The goal is for the speaker to feel heard and understood.

• If you need to take a time-out, be sure to schedule a reunion within 24 hours for further discussion. This gives both of you a sense of reassurance and safety.

If Bill and Carol follow these suggestions, here's what probably will happen. Bill will feel more in control, seeing how to give Carol what she needs without fearing it will never be enough. He'll grow more assertive in asking for what he needs, and less guilty about taking time for himself.

> Set a specific time to talk. This should thrill your spouse, since it represents a commitment to communicate.

Carol will feel less threatened, emotional, and needy. She'll be happier, more content. She'll know Bill loves her because he's been initiating doing things together—and even asking about her feelings.

—ROMIE HURLEY

Why Don't We Speak the Same Language?

Are men and women really from different planets?

Any marriage counselor can provide tons of examples of husbands and wives who, having lived together for 20 or 30 years (let alone just 4 or 5), are in some ways a complete mystery to each other. The obvious answer is that God chose to wire males and females very differently. Some would even suggest that this illustrates His sense of humor.

It's possible that the communication gender gap lies in how messages are perceived. But the style and content of the messages themselves differ, too. Men tend to use language to transmit information, report facts, fix problems, clarify status, and establish control. Women are more likely to view language as a means to greater intimacy, stronger or richer relationships, and fostering cooperation rather than competition.

In other words, it's "debate vs. relate." That means you and your spouse may be tuned in to very different "meanings" in what each of you is saying. This provides fertile ground for misunderstanding, hurt feelings, and conflict. What one of you thinks is the other's "hidden meaning" can be 180 degrees out of phase with what the speaker really intends to communicate.

> *Any marriage counselor can provide tons of examples of husbands and wives who are in some ways a complete mystery to each other. The obvious answer is that God chose to wire males and females very differently.*

This can easily lead to distorted conclusions about the other person's motivations.

She's an unreasonable, demanding nag who won't leave me alone to watch the football game, he thinks.

He's an insensitive, domineering bore who doesn't have a clue about my feelings and doesn't want one, she tells herself.

Nancy and Ralph are having this kind of conflict.

Nancy sits in the counselor's office in tears. Ralph, her husband of three years, sits stone-faced, two feet away on the same couch, his arms crossed over his chest. The atmosphere is thick with her fury and his defiance.

She begins the session with a litany of Ralph's alleged failures, the worst being his neglect of her needs. He is, she says, "never home." Self-employed, he works long hours and takes frequent business trips. Sometimes he leaves on the refrigerator lists of things for her to get done while he's gone. He also leaves her with the care of a one-year-old.

When he's home, she says, he's either restoring an antique car or wanting to jump into bed for a quick sexual romp—for which he seems to have plenty of energy. When she's dead tired and turns him down, he pouts and sometimes storms out to the garage and his beloved Chevy. She notes with undisguised sarcasm that he's always too tired to just talk to her.

The final straw: Last week, on her birthday, he was gone on another business trip. She feels abandoned and unloved.

When Ralph finally speaks up, it's to say that things are usually much more peaceful in the garage than in the bedroom. At least the Chevy doesn't treat him like he's some dirty old man.

He can't understand why Nancy is so angry about his long hours at work. She seems to him to have no concept of what it takes to earn the money needed each month to pay the bills. This is how a husband and father takes care of—loves—his family. And why would she be upset about his efforts to organize on a list the chores that need to be done when he's out of town?

When she caustically remarks that she isn't one of his employees, it makes no sense to him. What does that have to do with their family life? Of course he loves her, he says. Look at everything he does to be a good husband.

> What one of you thinks is the other's "hidden meaning" can be 180 degrees out of phase with what the speaker really intends to communicate.

Standing outside looking in, it seems easy to see that when it comes to understanding each other's languages, Nancy and Ralph are missing each other by a mile. In many respects, they exemplify stereotypical male-female struggles with differences in communication.

Of course, one size never fits all. Females don't all fit neatly into one communication-style box and males into another. Some men can be quite nurturing and emotionally empathic in their language; some women are aggressive and task-oriented in theirs.

Still, you needn't be surprised if you and your spouse sometimes seem to need a translator. In his book *How Do You Say "I Love You"?* (InterVarsity Press, 1977), Dr. Judson Swihart notes, "Often the wife comes in [to the marriage] speaking French and the husband speaking German—in an emotional sense. Unless you hear love expressed in a language that you can understand emotionally, it will have little value." The author goes on to say, "Fi uoy era gniog ot etacinummoc na edutitta fo evol drawot ruoy esuops, you must learn to speak his or her language."

It's hard to do that if, like too many couples, you enter marriage focused on being loved rather than on giving love. Try making it your goal not to change your spouse but to adapt to his or her style of communication. Turn your attention to hearing the heart of your partner rather than to the frustration you may feel about not being heard or understood.

If you feel stuck, and that your marriage is in a hole that just gets deeper, do something about it. Make a date with each other once a week to try a communication exercise. For example, the wife talks for 10 minutes about feelings or issues she has; the husband does nothing but listen. He may

> Make a date with each other once a week to try a communication exercise. For example, the wife talks for ten minutes about feelings or issues she has; the husband does nothing but listen.

respond only with, "I don't understand; could you restate that?" or "What I hear you saying is . . ."

Then he talks for 10 minutes and she listens. She can ask only for clarification or affirmation that she's hearing him accurately.

At the end of the exercise, neither of you is allowed to try to "straighten the other one out," react angrily to something you didn't want to hear, or debate the issue. During the next such "date," the husband will talk first and the wife second.

Other approaches to getting "unstuck" include attending a well-recommended weekend Christian marriage retreat, participating in a couples' support group through your church, or enlisting the help of a licensed Christian marriage counselor.

This is not a hopeless situation. In fact, compared to many marital conflicts, it's a state that can more quickly and remarkably improve—when two children of God who are committed to their marriage decide to work on it and seek appropriate help.

—Phillip J. Swihart

Why Does My Spouse Keep Hurting My Feelings?

Does your spouse ever claim to be teasing when you think he or she is really just being cruel?

Do you ever feel your wife's nagging about your weight stems from insensitivity, not concern for your health?

Ever wonder whether your husband's habit of pointing out your flaws in public has more to do with his mean streak than with the part of the country he's from?

> Many couples suffer from a perpetual case of individual or mutual heartlessness. As sacred as marriage is to God, you can rest assured that it displeases Him to see husbands and wives haphazardly wounding each other's spirits with potshots.

Many couples suffer from a perpetual case of individual or mutual heartlessness. Maybe you've seen an example in the ever-bickering Frank and Marie Barone on reruns of TV's *Everybody Loves Raymond*. Marie makes a brainless observation; Frank counters with a cutting remark. Marie comes back with a crude nickname. The pattern continues from one scene to the next.

The Bible instructs us repeatedly to treat each other with kindness, honor, and respect. These commands were designed to be applied to any relationship, especially marriage. As sacred as marriage is to God, you can rest assured that it displeases Him to see husbands and wives haphazardly wounding each other's spirits with potshots like these:

- "Can't you do anything right?"
- "You always make dumb choices like this!"
- "You act like your mother."
- "You are such a baby. Everything I say hurts your feelings."
- "How many times do I have to tell you to mow the lawn? Are you deaf or do you just not care?"
- "Can't you see I'm watching this show? Just let me unwind for a few minutes!"

If you look long enough, you'll find a counselor who'll label this kind of behavior with a diagnosis. But the simple fact is that some couples, like Frank and Marie Barone, are just plain cruel and have adopted uncaring spirits.

In many cases, though, ongoing patterns of hurt feelings can stem from two possible sources: a hypersensitive spouse or an insensitive one.

Being overly sensitive can be just as destructive as its opposite. If you take offense at every perceived slight, your spouse probably will walk around on eggshells, trying not to upset you. He or she will run everything through the "Will this hurt his feelings?" filter. People who live with hypersensitive mates often respond by withdrawing, becoming resentful, or being terrified to say or do anything.

Hypersensitivity is common in people who allow what they feel to become the primary factor in determining how they see themselves and others, and how they respond to criticism and perceived threats. It can be a precursor to deeper, more destructive emotional and relational problems. It also can be a symptom of Avoidant Personality Disorder, a condition marked by timidity, low self-esteem, and excessive sensitivity to rejection. If you or your spouse fits the criteria for this disorder, professional intervention is needed.

> Being overly sensitive can be just as destructive as its opposite. If you take offense at every perceived slight, your spouse probably will walk around on eggshells, trying not to upset you.

The opposite of being too sensitive is insensitivity, which can be just as debilitating. An insensitive person "throws" his thoughts, words, and behaviors out there and lets the chips fall where they may. He may experience a temporary feeling of freedom by "getting it out on the table," but doesn't realize the price of his liberation may be revolutionary war.

Insensitive people are habitual violators of the command to "be kind and compassionate to one another, forgiving each other, just as in Christ God forgave you" (Ephesians 4:32). Insensitivity sometimes indicates a serious personality disorder called narcissism. People with this problem are excessively self-centered, lacking concern or empathy for others. Often they're unable to recognize when they've hurt another's feelings, and don't control their hurtful behaviors without professional help.

Apart from personality disorders, if you or your mate has allowed insensitivity or hypersensitivity to set up camp in your marriage, beware that it can destroy your relationship if left unattended. Changes in attitude, behavior, and spiritual direction—including genuine remorse and repentance—are necessary.

If this is the case in your marriage, here are some practical steps to take.

1. *Educate yourself about the problem, whether it's yours or your spouse's.* Knowledge often leads to understanding, which often leads to resolution.

> An insensitive person "throws" his thoughts, words, and behaviors out there and lets the chips fall where they may. He doesn't realize the price of his liberation may be revolutionary war.

Melanie felt verbally abused by her husband, Larry. She decided to learn as much as possible about this problem and how others have dealt with it. Through sources on the Internet she discovered that one of the first steps in dealing with verbally abusive spouses is to understand what drives the abuse.

After several weeks of reading and seeking advice from people she trusted, Melanie realized that some of Larry's behavior stemmed from being raised by a physically abusive father. She began to respond with less resentment to Larry's hurtful words. As her responses became less threatening to Larry, the intensity of his verbal attacks lessened. A dialogue opened up between the two. Eventually this led to professional counseling.

2. *Make your concerns known to your spouse in a nonthreatening way.* Don't use accusatory language like, "It's your problem, not mine," or "You are just too insensitive." Describe how you feel when your mate uses hurtful words. Describe how long the hurt lasts and how it may possibly lead to inappropriate responses on your part—like ongoing resentment or withdrawal.

3. *Be transparent about your own sensitivity or insensitivity.* Often your willingness to admit a weakness will encourage your spouse to acknowledge his or her own flaws.

4. *Realize that God will judge us according to the way we treat others.* He doesn't approve of willful, malicious, hurtful actions. Jesus said, "But I tell you that men will have to give account on the day of judgment for every careless word they have spoken" (Matthew 12:36). Couples are not exempt from this warning.

5. *Consider whether insensitivity has escalated into abuse.* Any words can become abusive when they're intended to hurt someone else. God calls this malicious and forbids it (1 Timothy 3:11).

James described the tongue as being "full of deadly poison" (3:8). David said in Psalm 52:2 that the tongue is like a "sharpened razor" that works to bring about the destruction of others. Proverbs 12:18 states that "reckless words pierce like a sword."

6. *Seek professional help.* If this is an ongoing problem, locate a Christian psychologist or psychiatrist who can assess and treat personality disorders. Even if your spouse doesn't want to participate, a professional therapist often can offer direction on how to live with someone who has verbally abusive tendencies and how to manage the situation.

Abusive words can cause so much pain that neither you nor your spouse can be objective enough to develop solutions. That's where a counselor can help. If abusive language turns into physical abuse, seek shelter and professional assistance immediately.

7. *Pray for your spouse.* Prayer can change situations and people, even if nothing else can. Jesus told us to pray for those who hurt us (Matthew 5:44). If He commands us to pray for our enemies, surely He expects us to pray for an insensitive spouse.

Hurtful emotions have a way of overshadowing the need to do what's right. Jesus tells us to pray for people like these, even if we don't feel like it. Maybe He did that not just for the benefit of those whose words hurt us, but for ourselves as well.

—MITCH TEMPLE

> Abusive words can cause so much pain that neither you nor your spouse can be objective enough to develop solutions. That's where a counselor can help.

How Can We Make Time to Talk?

Caleb and Trina, recently married, didn't have much spare time. They had full-time jobs and took evening classes. Already active in their church, they were approached one day by a church leader who said there was a desperate need for a young couple to lead the junior high group. "We can't pay you anything," he added, "but we're sure that others will come alongside you two and support you in prayer and help you in this ministry. What do you think?"

Unfortunately, they didn't say no. How could they? After all, they'd been married in that church. And they were interested in doing "full-time" ministry someday.

After months of hard work, they found themselves overinvested in church work and underinvested in each other. They spent little time together, and found even less time to converse. When they did talk, it was mostly to argue and criticize each other. They even questioned whether or not they should be married because they were "falling out of love."

Caleb and Trina spent little time together, and found even less time to converse. When they did talk, it was mostly to argue and criticize each other.

One day, Caleb told Trina that he had to get out of the house. He went to a car lot and looked at the hundreds of sleek, clean vehicles. After some wistful daydreaming, he got back in his own sedan.

It was a glorious afternoon for a drive in the country, so he drove—and kept driving. Long into the evening, about two miles from home, the car suddenly stopped. It had run out of gas.

Something came to Caleb's mind at that moment: His marriage was running out of fuel, too.

He thought about how much he'd enjoyed the afternoon drive without his wife. This was an ominous sign, he knew, and his marriage was heading in a direction that would ultimately lead to separation or dissolution. He knew that he and his wife needed help, and needed it immediately.

Fortunately, they were referred to a marriage counselor. The first thing they learned was the "24-5 Principle"—based in part on Deuteronomy 24:5: "If a man has recently married, he must not be sent to war or have any other duty laid on him. For one year he is to be free to stay at home and bring happiness to the wife he has married."

Many couples don't take enough time to talk, bond, and firmly connect with each other during the early days of their marriage. If you're a newlywed, you can apply the 24-5 Principle by doing the following:

- Establish a special, exclusive covenant for one year.
- Refrain from all extra responsibilities during that year.
- Focus on and establish your marriage before you move out into career advancement, ministry, and further education.
- Invest in and bond with your spouse emotionally, spiritually, relationally, and sexually.
- Bring happiness to one another; limit your time with others during the first year.

You can expect some resistance from family members and friends on this decision. But ask them to pray for your marriage throughout this first year together.

What if, like Caleb and Trina, you're asked by your church to take on a major task during that time? One counselor advises his clients to say something like, "Thank you for thinking of us. We're so pleased with the church and so encouraged by all of you. But we've been strongly advised by our counselor to invest in each other this first year of our marriage—to really bond and connect with each other and limit our activities. We promised him we'd do that. But please ask us again in a year or so, okay? We really want to be involved."

What if you're past the one-year mark? You can apply the 24-5 Principle at any time in your marriage. Here are five steps to doing just that.

1. *Keep your promise.* Many couples, at their weddings, light a "unity candle" and blow out their individual candles. That symbolizes husband and wife dying to themselves in order to give birth to something new and much more intimate, beautiful, and mysterious—"two becoming one." One of the best ways to become one is to spend time together, and that can happen when you and your spouse talk, celebrate special occasions, set goals, go shopping, pay bills, play tennis, or study a devotional book.

Many couples don't take enough time to talk, bond, and firmly connect with each other during the early days of their marriage. Instead, you can apply the 24-5 Principle.

2. Be intentional and selective. Everyone has the same amount of time—24 hours a day. Avoid being sloppy with yours.

Manufacturing more time isn't possible, but you can make excellent use of what you have by allocating time to talk and do things together. When that time comes, make sure you're rested and not rushed or preoccupied. If talking really is a priority for you, you'll say no to time-stealers like sitcoms, reality shows, and the Internet.

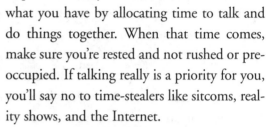

You can expect some resistance from family members and friends on this decision. But ask them to pray for your marriage.

3. Be creative and perseverant. Talk about a variety of subjects—solving problems, overcoming challenges, establishing goals and priorities, your spiritual life, preferences, and just having fun.

Start small and build. Some couples tend to have unrealistic expectations. This may result in discouragement, criticism, and blaming. Remember that bonding and connecting don't happen overnight.

4. Enjoy and encourage uniqueness. You and your spouse aren't alike. Think of how awful and boring it would be to be married to yourself! Those conversations wouldn't be very interesting, would they?

As you spend time together, resist the temptation to try remaking your spouse in your image. Let the Holy Spirit transform both of you into the image of Christ. Allow and encourage your spouse to be the person God has created him or her to be, and enjoy that person.

5. Be loving, respectful, and patient. The gift God has given you and your spouse is each other. In the end, He'll probably be less interested in your professional success or how much money you made than in how you nurtured the gift He gave you in marriage.

Taking time to talk is part of that. Choose wisely how you spend those minutes, hours, and days—especially in your early years together.

—James Groesbeck with Amy Swierczek

How Can We Talk About Feelings?

You were designed to have emotions and to validate your spouse's emotions. It was God's idea.

You need to talk about those emotions. But how can you do that without creating conflict?

Janeen wants to talk about feelings. She's having trouble with a coworker. Her husband, Jerry, is willing to listen for a while to her story, but then he proceeds to tell Janeen what she should do. For Jerry the subject is completed, closed; the problem is solved.

But Janeen doesn't want a problem-solving session. She only desires to be heard. She needs Jerry to be a safe sounding board, and she doesn't want this used against her later.

> Jerry is willing to listen for a while to her story, but then he proceeds to tell Janeen what she should do. But she doesn't want a problem-solving session.

Even though this "feelings discussion" didn't begin with an issue between Janeen and Jerry, it ends there. Janeen's response is resentment and bitterness. Next time she needs to talk about feelings, she may not confide in him.

A week later Jerry has a disagreement with his father. Janeen, wanting to be helpful, follows Jerry around and tries to get him to talk about his feelings. But Jerry needs to be by himself to give this situation some thought.

"Just leave me alone!" Jerry finally yells.

Jerry, like most men, needs space to work through problems. Not understanding this, Janeen triggers an argument. Next time Jerry may not reveal his pain to her, either.

Talking about your feelings is an art. Whether you're more like Janeen or Jerry, you want a partner who honors you by listening when you're ready. You want your spouse to acknowledge your pain, to hear the options you've formulated, to give you equal status. If these things don't happen, the relationship doesn't feel safe. The depth of the conversation becomes shallow and unsatisfying.

Intimacy in a marriage begins when each spouse takes responsibility for his or her emotions and behaviors. This is more likely to happen in a climate free from judgment, defensiveness, and blame.

When Janeen reports problems with a coworker and Jerry responds as problem solver, she can use "straight talk" with Jerry. For example: "When I'm not allowed to finish my sentences, I feel discounted and unimportant to you. What I need is to be heard."

When Jerry takes responsibility for the hurt he feels because of his father's comments, Janeen can promote intimacy by listening. She can draw him out to express what he's ready to say. Only when Jerry feels safe will he disclose to Janeen his deepest feelings and any related history. Their closeness will be enhanced.

Jerry, like most men, needs space to work through problems. Not understanding this, Janeen triggers an argument.

When you have feelings you'd like to express, it may be helpful to pray or journal about them first. Tell your heavenly Father how you're feeling before you address the issue with your mate. You can find comfort in looking to Him first.

What should you do when the feelings you want to talk about are likely to spark an argument? Once you've taken responsibility for how you feel, then conflict resolution can begin. A good place to start is by clarifying the issue, saying something like, "Is this what you meant?" Many arguments are about misunderstanding the actual issue.

For instance, let's say that Jerry tells Janeen, "We're really short on money this month."

Janeen responds defensively by saying, "It isn't my fault!"

It would have been better for her to get Jerry's clarification of the money situation. "What are you trying to tell me?" she could have asked.

That doesn't mean she'll agree with his answer. Clarifying simply enables you to understand your spouse's perspective. This honors your mate and allows both of you to start at the same place.

Talking about feelings is challenging enough in itself, but other factors can make it harder. First, there's the "child challenge." If you have kids, they're probably clamoring for attention often—even when the two of you need time and quiet to talk about emotions. Janeen and Jerry, who have eight-month-old twin boys, need to develop intimacy skills and schedule time to address feelings. If this doesn't occur, the emotions won't go away; someone else (coworker, friend, relative) will be selected as a confidant. A wedge may be driven between Jerry and Janeen, and counseling may be needed to repair the damage.

Then there's the "childhood challenge." Sometimes a person enters a marriage without having been nurtured as a child. Missy, for example, had a mother who was an alcoholic. Never experiencing unconditional love, Missy became the "parent" at age 3. When her husband, William, attempts to nurture her now by talking about feelings—even positive ones like love, joy, and peace—it feels foreign and uncomfortable to her. Missy and William may need counseling to address this unfinished business, so she can express feelings and receive nurturing.

> You want your spouse to acknowledge your pain, to hear the options you've formulated, to give you equal status. If these things don't happen, the relationship doesn't feel safe.

So how can you talk about feelings?

- By being respectful and honoring when your spouse takes responsibility for his or her emotions and behaviors;
- By understanding how the communication styles of men and women differ;
- By developing conflict resolution strategies;
- By intentionally nurturing one another;
- By committing yourself to make this an enjoyable marriage; and
- By keeping a prayer journal to release frustration.

This sets the stage for safe self-disclosure. What happens next is up to you.

—Betty Jordan

How Should We Talk About Sensitive Issues?

Let's face it: Some topics are trickier than others. Even in the happiest marriages, issues like in-laws, finances, and sex can quickly shake things up.

Corey and Jen are building their first house. Every time Corey shares an idea about changes to the plan, Jen gets angry. Even when he tries to apologize, she may still attack him.

Corey knows that Jen has a difficult relationship with her father, a contractor in another state. Corey wonders if this influences her reactions to him, but doesn't know how to bring it up without making her mad.

When tough topics come up, couples can find lots of places to veer into the ditch. Many mistakes come from inexperience as husbands and wives bounce from one conflict to the next, experimenting with various solutions.

When it comes to talking about sensitive topics, some pitfalls are dug way before marriage. If you didn't get the right skills in your family of origin, it's hard to manage conflict with a spouse. The twin ditches of (1) avoiding conflict at any cost and (2) escalating into chaos are often more familiar than the path itself.

Even engaged couples need to begin communicating and making decisions as if it will affect the rest of their marriage—because that's exactly what will happen. One couple encountered this challenge while preparing to choose a china pattern. The bride's mother assumed she'd go with her daughter to make the selection; the fiancé recognized this as his privilege and responsibility. Fortunately, communicating these expectations early on opened the door to greater harmony in the future.

In addition to the old habits you bring into a marriage, new challenges can quickly crop up. Even the idyllic honeymoon phase can raise a number of touchy topics. A major purchase or holiday tradition can seem bigger than your relationship if you aren't prepared.

> When it comes to talking about sensitive topics, some pitfalls are dug way before marriage. If you didn't get the right skills in your family of origin, it's hard to manage conflict with a spouse.

How can you prepare yourself to talk about those sticky subjects? Here are three suggestions.

1. *Get practical skills.* At the nearest Christian bookstore, you can find strategies for dealing with sensitive issues. Shelves of books on marriage address the role of communication. Improving body language, word choice, and tone of voice will greatly improve your results.

So will picking a better time and place for your discussion. After Corey and Jen made yet another frantic attempt to make decisions about the new house amid piles of laundry and the cries of their baby, they changed their approach.

"Look, Hon," Corey said. "We're never going to accomplish anything like this. Let's get away and just talk over a nice dinner tomorrow night when I get off work. What do you say?"

> If you're trying to talk about a sensitive issue, get rid of distractions like television. Find a time free of interruptions from children and pagers.

"If we can leave this discussion until then, I think I can handle it just fine," Jen answered. "I'll call a sitter if you'll just promise me I won't have to hear the words 'floor plan' or 'crown molding' until then. I'm sure we can work something out if we calm down and put our heads together."

If you're trying to talk about a sensitive issue, get rid of distractions like television. Find a time free of interruptions from children and pagers. Still, don't let things get worse while you wait for the "perfect" time. It may never come.

One of the most practical things to do is to start your discussion with prayer. This habit can transform your marriage as you invite the Holy Spirit to guide your conversation. It also helps you steer clear of the pothole of confronting your spouse impulsively.

Speaking of steering, remember that driving along a cliff is even harder going in reverse. In other words, don't bring up past issues while trying to resolve new ones. If many of your old conflicts lack closure, get a mediator—a pastor or Christian counselor—to help bring your marriage up to speed and moving forward again.

2. *Be principle-centered.* Don't ask *who's* right. Ask *what's* right.

Imagine a couple fighting over the perennially thorny issue of money. If both spouses take time to examine biblical principles of money management, they'll often emerge with a plan they agree on. The idea of attacking the problem, not the person, creates safety for sharing at a deep, effective level on any topic.

3. *Partner with your spouse.* "If only I could get a little help around here!" Kelli said to no one in particular as she stormed through the den.

Dan recognized that tone. His wife had been home with the baby all week while he was out of town. Her usually sweet demeanor had vanished after about the fifth day.

He came down the stairs to find Kelli had dropped into a chair. "I'm sorry I'm being so huffy," she said with a sigh. "I'd be grateful for any help you could offer."

He started gathering the newspapers from around the chair. "Why don't we try to come up with a plan before my next trip? Maybe we can arrange for my mom to take Haylie for an afternoon. Mrs. Duckett from church is looking for extra income. She'd probably be glad to help you around the house for an hour or two."

"Actually, that sounds great. You wouldn't mind?"

Dan shook his head. "Single parenting is hard, even if it's only for a week. When I can't be here to give you a break, I should at least help you find some kind of solution."

While it's critical to find the truth about issues affecting your marriage, relationship is always more important than issues. You're partners, not prosecutors.

That partnership doesn't end when you discuss sensitive topics. Ask yourself whether you're showing your husband or wife the same respect you show your coworkers and friends. If you're Christians, ask yourself whether you're acting first as brother and sister in Christ, and second as husband and wife.

> One of the most practical things to do is to start your discussion with prayer. This habit can transform your marriage as you invite the Holy Spirit to guide your conversation.

If the prospect of discussing a sensitive subject has you fearing (or worse yet, predicting) your spouse's reaction, you're losing focus. Your agenda should be to please God. If that's your goal, you won't hesitate to confront an issue like infidelity or addiction that tears your spouse away from Him.

That's what Elena did with Jacob. She'd debated for weeks whether to mention Jacob's new habit—playing online video games late into the night. She told herself that there were worse things he could do. But as a recovering bulimic, she knew firsthand that any compulsive behavior would eventually tear him down and damage their relationship.

Finally she decided to confront him: "Sweetheart, I know video games aren't immoral. But I'd like our day to end together." It was a first step toward a healthier relationship.

Talking about sensitive issues isn't easy, but it can make your marriage the vehicle that drives both of you closer to God. And two people with the same destination can't help but move closer to each other, too.

—ROB JACKSON

> If many of your old conflicts lack closure, get a mediator—a pastor or Christian counselor—to help bring your marriage up to speed and moving forward again.

How Can I Start a Conversation?

Heather emerged from the clothing store's dressing room and looked in the three-paned mirror. Keith would love this dress. But would it be enough to ease the way for the conversation they had to have?

How can I explain my feelings to him? she thought. *How can I get him to understand?*

Heather was convinced that she and Keith needed to wait one more year before they started a family. It was so important for her to finish college first. But she knew how much Keith wanted to be a father.

How could she begin such a delicate conversation without hurting her husband's feelings?

It had seemed easy to begin a conversation when they were dating, but saying the difficult things had always been hard. Heather sensed that the time to learn how to open a discussion was now, in the early days of their marriage.

She was right.

Perhaps you, too, are having trouble getting conversations started with your spouse. Maybe you're avoiding certain topics. Maybe you or your spouse isn't much of a talker. Maybe you just don't know how to begin.

> "I'm not sure how to say this. I'm afraid it might come out all wrong. But something is on my heart that I want to talk with you about. Is this a good time for you to listen to me?"

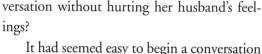

Fortunately, acknowledging that can be an excellent way to start a conversation. Be honest and state your lack of confidence. For example, Heather might begin her talk with Keith this way: "I'm not sure how to say this. I'm afraid it might come out all wrong. But something is on my heart that I want to talk with you about. Is this a good time for you to listen to me?" Stating your concerns and fears can open the conversational door.

As Heather thought about talking to Keith, she knew she'd have to "keep to the point." If she was too elaborate with details, he'd become frustrated and distracted. She also knew that giving too *little* information would frustrate her as well, leaving her feeling that the conversation was incomplete.

So she went home and spent a few minutes at the kitchen table writing out her thoughts. That would keep her focused and ensure she was "covering all the bases." If she got anxious, she could even read aloud what she'd written! That gave her confidence.

So did praying. After a quick request for help, she was convinced that the Holy Spirit would help her communicate what was on her heart.

If this is a problem area for you and your spouse, consider the following steps to beginning a conversation.

1. *Identify your concerns.* Put your thoughts on paper. Practice saying them in front of a mirror if that boosts your confidence. When you begin your conversation, you may even want to read aloud what you've written. That's okay.

As you talk, don't expect your partner to know what's on your mind—and don't make him guess. Keep clarifying things by asking your spouse what he's heard you say or read and what he thinks about it.

2. *Get the timing right.* None of us likes to be inconvenienced. Look for the right opportunity to begin your conversation.

Is your spouse tired or preoccupied? It might be wise to wait until she's rested and you have her full attention. If you have children, get them involved in some activity before you begin your conversation.

3. *Honor your spouse's time.* Don't waste it. Be succinct; don't belabor your point. Make sure you have sufficient time to complete the conversation well. Allow time for feedback during your talk, too.

4. *Use body language.* Look your spouse in the eye directly, lovingly, and respectfully, and state your desire to begin a conversation. Ask your mate to sit down with you; take her hand in yours and speak calmly. The eyes can truly be a window to the mind and soul, and touch can allow you to show loving feelings.

Put your thoughts on paper. Practice saying them in front of a mirror if that boosts your confidence.

5. *Keep your partner's communication style in mind.* People find us most attractive when we communicate in their style—in a way that's familiar and comfortable to them. If your partner likes facts, give him facts. If she likes details, tell the story. If she values warmth, take time to connect relationally. If he wants choices, give options.

If she needs time to process, slow down. If he likes a rapid pace, get to the point. If she's analytical, provide data.

6. *Include your partner's interests.* If your spouse is interested in football,

finances, movies—start with that subject. It's a most natural way to enter a conversation, even if the topic ends up veering in another direction.

7. *Be interesting.* Ask yourself why your spouse would want to listen to you in the first place. Be a creative and stimulating partner. Discover how to capture your mate's attention. If you're boring and negative, your conversation will be dull and depressing. If this is the case, you have some work to do.

8. *Be realistic.* Don't set yourself up for disappointment. If the two of you find it difficult to start a conversation, keep it simple. Don't assume you can have a deeply intimate, nurturing conversation immediately if you've never had one before.

Start with the basics. Do fun activities together. Laugh. Build a foundation for deeper conversations. Take one step at a time.

> Is your spouse tired or preoccupied? It might be wise to wait until she's rested and you have her full attention.

9. *Seek to accept and bring joy to your spouse.* Beginning conversations is much easier when your spouse knows you won't ridicule him or her. Learn to lovingly accept and enjoy each other, even when your opinions differ. Let your spouse know that you're on the same team and that you support him or her 100 percent. Be your mate's number one fan!

10. *Be appreciative and infuse hope.* Thank your spouse for listening to you. Tell him he encourages you and that you want to encourage him. Life on earth is difficult—sometimes awful—and we need to be "life-givers" to our mates. When we speak words of hope to our spouses, we speak life and love. Remember Philippians 4:8: "Finally, brothers, whatever is true, whatever is noble, whatever is right, whatever is pure, whatever is lovely, whatever is admirable—if anything is excellent or praiseworthy—think about such things."

If all of this seems overwhelming, don't be discouraged. Just start and be patient and persistent; pick one or two ideas and begin!

—James Groesbeck with Amy Swierczek

How Can We Communicate Without Talking?

When Paige and her husband, Steve, sit down to talk, she's usually intimidated. She knows Steve loves her, but he hardly ever smiles. *Is he mad at me?* she wonders.

Chuck isn't much of a conversationalist. He knows that's frustrating to his wife, Raina, who could talk the paint off the side of a barn. He wishes there were a way to let her know he cares—without having to chat for hours at a time.

Cherie doesn't understand why her husband, Brian, got so upset yesterday when she left him a Post-it note on the kitchen table. All it said was, "Remember, garbage day." She was just reminding him to take out the trash. Would he have been happier if she'd drawn a little smiley face on it?

> Unspoken communication can be at least as powerful as words. It can help build your marriage—or chip away at it.

Unspoken communication—a raised eyebrow, a folding of the arms across the chest, a hand on the shoulder, an e-mail—can be at least as powerful as words. It can help build your marriage—or chip away at it.

Communicating without talking can be tricky. You may not always realize what you're "saying." And your silent messages may contradict your spoken ones, confusing your spouse.

It's no wonder some wives begin to ask early in their marriages, "Why does my husband say one thing and act totally different?" Some husbands, on the other hand, ask, "If she's really attracted to me as she used to be, why does she act like a cold potato every time I approach her?"

The unspoken can be very difficult to interpret properly. Nevertheless, non-verbal communication has its positive side. To help you and your mate make the most of those silent messages, here are some principles to remember.

1. *Go low-tech when possible.* When it comes to communicating with your spouse, don't try to send important messages or work out sensitive issues over the phone or via e-mail.

When you read an e-mail or listen on the phone, you're not getting the whole message. You can't interpret facial expressions, maintain eye contact, or sense warmth or genuineness. If intimate, relationship-building conversation is needed, have it face-to-face.

2. *Don't be "all talk."* Remember this advice: "Faith by itself, if it is not accompanied by action, is dead" (James 2:17). Actions do speak louder than words. You can tell a hungry man you care about him and wish him well, but if you don't demonstrate your compassion the words are useless. The same is true for your spouse.

A church sign put it this way: "Actions speak louder than bumper stickers." Ask yourself whether the messages you've been sending your spouse lately have been through your actions—or the lack thereof.

3. *Don't rely on silence to send a message.* Silence can be one of the loudest forms of communication, but it's easily misinterpreted. What does it tend to say in your marriage? Is it "I don't want to fight"? "I'd rather not say anything that could stir up trouble"? "Don't bother me"? "I don't care what you think or what you need from me"?

The trouble with silence is that your mate may "fill in the blanks" with answers that aren't correct. Learning to communicate what you feel will help your spouse know what's in your heart—instead of encouraging him or her to take your silence and assume the worst.

>
> Silence can be one of the loudest forms of communication, but it's easily misinterpreted. Your mate may "fill in the blanks" with answers that aren't correct.

4. *Don't catastrophize.* In other words, don't overreact. What you *think* your spouse meant may not be what he or she intended to communicate.

Ask for clarification: "Remember the other day when I asked you about taking a vacation and you sighed real loud? Were you aggravated with me because I brought it up again, or were you frustrated with yourself for having forgotten about it?"

5. *Watch your body language.* Your facial expressions and eye contact send messages to your spouse about how interested you are in what he or she is saying.

Actions like looking away, cleaning your fingernails, yawning, or flipping channels on the remote say, "I have better things to do." To avoid getting distracted when your spouse is trying to communicate with you, turn off the radio, TV, computer, or other electronic devices.

6. *Use touch to communicate your love.* When Jesus wanted to communicate how valuable children were to His kingdom, He didn't just say, "Hey, kids, you are valuable!" He reached down and touched them and sat them in His lap.

People need touch. Babies left untouched become ill emotionally and physically. Spouses who fail to affectionately touch each other by holding hands, rubbing necks, putting their arms around each other, and hugging will not be as close—literally and figuratively—as those who make these patterns part of their everyday routine.

7. *Use your eyes to express warmth and caring.* Most mothers are experts at controlling their children's behavior by simply looking at them; sometimes it seems a mom's angry look in church can pierce 70 rows of bodies to reprimand a talking teenager. In marriage, your eyes can communicate warmth or disgust, contentment or dissatisfaction, love or hatred, approval or disappointment.

Actions like looking away, cleaning your fingernails, yawning, or flipping channels on the remote say, "I have better things to do."

Many men struggle with looking at their wives. Some are by nature shy and developed a habit in childhood to avoid looking directly at a speaker. Some fear seeing disappointment in their wives' eyes. Whatever the case, both men and women need to look their spouses in the eyes, especially when discussing sensitive topics or expressing love.

8. *Practice, practice, practice.* Make sure that what you feel in your heart is communicated clearly not just by your words, but also by eye contact, touch, and other "nonverbals." Don't assume that since you feel good about what you're communicating, your spouse must feel good about it, too.

—MITCH TEMPLE

Part 7:
Resolving Conflict

Is It Okay to Fight?

In a word, no.

That assumes "fighting" isn't just disagreeing and expressing negative emotions. Those things are inevitable in a marriage. But if fighting is trying to resolve those feelings and problems through abusive behavior, it's unhealthy.

Conflict occurs when two people have a difference of opinion that hasn't been resolved. This can happen when you and your spouse disagree over where to go for dinner, whose family to spend the holidays with, or what each person's chores were this week. All of these are normal marital conflicts that can be worked out.

When arguments turn into verbal or physical abuse, though, it isn't healthy for any marriage. If you consistently attack your spouse with statements like, "I'm sorry I married you," "You are so stupid," and "I hate you," you've moved from arguing to abusing.

> If you consistently attack your spouse with statements like, "I'm sorry I married you," "You are so stupid," and "I hate you," you've moved from arguing to abusing.

If you throw things at your spouse—pillows, silverware, pictures, vases—it only leads to more conflict and hurt. And you *never* hit, push, shove, kick, or spit at your spouse. This is physical abuse. Not only is it immoral and illegal, but it causes tremendous damage to your relationship. If this is the way you deal with conflict, you need to seek counseling to learn appropriate ways to reconcile.

Those appropriate ways don't include simply submerging your differences instead of dealing with them honestly. Many couples try to sidestep or hide their conflict because disagreements can be painful. That leads some spouses to think their own arguments are abnormal.

"I never see other couples fight," Gary told a friend. "It makes me feel like Katie and I have a bad marriage." Gary doesn't realize that some couples share their conflicts openly, while others are more private. Some couples appear to have no conflicts, but in time they often have distress in their marriages because they had just internalized conflict and allowed hurt and resentment to build. Their anger may explode, doing incredible damage to the relationship.

A husband we'll call Paul was one who tried to suppress conflict because he feared fighting. "I fell in love with Lucy because we never fought before we got married," he told his accountability group. "I am so afraid of divorce because of my parents. They fought all the time and look where it led them. If Lucy and I continue to fight, I'm afraid we'll end up like my folks."

Contrary to what Paul believed, divorce is most common when conflict is hidden or unresolved—not when it's dealt with openly. Conflict in itself doesn't lead to divorce. Lack of resolution has brought divorce at worst and unhappy marriages at best.

Conflict resolution may sound complicated, but it's possible. It's a skill that requires the commitment of both spouses and can be refined with practice.

Here are 10 things to remember about resolving conflict without fighting.

1. *Deal with disagreements as soon as possible.* Confront issues as they arise. The longer a conflict stews, the larger the issue becomes; time tends to magnify a hurt. As the Bible says, "Do not let the sun go down while you are still angry, and do not give the devil a foothold" (Ephesians 4:26).

2. *Be specific.* Communicate clearly what the issue is. Don't generalize with words like "never" or "always." When you're vague, your spouse has to guess what the problem is. Try something like, "It frustrates me when you don't take the trash out on Mondays," rather than, "You never do what you say you're going to do."

3. *Attack the problem, not the person.* Lashing out at your spouse leaves him or her hurt and defensive. This works against resolving conflict. Your goal is reconciliation and healing in your relationship. Let your mate hear what the problem is from your point of view. Say something like, "I'm frustrated that the bills didn't get paid on time," instead of, "You're so irresponsible and lazy. You never pay anything on time."

> ◆
>
> **Some couples appear to have no conflicts, but in time they often have distress in their marriages because they allowed hurt and resentment to build. Their anger may explode, doing incredible damage to the relationship.**
>
> ◆

4. *Express feelings.* Use "I" statements to share your understanding of the conflict: "I feel hurt when you don't follow through." "It makes me angry when you tease me in front of your friend." Avoid "you" statements like, "You're so insensitive and bossy."

5. *Stick with the subject at hand.* Most people can deal with only one issue at a time. Unfortunately, many spouses bring two or three issues to an argument, trying to reinforce their point. This confuses

the confrontation and doesn't allow for understanding and resolution. It's better to say, "It hurt my feelings when you didn't include me in your conversation during dinner with our friends," rather than, "You never include anyone, you always think of yourself. Whenever we're with other people, you always ignore me. Everyone thinks you're selfish."

6. *Confront privately.* Doing so in public could humiliate—or at least embarrass—your spouse. This will immediately put him or her on the defensive and shut down any desire to reconcile.

7. *Seek to understand the other person's point of view.* Try to put yourself in your spouse's shoes, an exercise that can lead to understanding and restoration. That's what Mia was doing when she told her sister, "Jeff had a hard day at the office today. His boss chewed him out. That's why he's quieter than normal, so I didn't take it personally. I know when I've had a hard day, I need time for myself, too."

8. *Set up a resolution plan.* After the two of you have expressed your points of view and come to an understanding, share your needs and decide where

> Divorce is most common when conflict is hidden or unresolved—not when it's dealt with openly. Lack of resolution has brought divorce at worst and unhappy marriages at best.

to go from here. That might mean saying something like, "In the future, it would help to discuss with me how we'll spend our savings—rather than telling me after the fact."

9. *Be willing to admit when you're wrong.* Sometimes a conflict occurs because one person's behavior was inappropriate. Be willing to confess and ask forgiveness from your spouse if you've wronged her or him. That process can help to heal the damage in your relationship. Try something like, "I'm sorry I was unkind to you. Will you please forgive me?" If you're the offended spouse, be gracious enough to accept your spouse's apology.

10. *Remember that maintaining the relationship is more important than winning the argument.* Winning an argument at the expense of losing the relationship is a defeat for both of you. Finding a solution that benefits both spouses lets everybody win.

What if the two of you just can't seem to find that solution? When you can't get past a specific conflict, seek the help of a counselor.

Fighting isn't healthy, but conflict isn't always bad. In fact, it can be a tool for strengthening relationships. When conflict is handled correctly, two people share their hearts with each other, trying to listen and be heard while connecting on a deep level. When you deal with conflict in a caring and positive way, the result can be a deeper relationship and greater intimacy.

> Attack the problem, not the person. Lashing out at your spouse leaves him or her hurt and defensive.

"In your anger do not sin" (Ephesians 4:26). God knew that we'd have anger and conflict in our relationships. But anger isn't a sin as long as we seek to resolve the conflict.

"If it is possible, as far as it depends on you, live at peace with everyone" (Romans 12:18). Instead of fighting, are you doing your part to reconcile and restore your relationship with your mate?

—SHERYL DEWITT

How Do Other Couples Handle Conflict?

You already know how you and your spouse deal with disagreements. Maybe you tend to knock a conflict over the head and bury it alive, hoping you'll never have to confront it again. Or maybe you let loose with verbal volleys that have plenty of volume.

Perhaps you've wondered, though, how your conflict management style compares to that of other couples. Since most husbands and wives avoid blowups in public, it can be hard to tell. Compared to them, are you normal? Average? Do they know something you don't?

Ben and Lisa are wondering that. As they look around the silent art gallery they're visiting, they don't notice any other couples who ooze hostility. Their own marriage, on the other hand, seems awfully turbulent. They argue often about how and where to spend their time and money. Lisa feels Ben's friends are always stealing him away. Ben thinks Lisa spends too much time on the phone, talking with her mother—and probably complaining about him. They've begun to withdraw from each other; when they do talk, their conversations usually end in a sarcastic verbal brawl.

Another couple, Luke and Jen, can't help observing how their neighbors, Bill and Mandy, handle conflict. Bill and Mandy have even dragged their fights into Luke and Jen's living room, loudly discussing the missing of garbage pickup day, dirty dishes in the sink, socks on the floor, and leaving the TV on when no one's watching it. If nothing else, Luke and Jen have learned how *not* to deal with disagreements.

Observing others' marriages, good and bad, may help you learn ways of resolving conflicts yourself. But the goal isn't to compare, compete, evaluate, or judge. It's to figure out what works best for you.

As you observe, you'll note that there are at least three kinds of marital clashes.

The first is domestic violence—physical conflict and words that threaten such conflict. This is extremely serious;

> Since most husbands and wives avoid blowups in public, it can be hard to tell how your conflict management style compares to theirs. Are you normal?

if things like hitting, pushing, words of harm, using or threatening use of weapons, or physical abuse are happening in your marriage, safety is of primary concern. Call 911 and report the situation in order to protect yourself and your family. Get to a safe place with safe people supporting you.

A second type of conflict is often referred to as "emotional abuse," which includes vulgar name-calling, dehumanizing statements, and behavior or gestures designed to emotionally hurt or intimidate. If these are part of your relationship, seek the help of a professional counselor immediately. Your marriage is in serious trouble.

A third type of conflict is what Lisa and Ben were experiencing—differing opinions, preferences, or points of view that were moving them toward marital crisis. This kind of clash is the most common of the three types; to build a lasting, enjoyable marriage you must learn to handle it well.

> Observing others' marriages, good and bad, may help you learn ways of resolving conflicts yourself. But the goal isn't to compete; it's to figure out what works best for you.

How do other couples handle these conflicts? In different ways, naturally. Some choose, after discussion, to set aside minor issues (how to put bowls in the dishwasher, as opposed to where to worship); others don't. Some couples consistently raise their voices—definitely not helpful.

Conflicts in marriage are common; unfortunately, handling conflict well isn't. But if you were to watch those who've learned how to resolve their differences, you'd see them taking some steps worth following. Here are eight of those steps.

1. *Face the facts.* All marriages—even healthy, vibrant ones—experience disagreements over issues like finances, jealousy, extended family, friends, sex, faith, and priorities. You and your spouse are imperfect; even at your best, you'll make mistakes. So it's important to develop a system of conflict resolution that fits your personalities and communication styles. Accept the fact that you'll face conflict—and commit to dealing with it.

2. *Take a time-out.* Rather than avoiding conversation or withdrawing altogether, take time-outs when things get dicey. When you're not making progress by talking, when you feel emotionally exhausted, or when the conversation becomes negative, step back and take a break. Time-outs can help you get a new

perspective. Agree to continue the discussion constructively or end it until you and your spouse can handle it well.

Here's the process of calling a time-out:

• Stop the conflict.

• Express your need to take a time-out.

• Affirm your intention to solve the problem together later.

• Communicate your respect and love to your spouse.

• Give each other "space" to gain perspective and think clearly.

• Establish a time to resume the discussion later the same day, if possible.

3. *Watch your words and gestures.* Don't let your statements become destructively intense and disrespectful. Control your tone of voice and facial responses. No whining, shouting, pouting, sulking, sarcasm, or blaming. Don't give "the look" or roll your eyes.

Couples can get lazy during discussions, using gestures, looks, words, or other behaviors that convey disapproval or dislike. Don't respond in kind, negative for negative; become proactive and encourage positive responses.

4. *Value each other.* No matter what the difference of opinion may be, see your spouse as precious. Eliminate disrespectful behavior and emotional put-downs. Choose to remove all name-calling, blaming, accusing, threatening, and manipulative speech from your conversation. Recognize that God has made every person unique and of eternal value.

It's important to develop a system of conflict resolution that fits your personalities and communication styles. Accept the fact that you'll face conflict—and commit to dealing with it.

5. *Think positive.* Choose to think the best about your spouse. When you find yourself consistently interpreting what your spouse says or does in a negative light, you're thinking the worst. Changing this can be a tough mental discipline that takes effort to establish.

To help you in this process, use the "Stop/Think/Decide" model. First, count to 10. Then identify the negative thought and question its validity. Replace it with a positive, accurate thought or belief—and say that to yourself and perhaps to your partner.

6. *Be a team.* Resolve to work together. Remember that you're on the same team with the same goal. Attack the problem, not each other.

Encourage each other through affirmation and acceptance. When you suffer a personal or family loss, for example, hold each other up. Recall your commitment to one another. If you need help to renew your effort, consult a marriage counselor or pastor.

7. *Listen intently and intentionally.* Take time to thoroughly talk and carefully listen to and understand each other. Distinguish between "relationship connecting" and "conflict confronting"; connect with each other before you confront problems.

Start by discussing only how you feel about the conflict; don't try to resolve it until both of you believe you've been clearly heard. Solving problems before connecting can cut off good discussion—temporarily reducing conflict but not truly resolving it.

No whining, shouting, pouting, sulking, sarcasm, or blaming. Don't give "the look" or roll your eyes.

8. *Keep getting together.* Establish weekly meeting times to deal with conflicts—and just to be with each other romantically and playfully. Plan "fun times" with no discussion of problems. Use those occasions to affirm each other.

No matter how other couples may handle conflict, you and your spouse are unique. Your Creator is the master artist, and the two of you are among His masterpieces. Keep learning about and enjoying your individuality, and you'll find it easier to deal with the differences.

—James Groesbeck with Amy Swierczek

Why Does My Spouse Avoid Conflict?

Not too many people actually enjoy conflict, especially in marriages. So it's not surprising that your spouse may prefer to avoid it.

But some clashes are inevitable in any marriage. No matter how similar you and your mate may be in basic interests, values, and personalities, men and women are wired differently. Spouses don't always agree; they have their own expectations and needs.

So when the honeymoon is over and tensions come to the surface, how do you handle conflict when one partner just wants to avoid it?

Karen and Bill needed to know the answer to that question.

They'd had few disagreements while they were dating. All were easily resolved because one would quickly defer to the other's wishes. After a few months of marriage, though, they discovered some areas of disagreement of which they hadn't been aware.

For example, Bill had expected to share a joint checking account without much discussion about family finances. Karen wanted to develop a tight budget, carefully managing expenses—and Bill's more casual spending habits. Bill began to resent what he considered her nagging about every last penny.

Then there was the issue of in-laws. Karen wanted to spend quite a bit of time—way too much, in Bill's opinion—with her parents and other relatives. He was bored with this and wanted much less family contact. As these tensions sharpened, she tried to insist on extended discussions about them so that some resolution could be found.

How do you handle conflict when one partner just wants to avoid it?

Bill found these "heavy" encounters extremely unpleasant. He wanted his time with Karen to be fun, and saw no point to the repetitious and increasingly shrill "fights."

Bill began to seek ways to avoid the discussions. Karen, anxious about his silent but increasing anger, grew more aggressive in seeking to engage him. He withdrew further, finding more reasons to stay away from home or to watch even more TV.

Karen became the furious nag. Bill became the hostile, cold, emotionally unavailable stoic.

Couples like Bill and Karen aren't uncommon. Many women prefer to deal with conflict by talking it out, only to find that their husbands prefer to withdraw—which the wives find maddening. Occasionally it's the opposite, with the wife doing the avoiding.

A number of reasons for these scenarios have been suggested. The wife may be better with language, better at articulating her thoughts and making cogent arguments. The husband may feel overwhelmed by the onslaught of her verbiage. Rather than "lose" in a straightforward exchange of opinion—which may seem unmanly—he may find it easier to disengage. He may view conflict as a battle for control, and believe he'll lose that control if he has to fight with verbal weapons.

> Many women prefer to deal with conflict by talking it out, only to find that their husbands prefer to withdraw—which the wives find maddening. Occasionally it's the opposite, with the wife doing the avoiding.

Another possibility: The avoiding partner may have grown up in a home where one parent verbally abused the other. The avoiding partner may fear that any hint of disagreement will escalate into a painful war of words—and try very hard to stay away from conflict.

It's also possible that the avoiding partner's parents never argued at all. There was no model of constructive and honest conflict resolution; everything was just papered over. That person "got it" early in life: There must be something very dangerous about any expression of negative feelings.

Whether the avoiding partner's parents fought or not, he or she may consciously or unconsciously believe the best solution is "peace at any price." But that price can become very high over time.

How? Unresolved anger, bitterness, and fear can bring serious medical and emotional consequences. The spiritual and sexual health of your marriage will be endangered. Your children may carry your example into another generation. Unspoken conflict can eat away at your relationship as a couple.

The apostle Paul implied that we should be honest about our anger, but not sin by expressing it in the wrong way. He advised not letting the sun go down before dealing with anger—because if we do, Satan may attack this weak point in our spiritual armor (Ephesians 4:26-27). Unpleasant as it may be to face conflicts, we're to try resolving them in timely and healthy ways—rather than allowing them to become hidden toxins in our relationships.

If your spouse has a strong aversion to discussing conflicts, ask him or her to try an experiment with you. It will take just 20 minutes once or twice a week.

During the first 10 minutes of that time, one of you will talk about issues that are bothering you. The other will only listen, with no argument or debate—no seeking to set the other person straight or change anyone's mind. The only response allowed is to ask for clarification.

During the second 10 minutes, the other spouse will talk. Again, a request for clarification is the only response allowed.

At the end of the 20 minutes, take a time-out from each other. Reflect on what your spouse said. Does it help you understand some of the reasons for his or her feelings?

If, having tried this, your spouse still seems intent on avoiding all conflict in your relationship, it's time to seek professional help. Seek the services of a Christian counselor who can help the two of you gain perspective on what's happening beneath the deceptively calm surface of your marriage.

> The avoiding partner may consciously or unconsciously believe the best solution is "peace at any price." But that price can become very high over time.

In the process, you can discover new tools for conflict resolution that allow a win-win outcome—so that no one loses and your marriage is strengthened and enriched.

—Phillip J. Swihart

Why Does My Spouse Overreact?

Arms crossed, Barry and Teresa sit in their minister's office.

Teresa says Barry intentionally provokes her with his annoying habits.

Barry says Teresa's overly sensitive.

"When he gets stressed out," Teresa declares, "he walks around sniffing all the time. It drives me crazy, and I blow up."

Barry says he doesn't realize he's doing it.

After exploring the situation further, the minister expresses his opinion: Barry is right. Teresa is being overly sensitive, overreacting.

He suggests that the couple try a different approach. When Barry is stressed out and begins the annoying behavior, Teresa should simply ask him, "Are you feeling stressed out?" In that way she'll make Barry aware of his sniffing habit without coming across as demeaning or overreactive.

Sounds simple? Yes.

But if it's so simple, why is overreacting such an easy pattern for spouses to fall into?

It's common for couples, especially new ones, to develop unhealthy ways of responding to minor irritations, miscommunications, and behaviors. Many couples develop destructive responses without realizing it.

> "When he gets stressed out, he walks around sniffing all the time. It drives me crazy, and I blow up."

They don't do this overnight, though. Often they bring into the marriage reactive tendencies that developed when they were children.

When you mix hypersensitive habits with the stresses of adjusting to marriage and the common pressures of life, you've got a bombshell waiting to detonate. Overreactions can cause words to fly and harmful behaviors to cut deep into the heart of a relationship. Things said and done on impulse can linger in the memory of your mate for decades. Your spouse may forget deeds done in kindness, but will remember negative, knee-jerk reactions.

Apparently God sees the danger of overreacting, because the Bible is replete with warnings about hasty responses. "A gentle answer turns away wrath, but a harsh word stirs up anger" (Proverbs 15:1). "A fool shows his annoyance at once, but a prudent man overlooks an insult" (Proverbs 12:16). "Reckless words pierce like a sword, but the tongue of the wise brings healing" (Proverbs 12:18).

God seems to be saying that instead of overreacting when we're irritated or hurt, we should exercise restraint and prudence. Why make a big deal out of something tiny? Why cut a wound deeper? Why stir the coal when that's not the goal?

Both Scripture and common sense encourage acting carefully when dealing with overreactive spouses. Here are some simple suggestions for doing just that.

1. *Seek to understand your mate.* This doesn't address his or her problem specifically, but helps you accept the reality of what you're dealing with. Understanding is often the first step toward acceptance, and can serve as a bridge to healthy changes.

Try talking with your spouse about what his or her home life was like during childhood. Start with a simple, appropriately timed question like, "Did your parents have misunderstandings like the one we're having?" That may help you discover whether Mom or Dad modeled overreaction. Knowing that your mate's mother regularly "flew off the handle," for example, helps you recognize where your spouse's tendency came from.

> When you mix hypersensitive habits with the stresses of adjusting to marriage and the common pressures of life, you've got a bombshell waiting to detonate.

Seeking understanding doesn't mean you approve the behavior. Jesus showed how to understand people's problems without approving their wrongs. When the woman with the alabaster jar of perfume anointed Jesus' feet and washed them with her tears (Luke 7:36-50), He looked into her heart and knew her motives. He accepted her without approving her sinful past.

2. *Model healthy behavior.* If you want a child to learn which behaviors are acceptable and which aren't, you have to reinforce the positive ones with praise—and model healthy alternatives to the rest.

If you overreact in response to your spouse's overreaction, you can be sure that a vicious cycle will follow. Your response can increase anger already present in your spouse, and gives him permission to continue his destructive ways.

Learn as much as possible about spouses with overreactive leanings. Find out how others deal with them rather than enabling yours by your own negative conduct.

3. *Create awareness and accountability.* Your spouse may not realize how reactive he or she has become. Habits aren't just hard to break; they're often difficult to recognize.

Next time your spouse overreacts, change the way you respond. If you typically overreact, turn and walk away. If you usually don't say anything, bring it up later and describe how it makes you feel.

If your spouse is volatile, allow at least an hour to pass before you bring up the conflict. This allows him or her to calm down and return to a normal heart rate, blood pressure, and other physiological levels.

In extreme cases, you might try writing your mate a letter and making him or her aware of how much of a problem this really is. Writing a letter underlines that you're addressing a real difficulty, and allows your spouse to read it without your presence or the pressure to immediately respond. It also gives you the opportunity to pray and think about what you're trying to communicate—not just settle for what typically comes out of your mouth during a heated exchange.

Why make a big deal out of something tiny? Why cut a wound deeper? Why stir the coal when that's not the goal?

4. *Be part of the solution, not the problem.* Ask your spouse how you can help.

Are you doing something that leads to your mate's reaction? If your spouse offers examples of how your behavior provokes him or her, don't get defensive. Simply thank your mate and commit to changing your behavior.

Don't imply to your spouse that this is only his or her problem, not yours. That makes you part of the problem again. Most marriage issues are not one-sided. Marriage is a system; what you do affects the other parts of the system. Intentional or not, your actions, aversions, or attitudes may be a major contributor to your spouse's overreactions.

Internal changes (yours) often lead to external changes (your spouse's). If that doesn't work and the overreactions continue, suggest that the two of you talk with a pastor or counselor who can offer direction on how to resolve the issue.

—MITCH TEMPLE

How Can We Work Out Disagreements?

Whether you've been married five years or five months, you've had disagreements with your spouse. *Having* them is not the issue. The real issue is whether you can deal with them in a healthy way. Destructive patterns of disagreement can leave behind emotional scars that never heal.

Most couples think their clashes are unique, but conflict has been around since Adam and Eve. Instead of learning from our ancestors' mistakes, though, we tend to copy them. If Mom screamed and threw CorningWare at Dad when she was angry, daughter will tend to do the same in her own marriage. If Dad withdrew by watching TV every time conflict arose, son will be inclined to follow his example.

No matter what was modeled by your parents, however, you can reframe your thinking. You can realign the way you handle disagreements to better reflect the pattern God wants to see.

Can you imagine Jesus dealing with disagreements as we often do with our spouses? How would He feel about the way you treat your mate during a heated argument?

"But that's just the way I am," you might say. "Besides, my spouse keeps provoking me!" Instead of justifying our behavior, we need to discover how to properly react to disagreements no matter how intense they may be or who's at fault.

Each time you work out a disagreement in a healthy way, you're better equipped to deal with the next one. Conflict handled properly can fine-tune a relationship: "As iron sharpens iron, so one man sharpens another" (Proverbs 27:17).

Resolving disagreements can also "unstick" a couple, moving the two of you to new levels of intimacy and growth. Some of the closest moments a couple can experience often arrive after resolving conflicts. It's like a lightning storm on a warm summer night; though the

If Mom screamed and threw CorningWare at Dad when she was angry, daughter will tend to do the same in her own marriage. If Dad withdrew by watching TV every time conflict arose, son will be inclined to follow his example.

lightning itself may be scary, it helps to clean the air. Negatively charged ions produced by the storm attach themselves to pollutants, which fall to the ground. That's why the air smells so clean at those times.

The same is true when you deal with disagreements in an appropriate way. Even if the discussion is loud and animated, it can help to rid relationships of contaminants and move you in a positive direction.

To understand how to handle disagreements effectively, let's first look at some techniques that *don't* work.

1. *Denial.* Why are so many married women in our society depressed? Quite a few psychologists believe it's because they don't feel free to discuss frustrations and disagreements with their husbands. That's because husbands tend to deny such problems and refuse to confront them.

> Each time you work out a disagreement in a healthy way, you're better equipped to deal with the next one. Conflict handled properly can fine-tune a relationship.

Some men simply don't know how to deal with disagreements properly, but many have discovered a payoff in not resolving conflict. They can maintain control by refusing to discuss problems, keeping their wives guessing about the state of their relationship. Wives then hold back because they've discovered that keeping peace with their husbands keeps the men in a good mood and increases the chances of intimacy.

This is not a healthy approach. Failing to resolve disagreements affects our relationships as arthritis does our bodies; it impairs movement, slows us down, and causes a lot of pain. The only way to deal with "relational arthritis" is to develop healthy responses to conflict.

2. *Downplaying.* This is the "Oh, it's nothing" response. This often happens when you feel that dealing with the issue is an exercise in futility. You tell yourself that things will only turn out like before—with your spouse not listening and with both of you upset.

But downplaying the significance of a problem doesn't make it go away. It only sets a negative precedent for dealing with future disagreements.

3. *Exaggeration.* Don't make a disagreement bigger than it is. Not every minor irritation and difference in perspective has to be dissected and "put to rest." Does it really matter if your spouse doesn't share your enthusiasm for sweet pickles and the Three Stooges? Does either of you have to win a debate over which brand of paper towel or route to your church is best?

4. *Nagging.* Don't fall prey to the idea that picking a fight is the best way to get your spouse's attention and deal with a disagreement. Constant nagging is a common example of such erroneous thinking.

A dad was watching the Atlanta Braves on TV one day when his four-year-old came up and wanted to wrestle. Just to see how the boy would respond, the father ignored him and stared at the game. The child made faces, waved, and jumped up and down, but Dad gave no response. Finally the boy knocked on his father's forehead and asked, "Hey, Dad, are you in there?"

Lesson: It's better to do a little gentle "knocking" than to incite a riot to get your mate's attention. "A gentle answer turns away wrath, but a harsh word stirs up anger" (Proverbs 15:1).

5. *Resurrecting the dead.* Bringing up lifeless issues from previous disagreements only "stirs the stink." Perhaps that's why the apostle Paul wrote that love "keeps no record of wrongs" (1 Corinthians 13:5).

When a disagreement is over, it's over! Don't rehash old arguments. Some counselors suggest that couples shouldn't bring up an issue that's more than a month or two old. In other words, don't get *historical* in your marriage by continually bringing up the past!

So much for the don'ts. Here are some positive ways to deal with disagreements in your marriage.

1. *Pick the right time and place.* Get away from the telephone, TV, pager, e-mail, and other distractions. Pick a soothing, peaceful environment; a Saturday shopping trip at Sam's Club isn't a good time or place to resolve conflict! Neither are moments when you're going out the door, sitting down to dinner, or lying down for a good night's rest.

Be willing to say, "I agree that this is important, but we need to wait till later to talk about it. Let's go out tomorrow night." Allowing 24 hours to cool down and think is often a wise alternative anyway.

2. *Be prepared.* Understand that emotional events like birthdays, weddings, holidays, anniversaries, and graduations are a natural breeding ground for disagreements. People tend to be "wired and tired"; little sparks can ignite big fires. Try to get plenty of rest before these events, and give your spouse extra grace and forgiveness.

> Does it really matter if your spouse doesn't share your enthusiasm for sweet pickles and the Three Stooges? Does either of you have to win a debate over which brand of paper towel or route to your church is best?

3. *Talk about yourself.* When discussing disagreements, learn to use "I" statements such as "I think" or "I feel"—rather than "you say" or "you always . . ." "You" accusations are usually meant to hurt, not to bring peace and understanding.

4. *Listen more than you talk.* Seek to understand where your partner is coming from, even when you may not agree with his or her viewpoint. Learn to listen instead of just trying to figure out what you're going to say next.

Temper and control what you think you have a right to say, too. As Ogden Nash put it, "To keep your marriage brimming with love in the loving cup, whenever you're wrong, admit it; whenever you're right, shut up."

5. *Keep your fingers to yourself.* Pointing fingers may be acceptable when correcting toddlers or pets, but it's not healthy between spouses. Pointing is a form of attacking, indicating that the recipient has done something terribly wrong—which often isn't the case. And no one, including your spouse, likes to have a finger wagged in his or her face.

6. *Keep your arguments out of the bedroom.* That's a place for unity and intimacy, not hashing out differences. Don't use sex (or lack thereof) to manipulate your partner. Sex was never designed to be used as a weapon, withheld without mutual consent (1 Corinthians 7:3-5).

7. *Remember that it's your problem, too.* It's tempting to say, "I don't have the problem, you have the problem!" But if there's trouble in your relationship, it belongs to both of you!

You're a vital part of a *marriage system.* When one part of the system is out of kilter, it throws the entire system off balance. It's like touching a mobile hanging over a baby crib; disturb part of it, and you affect the whole thing.

When you view your spouse's problem as your own, you're much more likely to get serious about helping to work it out. This makes a "double-win"—rather than an "I win, you lose" scenario—more likely.

8. *Learn to see through conflict.* Search for the real issues that often lie beneath the surface. Say, "Wait a minute. We keep arguing about all kinds of irrelevant stuff. What's the *real* problem here?"

You're a vital part of a marriage system. When you view your spouse's problem as your own, you're much more likely to get serious about helping to work it out.

9. *Bring God into the conversation.* Ask Him for wisdom when you can't seem to find the answers (James 1:5-6). And if the two of you are Christians, nothing will put a heated argument on "pause" more quickly than two small words: "Let's pray!"

10. *Remember your vows.* Don't threaten divorce during conflict. Threats will only intensify the pain—and leave scars. "For better or worse" will not be stricken from your vows simply because you're in the middle of a major disagreement.

Are you and your spouse disagreeing? Look for mutually beneficial solutions that resolve the tension. If the conflict is too intense to handle, or if one spouse gets extremely emotional, call a time-out until you've both calmed down. If that doesn't help, involve a counselor to assist you in getting perspective.

You can't eliminate disagreements in your relationship. But by taking a proactive approach early in your marriage, you can learn to address conflict in a way that makes everyone—including the Lord—smile.

—MITCH TEMPLE

How Can We Make Decisions Together?

One of the hardest things for many couples is making a decision—especially one that satisfies both spouses.

And why not? Most corporations have difficulty in decision making. Churches have split up because they can't make a choice that pleases everybody. It's no wonder marriages struggle in this way.

Take Kathleen and Clifford. As CEO of a large company, Clifford is accustomed to calling the shots. This way of running his family, however, is taking its toll on his wife. "Cliff treats me like I'm a child or his employee," she says. "My opinion doesn't count with him. I want to do God's will, but he feels that it's the man who always gets to make the decision. I was in the corporate world before we met and made decisions that affected many people. I feel like he doesn't trust me."

Then there's Sam, husband of Kelly. He has a different complaint. "Kelly allows me to make decisions. But if they aren't to her liking, she pouts and I feel guilty. I would rather she tell me what she wants and work together with her."

"Cliff treats me like I'm a child or his employee. I was in the corporate world before we met and made decisions that affected many people. I feel like he doesn't trust me."

If these couples can figure out how to make decisions together, their marriages will be stronger. Research shows that spouses who work together to make decisions are happier and more fulfilled.

Clifford and Kathleen would do well to follow the example of many couples who've learned to use each partner's strengths. If the woman is better at finances, then she's in charge of the budget. If the man is better at planning, he maps out family outings, vacations, and family devotions.

These spouses work together because they realize the goal is to make decisions in a way that's best for the family. Building on each other's strengths is the smartest thing to do.

It's like a football team. For the team to be successful, each player has a position to play based on his strengths. The offensive line needs big, strong athletes; the running back should be fast and agile.

Each player uses his talents and works with the rest for the good of the team. If one player tries to do it all, the team suffers. If one player insists on playing a position he's not gifted for, the same thing happens.

That's also true in a marriage. In Ephesians 5:22-30, Paul writes that the husband has a position to play—as "head" of the wife. He's to lead his wife as Christ led the church, doing what's best for his family out of love.

The husband, as "captain" of the team, recognizes his wife's strengths and enlists them to benefit the family. If he's truly looking out for the best interests of his wife and family and is willing to sacrifice for their good, wise decisions will be made.

Those decisions may be made jointly, or by each spouse in his or her area of expertise. Either way, your goal as a couple should be to make decisions that benefit your relationship.

>
> Many couples have learned to use each partner's strengths. If the woman is better at finances, then she's in charge of the budget. If the man is better at planning, he maps out vacations and family devotions.

Here are some guidelines on making decisions, which you can follow individually and together.

1. *Apply sound judgment.* God has given the two of you rational minds and the ability to investigate. He expects you to use them in your decision making.

2. *List pros and cons.* Sometimes seeing on paper the benefits and detriments of possible choices helps to put things in perspective.

3. *Consult God's Word.* When making a decision, study the Bible and see what God has to say on the subject specifically or in principle.

4. *Pray.* Many couples find that if both spouses are praying about a decision, God gives them a "peace" about taking one direction over another.

5. *Seek wise counsel.* "Pride only breeds quarrels, but wisdom is found in those who take advice" (Proverbs 13:10). Don't be afraid to talk to other couples, a pastor, or a mentor about your decision. Sometimes others can see more objectively than you can. This is especially helpful when the two of you have different points of view and can't seem to agree or compromise.

How does all this work in real life?

Alex and Eliza planned to buy their first home. They had two houses in mind. Both were within the budget they'd set beforehand, but one would stretch them to the limit.

They sat down and talked through their feelings about the houses, then wrote down the pros and cons of each. They prayed about the decision and sought counsel from wiser, older men and women. Already they'd searched for related principles in the Bible, and came to believe that buying either house would represent good stewardship of their money.

After considering all the facts, they decided to keep more margin in their budget by choosing the smaller house. They believe God guided them in this process, and are enjoying the house He provided.

Sometimes others can see more objectively than you can. This is especially helpful when the two of you have different points of view and can't seem to agree or compromise.

When most couples with a Christian commitment come to a fork in the road, they want to know their choice of direction reflects God's will. But decisions aren't always a matter of right or wrong; sometimes they're about preference. If consulting Scripture and other mature believers doesn't turn up a spiritual principle to follow, you're probably picking between two or more valid choices.

Some couples fear they'll miss the "one and only right choice," putting them "out of God's will" and dooming them to lives of misery. But God doesn't want to confuse you. As you seek Him, He promises to give you wisdom to make wise decisions.

"If any of you lacks wisdom, he should ask God, who gives generously to all without finding fault, and it will be given to him" (James 1:5).

God is waiting to give you wisdom for your next decision—both of you, working as a team.

—Sheryl DeWitt

How Can We Handle Racial and Cultural Differences?

Every couple has to deal with differences; racial and cultural contrasts add another dimension of potential conflict and adjustment. Cultural differences tend to cause more rifts in a relationship than racial ones do, but both can create problems.

Racial differences don't necessarily bring trouble on their own. Perceptions of and reactions to those differences are more often the culprit. Cultural differences, on the other hand, shape a person's belief system. When two cultures collide in a marriage, the results can be rewarding or devastating—depending on the flexibility of the spouses and their families.

Gloria, a white woman, wanted to marry an African-American man named Chris. Both were Christians. Gloria's parents were very upset, saying they were worried that their daughter would be alienated from the rest of the family. They were so concerned, in fact, that they were refusing to attend the wedding.

Gloria's parents were trying to force their daughter to choose between her family and the man she loved. It wasn't easy for Gloria to deal with the prejudices of her family and friends in addition to the usual challenges a relationship brings.

> When two cultures collide in a marriage, the results can be rewarding or devastating—depending on the flexibility of the spouses and their families.

As the wedding drew closer, the pressures increased. Gloria, who'd been drawn to Chris's personality, smile, and faith, began to realize that marrying him would mean having to withstand a lot of stress. Chris, meanwhile, began to feel isolated from his family and friends. Women he knew would tell him angrily that he was betraying them by dating a white girl.

Still, Gloria and Chris got married. They loved each other, and felt no one should be able to stop them. When they began to face the realities of cultural and racial differences, however, it was a struggle. There were many adjustments and compromises to make. They started to clash over holidays, church, food, how many children to have, and how to discipline them.

Andres and Wendy, on the other hand, had a happier experience.

Andres was from Mexico; Wendy lived in the United States. Wendy, wanting to be a missionary, had learned about Mexican culture and knew she needed to adapt to it. In a similar way, Andres realized that the "machismo" way of Mexico wouldn't work very well with an independent American female.

When they married, Andres took a path that was contrary to his cultural norms. He helped with household necessities, including washing dishes and cleaning. He encouraged Wendy to pursue her master's degree and career. Wendy, meanwhile, understood how important family involvement was to Andres and made it part of their lives.

Andres and Wendy made their marriage work because they were more committed to loving one another than to maintaining their own cultural norms and preferences. They compromised, sacrificed, and were patient with one another as they combined their two worlds.

When two cultural backgrounds meet in a marriage, the relationship can be enriched. But obstacles first need to be identified and addressed. Here are four barriers couples usually encounter during the learning phase of a multiracial, multicultural relationship.

1. *Customs and culture.* The way you're brought up is the way you'll live, unless you discover another option that seems preferable. Stress causes people to revert to the patterns they're most familiar with. Even without the influence of culture, you and your spouse have learned different ways to deal with stress. And even without stress, customs and culture have taught you different values and priorities. This means the two of you need to learn and compromise, especially if you haven't lived in similar areas of the country or world.

That was true of Andres and Wendy. At first, Andres couldn't understand why Wendy wouldn't eventually want to be home taking care of the house and children. At first, Wendy saw his perspective as arrogant, limiting, depressing, and controlling. She also felt his quietness during conflict, and his tendency to leave without looking at her, were rude and arrogant. Andres, meanwhile, thought of

> Andres and Wendy made their marriage work because they were more committed to loving one another than to maintaining their own cultural norms and preferences. They compromised, sacrificed, and were patient with one another as they combined their two worlds.

Wendy as too direct and disrespectful. It took time for them to understand each other.

2. *Pride.* This attitude displays itself when one spouse feels superior because he or she grew up in a "higher" socio-economic class than the other. Or a spouse may feel owed something for having legalized the other's citizenship through matrimony. Pride also shows itself when one spouse believes the other's culture or beliefs are inferior or strange, thereby discounting the other person's importance in the relationship.

3. *Communication.* This includes the challenge of literally speaking different languages. At first, couples tend to enjoy listening to another language being spoken; it can become a point of contention, however, when misunderstandings occur or the "foreign" language is spoken at family gatherings.

One man, Tom, decided to marry a woman named Olivia even though she knew no English; Tom could speak Spanish quite well. After a few years of marriage, he began to hint that Olivia should learn English.

Her desire was there, but the time wasn't. The couple had three children, two with Down syndrome. Despite this, Tom began to resent the fact that she was not learning English or assisting with finances. Eventually the relationship fell apart.

> Andres questioned the "machismo" attitude that had hampered his ability to resolve conflict with his wife. Wendy realized that her openness created pain when she didn't think before speaking.

Communication also becomes an issue when it affects the way in which couples solve problems. Andres was raised in a culture in which women "bit their tongues" and didn't openly complain at home. Wendy had grown up in a family in which women said whatever was on their minds. When Wendy would let loose with gripes and disagreements, Andres would boil inside. Sometimes he would then disconnect from the discussion; other times he would explode.

When Wendy and Andres couldn't resolve conflicts in the ways they were accustomed to seeing at home, they grew resentful. It took time to turn conflict into a learning opportunity and an avenue for growth in the relationship.

4. *Isolation.* Gloria and Chris, challenged because of their multiracial relationship, experienced isolation from family and friends. Gloria dealt with depression and loneliness, and Chris gradually became more irritable.

Both knew they wanted to be together. Their commitment to one another carried them through their dating and engagement years. But broken family relationships and friendships haunted them, too.

How can you handle racial and cultural differences in your marriage? Here are five recommendations.

1. *Educate yourself and your family about the other culture.* This can ease surprises and defuse potential conflicts. Ask questions of your partner. Research norms and expectations.

Because she loved Andres deeply, Wendy did a thorough study of the Latino culture. She talked with him about what she'd learned, pointing out where she and Andres were likely to experience tension in their relationship. This also helped clear up some misunderstandings Wendy had about Andres' family.

> All of us have bones that are the same color—and in the end, we all return to dust. The important thing in a cross-cultural marriage is uniting two individuals who are committed to making the relationship work regardless of other factors.

2. *Challenge false beliefs you or your family may have about the other culture.* Beliefs drive thinking; thinking drives feelings; feelings drive behaviors. The beliefs held by Gloria's parents about African-Americans, for example, clearly influenced their attitudes and actions toward their daughter and future son-in-law.

When two people marry, they generally "marry" each other's families as well. That's why it's a good idea to discuss as a couple the belief system each person has, and to explore the evidence supporting those beliefs. If the beliefs are held simply because the extended family has said so or "society is just that way," challenge them gently and respectfully. For example, you might ask, "How can you help me better understand this belief that you hold dear?"

3. *Discuss the positives and negatives of the two cultures and jointly choose which parts will best fit in your relationship.* Talk with your mate about the possible weaknesses and strengths of your own culture. Decide which attributes of both cultures might enhance the household you're building.

This worked for Andres and Wendy. Andres questioned the "machismo" attitude that had hampered his ability to resolve conflict with his wife. Wendy realized that her openness created pain when she didn't think before speaking.

4. *Adjust and adapt to one another's cultures through compromise and communication.* This takes humility and courage. It also takes a willingness to give up

some of your desires in order to meet the other person's needs. Listen to each other before identifying differences, problems, and solutions. Realize that both of you have equal influence in your relationship.

This process helped Andres see that Wendy's openness could be a tool for quickly identifying and solving problems. It helped Wendy tone down her explosions and listen to what Andres was saying before jumping to conclusions. She also decided to work with her husband to solve problems instead of working against him to prove a point.

5. *Be patient as your partner adapts.* If you continually correct your spouse, he or she may lose interest in adjusting to your culture. People tend to gravitate toward familiarity and success; provide both as your spouse tries a revised and expanded way of living and perceiving.

All of us have bones that are the same color—and in the end, we all return to dust. The important thing in a cross-cultural marriage is uniting two individuals who are committed to making the relationship work regardless of other factors.

Prejudices about race and culture have existed for thousands of years. It's up to the individual that holds a prejudice to change it. You and your spouse can't control what others think, but with God's help you can strengthen your own marriage.

—Daniel Huerta

How Should We Handle Friendships with Others?

Sam and Julie have been married almost two years. Sam has a group of buddies he's been hanging with since high school. Depending on the season, their softball league and early morning calls to the deer stand keep him pretty busy.

Julie is getting worried. She'd imagined cozy evenings together in their new home, and wonders why Sam doesn't spend more time with her. When he stays out late without calling, her anxiety turns to anger.

Sam argues that as long as he isn't doing anything "wrong," he should have the same freedom that he had when he was single. But Julie wants to be first in his life. What are they to do?

Friends are a big part of our lives. They've been with us through school, breakups, and job changes, and stood with us at our weddings. Every marriage inherits some from each spouse and gains more along the way.

But friendships can unsettle a marriage, too. How should you handle it when they threaten to destabilize yours? Here are five suggestions.

1. *Remember your most important earthly friendship.* As your priorities shift into "marriage mode," they're influenced for better or worse by outside relationships. Each friend brings to your life his or her own value system (see 1 Corinthians 15:33; Proverbs 22:24-25). Anything that affects you affects your marriage, too. And the longer you've waited to marry, the more likely that you've acquired friends who don't share all your values.

> Sam argues that as long as he isn't doing anything "wrong," he should have the same freedom that he had when he was single. But Julie wants to be first in his life.

If your friends put even an amoral activity like work or shopping ahead of their marriages, you may have to reconsider how much to invest in your relationship with them. If you're committed to Christ and they're involved in lifestyles that run counter to that, there's an even greater threat. Your friends' partying or gambling are dangerous enough to you, but can be a deathblow to your marriage.

Your relationship with your spouse is your highest-priority friendship on earth. Any marriage, especially a new one, needs consistent nurture. While you're learning to meet each other's needs, keep this relationship second only to the one you have with Christ.

2. *Look at the time.* When conflicts arise over time spent with friends, try applying the strategies you use with money. Both topics are often muddied by emotion but clarified by a budget. Sit down together and review the time you spend with others. Ask your spouse how he or she feels about your friendships and the time you invest in them.

Priorities identify what we should plug into our schedules first. Husbands and wives can reasonably expect to receive not *all* but the *best* of each other's time. After planning those quality slots for each other, you can commit to other healthy relationships without worry over offending or neglecting your spouse.

3. *Show respect for your mate.* Paul writes in Galatians 5:13, "You, my brothers, were called to be free. But do not use your freedom to indulge the sinful nature; rather, serve one another in love." It's your responsibility to make every reasonable effort to keep your spouse's respect and trust, even if it means not doing something you may be technically "free" to do.

Of particular concern are opposite-sex friendships. Opinions differ on this issue, but the safest approach is to avoid exclusive friendships or one-to-one time with a person of the other gender. Many people in today's culture will think these boundaries unnecessary, but that culture's sexualization poses real risk to a developing marriage.

> Your relationship with your spouse is your highest-priority friendship on earth. Any marriage, especially a new one, needs consistent nurture.

Safe friends, regardless of gender, will earn your spouse's trust. Single or married, they are *for* your marriage. This could mean they refrain from calling you if they're of the opposite sex—or, if the same gender, they won't expect to spend inordinate amounts of time with you on the weekend.

Staying accountable to your spouse for your time and activities can be a helpful safety net. Come home at a reasonable hour; call home if your plans change. Avoid the trap of forcing one spouse to parent or police the other. With respect and trust, greater flexibility will be there when needed.

4. *Set a new pattern.* Insecurity over any topic, including outside friends, tends to occur more often in new or immature marriages. That's why it's important to handle these issues responsibly early on. How you conduct yourself with others can make or break your spouse's trust.

Simple habit can cause conflict over friendships. It may be second nature from her single days for a new wife to accept a lunch appointment with a male friend. Not having "shifted gears" yet in her thinking, she may not realize until later that the invitation should now include her spouse or be turned down.

With consistent effort and calm resolve, you and your mate can forge practical friendship guidelines that will serve you for a lifetime. Once you find a set of principles you're comfortable with, though, carefully consider exceptions as needed. For example, when work requires you to spend time with a person of the opposite gender, keeping your spouse informed may be a better solution than changing jobs.

Husbands and wives can reasonably expect to receive not all but the best of each other's time. After planning those quality slots for each other, you can commit to other healthy relationships without worry over offending or neglecting your spouse.

5. *Strike a balance.* A healthy marriage consists of two healthy individuals. No one wants to be smothered, and God didn't design marriage to meet anyone's every relational need.

Some new couples make the mistake of spending nearly all their time with each other. When a spouse is too insecure to tolerate a mate going out with friends, he or she is undermining the marriage rather than protecting it. A good balance of time alone and time with others can foster marital health.

Each marriage is unique; outside of Scripture, there's no set of rules on friendship that will apply to everyone. You and your mate must work together to strike a balance of trust that works for you. As you find that balance, remember that it's not about rules—it's about relationship.

—ROB JACKSON

When Should We Agree to Disagree?

Some couples think every difference of opinion in a marriage has to be settled. They fear disaster lurks when spouses don't agree on every issue.

Frank and Lois know better.

It's bedtime, and the two of them are once again apologizing to each other for an argument they had earlier today. They almost get the giggles when they realize how stupid it was. They can hardly remember the subject—something about their upcoming vacation. Both were very upset and hurt by what was said, whatever it was.

A long time ago Frank and Lois made a pact to never go to bed mad, which is good. But they've wasted the better part of the day being upset over something they can barely recall—a conflict about which they could have agreed to disagree.

It's hard to guess how many arguments could be averted if couples would pray about their differences and let them go. This is hard to do, since most of us want to be "right" and justify our behavior.

Many couples, especially Christians, assume that if they're truly compatible and in love they'll agree on practically everything. They may even think that disagreement is a sign of drifting apart—or that agreeing to disagree means settling for second best.

That's a faulty judgment based on an unrealistic expectation.

> Sharing all opinions and preferences isn't going to happen, and you wouldn't want it to. Agreeing to disagree, when it's appropriate, is realistic.

Differences are usually what attract partners to one another. If you doubt that, take a personality test from a counselor—which can be fun—and highlight the differences that enrich your relationship. Sharing all opinions and preferences isn't going to happen, and you wouldn't want it to. Agreeing to disagree, when it's appropriate, is realistic—and can help each of you appreciate the other's uniqueness.

If you have children, agreeing to disagree also can set a good example for them. Watching you gives them a broader perspective. Children aren't usually confused or upset by parents disagreeing, but may feel threatened by the behavior they observe when there's no resolution of a conflict.

So when should you agree to disagree? And when should you "stick to your guns"?

The answers to those questions will depend on the importance you attach to each issue. There are certain decisions such as having children, setting life goals, and choosing where to live that may require outside help to negotiate if you can't agree. Other cases—whether to have pets, where to go on vacation, how much to spend on dining out, who cleans the bathrooms—may be easier to work out on your own. The key seems to be your willingness to not get defensive nor to insist on "winning."

> Certain decisions such as having children, setting life goals, and choosing where to live may require outside help to negotiate if you can't agree. Other cases—whether to have pets, where to go on vacation, how much to spend on dining out—may be easier to work out on your own.

Sometimes agreeing to disagree is a choice to accept your spouse's preference out of respect or love. For example, Dan doesn't really want to have a second child at this time. But his wife, Bonnie, does. After discussing it, Dan tells her that he won't stand in the way of her enthusiasm; he'll support and love her without resentment.

But when a disagreement can't be resolved and either of you harbors resentment that interferes with your relationship, agreeing to disagree may only be "stuffing" feelings. If that happens, get help so that the resentment can be released.

Very few disagreements are worth fighting for. But there are healthy ways to express your desires and negotiate resolution. When you make a request with respect and an open mind, your chances of being heard are that much greater.

Here are some principles to keep in mind when it comes to dealing with disagreements.

1. Don't expect to agree on everything.
2. Convey your desire without anger and without having to be "right."
3. Ask yourself if you're being selfish.
4. Remember that your relationship, not the issue, is most important.
5. Try not to take things too personally.
6. Remember that building a relationship takes time.

7. Forgive, forgive, forgive.

8. Keep a sense of humor.

When disagreements arise, try using that as a checklist. Often if these principles reflect your attitude, you'll find it easier to let go of the issue you've been struggling with.

Let's say that Frank and Lois love to go out to dinner and a movie. But Frank likes action movies and Lois likes romantic comedies. Frank would rather take poison than watch a romantic comedy; Lois would rather be skinned alive than see an action film. If they compromise by taking turns, one person always loses. How can they agree to disagree?

First, they give each other permission not to agree on everything. Then they listen to each other without judging. They feel secure in the knowledge that they're not trying to change each other, and that each has a choice to act in a loving way even when the two of them have different perspectives.

> When a disagreement can't be resolved and either of you harbors resentment that interferes with your relationship, agreeing to disagree may only be "stuffing" feelings. If that happens, get help so that the resentment can be released.

They brainstorm some creative options. Finally they decide that they'll go out to dinner, then pick a cineplex where each can see the movie of his or her choice.

It may not be the perfect solution, and they may change their minds after trying this approach. But it beats arguing over issues they can't even remember at the end of the day.

—ROMIE HURLEY

What If We Have a Lot of Unresolved Conflicts?

After only two years of marriage, Nancy and John are living very separate lives.

The problem? Neither of them likes conflict, so they avoid each other.

Nancy pours herself into hobbies and caring for their nine-month-old son. John is staying later at work, and often goes straight from there to the health club. On those nights he doesn't even see Nancy or his son before they go to bed. Using the excuse that he doesn't want to disturb his wife, he sleeps on the couch.

John and Nancy can't remember when they last had a night out together. Their sexual intimacy has dwindled to less than twice a month, with little tenderness or joy. Both are concerned about their marriage, but feel immobilized by the fear of getting angry, getting hurt, or hurting each other.

Maybe you can identify with Nancy and John. Unresolved conflict is hanging over your marriage like a thundercloud, threatening a storm you don't want to brave. Perhaps you've always resisted discussing problems. Or your efforts to resolve differences have ended in icy silence or shouting matches, experiences you don't care to repeat.

> Perhaps you've always resisted discussing problems. Or your efforts to resolve differences have ended in icy silence or shouting matches.

Not resolving conflict may give an initial feeling of peace or harmony, but it's like a wound that heals on the surface when underneath there's an infection that needs to be released. No one enjoys lancing the wound, but real recovery can't take place otherwise.

Fear of conflict can stem from having experienced too much of it as a child—or from never having seen any. Some parents shelter their children too much by not revealing disagreements nor demonstrating how they can be resolved. Others display only the arguments, not showing the process whereby disagreements are worked out, leading to a fear of the unknown.

In the case of John and Nancy, it would be good to share their childhood experiences with conflict and what their expectations were for marriage. They may discover that their expectations were unrealistic or mistaken—for example, thinking that Christians must never argue or disagree.

How couples deal with conflict is one of the greatest predictors of whether or not a marriage will end in divorce. In most marriages, conflict resolution is initiated by the partner who's more assertive or more of a pursuer physically and verbally. That can at least bring situations to the table, but the healthiest scenario requires freedom for both spouses to start conversations on areas of concern.

When both partners aren't assertive, or fear conflict, or lack the skills to deal with it, resentment can build quickly from the proverbial molehill into a mountain. It's crucial to get outside help in that case; you're dealing not only with personality issues, but most likely a lifelong pattern of avoidance. A good family therapist, or a pastor who has time and expertise to work with you on an ongoing basis, could coach you.

When unresolved conflicts are immobilizing your marriage, your goal should be to "get unstuck." Here are five steps in that direction.

> Not resolving conflict may give an initial feeling of peace or harmony, but it's like an infection that needs to be released. No one enjoys lancing the wound, but real recovery can't take place otherwise.

1. Forgive your spouse.
2. Pray together.
3. Appreciate each other in a tangible way (cards, gifts, special meals, etc.).
4. Discover and confess stubbornness and the desire to be "right."
5. Get help from a wise mentor or counselor.

In the case of Nancy and John, it took a crisis to get them to a therapist. Nancy grew severely depressed and ended up in the hospital. John's concern for her, along with her doctor's prescription, drove them to see a Christian counselor.

After working with the therapist for several months, Nancy and John are less afraid of conflict. They know there's still a long road ahead, but are encouraged by how honestly they're expressing their feelings—especially when they remember how carefully they used to avoid that.

In addition, Nancy has been working out at the health club with John twice a week—while their son stays with John's parents. They go out to eat on those nights, and find they have energy and excitement for intimacy—and staying up later than usual.

—ROMIE HURLEY

What If an Argument Gets Out of Control?

Once again, Sue and Ken have gone to bed angry. Each lies as far over on his or her side of the bed as is humanly possible.

Sue is thinking about the terrible things Ken said to her, and how afraid she was. She'll spend most of the night unable to sleep, remembering all their fights in almost three years of marriage.

Ken, meanwhile, is exhausted. He thinks about how unreasonable Sue is. Then, suddenly, he falls asleep.

Some couples, like Ken and Sue, have a habit of letting arguments get out of control. Others find it happening only once in a while. Still others try never to raise any sensitive subjects, fearing the resulting argument will degenerate into a verbal battle that leads inevitably to divorce.

Why do arguments spin out of control? Here are seven things couples need to understand about disagreements that go off the deep end.

1. Spouses become irrational for many reasons. It can stem from feeling overwhelmed, threatened, provoked, criticized, or just misunderstood. The emotions may not be wrong, but their out-of-control expression can be. As the Bible says, "A fool gives full vent to his anger, but a wise man keeps himself under control" (Proverbs 29:11).

> Some people seem only too glad to lose control during an argument. There's a kind of adrenaline rush that comes with expressing anger, and it can be addictive.

2. Some people seem only too glad to lose control during an argument. There's a kind of adrenaline rush that comes with expressing anger, and it can be addictive. That's one reason Ken could fall asleep easily once he came off the "high" of the argument; the adrenaline depletion had worn him out.

3. Fearing out-of-control arguments can cause a spouse to bury his or her feelings, so as not to provoke the other person. That may work in the short run, but ignoring explosive issues won't work long-term. They'll eventually come to a head.

4. A wife tends to remember situations much longer than a husband does, and the danger of her dredging up the past is not only real but common. This is overwhelming to the spouse who tends to forget, or wants to forget, things said and done in anger.

5. Both aggressive and passive/aggressive behavior can be dangerous. In most couples, one spouse tends to be more of an aggressive pursuer in arguments. This person usually gets more of the blame because he or she is easy to identify. But the passive, quieter mate who nags or blames is often just as destructive.

Here's an example of a passive/aggressive statement: "I know how smart you are, but you'll never really be able to get a good job since you didn't finish your degree." This behavior is harder to identify than outright aggression; even the person who uses it may not see the need to repent and change.

6. Bullying in a relationship can be intimidating, but it's important not to run from threats. It's better to find a constructive way to deal with the bullying and avoid living in fear. There are times when a gentle answer can turn away wrath (Proverbs 15:1), but this is presented in the Bible as an intentional, positive act—not one motivated by fear of provoking someone to anger.

> No matter how much you and your spouse love each other, no matter how understanding you try to be, and no matter how strongly you want to avoid hurting each other, there will be times when arguments get out of control.

7. Physical violence is never okay. Threats of physical violence must be handled immediately. If you feel threatened, get to a safe place. Put distance between you and the person endangering you; call the police if necessary.

Physical violence doesn't stop without intervention. Abusers must learn to manage anger. Once the danger is past, insist on counseling. Also, educate yourself about abuse cycles and how to protect yourself in the future.

Out-of-control arguments don't always involve violence, of course. No matter how much you and your spouse love each other, no matter how understanding you try to be, and no matter how strongly you want to avoid hurting each other, there will be times when arguments get out of control.

Here are some ways to prepare for those times and to minimize their negative effects.

1. Be aware of your physical reactions and triggers, to let you know when

it's time to back off. Most people tense up when uncomfortable or threatened.

2. Take responsibility to communicate how you're feeling and what you're thinking.

3. Never, ever bully, threaten, or intimidate your spouse.

4. Ask for a time-out when you need it; set another time to talk.

5. If you know a subject is too volatile to handle alone, discuss it in the presence of a neutral party such as a pastor or counselor.

6. If you're "walking on eggshells" or hiding in fear in order to avoid angering your spouse, get outside help.

7. Pray with your spouse when things get too intense, even if you avoid the immediate topic for the moment. The act of submitting to God's authority may bring some relief.

8. Pray individually—a prayer of repentance for your own attitude and actions.

9. Forgive your spouse. This doesn't mean agreeing with his or her position or excusing abuse; it means giving up your determination to get revenge.

Remember Ken and Sue? When they get up the next day, Ken apologizes for the mean things he said—as he's done many times before. This time, though, he admits that he's afraid of hurting Sue during one of these fights. He says he knows he has a problem and wants help in getting to the bottom of the rage he often feels. Since he and Sue have been talking about having children, the thought of hurting them scares him, too.

> Pray with your spouse when things get too intense, even if you avoid the immediate topic for the moment. The act of submitting to God's authority may bring some relief.

Until now, Sue has always retreated in fear. Now, because of Ken's admission, she feels safe enough to express some of her feelings. She acknowledges that she has a problem with fear and would be willing to see a counselor with her husband.

Don't let your anger, or your spouse's, dominate your relationship. And don't let fear of an out-of-control argument keep you and your mate from communicating honestly. For further help, see "How Should We Talk About Sensitive Issues?" and "Why Does My Spouse Overreact?" in this book.

—Romie Hurley

Do I Have to Forgive My Spouse?

The short answer, if you're a Christian, is yes.

Jesus Christ has been crystal clear on that subject: "And when you stand praying, if you hold anything against anyone, forgive him, so that your Father in heaven may forgive you your sins" (Mark 11:25).

The apostle Paul echoes this idea: "Bear with each other and forgive whatever grievances you may have against one another. Forgive as the Lord forgave you" (Colossians 3:13).

Short answers to profound questions, however, are not always completely satisfying. On the surface, they seem to gloss over the complexities.

After all, some offenses are so grievous that it's difficult to *want* to forgive a person who's betrayed your trust and his or her vows to God—much less actually *do* so. Putting things in perspective, of course, most offenses in marriage don't rise to that level of pain and destructiveness.

> The short answer, if you're a Christian, is yes. Short answers to profound questions, however, are not always completely satisfying.

Both Jesus and Paul answered this question by emphasizing that the most important reason to forgive is that we've been forgiven. If we've asked for God's forgiveness through Jesus' sacrifice, for our terribly long list of offenses against Him (and if we think we haven't offended Him, we're really out of touch with reality), He's already forgiven us. Why would we do less for those—including our spouses—who have wronged us?

Another good reason for forgiving a spouse is that it's in your own best interest to do so. As in art, what isn't positive space is negative space. What's left if we decide not to take the positive step of forgiving? The negatives of depression, anger, self-pity, and bitterness will be fertilized.

Not to forgive is costly—to the person who chooses not to do so, and to those around that person—even more than to the target of the person's chronic wrath.

Some husbands and wives seem highly invested in keeping minutes of all past sins and offenses of their spouses. *Ka-ching, ka-ching, ka-ching*—the cash register of marital history just keeps adding up the injustices, great and small, perceived and real.

One day that gunnysack of unforgiven hurts becomes so heavy that the aggrieved spouse, irritated by some insignificant infraction, feels the irresistible urge to dump them on the other's head. The pent-up poison of accrued bitterness blows out like a volcanic eruption. The recipient feels righteously indignant that a major injustice, a massive overreaction to nothing, has been perpetrated on him or her. This exchange, born of many choices not to forgive, solves nothing, resolves nothing, heals nothing.

Failing to forgive also gets a relationship stuck in an unending, repetitive cycle of blaming each other—rather than taking responsibility for one's shortcomings. This is a no-growth, slow-death strategy, again filling what could be positive space with negative space, which can doom marriages. It's also a terrible model for children to follow and to pass on to future generations.

But what about offenses that seem almost unforgivable? What about a father who sexually abuses his children, or an unrepentant wife who flaunts a lesbian affair? How do you forgive that?

Ultimately, forgiveness is an attitude—one that may be understood only by you and the Lord. It's giving up your insistence on getting revenge. It is not sweeping a crime under the rug or denying the enormity of what an offender has done.

> Some offenses are so grievous that it's difficult to want to forgive a person who's betrayed your trust and his or her vows to God—much less actually do so.

In the case of abuse, your first action may need to be ensuring your safety and that of your children, if any. Forgiving a violent or perverted spouse is not the same as being naïve or stupid about his or her potential to do further harm.

Forgiveness is also not equivalent to forgetting a spouse's track record. It doesn't mean that an abusive husband or wife will be immediately allowed back into the family home after a quick, superficial, even tearful "repentance." It doesn't mean that an unfaithful spouse must be welcomed back without a commitment to counseling and behavior change.

There are times, for example, when a wife is afraid to forgive her serially adulterous husband for fear that he'll only betray and hurt her again. Her instincts may be exactly right; he'll be chasing another skirt within a month.

Forgiving him does not mean that she must permit him to continue his sinful lifestyle and remain in a sham marriage to her.

One husband, Brent, began "staying late for work." His wife, Shannon, happened on a cell phone bill that included many calls to one number she didn't recognize. Some of these calls were made late at night and on weekends. When she called the number, a woman who turned out to work in Brent's office answered.

This all seemed heartbreakingly familiar to Shannon. Brent had been involved in two affairs—that she knew of—during their marriage. This was number three. The old feelings of hurt, betrayal, and anger came flooding back.

In the past, Brent had been very "repentant" when caught. She thought she'd forgiven him. Now she wasn't so sure. The only certain thing was that she wasn't about to forgive him again; she'd had it.

> Ultimately, forgiveness is an attitude—one that may be understood only by you and the Lord. It's giving up your insistence on getting revenge.

If you're at the edge of this cliff, married to an abusive spouse or a mate who's continued to trash you and your marriage vows through sexual infidelity, seek the help of a pastor or Christian marriage counselor.

If the situation isn't that grave, but you harbor an unforgiving spirit and find it impossible to let go, ask God to give you the power to *want* to forgive. Then commit yourself to doing so.

"But what good will that do?" you might ask.

First, it will restore your fellowship with God that may have been quenched due to this issue in your spiritual life.

Second, it will open the door—at least in relationships that haven't been irretrievably damaged—to the possibility of healing and restoration with your spouse. It may bring greater intimacy than you've had in a long time.

Finally, it can bring freedom from the bonds of resentment, allowing emotional health—perhaps even better physical health. It can build a greater sense of joy and peace to fill that negative space in your life—and displace the occupant of bitterness.

—Phillip J. Swihart

How Can I Get My Spouse to Forgive Me?

Rebecca and Mark stood in the church office after worship service. They were arguing about a topic that had surfaced during the sermon: forgiveness.

Mark couldn't seem to refrain from bringing Rebecca's mistake up again. Nine months ago, while Mark had been away on an extended business trip, she'd contacted an old boyfriend simply because she was lonely and curious about what he was doing these days.

Nothing else had occurred between the two. But when Mark had found the guy's number on her cell phone bill, he'd imagined the worst.

Rebecca had been penitent and tearful. She'd realized it was inappropriate and had asked Mark more than once to forgive her. But he seemed unable to do that.

Now they stood in the church office, clashing again over the incident. Almost everyone had gone home after the service.

James, an older deacon, could tell the young couple was having a fight as he walked by the office's glass door. After several moments he approached the pair and asked whether they were okay.

> When Mark had found the guy's number on her cell phone bill, he'd imagined the worst. Rebecca had asked Mark more than once to forgive her. But he seemed unable to do that.

They said they were, but admitted something had come up during the sermon that exposed old wounds. James figured it was connected with forgiveness.

"You know," he said, "when my wife and I were first married, I did something stupid which I regretted a long time. And though she is now gone on, she did something that I will never forget. She taught me a lot."

He gently placed his hand on Mark's shoulder. "If I can help you," James added with tenderness, "let me know. I will be praying for you." Then he walked away.

Curiosity got the best of the couple. That evening, Mark called James and asked if he and Rebecca could drop by Tuesday evening to hear the rest of the story. James quickly agreed.

After Mark and Rebecca arrived at the little house, James asked them to tell him a little about their problem. After several minutes of listening, he began to relate his own story.

While serving in the Korean conflict, James had been unfaithful to his wife. Overcome with shame, he'd confessed his sin to her the evening he returned from duty.

For the next several months, James worked to earn back his wife's trust. After proving his love through many difficult days, he received a special gift from her.

Now James pulled a piece of yellowed paper from his Bible and handed it to Mark. On it was the following:

"When my wife and I were first married, I did something stupid which I regretted a long time. And though she is now gone on, she did something that I will never forget."

"Let all bitterness, and wrath, and anger, and clamor, and evil speaking, be put away from you, with all malice: And be ye kind one to another, tenderhearted, forgiving one another, even as God for Christ's sake hath forgiven you" (Ephesians 4:31-32, KJV).

Under the Scripture passage was written the following: "James, I forgive you. If I were in your shoes, I may have done the same thing. God burned this verse on my heart and I have obeyed. You have proven yourself worthy of forgiveness and through the months I have learned how to forgive you. I love you and believe in you. Forever yours, Sue."

James wiped one lonesome tear from his eye. "The gift she gave me was forgiveness," he said. "I hope you two will learn to forgive each other like my wife did for me."

That night changed Mark and Rebecca forever. Though they both came from homes where forgiveness was sparse, they committed to learn how to forgive and be forgiven.

Like Mark and Rebecca, most couples struggle with learning how to forgive. It's not something that comes naturally for us; it's something we learn to do. Jesus must have known that when He commanded us to pray for our enemies. He knew it wouldn't happen by itself, but that a directive was needed.

Is your spouse having a hard time forgiving you? There are some things you can do to help.

1. *Recognize that forgiveness is a process.* It ebbs and flows; it starts, stops, and starts again; it gets better and gets worse. No matter what the issue is that caused

your spouse to be hurt, forgiveness can be more than just a one-shot decision. Understand that forgiving you may take time.

If your mate occasionally seems to struggle with or dwell on what you did, that doesn't necessarily equal a refusal to forgive. Sights, sounds, and memories can trigger an episode of struggle. If you're impatient or inconsiderate, it will only cause more hurt. Pursue understanding, not just the desire to put the conflict behind you.

2. *Realize that fear can be a barrier to forgiveness.* Fear often blocks mercy. Here are three kinds of fear that can delay the process:

- *Fear of losing control or power.* To help your mate let go of his or her need to control the situation, demonstrate your trustworthiness and show that you understand the seriousness of what you've done. Let your spouse see that you have to live with the consequences every day; assure him or her regularly that you've learned a great deal about how deeply your actions have affected him or her. Show how you're taking steps to prevent the mistake from occurring again.

- *Fear of not being able to punish the wrongdoing.* Maybe your spouse is still in the anger stage and wants you to experience some of the hurt he or she felt. Be patient during this stage of the process, whether your mate is right or wrong. Pray for your spouse; ask God to reveal your broken heart and your desire to make things right. Eventually your spouse may start asking himself or herself, *Why can't I forgive? What payoff am I getting out of not forgiving?* Questions like these often lead to healing, but it takes time.

- *Fear of forgetting what occurred.* Help your spouse realize that you don't expect him or her to not remember what happened. That's impossible. Explain that you simply look forward to the day when he or she will be affected less by your actions, and to the opportunity of proving your commitment to make your marriage healthy again. Be as understanding as possible. Impatience will only underline the suspicion that you don't care what your partner is struggling with.

3. *Seek outside guidance.* If necessary, ask a professional counselor or older Christian to help you and your spouse with the process. You might be surprised to know how many

> That night changed Mark and Rebecca forever. Though they both came from homes where forgiveness was sparse, they committed to learn how to forgive and be forgiven.

people you respect have struggled with and triumphed over issues of forgiveness. Make sure, though, that your spouse is open to this help. An outsider may be perceived as a threat or as an additional source of embarrassment.

4. *Be honest with yourself.* It's easy to see your spouse's failure to forgive when you're confident that your heart is genuinely remorseful. But keep checking your own attitude and actions during your journey to forgiveness. Ask the following questions:

- *What exactly caused my spouse to be hurt?* It's easy to forget what the real issue is and focus on distractions.
- *What behaviors or attitudes do I hold on to that cause more hurt?*
- *What's my plan to make necessary changes?*
- *What might God be showing me in my spouse's inability to forgive?*

—MITCH TEMPLE

What If the Same Conflicts Keep Coming Up?

"I cannot believe I married this man!" Cindy told the counselor. "I know that I love him, but right now I am so angry with him.

"Kent never follows through with anything he says he is going to do. Sometimes I wonder if I married the wrong person. We continue to have the same fights over and over again; nothing ever gets resolved.

"For example, last night I asked him to take out the trash. He told me he would do it when the basketball game was over. This morning the trash was still there, and so I took it out. Tonight we'll talk about it and he'll apologize and expect me to forgive him. But then the same situation will happen again.

"I am tired of his empty apologies when there is no change. I'm beginning to feel a lot of resentment, and we've only been married three years. I'm afraid that our marriage is going to be in trouble if we can't get a handle on this."

Cindy believes that when Kent agrees to take the trash out for her after the game, he'll do it that night. Kent believes that as long as the trash gets taken out in the next few days, he's lived up to his responsibility. Or he thinks that because he intended to follow through and just forgot, Cindy should remind him again. He can't understand why she took it out and then got mad at him; after all, it wasn't that full in the first place!

Cindy's frustration is a common one for recently married couples: The conflict that arises is temporarily resolved, but continues to creep up because no lasting remedy has been found. These unresolved conflicts leave spouses feeling as if they married the wrong person, or that their marriage is doomed.

Conflict in any relationship is normal. The problem occurs when you don't work through it.

What should you do if the same issues keep popping up, unresolved? Here are some steps to take.

> "I am tired of his empty apologies when there is no change. I'm beginning to feel a lot of resentment, and we've only been married three years."

1. Realize that you learn to work through conflict by confronting the issue—not by avoiding it.

2. Remember the purpose of confronting the conflict: resolution. Your ultimate goal is to reconcile and make your relationship even stronger. If you're aiming just to spout hurt and anger, you'll damage the relationship. Winning the battle isn't important, either. What matters is continuing to strengthen your bond.

3. Don't procrastinate. Conflict resolution should be done as soon as either party recognizes that he or she is feeling upset.

4. Set aside a time for discussion when each spouse can be at his or her best—not when one party is extremely tired or abnormally stressed. You want both partners to be willing and ready to seek reconciliation.

5. Take turns expressing your feelings about the conflict at hand. Listen carefully.

6. Use "I" statements instead of attacking the other person. Examples: "I feel hurt when you don't follow through," rather than, "You're so irresponsible. You never keep your promises."

A conflict is temporarily resolved, but continues to creep up because no lasting remedy has been found. This leaves spouses feeling as if they married the wrong person, or that their marriage is doomed.

7. Specifically express your need to your spouse. For instance, "It would help me if you'd take the trash out as soon as you agree to do it."

8. Come up with a plan of action. For example, write down chores that each person is responsible for and when each chore is to be accomplished. In the case of Cindy and Kent, they wrote that Kent is to take out the trash every Monday, Wednesday, and Saturday. Now both have the same expectation; Kent knows Cindy can't nag him, but she has the freedom to confront him if he doesn't follow through on his agreement.

9. Find another couple, a pastor, or a counselor to whom both of you will be accountable. Share the plan of action you've agreed upon. Knowing that someone is holding you accountable can help you follow through.

If your chronic conflicts have dragged on and on, never reaching resolution, you may be skeptical about whether these methods really work. Consider the cases of these two couples.

"Samantha and I always fought over money," Joe said. "She would spend without talking to me and write checks without logging them in the register. Every month when I sat down to do the finances, we would fight. We both hated the beginning of the month.

"We finally solved this conflict by setting up a budget. Sam knows how much we have to spend in each budgeted area. I got duplicate checks so if she forgets to write down the amounts, I still have a record. This has saved us numerous fights. Now neither of us dreads the beginning of the month."

Gail and Tom also discovered the value of coming up with a plan. Gail felt Tom never listened to her when she came home from work, wanting to talk about her day. They discussed the problem many times, with Gail in tears and Tom feeling nagged and then apologizing for his insensitivity. The conflict would die for a few days; then they'd be right back where they started.

Gail knew the repeated battles were harming their marriage. So she came home early from work one day, made Tom a great dinner, and shared her hurts with him. "I love you so much and I hate it when we fight," she said. "You are my best friend and I want to share my day with you. Would you be willing to give me 10 minutes of your night without the TV on, just to let me share?"

They agreed to talk after dinner every night. Now Tom turns the TV off and sits down with Gail for 10 to 15 minutes while she tells him about her day. Instead of arguing, they're closer. Gail, feeling cared for, has stopped nagging Tom—who's pleased that he can show love to his wife this way.

> Don't procrastinate. Conflict resolution should be done as soon as either party recognizes that he or she is feeling upset.

If you're driving to work and hit huge potholes that damage your tires and make you late, what do you do? You take a different route the next day.

The same should be true in your marriage. If a conflict keeps coming up, it's silly to keep going down that road. Take another path that will benefit your relationship. Instead of submerging the conflict, develop a plan that helps you resolve it once and for all.

—SHERYL DEWITT

What If My Spouse Abuses Me?

All marriages are sacred, but not all are safe.

Sean grew up with an abusive father. Vowing never to be like his dad, he made sure to avoid using physical violence toward his wife. But the anger he'd absorbed for years frequently led him to assault her verbally and emotionally.

Mia was crushed by his abuse, but told herself, "That's just Sean. He can't help himself." She'd learned to walk on eggshells as a child, blaming herself when her mom flew into a rage. Now she did the same thing with her husband.

How do you know when you're being abused? It can help to know that abuse comes in many forms. Author Paul Hegstrom, in his book *Angry Men and the Women Who Love Them* (Beacon Hill Press, 2004), counts 16 kinds of domestic violence—only one of which is physical. Many people assume abuse hasn't occurred unless there's a physical mark; but as creations with bodies, minds, and spirits, we suffer wounds on each level.

> Many people assume abuse hasn't occurred unless there's a physical mark; but as creations with bodies, minds, and spirits, we suffer wounds on each level.

Some spouses claim they can handle physical abuse more easily than being demeaned verbally and emotionally. Examples of ways in which partners misuse power without doing physical harm would include gambling away the grocery money or scolding a mate while compulsively auditing a supermarket receipt.

Statistics and stereotypes spotlight the abusive husband, but wives have also abused spouses. No matter who the abuser is, though, abuse can be manifested actively or passively. The categories are as follows:

- Active physical abuse, including hitting, slapping, punching, choking, pinching, shoving, hair pulling, and kicking.
- Passive physical abuse, including "posturing" violence, such as punching the wall, slamming doors, throwing or breaking things, and stomping.
- Active verbal abuse, including name calling, sarcasm, profanity, yelling, screaming, and poorly timed (in front of others) or unfair criticism or comparison.

- Passive verbal abuse, including the "silent treatment," muttering, sighing, and other derisive sounds or lack of verbal affirmation.
- Active emotional abuse, including "mind games," preferential treatment, double standards (which change from person to person), and inconsistent standards (which change from day to day).
- Passive emotional abuse, including chronic moodiness, holding someone "emotional hostage," and withholding appropriate emotional care or affirmation.
- Active sexual abuse, including forced anal, vaginal, or oral penetration.
- Passive sexual abuse, including indecent exposure and displaying pornography.
- Active spiritual abuse, including mockery, ridicule, overspiritualizing, and misusing Scripture as a means of control.
- Passive spiritual abuse, including refusal to participate in spiritually meaningful activities and failure to affirm spiritual involvement.

If your spouse is abusing you, here are four things you need to keep in mind.

1. *Abuse is always wrong.* Some try to excuse it. Most perpetrators have a sense of entitlement, thinking their actions are justified. Ironically, their victims may also believe they deserve to be mistreated. Some will even defend their abuser, citing his or her earnest apologies afterward.

> Abuse is always sinful, and few things destroy trust in a marriage as quickly. Regardless of childhood pain or marital conflict, mature spouses learn to set limits so anger doesn't become abuse.

But abuse in any form, for any reason, wounds both spouses. It's always sinful, and few things destroy trust in a marriage as quickly. Regardless of childhood pain or marital conflict, mature spouses learn to set limits so anger doesn't become abuse by frequency, degree, or duration.

2. *Abuse takes two to continue.* Domestic violence is a paradox. There's an active partner in crime and a passive one. One abuses, the other tolerates it. The cooperation of both parties drives the cycle. It's not fair, but abuse rarely stops until the victim makes choices to stop it.

Some spouses need protection and counsel before confronting their abusers. Depending on state law, an order of protection may be arranged through a private attorney. Families and friends can be a valuable support, but it's difficult for them to remain objective. In most cases, it's necessary to get additional aid from a therapist or shelter.

If you can't persuade your spouse to get help privately, call your pastor or other church leaders. They should be ready to help you find safety first, then offer ongoing support to help heal your marriage. For an overview of a biblical process of church intervention and discipline, see Matthew 18:15-17.

Remember that the first few hours of a domestic conflict are often the most dangerous. Get help sooner, not later. If you or your children are at risk, call the police. Focus on the Family's "Troubled-With" Web site advises, "Get out of the abusive situation. Even if you want to try to work things out, finding a shelter or a friend to stay with will stop the abuse right away. Leave quickly and without discussing your departure with your violent spouse. If you are in fear for your safety or your children's, contact your local law enforcement agency to find out what steps to take to get a restraining order against your abusive partner."[1]

One abuses, the other tolerates it. The cooperation of both parties drives the cycle. It's not fair, but abuse rarely stops until the victim makes choices to stop it.

3. *Abuse is a symptom of a deeper problem.* Mistreatment is bad enough, but it also indicates other trouble.

First, the abuser has an *intrapersonal* conflict inside. Healing his injured thoughts and emotions will help the abuser stop his behavior.

Second, the *interpersonal* conflict between husband and wife needs resolution. While the perpetrator is solely responsible for the abuse, both may have contributed to the escalation leading up to it.

4. *Marriage is for committed lovers, not hostages.* Marriage is a sacred relationship created for two people who complete each other spiritually. While it requires sacrificial service, it is not a call to martyrdom. In many cases of domestic violence, a therapeutic separation is necessary to gain safety and direct attention to the gravity of the need for change.

Laws affecting marriage are unique to each state; consult an attorney to find out more. Your options for recourse in the case of an abusive marriage include the following:

- Separation with no legal intervention. This provides no financial or physical safeguards. If you choose to leave without any children of the relationship, even temporarily, you may inadvertently harm your chances of gaining custody later.
- Some states also allow for an order of protection or temporary restraining order. These require the help of an attorney who will take the petition before a judge.

In the event of an emergency injunction, you'll usually go to a safe shelter. If you choose to have contact with your abuser during the course of the restraining order, it may become legally void, so you must approach this option with the determination to cooperate with the system.

- Separate maintenance or legal separation. Some states provide this option, which sometimes allows for protection against financial or physical harm.

While divorce may be a legal option, most Christians would hope to avoid this. If, after a period of separation for safety and a request for counseling, your spouse continues to be abusive and unrepentant, talk to your pastor about your church's view on this subject.

Abusive situations can be complex. But the question of whether to take action on them is relatively simple.

> Remember that the first few hours of a domestic conflict are often the most dangerous. Get help sooner, not later.

When Sean's rages started waking up their newborn son, Mia had a terrible vision of what the future might be if nothing changed. *I should have done this for myself,* she thought, *but I will certainly get help for Hunter's sake.*

The next day over lunch, Mia told Sean, "I love you, but you've got to do something about your anger. I've called the church and gotten the name of a counselor. If you want Hunter and me to stay, you'll go talk to him."

It was a hard step for Mia to take. But it was the right one.

—ROB JACKSON

**Part 8:
Spiritual
Issues**

How Can Faith Keep Us Together?

Every marriage needs a bond to sustain it during the trials that will surface. Is faith in Christ really the glue that can keep a marriage together?

After all, some statistics seem to indicate that evangelicals divorce at a higher rate than those with no connection to religion. As Glenn Stanton, director of social research and cultural affairs and senior analyst for marriage and sexuality at Focus on the Family, writes, "We often hear that divorce rates among people who identified themselves with certain denominations and lived in the Southern Bible Belt states had higher divorce rates than people with no religious affiliation. . . . [But] religious commitment, rather than mere religious affiliation, contributes to greater levels of marital success."[1]

Stanton notes that sociologists David Popenoe and Scott Stanley explain that the "Bible Belt" statistics result mainly from higher poverty rates and marriage at younger ages—not religious participation. In fact, University of Virginia sociologist Brad Wilcox found that evangelicals who attend church regularly have a divorce rate 35 percent lower than secular couples, after adjusting for factors like economic and educational status.[2]

Kay wanted to yell at Carl and tell him to defend her. Instead, she asked God to make it clear to Carl what his role as a husband should be in this situation. Before long, he took a more active part in supporting his wife, and did it in a loving way.

But how does faith make a difference?

When Kay and Carl married, they made a commitment to honor each other. They hoped nothing could break their bond. They had high moral values and a personal relationship with the Lord. Their security was in Jesus—not in themselves, not in each other.

They were beginning in the right direction. Could they stay the course?

It didn't take Kay long to realize that Carl had a lot of faults she'd failed to recognize. One was his inept handling of their money.

Kay had a choice. She could handle the problem in a way that was consistent with her faith, which took the authority of the Bible seriously. Or she could turn elsewhere for advice.

She decided to take an approach that echoed 1 Peter 3:3-6: "Your beauty . . . should be that of your inner self, the unfading beauty of a gentle and quiet spirit, which is of great worth in God's sight. For this is the way the holy women of the past who put their hope in God used to make themselves beautiful. They were submissive to their own husbands, like Sarah, who obeyed Abraham and called him her master. You are her daughters if you do what is right and do not give way to fear."

When Kay respectfully and graciously confronted Carl with their dilemma, he was able to hear her instead of being defensive. Now it was his turn to decide whether his response would reflect his faith.

He decided to apply principles he'd learned in 1 Timothy 3:3-6, especially the instructions to be gentle, not quarrelsome or proud or greedy. In particular, he didn't allow pride to get in the way of learning new budgeting methods.

In other words, faith helped keep them together.

Kay and Carl faced another challenge when it came to in-laws. Carl's mother had never really been excited about her only son marrying anyone—including Kay. Every family gathering was uncomfortable for Kay, and she began to feel resentful. She wanted to yell at Carl and tell him to defend her.

Instead, she prayed about the problem. She asked God to make it clear to Carl what his role as a husband should be in this situation.

> Faith helps keep couples together despite the challenges of everyday life. When Carl offends Kay, for example, her understanding of what the Bible says about forgiveness is activated.

Before long, Carl was choosing to follow 1 Corinthians 16:13-14: "Be on your guard; stand firm in the faith; be men of courage; be strong. Do everything in love." He took a more active part in supporting his wife, and did it in a loving way. Once again, faith helped keep these spouses together.

Then came another challenge. Carl and Kay moved to another state, leaving the church that had been an awesome support system for them. Knowing what a difference faith had made to them individually and as a couple, they looked in their new location for the nurturing and fellowship of other believers. They found it in a church with solid teaching, where they began to volunteer. Again their faith provided resources that strengthened their relationship.

Faith helps keep couples together despite the smaller challenges of everyday life, too. When Carl offends Kay, for example, her understanding of what the Bible says about forgiveness is activated. So is her commitment to apply those principles. She knows that God has graciously extended forgiveness to her, and expects her to do the same for others (Matthew 18:23-35). This helps her to have a forgiving heart toward Carl, preventing a root of bitterness—a marriage killer—from taking hold. Forgiveness is a vital ingredient of the glue that holds marriages together.

> Carl isn't blind, but the eyes of his heart are enlightened. Having received the gift of a relationship with God, he's not about to mess it up. His commitment to Kay flows from his commitment to the Lord.

So is fidelity. Carl and Kay have pledged to be faithful to one another, which might prove difficult for Carl in his job. He works with women who are congenial and attractive. All the temptations are there—travel, creative teamwork, the opportunity to share confidences. Carl isn't blind, but the eyes of his heart are enlightened (Ephesians 1:18). Having received the gift of a relationship with God, he's not about to mess it up. He chooses to "avoid every kind of evil" (1 Thessalonians 5:22). His commitment to Kay flows from his commitment to the Lord.

If you're a follower of Christ, staying together as a couple involves the same things that living your faith does—constantly putting aside pride, working daily on fully accepting God's forgiveness, and seeking to do what pleases Him. The following passage applies to marriage as it does to all of life: "Therefore, since we are surrounded by such a great cloud of witnesses, let us throw off everything that hinders and the sin that so easily entangles, and let us run with perseverance the race marked out for us" (Hebrews 12:1).

Can faith keep you together? God's Word says it can.

—BETTY JORDAN

What If We Don't Like the Same Church?

When you're newly married, and all is sweetness and light, it seems easy to overlook differences of preference—which restaurant to go to, what TV show to watch, where to go on summer vacation—in order to please your spouse. This time of agreement often extends to your choice of what church to attend.

As you settle into your relationship, however, feelings about some preferences gain importance.

For many couples, the birth of their first child seems to trigger a closer look at the church or faith tradition in which they want their children to be reared.

Differences of opinion about what church to attend become more intense when the debate centers not just on varying worship styles but also on differences in deeply held doctrines and worldviews—even if those differences never had seemed all that serious before.

> Jim found himself attracted to a different form of worship. Janet was completely turned off and wanted nothing further to do with it.

Frequently spouses discover a desire to return to the traditions in which they were raised. Or they want just the opposite—avoiding reminders of unhappy religious experiences in their own childhoods, against which they rebelled.

Jim and Janet met at a large "seeker" church. They were happy with the casual services and the charismatic emphasis.

Things seemed fine until, after three years of marriage, Jim was invited by a Christian coworker to a vesper service at an Eastern Orthodox congregation. Both Jim and Janet found it totally unfamiliar; people stood most of the time, didn't raise their hands or make other expressive gestures, used incense and icons, and followed a formal, liturgical order of service.

Jim found himself attracted to this different form of worship. Janet was completely turned off and wanted nothing further to do with it.

Jim began to meet with his friend and the priest to learn more about this church. He insisted that Janet reconsider her objections. He wanted to switch churches for what he thought were sound doctrinal reasons.

Janet thought Jim's enthusiasm must be due to some sort of emotional need for more structure and a heightened sense of church authority. When he told her that he now believed this Orthodox church was the one, true church, she became even more concerned and even offended.

After considerable struggle over the issue, Jim continued to attend the Orthodox church. Janet often accompanied him, but didn't share his passion for the experience. In consideration of her feelings and needs, Jim sometimes chose to go with her to a church in which she felt more at home.

This compromise wasn't totally satisfying to either. But it did keep them together for worship.

The dilemma of Jim and Janet suggests a few principles you might want to consider—especially if you and your spouse are having trouble in this area.

1. *Husbands have a spiritual leadership role—within limits.* Generally, the biblical standard is that the husband has a responsibility to lead spiritually at home. Whenever possible, the wife is to respect and follow that leadership rather than openly rebelling against it or passively under-cutting his efforts. The husband also is to love his wife "as Christ loved the church and gave himself up for her" (Ephesians 5:25). He has a sacred duty not to trample on or ignore his wife's needs, preferences, and feelings.

> Give your relationship priority. God doesn't want a dispute over church choice to tear your marriage apart.

If a husband is "leading" his wife and family into churches or practices that are heretical or cultic, of course, the wife has to put her spiritual foot down and refuse to participate. Her first allegiance is to God and His truth. Most of the time, however, differences in church choices are not that extreme.

2. *Give your relationship priority.* God doesn't want a dispute over church choice to tear your marriage apart. Try to compromise in a way that both of you can live with. Perhaps you've considered only a few churches, and there are more you can visit. Keep looking for a place of worship that provides for the spiritual growth of both spouses—and your children, if you have any.

Expect that if you're both seeking what God wants, have a spirit of unselfishness, and genuinely wish to serve the needs of your spouse rather than your own needs first, God will lead you to a good solution.

3. *Try creative alternatives.* For example, you might try the "mix and match" approach. Many churches provide both "traditional" and "contemporary"

services. Some couples attend a Saturday night "contemporary" meeting but also occasionally a Sunday morning "traditional" service at the same church.

Some spouses attend completely different churches. This is rarely a positive, long-term solution, however; it separates partners rather than engaging them together in a marriage-enriching, spiritual experience.

Some husbands and wives decide to "solve" the problem by skipping church altogether. Clearly this is not a decision God would want for them; Scripture states that Christians are not to abandon fellowship with other believers (Hebrews 10:25).

Expect that if you're both seeking what God wants, have a spirit of unselfishness, and genuinely wish to serve the needs of your spouse rather than your own needs first, God will lead you to a good solution.

If you're at an impasse on this issue, don't despair. Keep praying with each other that God will give you a solution. Examine your own motives, asking yourself why you find it so hard to accommodate your spouse. You may discover that this argument is a symptom of deeper problems in your relationship—control needs, conflict management, or plain old selfishness. Address these issues—in Christian marriage counseling, if necessary.

Most couples, if they're seeking to please God and not just themselves, do eventually find a church where both spouses are satisfied. You can, too.

—Phillip J. Swihart

Do We Have to Pray Together?

In *Complete Marriage and Family Home Reference Guide* (Tyndale, 2000), Dr. James Dobson writes, "You and your fiancée need to develop a meaningful prayer life even before the wedding. . . . My wife, Shirley, and I did that, and the time we have spent on our knees has been *the* stabilizing factor throughout nearly forty years of marriage."

Would praying together really make a difference in your marriage? What if one or both of you aren't comfortable with the idea?

Beth was overjoyed when her boyfriend, Don, became a Christian. She'd told him she couldn't marry a non-Christian. But she didn't know what lay ahead.

From the time he received Christ as his Savior, Don knew he was different. Within a few weeks he was talking to Beth—and anybody else who would listen—about Jesus and his new life.

Don was so enthusiastic, in fact, that Beth wasn't sure what to do with him. He wanted to pray with her—out loud! That was something she'd never done with a man. He thought they ought to bow in prayer at meals, even in restaurants.

When Don finally convinced Beth to marry him, she was still concerned about his exuberance over his new faith. She didn't feel comfortable with his desire to read the Bible together, much less pray.

Don didn't get it. Why wasn't Beth as thrilled as he was that they were both Christians? After all, the guys in his men's Bible study group all had been applauding his spiritual growth.

When he asked her about it, she tried to explain that her personal devotional life always had been just that—personal. Did they have to pray aloud together all the time?

Would praying together really make a difference in your marriage? What if one or both of you aren't comfortable with the idea?

Nick and Margaret had differences on this issue, too. A busy airline pilot, Nick found it tough to keep up with regular church attendance and personal prayer and Bible reading. Margaret, on the other hand, was more devoted to those disciplines. She wanted to pray before meals and on other occasions. The fact that praying together was so important to her made Nick feel uneasy—even irritated.

In premarital counseling, the two of them met with a mentor couple. Nick admitted that when it came to prayer, Margaret had expectations that he might not be interested in fulfilling. "I feel awkward doing that with her," he said of prayer. "Is it really better than praying by yourself?"

Deep down, Nick felt praying as a couple was something people did in "the olden days." What was the value in doing it now?

Sometimes spouses agree that praying together is a good idea, but don't know how to do it.

Bill and Sue were in that category. Bill had grown up in a Christian home, watching his dad pray at the dinner table—mainly on Sundays. At other times, his mom or a sibling would return thanks.

> When Don asked Beth about it, she tried to explain that her personal devotional life always had been just that—personal. Did they have to pray aloud together all the time?

Sue, meanwhile, had come from a non-Christian home. She'd become a believer before marriage, but neither she nor Bill had thought much about praying together.

That changed when they attended a weekend marriage retreat. The pastor challenged all the couples to consider praying and reading the Bible together. Sue and Bill thought it sounded like the right thing to do, but weren't sure how to begin.

If you and your spouse are struggling with the idea of praying together, here are some things to keep in mind.

1. *Start with yourself.* A joint prayer and devotional life for a married couple works best when it's a natural outgrowth of each partner's personal time with God. If you haven't been praying much yourself, you might practice on your own for a while.

2. *Don't rush it.* If you're the more interested spouse, be patient. Praying together, like any family tradition you establish, must emerge from what both partners agree to and feel at ease with.

It took time for Beth to get on the same "page" as Don when it came to prayer. But as he matured in his faith and they found some devotional materials at the bookstore, she began to relax. Eventually their joint prayer and Bible reading times came more naturally.

In the case of Nick and Margaret, it took patience on Margaret's part to gently nudge Nick to consider his role as a spiritual leader. When he saw how important it was to her, he determined to learn more about praying together and to become more at ease with it. They began with "saying table grace," then added other requests Margaret had shown concern for. She was overjoyed at Nick's efforts, which in turn encouraged him.

3. *Start small.* Many couples, never having seen their parents pray together, find it an uneasy, challenging experience. Bill and Sue met the challenge by starting with what they knew.

They began by praying before meals. One day, after Sue's girlfriend at work had a miscarriage, Sue prayed about that right after Bill asked the blessing. That seemed easy enough. In time they began to kneel beside their bed at night and ask God to deal with other concerns. "Actually," Bill eventually told a friend, "it really hasn't been that hard. We even read the Christmas story together from the Bible, before opening our gifts."

4. *Use the resources available.* Can a mentoring couple or role model help you get started? Don's Bible study friends helped him get oriented, and his pastor suggested materials he and Beth could use.

A joint prayer and devotional life works best when it's a natural outgrowth of each partner's personal time with God. If you haven't been praying much yourself, you might practice on your own for a while.

Devotional books, pamphlets, and magazines can help take the pressure off by structuring your prayer times. Check your local Christian bookstore for examples, like *Night Light: A Devotional for Couples* by Dr. James Dobson and Shirley Dobson (Multnomah, 2000).

As for Beth, she came to realize that praying together had its benefits. When Don prayed, her heart resonated with his. She liked the idea that he might be inspired and helped by hearing her concerns and praises, too.

She also came to see that praying together wasn't a test in which she had to impress Don with her spirituality. *After all,* she reminded herself, *God is the audience.*

—LON ADAMS

What Does a Christ-centered Home Look Like?

When Tyler married Kat, he thought he knew what a Christian home looked like.

He didn't want one.

When he was growing up, his family went to church regularly and adopted many cultural symptoms of Christianity. They had plaques with Scripture verses and cars with fish symbols, and attended religious conferences.

Behind closed doors, however, family members rarely spoke of Christ. They prayed only at mealtimes, and lost track of their Bibles between Sundays. Unlike their winsome public image, they were often in conflict.

If that was a Christian home, Tyler wasn't interested in re-creating it.

> When Tyler was growing up, his family had plaques with Scripture verses and cars with fish symbols, and attended religious conferences. If that was a Christian home, Tyler wasn't interested in re-creating it.

Many couples would like to create a "Christian home." Or they've been told that it's important to do so. But what is a Christian home really like? Here are some ideas.

1. *A Christian home is (mostly) happy.* How to have a happy home is the $64,000 question, isn't it? We know it's not going to be all good or bad. Most families rank somewhere in the middle, often resembling a roller coaster between the two.

While we could argue the definitions of "happy" versus "joyful," the bottom line is that most couples want a happy home when they marry.

You may worry, "But I've brought along the chaos I grew up with. Can our new home ever be happy?" You may struggle to cooperate with God as He works things out for good—because, frankly, things still feel bad.

If you're a Christian, you probably agree that the source of joy is Christ. You probably believe that when you're busy enjoying Him, your home will be happy. But that's pretty lofty. We need some handles to really pick up this idea.

To have a happy home, you must be "here now." You need to be plugged in—working when you're at work, being home when you're home. You need to pay attention to the kids when it's time and fully experience sex with your spouse when it's time.

A happy home is somewhat simplified. It's purposely *not* in chaos. The tyranny of the world and its bedlam is required to stay outside; you review regularly everything that's allowed in. Should it stay? Does it build up your family? Are you valuing each other over things?

2. *A Christian home is gracious.* Home should be a safe place to mess up. Family members need the ointment of grace on the wounds of their hearts, remembering perfection is not the goal. With the world firing at you, make your home a foxhole for retreat and healing.

Grace invites humility and repentance. Scripture tells us God's kindness leads us to repentance (Romans 2:4). When a spouse or other family member wrongs you, approach that person gently. Offering grace will come back to you many times as you mess up in the future.

Gracious language says, "I expect the best of you." It avoids criticism, sarcasm, and snide humor at all times. Instead of praising only performance, it encourages, notices, and rewards effort.

3. *A Christian home is a place of service.* If you're a parent, you've tasted sacrificial service. Anyone who cleans a helpless, soiled infant or forgoes sleep to feed a hungry baby knows servanthood on a very practical level.

But why wait until parenthood? What would happen if you served your spouse from betrothal forward? Acts of kindness, respect, and self-control should flavor the Christian home. This is where husbands and wives find that serving each other in Christ is primary. Serving others is important, too—but integrity at home is foundational.

Christ-centered couples can discover that all of life is sacred. The mundane duties of laundry, bill paying, housekeeping, and lawn mowing become opportunities to serve God. This can transform your marriage, teach your children by example, and bypass many conflicts.

>
> Home should be a safe place to mess up. Family members need the ointment of grace on the wounds of their hearts, remembering perfection is not the goal.
>

4. *A Christian home practices spiritual disciplines.* Happy families are growing spiritually. Fellowship with Christ through the Scriptures plays a central role in a home's peace. A Christian home is where

you learn how to live as you study, meditate, and pray your way through the Bible.

When you're learning to treasure Christ, He empowers you to live more simply. Your checkbook and calendar reflect your appreciation for God. Home becomes the least harried place in which you spend time.

Spiritual growth includes discovering the high value of worship. No longer relegated to certain times in a certain building, worship of God breaks into your day at home, too.

So does prayer. Individually and as a couple, spending focused time with God should sometimes be spontaneous, sometimes planned. It should be relational and meaningful, not formulaic.

5. *A Christian home is based on God's purposes for you.* Maybe you dream of how your kids will grow up and what retirement will be like. But does your vision of the future match God's?

You're probably familiar with the concept of a mission statement. This clarification of purpose is as valuable for families as it is for corporations. Developing one is a wonderful place to start crafting your Christian home. These core values and guiding principles should be flexible but consistent. They can reflect not just what you want for yourselves and your children, but also outline how you want to influence the home in which your grandchildren will be raised.

Christ-centered couples are driven by the hope of seeing Jesus one day. They avoid cluttering their eternal focus—and their homes—with possessions and people-pleasing.

When your marriage joins with God's purposes, you get a vibrant partnership. Instead of a contrived, rule-bound facade, you discover a rich and satisfying home life.

As Tyler entered marriage, he and Kat talked about what they wanted to do differently from their parents. Used to reacting to the past, he began to respond more and more "in the moment." Moving past angry cynicism, he caught a vision for what his new home could be. He started running *toward* something instead of *away* from it.

By the time they became parents, Tyler and Kat had begun to enjoy a more

> Christ-centered couples can discover that all of life is sacred. The mundane duties of laundry, bill paying, housekeeping, and lawn mowing become opportunities to serve God.

authentic Christian home. Watching other believing couples, Tyler saw the balance he'd missed growing up. Now relating to God took the place of the ineffectual religion he'd observed as a child.

Headquartered in a Christ-centered home, Tyler and Kat slowly grew into enjoying Him together.

—Rob Jackson

Christ-centered couples are driven by the hope of seeing Jesus one day. They avoid cluttering their eternal focus—and their homes—with possessions and people-pleasing.

How Can I Help My Spouse Grow Spiritually?

Lately Jessica has noticed that her husband, Mason, is withdrawing from her. His faith seems less important to him, too.

She's tried to encourage him to attend one of the men's groups at church. Recently, at the local Christian bookstore, she picked up a couple of books for him.

The signs are ominous, though. Mason still attends church with her, but he's made it clear: When it comes to faith, he wants her to back off.

> What can you do when you and your spouse don't have the same level of spiritual maturity or interest?

What can you do when you and your spouse don't have the same level of spiritual maturity or interest? The answer doesn't lie in lecturing or manipulating your mate. Instead, consider the following five actions you can take to better understand your spouse and make the concept of spiritual growth more intriguing to him or her.

1. *Be patient.* Whether your spouse is a new Christian, a non-Christian, or just a nonplussed Christian, it's hard not to overreact when he or she doesn't seem to care about the most important thing in your life. But try to remember that God loves your mate even more than you do. He may even be taking your partner on a journey that will ultimately produce a deeper faith.

In any event, be careful. God may *choose* to reach out to your spouse through you, but He doesn't *need* your help. Sadly, spiritual conflicts are often made worse by a spouse attempting to jump-start a mate's conscience or play the role of the Holy Spirit.

2. *Don't stand in the way.* "I need you to be the spiritual leader in our home, Mason," Jessica declared. "You say you're a Christian, but you don't do any of the stuff spiritual leaders should do. You hardly ever lead us in family devotions at night."

Shoulders hunched, Mason countered, "I'm doing my best to be real with you, Jess. I want to be what you need, but mostly you seem to think *I* need another mother!"

While perfection isn't possible or even necessary, your behavior can attract or repel your spouse where spiritual growth is concerned. You're living out what you're experiencing with God. Is it appealing? Is your relationship with Christ making you a more enjoyable person to live with—or just a more religious one?

Those who languish spiritually especially need to see the real deal. Your mate will benefit from your companionship when you're serious about your devotion to Christ *and* realistic about your struggles, too.

One young wife floundered spiritually for years, trying to reconcile her faith with the hurtful, religiously abusive family that had raised her. Here's how she describes her husband today: "He made it safe for me to mess up and admit it. I saw how much he enjoyed God and that he loved me like God does. I couldn't *not* respond to that."

3. *Be authentic.* You should not only share your faith with your spouse, but your concerns as well. It would be hypocritical to pretend you're not worried when a spouse struggles spiritually. But *how* you share may be as important as *what* you share. Very few spouses would react negatively to comments like, "I know you're going to be safe to share this with, but it's still not easy to admit I'm worried about you."

The spouse who struggles with faith issues needs a gentle partner to come home to. A holier-than-thou approach is sure to deepen the divide—not only between your partner and yourself, but also between your partner and God (and it can't do much for your own walk with Christ, either). Nobody wants to be smothered or judged or patronized. It's not an issue of spiritual leadership or authority; it's just human nature to pull away when someone invades your space physically or emotionally.

God loves your mate even more than you do. He may even be taking your partner on a journey that will ultimately produce a deeper faith.

When you're honest about your own faith issues, you assure your spouse that it's part of the journey to have questions and doubts. Your transparency can be especially healing if your mate has felt—accurately or not—that spirituality has become a competition in your marriage. This process applies the scriptural idea of comforting others with the same comfort you've received (2 Corinthians 1:4).

4. *Stay balanced.* There's no doubt about the importance of faith. But it's possible to lose a healthy perspective, especially when you feel your mate's Christian commitment is at stake. Even though you believe you can trust God

with your partner's spiritual development, you may try to take matters into your own hands.

Sometimes a concerned spouse drops hints or invites others to offer unsolicited counsel to the spiritually indifferent spouse. While well intended, these approaches are manipulative. Others withdraw from a mate and become excessively involved with church or other religious endeavors.

Make no mistake: You can't be too devoted to Christ. Nor should you minimize your faith to accommodate your spouse. But overspiritualization and hyper-religiosity will hinder your efforts as much as falling into the opposite ditch of apathy.

5. *Examine the reasons.* Before you sum up your spouse's struggle as merely a "sin issue," take some time to consider his context. What was his religious experience as a child? Was his faith nurtured or hindered? Was his parents' faith meaningful or a chore? Has he experienced a personal relationship with Christ or mere religion?

The Bible is clear: We're not authorized to judge others (Matthew 7:1). Sometimes in marriage we're prone to judge because of what we know—or *think* we know—about our spouses.

We do know, however, that God cares about our mates. The struggle may take time, and may even challenge our faith. In the meantime, we can trust Him to nurture our spouses and our marriages.

Jessica is holding on to that hope. She's seen progress since she and Mason talked honestly about his spiritual shakiness.

> Your behavior can attract or repel your spouse where spiritual growth is concerned. Is your relationship with Christ making you a more enjoyable person to live with—or just a more religious one?

"I'm sorry I criticized you," she said. "I was out of bounds."

"Thanks," he answered warily. "I don't want to lose your respect, but I can't pretend anymore. I feel like part of getting honest with God is being honest with you, too."

"Well, I do want your honesty. And I do respect you, I really do," she added, putting her hand on his shoulder.

Mason hesitated, then offered an idea. "Look, you know Mr. Rodriguez at church, right? Well, he and I talked one Sunday after he taught our class. I felt really safe with him, like I could talk about whatever I needed to—you know, spiritually and all. I was thinking I might give him a call and see about doing something weekly. Kind of a mentoring thing, I guess."

"That sounds like a great idea, Honey," Jessica replied, trying not to seem overzealous.

"I can see why you've been worried about me," Mason admitted. "If you're still frustrated with how things are going a month from now, I'll give Mr. Rodriguez permission to talk to you. I don't plan to give up, though."

—Rob Jackson

How Can We Serve God Together?

"Hi, Kerri, this is Susan. Is there any way you can help us out tonight at church? We have to have our care bags put together by tomorrow. Could you possibly help out? If you can, just show up at seven o'clock. Hope to see you there. Call me back if you get a chance. Bye."

"Bart, this is Eric. I hope you're planning to be there Saturday. Mrs. Mullins needs some help moving into her apartment. I know you said you were doing something with Donna, but we sure could use you. Send me an e-mail. Thanks, man. See you Saturday."

> Isn't it amazing how you never run out of opportunities to serve? If you're connected to a church, there's always a need beckoning.

Isn't it amazing how you never run out of opportunities to serve? If you're connected to a church, there's always a need beckoning.

When your marriage is relatively new, though, it can be a challenge to balance Christian service with your relationship. Even worthy projects can deprive couples of the time they need to be alone.

Other couples struggle when one spouse is more interested than the other in Christian service. The spouse who wants to be involved may feel alone and unsupported, longing intensely for the day when both mates can serve the Lord together.

Still other couples find it hard to serve together because their interests don't match. One may want a visible role such as performing on the drama team, while the other prefers behind-the-scenes work like setting up chairs. Having different interests doesn't mean there's something wrong with your relationship; it just means you aren't the same.

How can you serve God in a way that strengthens your marriage instead of stressing it? Here are some things to remember.

1. *Champion your differences.* It's okay to serve the Lord in different ways. Paul endorsed this idea in 1 Corinthians 12:4-6: "There are different kinds of gifts, but the same Spirit. There are different kinds of service, but the same Lord. There are different kinds of working, but the same God works all of them in all men."

Every talent, gift, and interest is important. God gave you and your mate varied strengths and weaknesses. Celebrate these differences and let God use them to His advantage.

Commend your spouse for his or her interest in a certain area, even if you don't share it. For example: "Beth, I really admire you for giving time to the children's ministry. I wish I had the patience you have with kids. That must be your gift."

When differences arose among the early Christians, they came together and worked side by side to accomplish crucial tasks (see Acts 6:1-7). Couples can do the same.

2. *Help each other out.* Having contrasting interests, skills, and levels of enthusiasm for service doesn't mean you can't enjoy working together in each other's "specialties" from time to time.

Jason, for instance, enjoyed overseas mission trips during the summer. Val liked planning an annual couples' retreat in the fall. Was this a problem? Not necessarily.

One may want a visible role such as performing on the drama team, while the other prefers behind-the-scenes work. Having different interests doesn't mean there's something wrong with your relationship; it just means you aren't the same.

Their solution began with sitting down at the start of the year and discussing service projects they'd like to undertake. They decided Val would serve on the retreat committee; Jason would take on added domestic chores to give Val extra time to do that. Val, in turn, would help Jason write and mail letters in the spring to gain financial backing for Jason's mission trip.

They also decided that throughout the year they'd volunteer in a Monday night inner-city program. Jason would drive the bus; Val would teach a class for five-year-olds.

Jason and Val are playing different roles, but supporting each other. Managing their varying interests simply calls for acceptance, imagination, and mutual give-and-take.

3. *Look for common opportunities to serve.* Ask yourself: "Are there areas of service in our church or community where we could serve God together?" Here are some ideas:

- Be hospitable. Invite a new couple from church, or a neighbor, to come for dinner. You might be surprised to know how many individuals and couples are looking for Christian friendships.

- Get involved in your church's youth group. Most need role models and mentors for their young people. Ask the youth leader whether you can host a movie night for teens in your home.
- Work in the church nursery. Some people joke that this is good birth control for young couples. But caring for babies could help you determine whether your marriage is ready for children or not.
- Volunteer to work at a soup kitchen or community center.
- Get involved with a local AIDS outreach program. Drivers are often needed to transport HIV-positive children for treatment at children's hospitals.
- Check your local newspaper for a list of community volunteer opportunities.

There are ample opportunities to serve together. Simply decide on one project together and get busy!

4. *Don't overdo it.* Yes, the needs are great. But your needs as a recently married couple are important, too.

Feelings of closeness can be built as you serve together. Still, new marriages need "down time." This is for simply being together—talking, holding each other, serving one another, and building intimacy. As you serve together, don't let even a good thing rob you of the bonding time your relationship requires.

—Mitch Temple

What If My Spouse Seems to Be Losing His or Her Faith?

Chuck had been an engineer at an automotive manufacturing company for four years. Because of declining auto sales, his company announced layoffs. Within six weeks, Chuck was without a job.

It wasn't just a job to him, though. He'd dreamed for many years of working with a major corporation and designing auto parts. He'd looked forward to going into work every day and watching concepts come to life on his computer screen. Now the dream had come to an end.

Stuck at home, he had to force himself to look for a job. He was irritable, moody, and hypersensitive to everything his wife, Tara, said or did.

Chuck began to change in other ways, too.

He no longer cared about going to Sunday school. He stopped meeting with his men's accountability group every Tuesday morning. He seemed to always be asleep or watching television when the time came for the nightly prayer he and Tara usually shared before bed.

> Chuck stopped meeting with his men's accountability group every Tuesday morning. He seemed to always be asleep or watching television when the time came for the nightly prayer he and Tara usually shared before bed.

Tara could see a pattern: Chuck seemed to be losing his faith. His self-esteem was tied to his job; when the job went away, so did his sense of worth and his faith.

Tara began to worry that the downward trend in Chuck's spiritual life was only going to get worse. She felt powerless to help.

Maybe something similar has happened to your spouse. Perhaps he or she has recently lost a job, a parent, or another close relative. Perhaps a close friend committed suicide. Maybe a church leader was discovered having an affair with a coworker.

Whatever the crisis, the probability is high that it will negatively affect your mate's faith. At times like these we question why something like this could have happened; we wonder why God would allow such tragedy in our lives. When we can't rationalize or explain it, we may doubt whether the energy and commitment we put into this "faith thing" is really worth it.

The strongest belief can be weakened through prolonged, painful experiences. Elijah is an example of this in 1 Kings 18–19. The prophet had recently displayed great faith on Mount Carmel, only to hear that wicked Queen Jezebel had vowed to kill him.

Almost immediately Elijah was overwhelmed with fear. He began to lose his faith. He ran for his life until he was completely exhausted, and even prayed that he would die.

Elijah's thinking became so distorted and his emotions so tattered that he felt he was the only one left in the world who was trying to stand for God's cause. He felt alone, rejected, and let down by his people and his God.

> We wonder why God would allow such tragedy in our lives. When we can't rationalize or explain it, we may doubt whether the energy and commitment we put into this "faith thing" is really worth it.

While Elijah lay in this state of depression and despondency, God went to work to restore the prophet's faith.

How? The answers shed light on how you can help your struggling spouse.

1. *God restored a sense of safety for Elijah.* The Lord sent one of His highest-ranking angels to protect the prophet. This sent Elijah a signal: "I care about you, and I am here with you."

Any low point in your life has a way of creating intense vulnerability. It can leave you feeling alone and hopeless. If your spouse seems to be losing his or her faith, he or she may feel that God is far away, uninvolved, uncaring—or even nonexistent.

Assure your spouse that even though things look bleak and it may be hard to sense God's presence, He is there and He is working. He knows when to speak and move and when to be silent and still. Both approaches can work for our good when we're struggling.

How can you support your spouse in this way? Here are some examples:

• Write your mate a daily note of encouragement. Each day, focus on a different aspect of hope. This might be an e-mail, postcard, or sticky note. It doesn't have to be long or preachy. A simple message like, "Everything will be okay, and I love you," is often enough.

- Remind your spouse that he or she is not alone. Affirm that you'll always take those wedding vows seriously: "For better or for worse, for richer, for poorer, in sickness and in health." Point out that Jesus has made the same kind of promise: "And surely I am with you always, to the very end of the age" (Matthew 28:20).
- Let your mate know you're praying that God will protect him or her and restore his or her joy and hope.
- Gently remind your spouse of times when it seemed God was absent, but later it was clear He'd been present. For example: "Honey, remember when your best friend, Allan, died in the car accident, and how alone you felt? You wondered why God seemed so distant and quiet. You said you learned some things by reading the Bible and talking to Mr. Morgan at church. Maybe that's something you'd like to try again."
- Be honest about your concern. You might say something like, "I love you so much and know you're going through a tough time. I'm really concerned about your faith right now. Would you mind talking about it? What can I do to help you?"
- If your spouse exhibits such signs of depression as lethargy, insomnia, sleeping too much, loss of appetite, or a strong sense of hopelessness, encourage him or her to see a doctor or counselor. Depression can stand in the way of responding to encouragement, teaching, and direction.

> ✑
> Write your mate a daily note of encouragement. A simple message like, "Everything will be okay, and I love you," is often enough.
> ✑

2. *God provided what Elijah needed to restore his strength and perspective.* The Lord sent ravens with bread and water. When issues like stress, physical weakness, illness, and lack of sleep enter the picture, they can affect your mate's emotional outlook and ability to see things as they really are. When this happens for an extended period, the result can be despair concerning oneself, others, and God.

Here are some steps toward helping your spouse regain strength and perspective:

- Encourage your spouse to get the proper amount of sleep. Crisis has a way of robbing one's ability to rest; it can also sap one's motivation to get out of bed at all.

- Promote the idea of eating properly—not too much and not too little. Sound nutrition is vital in restoring health, both physical and mental. These in turn support good spiritual health.

- Do what you can to maintain habits like exercising, hobbies, service, church activities, and Bible reading. Even if your mate doesn't always feel like it, encourage him or her to remain active in these areas.

> Sometimes it's difficult to say the things your partner needs to hear, especially when it involves something as sensitive and personal as faith. This is especially true when you haven't been married very long.

3. *God reminded Elijah who he was as a person and what his purpose in life was.* He also reminded Elijah about Himself. God listened to Elijah's cries of pain, but also worked to realign the man's thinking.

When trouble comes, it's easy to forget that we're here for a purpose. Part of God's plan involves being faithful no matter what; difficulty isn't a license to give up. "Be faithful, even to the point of death, and I will give you the crown of life" (Revelation 2:10).

Despite suffering and disappointment, God is still God. And nothing can separate us from His love (see Romans 8).

Preaching this message to a doubting spouse may not help. But you can make it easier for him or her to be open to God's reminders. Here are a few suggestions:

- Listen to your spouse as God listened to Elijah. Let your spouse know that you really want to hear what's going on inside him or her. Expressing those feelings has value in itself. Furthermore, if you listen to your spouse when you don't agree with what he or she says, your words of guidance are more likely to be heard.

- Help your spouse find a mentor. Sometimes it's difficult to say the things your partner needs to hear, especially when it involves something as sensitive and personal as faith. This is especially true when you haven't been married very long. If you don't feel equipped to do this, encourage your spouse to talk to your pastor or an older brother or sister in Christ.

- Encourage your spouse to read books that address faith struggles, like *Where Is God When It Hurts?* by Philip Yancey (Zondervan, 2002),

The Case for Christ by Lee Strobel (Zondervan, 1998), and *When God Doesn't Make Sense* by Dr. James Dobson (Tyndale, 1997). Attend a conference together that teaches people how to rebuild their faith. The Navigators is one organization that offers faith renewal retreats. Ask your pastor for advice on books, Web sites, and conferences designed to reinforce belief.

As uncomfortable as you may feel in talking with your spouse about this issue, it's important. God held Elijah accountable while creating an environment in which his faith could be rebuilt. When it comes to helping your spouse with doubts, He expects nothing less.

—MITCH TEMPLE

What If My Spouse Isn't a Christian?

Let's say you've made a personal commitment to follow Christ. Your mate hasn't. The two of you clash over a variety of issues—whether to go to church or go skiing, what to tell your kids about God, whether to follow biblical guidelines on everything from drinking alcohol to donating money to caring for your parents.

What should you do?

In some respects, you need to treat your spouse as you would if he or she were a believer. If you're the husband, you're to love your wife as Christ loved the church and gave Himself for it (Ephesians 5:25). If you're the wife, you're to treat your mate with respect as the head of the house (Ephesians 5:22-23).

In fact, precisely because your spouse is not a Christian, it's especially important to demonstrate daily what a Christian is. Your purpose: to attract him or her to a relationship with the Lord.

Paul the apostle advises that as the believer in the marriage, you're to go the extra mile: "If any brother has a wife who is not a believer and she is willing to live with him, he must not divorce her. And if a woman has a husband who is not a believer and he is willing to live with her, she must not divorce him. . . . How do you know, wife, whether you will save your husband? Or, how do you know, husband, whether you will save your wife?" (1 Corinthians 7:12-13, 16).

> You live in two different worlds. You've made yourself subject to God's authority in decision making; your partner hasn't.

In other words, the first priority is your spouse's spiritual welfare—not your own comfort level. Paul also implies that your choices affect the spiritual state of your children, if any (1 Corinthians 7:14). This is no time for a selfish decision.

Does this mean it will be easy for you to live with a nonbelieving spouse? On the contrary—it's usually difficult and demanding.

Why? Because you live in two different worlds. Not only do you experience the normal differences between the sexes, but your views are informed by the teachings of Scripture and the presence of the Holy Spirit in you. You've made yourself subject to God's authority in decision making; your partner hasn't. This causes a severe "disconnect" between the two of you.

Trying to explain to a non-Christian spouse your deepest spiritual insights and feelings is like trying to explain what red is to a person who's been completely color blind from birth. You're speaking a language that probably sounds like pure gibberish. In 2 Corinthians 6:14 Paul asks the question this way: "What fellowship can light have with darkness?"

That was true of Seth and Carol. They were wildly in love at age 19. Strongly attracted to each other, they didn't realize what a major role hormones played in this magnetic response.

They didn't discuss spiritual issues much. Carol had attended church as a child, but the idea of a personal relationship with God was foreign to her. She assumed she would go to heaven because she was basically a "good person."

Seth had received Christ as Savior at age 13 in a summer camp, but drifted away from church during his teen years. His commitment was shallow and lukewarm, but he considered himself a believer.

Once the two of them married, few spiritual concerns surfaced—until Seth wanted to regularly attend an evangelical church.

Carol wasn't interested; the church was too "strong," she said. She resented his insistence that they become more involved. She also had no enthusiasm for his idea of praying with her and doing Bible studies together.

> Don't nag your spouse to "get right with the Lord" (which may seem like Greek to him or her), to go to church, or to read tons of good Christian books. If your mate is to be won, it will more likely be through your love, respect, and quiet example.

One day Carol came home from work and announced that she "wanted out." Her explanation: She didn't feel she was in love with Seth anymore.

He suggested they see a Christian marriage counselor. Carol, seeing no point in this, moved out.

Soon the suspicions Seth had harbored for some time proved to be true. Carol had been carrying on an affair with a coworker, who now promised to divorce his wife and marry her.

Your own marriage may not be undergoing such a total "disconnect." But if you and your spouse don't share a common faith, chances are that there's trouble in your marital paradise.

Perhaps you married someone you knew or suspected didn't have a personal relationship with Christ. You told yourself this would be the exception to the biblical rule; you'd "fix" him or her after you were married. Instead, you've found you can't argue that person into the Kingdom. The more you try, the more resistance you encounter.

Or maybe neither of you knew the Lord before getting married. Then you became a Christian and your partner didn't. Now you're seeing how great a gulf that can open in your relationship.

In some situations, like that of Seth and Carol, it seems virtually impossible to continue a marriage. Wedding vows are broken by adultery with no repentance, or the nonbelieving spouse abandons the Christian mate—by physically moving out or deliberately making married life a living hell of physical, verbal, or emotional abuse.

In such cases, Christians are instructed as follows: "But if the unbeliever leaves, let him do so. A believing man or woman is not bound in such circumstances; God has called us to live in peace" (1 Corinthians 7:15).

Frequently, though, the nonbelieving spouse is content to remain in the marriage. If this is your situation, consider the idea that God has given you a "mission" in your own home.

This is not a "preaching mission," however. Don't nag your spouse to "get right with the Lord" (which may seem like Greek to him or her), to go to church, or to read tons of good Christian books. If your mate is to be won, it will more likely be through your love, respect, and quiet example of what a Christian really looks like. In no other situation is it truer that actions speak louder than words.

> Look for ways to sincerely affirm his or her good qualities. In some areas your spouse may be more mature than you are.

Don't concentrate on your spouse's spiritual deficits. Look for ways to sincerely affirm his or her good qualities. In some areas your spouse may be more mature than you are; it's good to acknowledge that.

You'll also need a prayer partner or group of believing friends who'll encourage you and pray for your spouse and your marriage.

Keep talking with God about your situation. Many have had the joy of seeing a spouse come to know Christ—but sometimes only after years of patient prayer.

—Phillip J. Swihart

**Part 9:
In-laws**

What Do I Owe My In-laws?

That's an interesting question. Another way to phrase it might be, "As a son-in-law or daughter-in-law, what's required of me? What are my obligations, whether I feel like it or not, in relating to my spouse's parents?"

Put this way, it doesn't sound like a very warm or relaxed relationship. It sounds more like your in-laws are a burden in your life. Perhaps you feel caught between trying to please them (or trying to avoid offending them) on the one hand, and just wanting to be yourself or wanting your own "space" on the other.

The first principle that applies here is that, if you're a Christian, you owe your in-laws behavior that's consistently Christian in character—as you do anyone else. This doesn't ignore the reality that if your in-laws are "difficult" people, are controlling and manipulative, are emotionally or mentally dysfunctional, or don't share your faith, this may be a particularly hard challenge. The problem is that they're not just anyone. They're connected to your spouse through genetics, history, and complex psychological dynamics.

> If you're a Christian, you owe your in-laws behavior that's consistently Christian in character—as you do anyone else.

If you have disagreements with your in-laws, your spouse may feel caught in the middle between parents and you. You, meanwhile, have obligations to in-laws and spouse—and children, if you have any.

If you feel your in-laws are intruding into your married life, the old saying, "Good fences make good neighbors," may apply. In concert with your mate, set reasonable boundaries; ask that he or she firmly and kindly insist that your in-laws respect these limits.

For example, in Herb's family, relatives just "drop in" for visits, not bothering to call in advance. Tina finds this upsetting and unacceptable. She doesn't want to be rude to her in-laws, but feels increasing resentment toward them—and toward Herb for not "doing something about it."

So far she's tried to be a "good Christian wife" by letting anger and frustration build while she puts on her best hostess smile. Instead, she needs to sit down with Herb and put the issue on the table.

Herb and Tina need to agree that he will explain to his parents that he and

Tina prefer to be asked in advance about visits. The couple should also agree on how many parental visits per week or month would be welcome—and Herb should communicate this, too.

If Herb's parents are mature, they'll respect the feelings of their daughter-in-law and son. If they're not so grown-up, they may take offense. They may even choose to pout for a while, perhaps offering cold shoulders to show their displeasure.

You may not even like them, but you need to choose to act in a loving manner toward them.

Herb and Tina would be making a big mistake if they let his parents divide them, or force Herb to "choose up sides," or manipulate the couple with false guilt into backing down. And once the boundaries have been communicated clearly, it's essential that Herb and Tina not let the in-laws ignore or violate those limits with impunity.

"Honoring" one's parents (Exodus 20:12) does require showing them patience, kindness, gentleness, and respect. This applies to in-laws, too. You may not even like them, but you need to choose to act in a loving manner toward them. For instance, you might choose to adopt their tradition of having an Easter egg hunt, despite the fact that you don't want your kids to think the Easter bunny is real. Enjoying the family event is possible, even if you follow it with a reminder to the children about the real meaning of the holiday.

When you married, you also became part of another family with its own set of expectations. You need to recognize and respect those—within limits.

What are those limits? Here are three things that "honoring" your in-laws does *not* mean:

- It doesn't require that you submerge all your own feelings, desires, preferences, and needs in the service of "doing things their way."
- It doesn't mean you must permit them to disrespect, control, or manipulate you for their own selfish ends.
- It doesn't entail "obeying" all their "parental" requests or requirements—which, in some instances with some in-laws, may get pretty crazy.

For example, if Herb's parents were to insist that Tina and Herb go on every family vacation with them, like it or not, it would be emotionally pathological and ultimately toxic for Herb and Tina's relationship. Sometimes the most honoring response is to diplomatically but firmly say, "No." Letting in-laws split, manipulate, or control you by silently acceding to their nutty, neurotic, inappropriate demands isn't necessarily showing Christian love.

In-law conflicts grow more complicated when a spouse seems to side with his or her parents and against his or her mate. The mate may rightly feel outnumbered or "ganged up on."

This isn't so much an in-law problem as a marital one. If one spouse remains too dependent upon his or her parents, that needs to be addressed in a straightforward way. If one spouse is blaming the in-laws for a disagreement the couple is experiencing, that should be dealt with, too.

> When you married, you also became part of another family with its own set of expectations. You need to recognize and respect those—within limits.

If you've become engaged in a quiet (or not so quiet) war with your in-laws—and maybe also with your spouse—about these tangled issues, don't let it erode your marriage further. Do the healthy thing and seek out a Christian therapist.

—PHILLIP J. SWIHART

How Should We Handle the Holidays?

How have you dealt with special days like Christmas, Thanksgiving, Fourth of July, Easter, Memorial Day, and birthdays? Most of us might think only in terms of the way we grew up, perhaps with Mom and Dad, and expect these occasions to be celebrated the same way.

The only problem, now that you're married, is *whose* mom and dad's celebration of the holidays you're going to adopt. An added challenge confronts blended families, who may have a host of combinations of relationships and traditions to consider.

One husband and wife, like many others, found themselves in a quandary. Where should they go for Thanksgiving? In an effort to respect the desires of both sets of parents and a grandmother, they ended up rushing from house to house. The result: They didn't enjoy the food *or* the time together.

Sometimes practical considerations minimize this conflict. If family members live far apart, the question of where to spend the holidays may be answered when travel costs are taken into account. Often, though, the solutions aren't quite so clear.

Premarital counseling may be the best place to start addressing this question; it's frequently covered in that setting. Whether you discussed this important area of family relationships before you were married or are just now beginning to deal with it, here are some key concepts that can help you decide how and where to spend your holidays.

1. Sit down with your spouse and share—orally and in writing—how each of you feels about holidays and how they're spent. Include major national holidays, birthdays, anniversaries, and other occasions that are special to you. If it's your family's tradition to take a drive to see the changing autumn leaves, for instance, don't hesitate to mention it. The same goes for marking the start of fishing season, the last day of school, or the Super Bowl.

> In an effort to respect the desires of both sets of parents and a grandmother, they ended up rushing from house to house. The result: They didn't enjoy the food or the time together.

2. Explain how you spent the holidays as a child. Which aspects did you enjoy? Which would you like to change? If the two of you were raised in different countries or cultures, what holidays could you learn more about? For example, a spouse who grew up in England might not realize the significance of Thanksgiving and Independence Day to a mate who was raised in the U.S.

3. Consider how your parents and other relatives may wish to have you involved. Perhaps a Christmas Eve service together is important to the wife's parents, while Christmas dinner is central to the husband's. Try to be open to the desires of family members—but not controlled by them.

4. Agree on how you as a couple would like to establish your own holiday traditions. Work for balance and fairness. For example, you might decide to spend Christmas morning with your parents and Christmas evening with your spouse's (if both live close by). The following year you might spend the whole day at home as a couple—or, if you have children, with them.

5. Be open to changing your plan as needed. Flexibility and variation can help to avoid hard feelings when the in-laws' expectations aren't met. For instance, you might invite relatives to gather at your place instead of agonizing over which ones to visit. You might even take a vacation during the holidays to add variety and break the cycle of expectations.

> Explain how you spent the holidays as a child. Which aspects did you enjoy? Which would you like to change?

Despite the usefulness of these steps, holiday observances still can be an emotional minefield for couples and in-laws. Here are some cautions to keep in mind.

1. It may be a lot easier for you and your spouse to change what you want for the holidays than for parents to adjust what's been important to them for many years. Share openly with them some of your ideas and hopes for holiday times, letting them know that you value being with them. One young husband and wife, always expected to be at the wife's parents' house for Thanksgiving, ran into a potential problem when they received tickets and hotel accommodations for a November football championship at the husband's college. By sharing both the excitement of the opportunity and the disappointment of missing the family time, the couple poured oil on what could have been troubled waters.

2. Develop realistic expectations of how the holidays should be spent. Wishful thinking generally leads to hurt feelings and disappointments. Personality differences, physical limitations, and philosophical disagreements don't

disappear just because a particular date on the calendar has arrived. On the contrary, these factors often become more pronounced under stress—and most holidays provide plenty of that.

3. Holiday gift-giving can be a source of conflict and hurt. While it's better to give than receive (Acts 20:35), most people seem to prefer a balance of the two. Exchanging presents can easily get out of hand, creating hardship for family members who can't afford the expense. Try creative options. For example, you might give Christmas or birthday gifts to immediate family members, exchange names for other relatives, or give single gifts to family units.

Try to be open to the desires of family members—but not controlled by them.

There may be no specific right and wrong ways for families to spend the holidays together, but there could be better ways for you to approach holiday traditions and expectations. To keep those days worth celebrating, remember these tips:

- Aim to make holiday times enjoyable and memorable.
- Balance the development of your own traditions with those of the homes you came from.
- Keep the focus on time spent together rather than amount of money spent.
- Invite Christ to be your honored guest in all your plans and celebrations.

—WILFORD WOOTEN

How Can I Cut My Spouse's Apron Strings?

"Julie, you'll never believe it!" exclaimed Susan. "Tom wants his parents to come live with us!"

"Whoa, Susan," Julie replied. "Slow down. Tell me what exactly is going on here. What did Tom say?"

Susan took a deep breath. "Well, the other night we were talking about our finances, and the kids, and how things are really tight right now. He thought it would be a good idea for his parents to move in with us to share some of the expenses. Maybe we could even charge them rent, or the kids could stay with them instead of going to day care. Julie, I just can't believe it!"

> "Oh, yeah," Susan said with sarcasm. "We have a real problem with the 'leave and cleave' thing."

Julie wondered why Susan was so upset. After all, having extended families live together wasn't exactly a new idea. "In Bible days, multiple generations lived together all the time," Julie said. "Just because we don't usually do it here, I don't quite understand why you're so freaked out."

The resentment in Susan's voice was clear. "Well, it would be just one more way for his mom and dad to try to influence our decisions."

"Oh! The issue is about boundaries and leaving and cleaving."

"Oh, yeah," Susan said with sarcasm. "We have a real problem with the 'leave and cleave' thing."

Susan and Tom aren't the only couple to have a problem in this area. Genesis 2:24 says, "For this reason a man will leave his father and mother and be united to his wife, and they will become one flesh." The King James Version calls being united "cleaving." This refers to God's invention of a unique bond between husband and wife that's not to be compromised by their relationship with their parents.

Does this mean that we cut ourselves off from our families of origin? Not if they're reasonably healthy. Maintaining relationships with our parents usually is beneficial. But problems arise if factors like the following are present:

- One spouse relies too heavily on the parents to help in decisionmaking, leading the other spouse to feel insignificant.
- One spouse looks to the parent, not the partner, to get his or her emotional needs met, leading the partner to feel ignored.
- One spouse reveals details of marital conflict with his or her parents, leading the other spouse to feel betrayed.

Let's take a closer look at these and what you can do about them.

1. *Decision-making dysfunction.* Couples need the freedom and autonomy to make their own decisions. Some parents are better than others in this area; many wait for their adult children to ask for advice, but others try to inject unsolicited wisdom. The latter are often deeply caring people who want the best for their children, but their behavior communicates a lack of respect and trust in the judgment of their child and his or her spouse.

Family history can make this difficult water to navigate. Some spouses are used to asking their parents for direction; others make decisions more independently. If you and your mate have different habits on this score, conflict may result.

If you're frustrated because your spouse consults with his or her parents on decisions more than you'd like, the two of you need to work through this issue. If you feel threatened by your spouse's behavior, share that diplomatically but honestly. Talk about how the two of you would like decision making to work. Would you prefer that the two of you make choices without getting input from either set of parents? Are there some decisions you'd ask one set of parents about, but not the other?

Be aware that asking for parents' advice can be a slippery slope. It may leave them feeling the door is open for them to give you input into other areas, or even to "correct" decisions you've already made.

> Asking for parents' advice can be a slippery slope. It may leave them feeling the door is open for them to give you input into other areas, or even to "correct" decisions you've already made.

Credit each other and your in-laws with goodwill toward your marriage unless they've demonstrated otherwise. Sadly, some in-laws don't seem to have a vested interest in the success of their child's marriage. If this is true of you, you and your mate may want to recommit yourselves to "leaving and cleaving." You may also need to seek professional advice to determine how best to establish and maintain appropriate boundaries with your in-laws.

2. *Emotional apron strings.* If your spouse gets his or her emotional needs met in his or her relationship with parents instead of with you, there's a problem. You may even feel as if your spouse is having an affair.

Sometimes this problem begins when a wife feels frustrated over her husband's seeming lack of interest in conversing about her day; she starts talking with her parents instead. Sometimes the husband is the frustrated one; it's common for mother and son to have long or frequent conversations that leave the wife feeling ignored. Neither scenario is appropriate.

Respect for each other is the key. In this situation, respect might require that the spouse maintaining an overly close relationship with his or her parents will decrease that contact in order to show love for the spouse. For example, a son whose mother is too close might say, "Mom, let's limit our conversations to once a week about general things." Or he may simply make the change himself, explaining it only if his mother asks him about it. In either case he would do well to save discussions of his goals

> A son whose mother is too close might say, "Mom, let's limit our conversations to once a week about general things." Or he may simply make the change himself, explaining it only if his mother asks him about it.

and disappointments for times with his wife; these are the things that build intimacy in a marriage.

This is not to suggest that children and parents should cut off their relationship under the guise of leaving and cleaving. But your primary human relationship now is with your spouse, not your parents. Your commitment to God comes first; then your bond to your spouse, then to any children you might have, then to your family of origin, and then to extended family and friends.

3. *Betrayal.* It's a common story: After a fight with his or her mate, a spouse goes "home to mother" or calls the parents on the phone and spills the details.

This is detrimental to a marriage. It communicates disrespect to your spouse and makes it hard for the parents to maintain a healthy relationship with him or her.

Even if you and your spouse reconcile within hours or days after your argument, family members may not know that. They might carry that memory of the fight you had, have a hard time believing that everything is okay, and remain suspicious of your partner.

Expecting parents to referee your conflicts isn't realistic or wise. It would be hard for them to be objective about your marriage. The best thing they can do when you come to them in the midst of an argument is to send you home to work it out.

One exception would be conflict that involves violence. Getting to safety is the first priority. Taking time to be apart and see your parents can give you an opportunity to think and establish a plan to repair the marriage. It's not helpful to just go home to Mom and Dad to vent, however.

If you have an "apron strings" problem in your marriage, keep the following tips in mind as you talk with your spouse about it.

1. Pray for wisdom and insight about what to say and how to say it.

2. Tread lightly when it comes to criticizing your in-laws. Your spouse knows more negative things about his or her parents than you do, whether or not they're expressed. Even repeating a complaint your spouse has made about his or her parents could be taken as an offense by your mate.

3. Approach your spouse when you're both rested, fed, and healthy. Right before falling asleep at night is not a good time to have this conversation.

4. Remember that you're a team. Because you're committed to each other, you can work through this even if you don't agree on the details—like your in-laws' intent, how to best meet your spouse's needs, or exact limits to place on parent-child conversations.

If parents need to be confronted or informed, agree that their own child—not the son- or daughter-in-law—will do the talking.

5. If parents need to be confronted or informed, agree that their own child—not the son- or daughter-in-law—will do the talking. Protecting your marriage is a priority; the newest addition to the family doesn't need another reason to be dissected by in-laws. Each spouse needs to know that he or she will be protected by the other, even if husband and wife disagree and the in-laws are meddlesome.

If, after following these steps, you and your spouse are at an impasse about your in-laws, get the objective input of a therapist.

Leaving and cleaving is tricky, but doable. The love and respect you communicate to each other when you value your marriage over your relationship with your parents are essential.

After Susan and Julie talked, Susan realized why she felt threatened by the idea of her in-laws moving into her home. It was because she believed her mother-in-law wanted more contact with Tom than Susan was comfortable with.

As Susan and Tom talked about it, she became less defensive. Tom was able to listen more easily and understand her heart. In turn, his own heart softened. He began to evaluate how much time he spent with his mom—and what he could do about those apron strings.

—SANDRA LUNDBERG

What If the In-laws Aren't Christians?

If you have a relationship with Jesus Christ, you probably long for your family and friends to have one, too. If your in-laws haven't chosen to follow Christ, what should you do? How can you accomplish the often difficult tasks of living out your faith, sharing it with those you love, and maintaining meaningful relationships with them?

One couple, married for three years, recently had become Christians. They faced a dilemma—wanting to spend time with their non-Christian parents without participating in behaviors like drinking alcohol and gambling.

The husband and wife met with their parents, making it clear that they valued the relationship and wanted to spend meaningful time together. They worked out alternate activities that all of them could accept and enjoy.

That couldn't have been an easy conversation to start. But it was worth the effort.

As that couple found, there are ways to work out such differences respectfully and without withdrawing or preaching. As you face this challenge, consider the following principles for responding in a God-honoring way to in-laws who aren't Christians.

1. *Pray for them.* "If you believe, you will receive whatever you ask for in prayer" (Matthew 21:22).

Hudson Taylor is credited with the statement, "When we work, we work. When we pray, God works." It's no small thing to put God to work in the lives of family members who aren't yet Christians. Keep bringing them before the Lord and asking Him for wisdom about how to touch their lives.

2. *Beware of having a critical or judgmental attitude.* "Do not judge, or you too will be judged. For in the same way you judge others, you will be judged, and with the measure you use, it will be measured to you" (Matthew 7:1-2). "Stop judging by mere appearances, and make a right judgment" (John 7:24).

> How can you accomplish the often difficult tasks of living out your faith, sharing it with those you love, and maintaining meaningful relationships with them?

Judging the behavior of in-laws is one of the surest ways to push them away from God and church activities. Instead, we're commanded to love one another (John 13:34).

3. *Be open and real about your own faith.* "But in your hearts set apart Christ as Lord. Always be prepared to give an answer to everyone who asks you to give the reason for the hope that you have. But do this with gentleness and respect" (1 Peter 3:15).

It's possible to be clear and candid about your values and principles while caring deeply for and being respectful to your in-laws. It also allows God to work in their hearts.

> One couple faced a dilemma—wanting to spend time with their non-Christian parents without participating in behaviors like drinking alcohol and gambling.

The importance of prayer in relating to non-Christian in-laws can't be overemphasized. Ask God to help you respond in love and wisdom.

If your in-laws continue to resist the good news about Jesus, you may wonder whether prayer really makes a difference. Consider the story of a staff member at Focus on the Family who ran into a woman at church with whom she'd been close friends in high school. The staff member, who hadn't seen the woman in many years, asked what she was doing in church.

"I recently have accepted Christ as my Lord and Savior," she answered.

Pleasantly surprised, the staff member said, "Call my mother!"

"Why?" the woman asked.

"Please, just call her."

The woman did as she was asked. Upon reaching the staff member's mother, she explained that she'd become a Christian.

The elderly lady shouted with joy.

What followed revealed a remarkable act of love and obedience. "When you were close friends with my daughter," the older woman said, "the Lord impressed upon my heart to pray for you especially. I have done this every day for the last 50 years!"

Never stop praying for those you want to come to the Lord—never!

In addition to prayer, here are some do's and don'ts for relating to in-laws who aren't Christians:

Do . . .

• Ask God for wisdom to share your faith with them.

- Look for opportunities to invite them to spiritual activities and special events at church.
- Give thanks at mealtimes when in-laws are in your home.
- Bring up topics that relate to values and faith.
- Offer to pray for them during times of illness, sorrow, and concern.
- Take part in activities they enjoy, as long as those activities don't cause you to compromise your own convictions.

Don't . . .

- Push your faith on them when they make it clear they're not interested.
- Criticize their more "secular" celebrations or traditions.
- Complain about things they value or hold dear.

It's no small thing to put God to work in the lives of family members who aren't yet Christians. Keep bringing them before the Lord and asking Him for wisdom about how to touch their lives.

One Christian husband and wife with non-Christian parents made a crucial decision early in their marriage. It served as an anchor for their future relationship with their parents. The decision: that they would intentionally love and accept and pray for their parents.

That couple has developed positive relationships with both sets of unbelieving moms and dads. Their decision has a lot to do with it.

You can make that kind of choice, too. Purposely loving, being kind to, and understanding your in-laws who aren't Christians shrinks conflict and can draw them in God's direction. It also honors your heavenly Father.

—WILFORD WOOTEN

What If an In-law Tries to Run Our Lives?

Savannah cringed at the sound of the phone. Her mother called at least once every day. Sometimes she'd talk for an hour.

Listening was hard enough. But managing the questions was harder.

"How's Jimmy treating you?"

"Are you going to finish your degree before you have babies?"

"Why don't you two come visit our church instead of going to that 'contemporary worship center'? Why, they don't even have a steeple!"

"When are you going to try that diet book I got you for Christmas?"

Savannah's husband, Jimmy, had made it clear that he'd had enough of her mother calling and getting her upset. "You have got to stand up and be an adult," he'd said the last time. "I'm tired of seeing you hurt under her thumb, and I'm ready to be married to an adult instead of a child."

But to Savannah, the thought of opening that can of worms seemed a lot worse than the slow trickle of torture she got in the daily phone calls.

Savannah and Jimmy probably would agree that relating to a controlling in-law is one of the trickiest problems a marriage can face. Some might even say that God offers preemptive advice on the topic—by directing us to leave our father and mother and "cleave" to our spouse (see Genesis 2:24, KJV).

How do predicaments like these happen?

Since we no longer have a traditional rite of passage in which a young person officially enters adulthood, marriage often ends up serving that role by default. Sometimes, though, even marriage doesn't trigger an appropriate emotional separation from a parent.

If parent and adult child are enmeshed in an unhealthy way, there can be runners of that vine throughout the marriage—gradually choking it to death. A prime example: the married daughter who still allowed her mother to balance her and her husband's joint checking account!

It helps if both sets of parents give the new couple their blessing—thereby affirming the newlyweds' independence. While this may seem

>
> If parent and child are enmeshed in an unhealthy way, there can be runners of that vine throughout the marriage—gradually choking it to death.

unnecessary with today's career-delayed first marriages and blended second or third marriages, it's a valuable gift for any husband and wife.

If you believe an in-law is trying to run your life, consider how the following principles might help.

1. *Honor—but don't necessarily obey.* Scripture directs us to honor parents (Deuteronomy 5:16; Matthew 15:4). Their wisdom, years of sacrifice, and role in the family are reasons to respect them in our hearts and our actions.

> "You have got to stand up and be an adult," Jimmy had said the last time. "I'm tired of seeing you hurt under her thumb, and I'm ready to be married to an adult instead of a child."

Obeying parents, however, is clearly time-limited. If we're still trying to obey Mom and Dad, we're not leaving them and cleaving to our spouse. While it may be difficult to defy their spoken or unspoken wishes, there may be times when it's necessary.

Take, for example, the question of where to live. Some parents attempt inappropriate—though sometimes well-meaning—control over their adult children in this area. Promises of houses or land ("Adjoining ours, of course!") or simply taking the children hostage emotionally ("You can't move our grandchildren away from us!") can result in significant generational strain. This and other issues must be dealt with quickly and directly, lest the marriage suffer the consequences.

2. *Maintain mutual respect.* Healthy parents have many opportunities to do this. Decisions about grandchildren, finances, careers, and many other important issues are chances to honor adult children's autonomy.

The need for respect goes both ways, of course. Healthy sons- and daughters-in-law attend responsibly to their new duties, making sure issues like money and child care aren't dumped in their parents' laps—on purpose or by default.

Sometimes spouses need to ask for their parents' respect—even if it's uncomfortable to do so. If a controlling parent is sharing private information without permission, raging verbally, or otherwise acting inappropriately, it's up to the adult children to ask the parent to observe safe relational boundaries.

3. *Check your assumptions.* Especially when a first child marries, it's common for all involved to have immature expectations. Visions of "one big happy family" can quickly turn to disillusionment, as each generation operates from its own perspective.

Assumptions lead to misunderstandings. Parents shouldn't assume that because they've always liked a particular brand of car, their kids will want to buy the same. Husbands and wives shouldn't assume Mom and Dad will do all the cooking at Thanksgiving.

4. *Be open to mediation.* When things break down on either side of the generation gap, a third party may be helpful. While not trying to provoke a feud, spouses should solidly back each other and respond as a team. Mediation should be God-honoring and principle-centered, and should support the marriage.

For mild or short-term conflict, one side might let the other choose a trusted minister or other third party that all can agree on. In the case of more complex, severe, or ongoing conflict, the services of a professional counselor will be valuable.

Some participants may see mediation as embarrassing or meddlesome. Encourage them to view it as a chance to cooperate for the good of the entire family. If total agreement isn't reached, that's okay; the goal isn't a merger of the generations, but a partnership between them.

> Relating to a controlling in-law is one of the trickiest problems a marriage can face.

Dealing respectfully but firmly with a controlling in-law takes fortitude, especially on the part of the son or daughter whose parent is the offender. That was the case the next time Savannah's mother called with another interrogation.

Swallowing the acid that threatened to eat through her esophagus, Savannah thought through the words she'd practiced so many times. This time she would say them.

"Mom," she interrupted, "when you call and say these things it makes me very stressed. I need for you to not call unless you can be pleasant and appropriate. I'm an adult now. My marriage, education, family planning, church attendance, and weight are not your concern anymore."

There. She'd said it.

She waited for a response, afraid she might faint. When there was no sound from her obviously stunned mother, she continued, "I'm going to hang up now. In a few days, when you've had a chance to think about what I said, I'll call you and we can discuss it like adults if you're ready. I love you. Good-bye."

The next step was up to Mom. But Savannah had taken an important one toward a healthier family dynamic.

—ROB JACKSON

What If an In-law Doesn't Accept Me?

Heather and Steve have been married almost four years. They love each other very much, but relationships with their in-laws have always been strained.

Heather feels Steve's mother is overly critical of how Heather parents the children. She also gets upset over her mother-in-law's statements about how Steve works much too hard; she sees them as attacks on her choice to be a stay-at-home mom.

Steve has great difficulty connecting with his father-in-law, who seems to live for sports. When Steve and Heather visit his in-laws, Steve is especially disturbed to see Heather share her father's sports mania—leaving Steve feeling like an outsider.

It's normal to want to be accepted by your in-laws. But feeling that you *need* to be accepted can bring complications, causing you to be uncomfortable and unnatural around them.

Unrealistic hopes cause problems, too. Many parents are initially over-protective of their own child, or have expectations that no spouse can meet in the beginning.

Often new husbands and wives assume they'll be loved and accepted by in-laws on the merit of having married the in-laws' child. This may be the case, but it usually takes time to establish trust and respect. Just as it takes time to build other close relationships, gaining acceptance into a family doesn't happen instantly.

After all, you're stepping into a family with a long history of established bonds. Don't be too hard on yourself and expect too much. If your relationship with your own parents is wonderful, the one with your mother- and father-in-law may never measure up. If your relationship with your parents isn't good, you may be too needy and demanding in trying to make up for it.

The number-one factor in resolving problems of acceptance by in-laws is

Just as it takes time to build other close relationships, gaining acceptance into a family doesn't happen instantly. Don't be too hard on yourself and expect too much.

your spouse's support. As with all close relationships, it's an art to support your spouse without jumping into the fight or feeding his or her discontent.

Let's say that Heather and Steve have just returned from an extended visit with his parents. She declares: "I never want to stay with your parents again! Why doesn't your mother like me? She told me that she had you potty trained by age two and that you obeyed her without question."

In this case, Heather is being a little overdramatic and overly sensitive. How can Steve support her without reinforcing her exaggeration or condemning his mom?

He could say something like this: "Honey, I'm so sorry that you feel hurt by the things my mom says. But I know you're a terrific mother, and she'll come to see that, too. She also seems to remember me as much more perfect than I was. I can remember plenty of frustration and grief, but it's probably good that she doesn't remember all the tough times. I'll always support you in finding a time to share your feelings with my mom. I really think she likes you and can't help but love you as time goes on."

> The number-one factor in resolving problems of acceptance is your spouse's support. It's an art to support your spouse without jumping into the fight or feeding his or her discontent.

Or imagine that Steve has the complaint. "I don't want to spend more than one day at your parents' house ever again," he says. "I always feel like a third wheel. I know your dad hates the fact that I don't enjoy sports. You and he seem to be in your own little 'sports world.' What am I supposed to do, spend my time helping your mom in the kitchen?"

Heather might respond by reassuring Steve along these lines: "I'm so sorry that I haven't been more sensitive to your feelings of being left out during those times. You're right—sports has been the major thing dad and I share. I know even Mom has felt a little left out when we obsess about it. Let's see if we can think of ways to connect when we're at my parents—all of us, including my mom. I know my dad primarily cares how I'm loved and taken care of, and there's no question about those things in my mind. Please give me a little sign if I forget it next time."

When it comes to dealing with an in-law who doesn't seem to accept you, here are the main principles to remember:

- Learn to support your spouse without getting hooked into taking sides.
- Encourage your spouse to share his or her feelings directly with you.
- Keep a sense of humor.

- Show your spouse that he or she is number one in your eyes.
- Don't take things too personally.
- Remember, building a relationship takes time.
- Forgive, forgive, forgive.
- Remember that you're loving your spouse by honoring his or her parents.

One more idea: When confronted with what feels like a no-win situation involving an in-law, use the "drop the rope" theory. Imagine a rope, the kind used in a tug-of-war. If you find yourself provoked, see that rope in your hands. You can choose to continue yanking on it—or drop it. Dropping it may sound as though you're giving in or giving up, but it's actually very empowering. It's also much more effective than tugging back and forth.

For Steve and Heather, a solution may look something like this:

- They discuss the things their in-laws say and do that tend to trigger anxiety and anger.
- They agree to act as "buffers" for each other against possible hard spots.
- They commit to forgiving any offense quickly.
- They plan to give the relationships time to develop.
- They start working as a team.
- They can even see some humor in learning to drop those "invisible ropes."

As a result, each of them feels more loved and supported. That helps them enjoy getting to know and appreciate each other's parents.

—ROMIE HURLEY

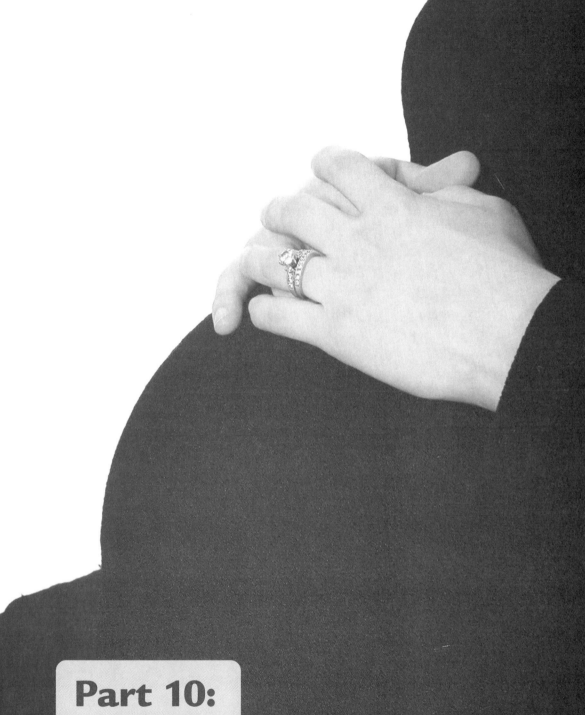

**Part 10:
Children**

Do Children Really Change Everything?

"I haven't slept one night in a year and a half," says a mom to a newly pregnant friend. "But I wouldn't change it for anything." She smiles and sighs wearily.

"*No*," says the mom-to-be, disbelieving. "You *had* to have slept through the night *some* time in there. And you get naps during the day, right?"

She just doesn't understand—yet.

Children really do change your life.

First comes the blur of infancy, then the vexations and victories of potty training. Before you know it you're trying to save for college. The new car and corporate ladder-climb are sacrificed for braces and soccer practice.

Whether it's trading sushi for macaroni and cheese or driving to piano lessons for the five hundredth time, you can't help noticing some alterations when you have children. They're a blessing from God, and it's an honor and privilege to have the responsibility of raising them—but your life will never be the same.

So how will you deal with the changes? Are they so unpleasant that you should abandon any plans to reproduce?

Here are some suggestions that may help to buffer the shocks of parenthood.

1. *Be prepared to adjust your assumptions.* Some parents-to-be talk about how they're going to take their kids with them wherever they go. You can try this approach with an infant or a somewhat older child, but much parenting experience shows that children do better with a routine. If you've assumed that your baby simply will tag along as you follow your usual schedule, you may have to think again. This may be a time in your lives when you have to give up some of your usual activities in order to provide the structure that your small children need.

2. *Be prepared to make sacrifices.* The truth is that you'll lose some of your freedoms if you choose to be parents. Most parents find the joys of parenting well worth the sacrifices of redirecting time, money, and energy into their children's lives, but the costs are still quite real.

If you or your spouse can't picture yourselves making

Whether it's trading sushi for macaroni and cheese or driving to piano lessons for the five hundredth time, your life will never be the same.

these sacrifices, right now may not be the time to have children. It's one thing to be realistic about the costs of parenting. It's altogether different to resent your child because you have to make those sacrifices.

3. *Be prepared to work harder at your relationship.* You and your mate will need to adjust your expectations and be intentional about connecting. Just as your child grows through developmental stages, you'll grow as a couple.

You won't know exactly how your expectations will have to change until your first child arrives. It's a sure thing, though, that if you've been dating, socializing, and hanging out for hours with friends, you'll need to adjust your timing and plan for child care. You'll still need these outlets, especially dating each other—but they will be different. You may want to start thinking now about creative ways to locate babysitters. For example, you might find yourself becoming closer friends with other new parents with whom you can exchange child care.

What should you do during those deliberate dates? If tight finances put movies and restaurants out of reach, try window-shopping, hiking, or coffee at the kitchen table. The most important thing is that you're together—and that you don't spend the whole time talking about the baby.

4. *Be prepared to see each other at your worst.* Since the wedding, you've probably started to see some self-centeredness in yourself and in your spouse. When the two of you are required to fill the stressful roles of parents *and* spouses 24/7/365, you'll see a lot more of these tendencies.

How can you get ready for that? Choose now to consider your spouse's needs as more important than your own (Philippians 2:3-4).

5. *Be prepared to lose sleep.* When your children are infants, they depend on you to meet every need. For some parents, that means getting up several times a night.

During this stage of parenting, both of you are likely to be sleep deprived. This can hamper your ability to communicate, among other things. Watch for ways in which resulting misunderstandings can erode your relationship.

6. *Be prepared to feel conflicted.* Sometimes you'll feel torn. For example, you may have mixed emotions about leaving for work if you're employed outside the

>
> Some parents-to-be talk about how they're going to take their kids with them wherever they go. If you've assumed that your baby simply will tag along as you follow your usual schedule, you may have to think again.

home. You won't want to leave your little one and miss the new things he or she will do today while you're gone. Yet your workplace may hold attractions of its own; it's more familiar, you don't have to sort through what your baby's cries mean, and you certainly need to earn a living.

7. *Be prepared for things to get easier—eventually.* The demands of parenting change throughout a child's life span. As he or she gets older, sleeping through the night may become more common. But there will still be interruptions: calls to help a little one go to the potty, calls from a first slumber party when your child wants to come home, calls from a date that's gone awry and requires you to pick your child up.

> Be prepared to see each other at your worst. When the two of you are required to fill the stressful roles of parents and spouses, you'll see a lot more self-centeredness.

Parenting will never be stress-free. But most parents see the challenges as well worth it. They take satisfaction in watching their children grow and change, encouraging them to know and serve the Lord, and developing an adult-to-adult friendship with them.

So, do children change everything? Absolutely!

Is parenthood worth it to most couples? Yes!

Children will change you, your spouse, and your marriage. But it doesn't have to be for the worse. Making your marriage a priority is a gift to your kids. Knowing that Mom and Dad are committed to each other for the long haul provides them with the security every child needs.

—Sandra Lundberg

When Should We Have Children, and How Many?

The obvious answer for the Christian couple is, "After you've gotten married!"

That's not very specific, is it? Still, it may be the only point of agreement you'll find on this subject.

God told Adam and Eve, "Be fruitful and increase in number" (Genesis 1:28). Children are a gift from God, and the fulfillment of His plan for married couples who are able to give birth to them.

But what about timing and numbers? Many Christian couples marry and bring children into the world just as soon as God allows. Others, no less committed to God's will for their lives, wait until they complete their formal educations or professional training. Quite a few seek to achieve a certain level of economic stability before having their families.

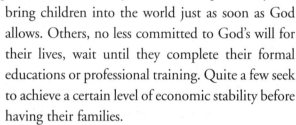

During the first five years of their marriage, this event repeated itself quite regularly. By their fifth anniversary Celeste was expecting baby number four.

Jerry and Celeste were a couple who, seeing God as the "author and provider" of children, felt He could best decide when to bring some into their home.

Celeste wanted a larger-than-average family, and prayed that Jerry would be open to that possibility. She was thrilled when Jerry agreed to use natural family planning techniques, and to trust "God's timing."

Before long, Celeste found herself expecting baby number one. Jerry was beside himself with glee. He'd never given a great deal of thought to becoming a family man until he and Celeste talked about it, and now it was happening. They couldn't have been happier.

During the first five years of their marriage, this event repeated itself quite regularly. By their fifth anniversary Celeste was expecting baby number four. She and Jerry saw each baby as God's blessing for their family.

Fortunately, Jerry's business ventures went well. He and Celeste continued to increase the size of their home. By their tenth anniversary they had six children. They didn't see the size of their family as anything but normal. Many of their friends had large families, too. God had indeed blessed them.

Bart and Margaret, on the other hand, believed that planning for their children's arrival was simply good stewardship. They wanted their marriage and finances to be grounded enough to handle the additional responsibilities that childrearing brings, and felt that carefully spacing their offspring would best allow for emotional and fiscal balance.

Bart had finished graduate school and had a good job. He and Margaret had bought their first home and were finding their places in the community and church. Four years into their marriage, they decided to try for their first child.

Margaret had a job, too, and liked it. She didn't want to leave it altogether. Bart, meanwhile, was expecting her to be home full-time with their child. *After all*, he thought, *we've been planning this for four years, and we want to do it right.*

> As some couples discover the hard way, it's important that both spouses agree on when to have children and how many.

When their daughter arrived, Margaret decided that she loved being a mother and didn't want to leave her baby in anyone else's care if she could avoid it. At the same time, she didn't want to abandon her career entirely. So she arranged work part-time from home as long as her boss would allow.

Bart and Margaret also planned to try again in a couple of years for a brother or sister, not wanting their daughter to be an only child. That would be it, they decided; two children would be best for their family.

As some couples discover the hard way, it's important that both spouses agree on when to have children and how many. No one can be completely prepared for child-rearing, but it's best if both partners are as emotionally ready as possible.

Leon was a music teacher and choral director; Brandy was a school social worker. Both were in their thirties. Brandy had decided that 10 years in the professional world were enough, and she wanted to become a mother.

When they talked about having a baby, Brandy was more willing than Leon to modify their budget and lifestyle. Leon had hoped to keep his "freedom" during summer months and school vacations, and to be involved in projects like the two short-term mission trips he'd taken. Parenthood might put a crimp in those plans.

As they discussed the idea of Brandy resigning her job, it became clear that Leon wasn't emotionally ready to start a family, even though the two of them had been married for nearly four years.

Brandy was shocked. She asked her husband exactly what she was thinking: "Why would I ever choose not to have my own children? Women in the Bible considered that a curse."

Diplomatic or not, that remark was a wake-up call for Leon. He realized that the challenges of accepting his wife's feelings—and being willing to modify his own—were really part of being a Christian husband. It didn't happen immediately, but as they talked to family and friends about Brandy's yearning to become a mom, Leon decided that he, too, wanted to start a family.

Ten years later, he reflected on what had happened next. He'd become a school administrator, a field he probably wouldn't have moved into if he and Brandy hadn't started planning for a child. And they had eight-year-old Kara, bright and beautiful, with whom both of them were thrilled.

> Spacing children depends more on the parents' emotional and economic stability than on an arbitrary number of years between kids.

Not every couple can choose whether and when to have children, of course. Those who are infertile but want children know the pain that childlessness can represent. For those couples and others adoption is still an option, and many have made that decision happily.

If you face choices about the timing of having children and the number you'd like to have, here are some principles to keep in mind.

1. Children need to be born into secure homes with loving parents.

2. If God permits couples to be fertile, bearing children according to the dictates of their consciences is in accordance with Scripture—and should be by mutual agreement.

3. Spacing children depends more on the parents' emotional and economic stability than on an arbitrary number of years between kids. Consider your emotional steadiness as well as your budget. Has either of you struggled with depression or chronic anger problems? Is either of you a recovering alcoholic or drug addict with potential for relapse?

4. Children need your time. Are you committed to frequent business travel or generally overcommitted to your job? If so, you need to reconsider your lifestyle before becoming a parent.

5. Postponing parenthood has a price. As couples put off childbearing, they often discover that it's harder to conceive—and the chances of miscarrying

increase.[1] Female fertility generally declines with age, starting in a woman's late twenties.[2] The likelihood of having a baby shrinks by 3 to 5 percent each year after age 30, and more than that after 40.[3]

6. Making good decisions takes wisdom. God offers it to those who ask (James 1:5), so don't forget to pray about your procreation plans.

—LON ADAMS

Postponing parenthood has a price. As couples put off childbearing, they often discover that it's harder to conceive—and the chances of miscarrying increase.

Is It Okay Not to Have Kids?

"A growing trend among young couples is to rethink the whole parenting thing," says Steve Watters, Director of Family Formation at Focus on the Family. "Unlike their parents, who often moved into the parenting season with little hesitation, couples now often ask, 'What if we don't want to have kids?'

"As Christians, it's important to consider our motivations. What is behind those kinds of sentiments? While some couples are excited and motivated to have kids, others don't feel a natural tug—and when friends and relatives ask them about kids, they're not quite sure what to say. They can see many natural benefits of *not* having children—cost savings, ability to pursue interesting work options, ability to travel, etc. Other parents may be frightened by the pain and hardship of childbirth, or feel like they just can't fit children into their current financial situation."

> "A growing trend among young couples is to rethink the whole parenting thing. Couples now often ask, 'What if we don't want to have kids?'"

Are you considering deliberately not having children? Maybe you're asking yourself questions like these:

"Is it selfish not to have children?"

"What if we think we don't have the money or the energy?"

One Christian therapist notes that in more than 25 years of marriage and family counseling, he's never had to convince anyone to have children. Still, in recent generations Western thinking has shifted, accepting an attitude of ambivalence toward children or an outright dismissal of parenthood. Couples are not only marrying later in life, thus abbreviating the childbearing years; they're choosing not to factor children into their relationship at all.

Some two-career households have elected to wait on having children—or skip it altogether—so that full attention can be given to their jobs.

Carson and June, for example, made it clear that they would get their socioeconomic status settled before having kids. June was a sales rep; Carson was starting his own software design company. Neither felt any particular emotional tug about starting a family.

Their travel-filled lives didn't seem to leave any room for talking about having kids. The more successful they became, the less time they seemed to have.

On a tenth anniversary trip to South America, they finally discussed whether they would ever try to start a family. Both agreed that finding sitters for their house and dog was hard enough. Maybe they'd have time for kids someday—but not now.

Are Carson and June choosing wisely?

Biblically speaking, we can't ignore the fact that God considers parenthood an incredible blessing. As Psalm 127:3 says, "Sons are a heritage from the LORD, children a reward from him." Even more striking is the silence of Scripture with regard to a chosen state of childlessness. It doesn't appear that the Bible ever envisioned married couples who denied themselves children. On the contrary, Genesis 1:28 declares, "Be fruitful and increase in number; fill the earth and subdue it."

The current tendency to ignore or dilute that command demonstrates a rejection of God's design for humanity. From the beginning of time, in most cases adulthood meant marriage and marriage meant children; in most circumstances, today's couples should carry on that pattern and look toward a future that includes children.

Certainly there are medical conditions that prevent childbearing. Encouraging couples to have children is not meant to imply that those who suffer the pain of infertility are less obedient to God or less valued by Him.

There are also conditions that pose genetic risks. Those with a family history of a hereditary illness might choose not to bear children, perhaps deciding on adoption instead. Julie, for instance, is being treated for bipolar disorder. She believes it's hereditary. She and her husband, Stan, are praying about the wisdom of producing their own kids versus the possibility of adoption.

If you struggle with this issue, make sure you have all the information you need. Get genetic counseling from a specialist who can tell you what the risks really are.

For most couples, however, medical concerns don't play a major role. Preserving a lifestyle or standard of living is more likely to be an issue.

Some couples, for instance, are convinced that kids are just too expensive. If that's your objection, ask yourself questions like these: "How do other people

> Finding sitters for their house and dog was hard enough. Maybe they'd have time for kids someday—but not now.

afford children? Do I need to trust God to provide for our family? Am I simply refusing to alter my own financial goals? If we really can't afford children now, might that change?"

If you're just guessing that children are beyond your budget, get the facts. A good financial planner could tell you how much it costs to raise kids, and may be able to help you come up with a plan to raise the money as well.

Other couples want to avoid the messiness of infants and toddlers. As one woman wrote, "I have a Christian friend who's married and absolutely loathes small children. The thought of changing a diaper is disgusting to her. She will probably never have children even though she's found the man she wants to spend the rest of her life with."[1]

No doubt about it: Parenting is inconvenient. Hesitations about starting a family are understandable. The responsibilities of parenthood can't be taken lightly, and there's no denying that children will bring major changes to your marriage and your individual lives. But the difficulties associated with rearing children aren't reason enough to choose childlessness.

Children bring a new dimension of joy and fulfillment to a marriage that can't be found elsewhere. Parenthood ushers in a spiritual transformation that we might otherwise forgo; it forces us to look outside ourselves and act sacrificially for the benefit of another.

Self-sacrifice isn't the only fear that makes couples wary of having kids, of course. Some husbands and wives, knowing their flaws or those of their own parents, are afraid they'll make a mistake that could misshape their children's lives.

Carson's growing-up years had left him and his sister emotionally scarred. His parents had divorced when he was 12. Fearing that could happen to him and June, he didn't want to hurt children the way he'd been hurt. Besides, with his temper, what kind of dad would he make?

No parent is perfect, and children can learn from our weaknesses as well as our strengths. If you have abusive tendencies or a family history you're afraid you'll repeat, let a counselor help you. But if you're waiting to "get your act together" 100 percent, you'll wait forever.

There are many factors involved in family planning, but the most impor-

>
> We can't ignore the fact that God considers parenthood an incredible blessing. As Psalm 127:3 says, "Sons are a heritage from the LORD, children a reward from him."
>

tant aspect of parenthood may be this: God gives wisdom and guidance to those who seek His help, and most parents agree that with the Lord to support them the joys of parenthood far outweigh the trials.

God is the One who ultimately gives children. Be sure to consult Him in prayer; may His blessings rest on you as you look to Him for direction.

—Lon Adams

> God gives wisdom and guidance to those who seek His help, and most parents agree that with the Lord to support them the joys of parenthood far outweigh the trials.

What If I Want Children, But My Spouse Doesn't?

Todd and Amanda were having *that* argument—again.

"I'm just not sure I'm ready to be a father!" Todd protested. "And I don't know if I can provide for a family."

"Todd, there's never going to be a perfect time for us to have kids. We need to look at starting our family now."

"We've always talked about you staying home if we have kids," Todd said. "We're spending more than we're making with *both* of us working. I just don't see how we can do it."

> "I'm just not sure I'm ready to be a father!" Todd protested. "And I don't know if I can provide for a family."

"Well, let's take another look at the budget and see what we can cut," Amanda countered. "We can try living on just your income for a few months and saving mine."

"We tried that. We couldn't pull it off."

"But this time I'm really committed."

Todd tried a different approach. "Well, what about the kind of parents we'd be? I mean, we don't want me to be like my dad."

"You're not like your dad."

"I might turn out to be."

And so it went—again.

Todd and Amanda may not be handling their conflict very well, but they're asking some important questions. When one spouse wants to start a family and the other doesn't, it's vital to work through that disagreement and find a way to proceed that's comfortable for both of you.

How do you work it through? Here are some suggestions.

1. *Realize that men and women approach this issue differently.* Many wives talk about the "ticking" of their "biological clock." This has different meanings for different women. Some are describing their longing for a cuddly infant, a longing they feel every time they see a baby and are reminded of the fact that they're not pregnant. Other women are concerned about their age and fertility.

Husbands, meanwhile, tend to have other concerns. They may be reluctant to have children because they're worried about providing for the family financially—or about what kind of fathers they'll be.

That's not to say men are always the reluctant ones. A wife might be concerned about finances or about how she'd care for the baby. She may fear the death of her career, or the possibility that her freedom to stay home with the baby will be a huge strain on her husband, or that her body won't stand up to the changes and stresses of pregnancy.

2. *Remember that "not now" doesn't always mean "never."* There's a big difference between wanting to have a baby and wanting to have a baby *now*. This may not be the best time; it certainly isn't if your spouse isn't comfortable with it.

If you're concerned that waiting may cause problems with fertility due to your age, talk with your physician—and then with your spouse. It's better to approach your mate with information, not just emotion.

> Many wives talk about the "ticking" of their "biological clock." Some are describing their longing for a cuddly infant. Other women are concerned about their age and fertility.

3. *Don't pressure your spouse.* Avoid placing undue pressure on an uncertain partner. To assert, "If you loved me, you'd change you mind," is a sophomoric argument. This is a lifelong commitment for both of you; playing emotional games over the creation of a new life is not the answer.

Pressure can actually make the problem worse. A spouse may say, "No, I don't want kids," in order to avoid further prodding and questions he or she can't answer.

4. *Don't deceive your spouse.* Respect each other and seek honest agreement. Do *not* surprise your spouse with a pregnancy by sabotaging the contraceptives. Parenting is far too important for deceptive behavior to be part of it.

If having children continues to be your desire, keep praying and talking about it. Given time, your spouse may have a change of heart. Instead of manipulating, trust God for the outcome.

5. *Act on accurate information.* Some reluctant spouses are worried about passing on a genetic problem. If this is the case with yours, both of you should meet with a specialist. Ask your doctor to refer you. The specialist can evaluate your families' medical histories and often can test to determine the likelihood of passing on a disorder. Then you can make a prayerful decision based on the most complete information available.

Be aware, however, that any genetic counseling you receive will have a margin of error. Ask the specialist about rates of false positive and false negative test results. We can plan and predict, but we can't control. Only God can do that.

6. *Aim patiently for consensus.* A "no" right now is not necessarily permanent. But it may take time to get to "yes."

Consider this analogy. Let's say you want to have sex tonight and your spouse doesn't. If he or she says, "Not right now, Honey, I'm really tired and stressed," would it be a good idea to say, "It's now or never"?

> Avoid placing undue pressure on an uncertain partner. This is a lifelong commitment for both of you; playing emotional games over the creation of a new life is not the answer.

With patience, you soon may find your spouse taking you up on your offer. You may have to bring it up when he or she is more receptive. Or the two of you might set a date in the not-too-distant future.

So it is with starting a family. You don't want to coerce your spouse into having a child; you want him or her to be an eager participant. If you're not jointly committed to this, you need to wait.

In the case of Todd and Amanda, they kept talking about becoming parents. They agreed that Todd's biggest reservations centered on finances and being a poor role model. So they took action in both areas.

On the financial front, they decided that for one year they'd live on Todd's income and save Amanda's. They put her pay in a separate account so they'd be less tempted to spend it.

During that year they also read four books on becoming parents and developed friendships with two couples who had children. Todd and Amanda babysat for the other couples and saw how exhausting—and what a joy—it can be to care for little ones.

By the end of the year Amanda and Todd felt much better prepared to have children themselves. They didn't have *that* argument anymore. And even Todd looked forward to parenting as the next stage of their lives.

—SANDRA LUNDBERG

Why Can't We Have Children?

Maybe you feel like Rachel when she cried, "Give me children, or I'll die!" (Genesis 30:1). If you've been trying unsuccessfully to have children, it's easy to have that outlook. You may also feel uncertain, wondering when you should begin to worry about the inability to conceive.

"I can't go to one more baby shower!" Sara cried to her husband, Josh. "It's too heartbreaking for me. I always end up leaving in tears."

Sara and Josh, both in their early thirties, had waited to have children until they were established in their careers. Now they were ready. But after six months of trying, nothing was happening.

They were full of questions. Were they doing something incorrectly? Was God punishing them?

> "I feel like God is mad at us. Many women who don't even want children become mothers."

Sara especially was struck by the unfairness of it all. An emergency room nurse, she'd observed many unwanted pregnancies of mothers who seemed unfit. She'd seen babies born addicted to their mother's drug of choice. "I feel like God is mad at us," she told Josh. "I feel abandoned by Him. Many women who don't even *want* children become mothers. I don't understand why God doesn't want us to have a child when we'd love and care for the baby. Our child would be *very* wanted."

When you struggle with infertility, you face many emotional issues. Here are some of the feelings you and your spouse may encounter.

1. *Grief.* If you want to conceive but are unable to, you'll experience grief over the loss of the dreams you've had for your future children. Allow yourself to feel the grief and deal with the pain by admitting you're sad. Talk it through with someone you trust. Let yourself cry. It usually helps to verbally express the immense hurt you feel.

2. *Anger.* This is a valid emotion when dealing with grief. You may wonder why God seems not to listen to your pleas for a child. You're mad that He hasn't intervened and answered your requests.

This is a natural response, and God is aware of your anger. He's the One who created you with the desire for a child in the first place. Express your frustration to the Lord, to your spouse, and to a counselor if needed. Accept the comfort and support of others.

3. *Low self-esteem.* You may begin to feel that you're defective, that you're less of a woman or man because you can't conceive. Seek a proper perspective on your value in God's eyes. You might want to start by reading passages like Matthew 10:29-31 and Psalm 139:13-16.

4. *Loneliness.* If you don't want to be around pregnant women, go to baby showers, or answer questions about why you and your spouse don't have children, you may find yourself feeling isolated. Joining a support group for couples dealing with infertility and sharing your heartache with them can be a healing experience.

One place to locate such groups is www.bethany.org/step. This Web site, presented by Stepping Stones, Bethany Christian Services' ministry to infertile couples, lists local support groups. You can find secular groups through RESOLVE, a national infertility support organization with local chapters, at www.resolve.org.

Uncertainty is another emotion common to couples struggling with infertility, especially in the early stages. If, like Sara and Josh, you've only recently started trying to conceive, it may still be a matter of time—and timing. Here are a few things a couple can try at home to maximize the likelihood of conception.

> God is the One who created you with the desire for a child in the first place. Express your frustration to Him, to your spouse, and to a counselor if needed.

1. *Identify your most fertile time of month.* One way to do this is with an ovulation predictor test, available in drugstores. This over-the-counter kit, which has a high degree of accuracy if used correctly, is a seven-day urine test. It signals when ovulation—the time when a woman is most likely to conceive—is probably about to occur.

A Basal Body Temperature (BBT) chart is another way to track ovulation. Available from a doctor, a drugstore, or online, this chart and a specially calibrated thermometer are used over a span of several months to discover the wife's ovulation pattern. This indicates when intercourse should occur for the best chance of conception.

Still another indicator of ovulation is the condition of the wife's cervical mucus. This substance changes when female reproductive hormones start to cycle in the body. The wife may usually notice thick, sticky, opaque mucus—or none at all—when wiping away urine. Just before ovulation the mucus turns clearer and more watery, stringy and resembling egg whites. This generally indicates that she will soon ovulate.

2. *Take care of your body.* For the wife, being obese or too thin makes it harder to conceive. A healthy body before pregnancy increases the likelihood of conception—and makes for an easier pregnancy if one occurs. This means nutritious eating, consistent exercise, and getting seven to eight hours of sleep per night.

3. *Reduce stress.* While it's not true that you'll conceive if you "just relax," stress can hinder the process. It can affect a man's ability to "perform"; it can even affect a woman's ability to conceive.

> While it's not true that you'll conceive if you "just relax," stress can hinder the process. Stop putting pressure on yourselves.

Stop putting pressure on yourselves. You may need to take time out from "trying" for a while and just enjoy being a couple.

In most cases, if you've tried for one year without conceiving, it's time to seek medical treatment. Find out what the problem is and what your options are. For most couples, infertility can be treated.

If it turns out that you and your spouse are unable to have a baby, it will take time to reach a point of acceptance. It will mean understanding that God is real, that He is there, that He understands, and that He is not punishing you. If needed, a pastor or Christian counselor can help you on this leg of the journey.

You may have sad days and angry days along the way. But there is hope for joy and contentment again as you and your spouse learn to enjoy the life God has given you. It may mean making new plans—perhaps adoption, or redefining yourselves as a family of two. Either way, deciding whether to believe that your heavenly Father truly wants the best for both of you is a choice that's in your hands.

—Sheryl DeWitt

How Can a Doctor Help Us Conceive?

"Kevin thinks I'm being overly anxious about getting pregnant," Shelly told her doctor. "But we've been trying for three years. He says we're young and have plenty of time ahead of us. But what if something is wrong?"

Shelly's doctor sent her to see an infertility specialist. The diagnosis: endometriosis.

After treatment, Shelly and Kevin tried again. Eighteen months later they had baby Jonathan.

The chances that they would have conceived without treatment: very slim.

If you've consistently tried to conceive for a year without success, seek medical help. A couple struggling with infertility needs to see an infertility specialist.

But what should you look for in this person?

If you've consistently tried to conceive for a year without success, seek medical help. A couple struggling with infertility needs to see an infertility specialist.

- If possible, find an obstetrician/gynecologist who is board-certified in the subspecialty of reproductive endocrinology. If you choose an ob/gyn who is not board-certified in reproductive endocrinology, ask about his or her specialized training and experience.
- Expect a plan of action and a time frame for the treatment.
- Since infertility treatment can be stressful, find a doctor who understands the emotional pain and treats patients with compassion.
- You'll need a good communicator. Be sure you feel free to ask questions; hold out for honest answers.
- Both spouses need to feel comfortable with the doctor. Do you and your mate like and feel safe with him or her?

In addition, a recommendation from a trusted friend may be valuable.

One wife, Melissa, reported, "My infertility doctor answered all our questions and became like one of our family. He assured us that less than 5 percent of infertility is untreatable. He told us what the problem was and what our options were. . . . We felt very hopeless, and he continued to encourage us and give us a sense of hope. He had pictures of all the babies he delivered after their parents dealt with infertility. His emotional support was as important to us as the medical help."

That's the kind of physician you want.

What will the specialist do?

He or she will want to know your medical histories—including use of alcohol or other drugs, miscarriages, abortions, significant weight gains or losses, and diseases (sexually transmitted and otherwise).

If both partners have a clean bill of health, the doctor will perform infertility tests. There are separate tests for men and women.

For the husband, this includes semen analysis. Semen is evaluated for count (number of sperm cells), morphology (shape of those cells), and motility (ability of the cells to travel). A normal semen analysis shows results of over 20 million sperm per cubic centimeter, 30 percent with normal shape and 50 percent showing normal forward movement. Lower numbers may indicate reproductive problems.

For the wife, several tests can be performed to determine the health of the ovaries and uterus. In an endometrial biopsy, the uterine lining is evaluated. Laparoscopy, an outpatient surgical procedure, is used to better view the reproductive organs and can be used to remove existing scar tissue. Imaging studies, such as ultrasound, may also be used to evaluate possible causes of infertility.

Depending on the outcome of the tests, your doctor may suggest further action to help with conception.

For the husband, these could include medication to increase sperm production, surgery to correct a problem such as a varicose vein on the scrotum that may have increased scrotal temperature enough to lower the sperm count, or sperm washing—a procedure in which sperm are gathered, cleaned, concentrated, and used to inseminate the wife. The doctor may also recommend that the husband wear boxer shorts and avoid hot tubs, since overheating the genital area inhibits sperm production.

Since infertility treatment can be stressful, find a doctor who understands the emotional pain and treats patients with compassion.

For the wife, fertility drugs may be prescribed. The type of medication depends on the diagnosis. Surgery, such as laparoscopy—a minor abdominal operation that often can correct problems with the uterus, fallopian tubes, or ovaries—may be recommended.

In-vitro fertilization (IVF), involving fertilization of eggs in a laboratory, may also be presented as an option. This is a costly procedure, though, and isn't always successful. There are also moral considerations; some Christians believe IVF is "playing God," while others believe it's acceptable as long as the sperm and egg are from the couple and not from outside donors. For a more complete discussion of assisted reproductive technologies like IVF—and their moral implications—see the book *When the Cradle Is Empty* by John and Sylvia Van Regenmorter (Focus on the Family/Tyndale, 2004). Seek the counsel of your pastor on these issues, and ask God for guidance.

> If both partners have a clean bill of health, the doctor will perform infertility tests. There are separate tests for men and women.

If nothing works, you still have the option of adoption. Adoption isn't a "cure" for infertility, but many couples have discovered that an adopted child is an incredible blessing to a family—just as a biological child would be.

You also have the choice of redefining your household as a family of two. As Helen Keller put it, "When one door of happiness closes, another opens: but we often look so long at the closed door that we do not see the one that has been opened for us."

If having a child is not the next step in your journey, you can use that time to try out your gifts, enjoy your spouse, and discover other meaningful things that life has to offer. God has a plan for you and your mate; begin to pray for direction and the ability to find that fulfillment. As hard as that is, you can choose to believe as the psalmist did, "For the LORD God is a sun and shield; the LORD bestows favor and honor; no good thing does he withhold from those whose walk is blameless" (Psalm 84:11).

—SHERYL DEWITT

What About Adoption?

Most newly married couples plan to have children. They assume that when the time is right, they'll simply put a bit of special effort into promoting the process of conception—and a baby will result. But for some, that doesn't happen. These couples may find themselves asking, "Should we adopt instead?"

Other husbands and wives consider adoption for different reasons. They believe it's better to care for children who are already here and may be unwanted than it is to bring new ones into the world. Or they feel compassion for children orphaned by war, famine, or neglect. Whatever the reasons, they're embarking on a course that can be challenging—and very rewarding.

In their book *When the Cradle Is Empty*, authors John and Sylvia Van Regenmorter warn against adopting for wrong motives like these:

"We will be doing the poor child a favor."

"Our other children will have a playmate."

"We've been through a difficult infertility experience and we deserve a baby."

"Raising a baby will help our marriage."

"Having a baby to love will make me feel completed."[1]

If you've made sure those aren't your reasons, here are some steps you can take to start exploring the subject of adoption.

1. *Process your emotions, but don't expect to resolve every issue.* If you'd expected to have biological children but infertility dashed that dream, you'll need to work through feelings of hurt, disappointment, and loss. It's especially important to recommit to your relationship with your spouse, which now includes the reality that having children biologically is unlikely.

Does that mean you must completely erase all grief and pain before you're qualified to adopt? No. But working through your feelings can lead to a clear-cut, clear-headed decision to accept life without children, or to adopt. If this takes the help of a Christian therapist or pastor, don't hesitate to get it.

2. *Expect uncertainty, but don't let it stop you.* Some couples considering adoption worry that after going through considerable effort, they might find at

> If you'd expected to have biological children but infertility dashed that dream, you'll need to work through feelings of hurt, disappointment, and loss. It's especially important to recommit to your relationship with your spouse.

the last moment that the birth mother is reversing her decision to relinquish the child. It's important to know that there are legal time frames within which this could happen. It's also important to know that reputable adoption agencies work carefully with birth mothers to assure that their rights are protected, *and* that those who are seeking to adopt are dealt with sensitively.

Uncertainty is part of starting every family, whether or not adoption is involved. This concern alone shouldn't prevent you from pursuing adoption.

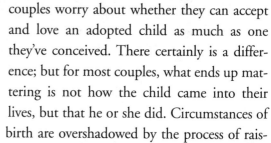

Uncertainty is part of starting every family, whether or not adoption is involved. This concern alone shouldn't prevent you from pursuing adoption.

3. *Believe in your ability to bond.* Some couples worry about whether they can accept and love an adopted child as much as one they've conceived. There certainly is a difference; but for most couples, what ends up mattering is not how the child came into their lives, but that he or she did. Circumstances of birth are overshadowed by the process of raising and caring for a child, loving him or her, helping him or her grow, and passing along values and beliefs.

For the vast majority of adoptive parents, the moment they meet and begin to relate to the child, the bonding begins—just as it does with birth parents.

4. *Don't look for perfection.* The so-called "perfect baby" doesn't exist, and never did—adopted or otherwise. All children have unique personalities and needs.

Children need loving parents who can provide a safe home in which to grow. You'll never locate a flawless child, but finding one who needs you is very achievable.

5. *Be prepared to spend some money.* Adoption costs. Thousands of dollars may be required—especially in the case of foreign adoption, when international travel may be necessary.

Still, the price should not prevent you from pursuing adoption. Many agencies have ways of subsidizing some costs in proportion to your financial resources. Many states in the U.S. have begun to help pay for the care of special-needs children. And to find out whether you might also qualify for an adoption expense tax credit, ask your financial advisor.

6. *Expect to be evaluated, but don't fear it.* Agency-sponsored adoptions require a "home study," which assesses the adoptive family. It's a fairly straightforward process, involving interviews and filling out forms.

It's easy to get anxious about being evaluated. But no one expects you to be perfect. Try to remember that the goal of a home study is to help the agency place children in the families most suited to their needs.

7. *Start gathering information.* Find out about the opportunities available. For example, you'll want to know how "closed" adoptions (the norm in Canada) and "open" adoptions (the norm in the U.S.) differ. The former keep the identities of the relinquishing and adoptive parents legally sealed and unknown to the parties involved, including the adoptee until the age of majority. The latter allow the parties to know each other, often giving the relinquishing mother an active part in selecting the adoptive parents.

> For the vast majority of adoptive parents, the moment they meet and begin to relate to the child, the bonding begins—just as it does with birth parents.

You'll also want to learn about such issues as adopting through public and private agencies, involving an attorney or physician, seeking a younger or older child, adopting children with special physical or emotional needs, choosing kids of your race or another, and domestic versus foreign adoption.

There are many resources and organizations that can help you. Here are a few.

Adoptive Families Magazine
Editorial and advertising offices, 39 West 37th St., 15th Floor, New York, NY 10018
www.adoptivefamilies.com
(646) 366-0830

Bethany Christian Services
901 Eastern Ave. NE, P.O. Box 294, Grand Rapids, MI 49501-0294
www.bethany.org
(800) BETHANY

Holt International Children's Services
P.O. Box 2880, Eugene, OR 97402
www.holtintl.org
(541) 687-2202

National Adoption Information Clearinghouse (NAIC)
Children's Bureau/ACYF
1250 Maryland Ave., SW
Eighth Floor
Washington, DC 20024
http://naic.acf.hhs.gov/
(888) 251-0075

The North American Council on Adoptable Children
970 Raymond Ave., Suite 106, St. Paul, MN 55114
www.nacac.org
(651) 644-3036

8. *Start creating your support network.* Once you've decided that adoption is a good way to form your family, begin sharing that decision with extended family and friends. These people are part of your support system; if you've struggled with infertility, they, too, need time to grieve for you and their expectations for you.

> Children need loving parents who can provide a safe home in which to grow. You'll never locate a flawless child, but finding one who needs you is very achievable.

You'll want and need their support in the future. Telling them how God has been leading you in this decision will help them to make the same transition.

—GAIL SCHRA

How Will Pregnancy Affect Us?

Katie is crying.

Her husband, Josh, thinks, *Not again! What is it this time? Where did my wife go? Where's that happy-go-lucky best friend of mine?*

With trepidation he asks, "Katie, what's wrong?"

"Nothing."

"You're crying. There has to be something."

"It's stupid. I'm just so tired. I want to go hiking with you, but I want to sleep. We never get to spend time together anymore because I'm always sleeping."

Josh manages a chuckle. "Honey, you're blowing this out of proportion. It's okay with me if you take a nap."

"But we never talk anymore," Katie wails.

What's wrong with Katie?

She's pregnant, that's all.

If you're expecting, have a wife who is, or are just thinking about starting a family, you may wonder what it's like to be pregnant. What will it do to you? What will it do to your relationship?

The ups and downs of pregnancy take many couples by surprise. Most people seem to know that the wife's abdomen will swell and that she may crave odd combinations of foods at the most inconvenient times, but what else should you be prepared for? Here are eight things you're likely to face.

> It's not uncommon for a pregnant woman to nap in the evening, get a full night's sleep, and want to go back to dreamland a few hours after awakening.

1. *Differing reactions of husband and wife.* Men and women experience the early stages of pregnancy in their own ways. A wife tends to be more aware of the new life inside, since she's inescapably connected to the baby.

For a husband, this is a mystery. Someone he can't see or feel is dramatically changing his wife and his world. When he hears the baby's heartbeat for the first time or sees an ultrasound image, it's often a turning point if the pregnancy hadn't seemed "real" yet. Now he feels proud of his role in giving life to this child, and his "hunter instincts" may kick in as he gets ready to provide for his family.

2. *Morning sickness.* Nausea may become an issue for the wife, especially during early pregnancy. Each woman and couple has a different experience of this, and you'll have to find your way through it together and with your doctor's help.

Symptoms may be minor, or severe enough to require medical attention. If it helps to eat saltine crackers before getting out of bed in the morning, as it does for many women, the husband can assist by bringing them to the wife's bedside.

3. *Fatigue.* You can't see it, but the wife's body is working very hard. She's likely to need much more sleep than either spouse anticipates. It's not uncommon for a pregnant woman to nap in the evening, get a full night's sleep, and want to go back to dreamland a few hours after awakening.

Use some of these "tired times" to snuggle. The husband may not feel like sleeping, but can talk with and hold the wife as she falls asleep. Eventually you may feel the baby move during these times of closeness.

4. *Mood swings.* Very common for pregnant women, these usually are related to hormonal changes. This can be difficult for husbands to understand. Why is that calm, stable woman sobbing for "no reason" or becoming frustrated and argumentative?

Remember that these changes pass. Give each other the benefit of the doubt. If you're the wife, wait a few hours or even a day before telling your husband why you're upset with him; you may decide it's more about your hormones than his behavior. If you're the husband, try not to take these mood swings personally. Listen to your wife; validate her concerns; let her know you love her and that you'll be there for her and the baby.

Give each other the benefit of the doubt. If you're the wife, wait a few hours or even a day before telling your husband why you're upset with him; you may decide it's more about your hormones than his behavior.

5. *Sleep problems.* These increase as the unborn baby grows. It can become more and more difficult to find a comfortable position in which to sleep.

Ask your doctor about the special pillows designed to help women with this problem. Try a variety of sleeping positions. The husband may find his rest interrupted by a restless wife, or see the "invading" pillows as taking over his space. Work together on this, reminding yourselves that it too will pass. Getting a reasonable night's sleep will help both of you get along during the challenges of pregnancy—and better prepare you for the famously sleepless nights of infant care.

6. *An interrupted sex life.* Your physician is the only one who can accurately advise you about sexual relations during pregnancy. Couples may be instructed not to have sexual intercourse toward the end of pregnancy. In some cases, your doctor may advise against sexual relations at other stages, too.

If your doctor okays sexual intercourse, you and your spouse may have to experiment with different positions in order to find something that's comfortable and workable. If your physician tells you not to have sexual intercourse at any stage of the pregnancy, it's still important for you and your spouse to continue having physical closeness.

> Getting a reasonable night's sleep will help both of you get along during the challenges of pregnancy—and better prepare you for the famously sleepless nights of infant care.

During this time, the two of you may find yourselves talking about physical intimacy in a way that you never have before. If you're the wife, you may need to know you're still attractive to your husband—despite the changes pregnancy brings. If you're the husband, you might feel like avoiding sexual activity even if the doctor okays it, out of concern over hurting your wife or the developing child. (It's worth noting, however, that if intercourse is permitted by your doctor, it's highly unlikely to harm the mother or baby.) Pregnancy can be a vulnerable, scary time for many couples—but talking about these issues can lead to an increased sense of connection and bonding.

7. *Fears about the baby's health.* This is a common experience during pregnancy. It's best to direct questions to your physician—and pray through your concerns. "Do not be anxious about anything, but in everything, by prayer and petition, with thanksgiving, present your requests to God. And the peace of God, which transcends all understanding, will guard your hearts and your minds in Christ Jesus" (Philippians 4:6-7).

Some couples seek to deal with the uncertainties of pregnancy by undergoing tests to determine the health of their unborn baby. Many Christian couples avoid this, however, because a test might inaccurately predict an abnormality or because they might be encouraged to terminate a "problem" pregnancy. Other Christians take the tests in order to prepare for any difficulties the child might have. It's helpful to understand that screening tests are not perfect and do have limitations. The decision of whether to take these tests should be made prayerfully by husband and wife, who need to determine in advance what they would do with the results.

8. *Worries about parenting.* Will you be able to handle your role as a mom or dad? It's normal to wonder whether you're up to the job.

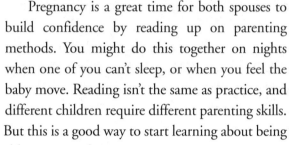

> Will you be able to handle your role as a mom or dad? It's normal to wonder whether you're up to the job.

Pregnancy is a great time for both spouses to build confidence by reading up on parenting methods. You might do this together on nights when one of you can't sleep, or when you feel the baby move. Reading isn't the same as practice, and different children require different parenting skills.

But this is a good way to start learning about being a steward of the little life God has entrusted to you.

Remembering that God designed pregnancy can help you develop a new appreciation of Him as your Father—and as Creator of your child. Pregnancy is a time to grow—in more ways than one.

—SANDRA LUNDBERG

What's Childbirth Really Like?

"I feel so sorry for you," the woman told Jeanne, who was pregnant. "Labor is horrible! It was the most painful experience of my life. I never want to go through that again."

Jeanne groaned inwardly. Why did so many women feel the need to tell her how awful childbirth was, especially when she was just weeks from experiencing it for the first time? She was already terrified; their discouraging comments only made her more nervous.

Most first-time mothers fear labor and delivery. Maybe you've heard horror stories about incredible pain, fainting husbands, and screaming wives. These increase a couple's anxiety, even though the reality of childbirth can be quite different.

Here are some things to remember about that reality.

1. *Labor pain is manageable.* Whether labor is wonderful or an ordeal may depend greatly on the mother's expectations. Uterine contractions *are* painful. But they're manageable.

> Most first-time mothers fear labor and delivery. Maybe you've heard horror stories about incredible pain, fainting husbands, and screaming wives.

Some women, believing the pain of labor detracts from the joy of childbirth, choose to take medication so they can be more relaxed and enjoy giving birth. Others choose not to take painkillers, and manage the pain with breathing and relaxation techniques. Many of them want to experience childbirth without medication that "dulls" the process.

Whatever a woman decides, the pain can be managed because she looks forward to the result of her labor. As Jesus put it, "A woman giving birth to a child has pain because her time has come; but when her baby is born she forgets the anguish because of her joy that a child is born into the world" (John 16:21).

As for those who may inflict childbirth horror stories on you, remember the words of this mom: "I realized labor could not be as bad as other women told me. Many of these moms were moms of multiple children. If labor was as bad as they said, you would think they would stop with only one child."

2. *A C-section is a possibility, not a disaster.* In some cases, a woman is unable to have a vaginal delivery. This can include situations like these:

- the baby is in the "breech" position (feet or buttocks first instead of head first);
- the baby or mother is in physical distress that's potentially harmful;
- the mother's pelvis is too small;
- the mother has *placentia previa* (a condition in which the placenta lies unusually low in the uterus);
- the existence of other health issues such as diabetes or heart disease.

In such cases, the baby may be delivered by Cesarean section (C-section). In this surgical procedure the doctor makes an incision in the mother's lower abdomen and uterus and delivers the baby through this opening. The doctor then repairs the incision. This surgery is not unusual, and is not a reason for panic.

> "I realized labor could not be as bad as other women told me. Many of these moms were moms of multiple children. If labor was as bad as they said, you would think they would stop with only one child."

3. *Don't worry, you'll bond.* Some women fear they won't bond with their babies. Most feel an immediate connection with their newborns; others, due to factors like the exhaustion of a long labor or fear of failure as a parent, don't sense a link right away.

All these feelings are normal. They don't mean that bonding isn't happening. As the woman gains strength and spends time caring for her child, the connection will come. As in any relationship, the more time you spend with a person, the closer you feel.

4. *You can prepare.* The start of contractions may take you by surprise, but there are several ways to make sure you're ready for childbirth. The more you prepare, the more confident you'll feel. Here are some things you can do:

- Attend prenatal classes. These are offered at most hospitals. Led by medical professionals, they teach practically everything you need to know about childbirth—stages of labor, differences in contractions, and breathing and relaxation techniques. Fears are addressed, and learning with other couples encourages mutual support.
- Talk to moms who are positive about their birthing experiences. Patty, nine months pregnant, felt apprehensive about contractions she was

having. "I read about Braxton-Hicks contractions in my birthing book," she said later. "But talking to Shelly, who just had a baby two years ago, has helped more than any book could. She reassured me that the feelings I had were perfectly normal [and] encouraged me that the pain was all part of the process. Knowing I could call her anytime made my labor experience more manageable."

- Write down questions for your doctor. It's common to think of questions after you've left the doctor's office or between visits. Putting them on paper is a great way to make sure you get answers at your next appointment. Being informed helps eliminate anxiety.

> Write down questions for your doctor. Being informed helps eliminate anxiety.

- Pre-pack a suitcase. When it's time to head for the hospital, you don't need the added stress of packing. Because many hospitals allow the husband to spend the night, pack for both spouses. Include pajamas, undergarments, toothbrushes, toothpaste, other hygiene items (shampoo, blow dryer, lotions, hairbrush, makeup, etc.), medicines you're taking, a Bible, camera, extra clothes to change into, and anything else you need to make you comfortable.

- Discuss your anxieties as a couple ahead of time. If you're the wife, are you concerned that you'll yell at your husband during contractions? Many wives do! Talk about the fact that if it happens, it's not because you're angry or your husband isn't doing a good job at coaching you. It's because this is a very emotional time and your concentration is on managing your pain.

If you're the husband, are you worried that you'll fall apart at the sight of blood or at seeing your wife in pain? Talk about it. Let your wife know that you'll be there to support her, despite your nervousness, and that you don't expect to do things perfectly. Discuss other concerns, too—whether to have others in the delivery room, picture taking, and whom to call after the baby arrives.

Childbirth is a miracle that reminds us of our amazing heavenly Father. Watching a little one come into the world is truly one of life's greatest moments. It may seem hard to believe now, but the pain of delivery will soon be outshone by the blessing of meeting your child.

—Sheryl DeWitt

What Can We Do About Postpartum Depression?

Getting depressed after your baby arrives isn't a rare malady. If you're a new mother suffering from this condition, you're hardly alone.

According to Dr. Byron Calhoun, vice chair of the Obstetrics and Gynecology Department at West Virginia University, up to 80 percent of new moms experience the temporary emotional slump of "postpartum blues." A smaller but significant number—10 to 40 percent—fall victim to clinical postpartum depression.

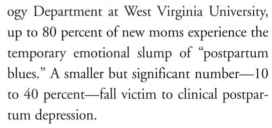

One report indicated that when women with postpartum depression knew "something wasn't right," only about 20 percent actually sought appropriate medical and psychological assistance.

Postpartum psychosis—which sometimes involves behaviors such as hallucinations and delusions—is much less common, occurring after about 1 in 1,000 deliveries.[1] But it has the potential for extremely serious consequences.

The first thing to do about postpartum depression is to recognize its signs. What are they?

- Feelings of sadness, unhappiness, or overwhelming despair just when a mother is "supposed to feel" happy and fulfilled.
- Difficulty sleeping, even when the baby is asleep.
- Loss of appetite or wanting to eat much more than normal, which can lead to significant changes in weight that aren't consistent with pregnancy or birth.
- Fits of crying, seemingly "for no reason."
- Trouble concentrating, with a very short attention span.
- Turning from being even-tempered and easygoing to irritable, chronically angry, or anxious every day.

When the more severe postpartum depression is present, thoughts of suicide or the impulse to harm the baby aren't uncommon. These feelings need to be taken very seriously and reported to a healthcare provider immediately—if not by the mother, then by her husband or other relatives or friends.

After recognizing the symptoms, it's time to take immediate and aggressive steps to find professional help. Yet one report indicated that when women with postpartum depression knew "something wasn't right," only about 20 percent actually sought appropriate medical and psychological assistance.[2]

Why do so many new mothers avoid seeking the help they need?

One reason is a sense of shame. Karen, a new mom, feels like she's going completely crazy. Her thoughts are irrational, even bizarre, and she knows it. Yet she feels the pressure of cultural expectations; they're particularly strong because she's a Christian. She's expected to feel happy, not sad and depressed, at this special time in her life. Unfortunately, she feels quite the opposite—and guilty that she does.

Fearing exposure, she hides her terrifying emotions—even from her husband, friends, and relatives. She doesn't feel comfortable telling her doctor about this ordeal. She tells herself that if she can just tough it out, the disturbing thoughts and feelings will soon go away.

Women like Karen tend to blame themselves, assuming their feelings indicate weakness or that they're "bad mothers." Yet such self-blame wouldn't be present if the mood swings were associated with other causes such as a thyroid imbalance.

You don't have to suffer postpartum depression in silence. You can take action, even before it strikes.

1. *Plan ahead.* Being prepared before the birth of your baby can really make a difference. Be aware that a wife is at greater risk if she has a history of even minor postpartum depression, if she's facing stressors like marital problems or the recent loss of a loved one, or if she has bipolar disorder or a family history of depression.

Early in the pregnancy, discuss these factors with your physician and with a professional mental health therapist. They can help you plan appropriate preventative care.

2. *If you're the wife, don't hide.* If you had no reason to expect problems when your baby arrived, you may find yourself blindsided by overwhelming "crazy feelings." Enormous guilt and shame may have come seemingly out of nowhere; you may feel you've been run over by a Mack truck.

Don't try to hide these emotions. Talk about them. Consult your doctor; if indicated, seek a psychiatrist who can prescribe the best medication to address

Karen is expected to feel happy, not sad and depressed, at this special time in her life. Unfortunately, she feels quite the opposite—and guilty that she does.

the biochemical imbalances that lie behind the reactions you're experiencing.

Find a Christian counselor who can help you put your feelings into perspective, and who may be able to assist you in finding a good support group. You may want to talk to your pastor, too.

Be honest with your husband about what you're going through. Let friends and relatives know that they can help by giving you some breaks from the constant demands of your infant.

> Don't try to hide these emotions. Consult your doctor; if indicated, seek a psychiatrist who can prescribe the best medication to address the biochemical imbalances that lie behind the reactions you're experiencing.

3. *If you're the husband, be proactive.* Men can play a pivotal role in helping—or hindering—their wives' battles with postpartum depression.

While your wife is still pregnant, review the signs of postpartum depression. After the baby arrives, you'll be more sensitive to subtle indicators that your wife may be hiding a strong undercurrent of feelings. If she begins to display some of the more severe symptoms, but won't address them, you need to intervene. Ask, or even insist, that she see her physician or a counselor with you.

You can also help arrange for support from others, especially in giving her respite from baby care.

Even though you may sometimes feel overwhelmed yourself, it's important that you not run away from your wife's struggle. She needs your sensitive, patient support.

4. *Nurture yourself and your relationship.* If you're the new mother, don't expect your husband to provide for all your needs. Your depression is undoubtedly creating considerable stress for him and for your other children if you have any.

Take care of yourself; you're worth it. You'll need some personal "down time" to do that, and some "date nights" with your husband.

Postpartum depression isn't unusual, but it's a serious matter. Don't hesitate to ask for help from both loved ones and professionals. Those who seek treatment when symptoms appear usually have a very favorable outcome—and spare themselves and their families untold stress and damage.

—PHILLIP J. SWIHART

What If Our Child Has Special Needs?

"Never let a problem to be solved become more important than a person to be loved."

—Barbara Johnson

Laura and Pedro had been married four months when they found out Laura was pregnant. Their families were excited; the couple was overjoyed. The pregnancy was normal, with no complications. Laura took good care of herself as she awaited the baby's arrival.

But after the child was delivered, he was taken into another room. Laura knew something was wrong. The hospital staff waited for a pediatrician to get there. Laura demanded to know what was going on, but couldn't get answers. She wondered whether her baby was dead. Pedro was kept in the waiting room.

When the pediatrician arrived, he looked at the baby and then came to speak with Laura. A nurse came, too, carrying a hypodermic needle containing a sedative. The nurse watched Laura to see whether the sedative would be needed as the doctor broke the news: Laura and Pedro's son had been diagnosed with Down syndrome.

For many families, the news of having a special-needs infant is an instant crisis. The most common initial reactions are sadness, disappointment, fear, anger, and uncertainty. Unmet expectations and anxiety about added costs and responsibilities add to the stress. So do questions like, "Why is God punishing me?"

Children's special needs can range from learning disabilities and speech impediments to quadriplegia and mental retardation. They can appear at birth or as the result of accident or illness. And they can present stiff challenges not only to the child but to the parents' relationship.

Unfortunately, many spouses in this situation internalize their feelings—not wanting to hurt the other further or complicate things. Laura, for example, thought Pedro had accepted the situation and was ready to approach the

> For many families, the news of having a special-needs infant is an instant crisis. The most common initial reactions are sadness, disappointment, fear, anger, and uncertainty.

challenge as a team. As the months and years passed, however, Pedro experienced an inner battle that he didn't share. He tried to escape the pressures through alcohol and drugs. Eventually the marriage fell apart.

Martha's experience was similar in some ways, but different in others. She'd been married six months when her son, Caleb, was born. Three months later, her husband left and the marriage ended. Not until Caleb was a year old did Martha notice that the little boy was "different." He flapped his hands, rocked back and forth, would not look at other people, and seemed to fear them.

A few months later Martha met another man and married him. The two of them faced the challenge of taking care of Caleb, who was eventually diagnosed with Asperger's Syndrome—one of the "autism spectrum" disorders. They worked to keep their marriage alive by using free respite care for a few hours each month, a rare opportunity for "alone" time.

The stories of Laura, Pedro, and Martha provide snapshots of the difficulties couples face when they have a special-needs child. Those difficulties are only intensified when the couples involved believe the misconceptions surrounding this challenge. Here are four of those myths.

1. *"My life is over."* On the contrary, this can be where a new chapter of your life begins. Watching a special-needs child develop can deepen and strengthen your faith. Some parents of these children feel a new freedom, finding there is less to fear in this world than they thought. Crisis creates change, and change provides an opportunity for growth, character strengthening, and hope.

> Martha and her husband worked to keep their marriage alive by using free respite care for a few hours each month, a rare opportunity for "alone" time.

2. *"God is punishing me."* Actually, God is unfolding His plan. Laura—who now has *two* Down syndrome children—acknowledges that the struggle is sometimes overwhelming. But, she adds, there's nothing God can't pull her through. Her fears about the fragility of her children have increased her dependence on Him and provided freedom from other anxieties.

Rather than feeling condemned, Laura considers herself fortunate. She says she doesn't know what kind of person she'd be had she not had these children. She believes this has been a perfect fit and God-ordained.

3. *"We can just have an abortion and try again."* Abortions are final, irre-

versible. Each ends a life. Some women who've had them spend years in regret, thinking about what their child might have been like.

Laura seriously considered abortion, but is happy and thankful she chose otherwise. She's seen her son and daughter persevere and beat all odds and predictions.

4. *"I'm all alone."* Martha and Laura both had to pick up the pieces and keep moving forward. The fathers of their children, unfortunately, decided to run.

No parent who has a relationship with God is truly alone. Often family and friends are ready to offer support, too. Ironically, depression causes some new parents of special-needs children to reject that support in favor of isolation.

> Watching a special-needs child develop can deepen and strengthen your faith. Some parents of these children feel a new freedom, finding there is less to fear in this world than they thought.

If you've recently learned that your child has or is expected to have special needs, you're on an emotional roller coaster. Your reactions following the initial shock and disappointment may set the tone for how you handle your feelings in the days and years ahead.

How can you get started on this journey in the healthiest possible way? Here are some suggestions.

1. *Remember that what seems like the easy road is not necessarily the best.* Pedro chose the "flight" response and ended up trapped in substance abuse. Laura rejected abortion and faced the risks, and has seen God's miracles every day in the lives of her daughter and son. She thanks God that she chose to "climb the mountain."

2. *Eliminate expectations.* Replace them with love and acceptance. Celebrate when your child reaches milestones, but don't insist on them. Expectations set parents up for disappointment, while love and acceptance allow blessings to be seen.

3. *Avoid blaming.* Your child's special needs are not anyone's fault. There's a tendency to point fingers and become disconnected as a couple in times of intense stress, but that won't take away the reality of the challenges. You and your spouse need to become more united than ever as you face uncertainty.

4. *Look to the future.* Make sure you understand your child's diagnosis and prognosis so that you can effectively participate in his or her growth. Many

special-needs children will function normally; others will have limitations or delays throughout their development.

5. *Communicate.* You and your spouse need to share your feelings and thoughts with each other openly. Encourage one another; establish a pattern of honest, safe communication. This can be hard when your child's needs require a great deal of time; there may be appointments to keep, conditions to monitor, procedures to learn. But that makes positive, effective communication more important than ever.

There's a tendency to point fingers and become disconnected as a couple in times of intense stress. You and your spouse need to become more united than ever as you face uncertainty.

6. *Form a support network.* Seek and accept the help of family members, acquaintances from church, friends, and neighbors. People usually don't know how to help unless you tell them; they may feel awkward, afraid to say anything. If you want them to just listen or help you fully understand what's happening, tell them. If you'd appreciate a hug, let them know.

7. *Realize that every problem has an end, but not necessarily an explanation.* Laura continues to struggle with the possibility that her firstborn son could die at any moment. She lives in constant vigilance, even pulling over when she's driving to make sure her sleeping son is okay. She no longer strives to find out why her children have Down syndrome. She accepts, loves, and trusts God.

8. *Gather information that builds your confidence in dealing with the challenges.* Listen to the information professionals (doctors, nurses, speech pathologists, hospital social workers, occupational therapists, physical therapists, etc.). Ask questions.

Investigate resources in your community; some early childhood programs funded by state and federal governments are overseen by each state. Hospital staff may be able to help you track these down. They may also know of support groups in your area that deal specifically with the kinds of needs your child has.

Here are a few of the many resources you may want to explore.

Adaptive technology for those with special needs: www.abledata.com, www.adaptivemall.com, and www.abilityhub.com

The Family Center on Technology and Disability: www.fctd.info

The National Dissemination Center for Children with Disabilities:
www.nichcy.org. Phone: (800) 695-0285. Offers free information about
many special needs. Ask for the resource titled, "A Parent's Guide: Access-
ing Programs for Infants, Toddlers, and Preschoolers with Disabilities."

National Center on Birth Defects and Developmental Disabilities:
www.cdc.gov/ncbddd

Having a special-needs child is dreaded by some. Yet many families who've
lived through the challenges and opportunities of raising such a child wouldn't
trade the experience for anything—nor would they change the past. Persevering
in this situation depends on your perspective. It also develops character and
hope, leaving a lot less room for fear.

—DANIEL HUERTA

What If We Disagree over How to Raise the Kids?

Most parents don't agree on every aspect of parenting. This is especially true of new moms and dads. They arrive on the parenting scene with little know-how—and often very different experiences.

Ben was raised in a traditional, conservative, even rigid type of home. His wife, Robyn, on the other hand, had parents who traveled and worked full-time and were quite lenient in their parenting style. When the two of them discussed having their first child, there were immediate disagreements on how they would raise him or her. Would their style be very structured or very relaxed?

> Ben believed in spanking; Robyn was strictly opposed. Ben wanted to develop a strict set of guidelines for their child to follow as a toddler and preschooler. Robyn felt rules couldn't be written for children that age.

Spanking was only one issue on which they differed. Ben believed in it; Robyn was strictly opposed. When it came to rules, Ben wanted to develop a strict set of guidelines for their child to follow as a toddler and preschooler. Robyn felt rules couldn't be written for children that age.

Ben and Robyn made a wise decision. They sought advice from an older husband and wife at church who'd experienced this problem early in their marriage.

The older spouses explained that they'd read everything the Bible said about parenting—and every Christian parenting book they could get their hands on. They'd attended every parenting seminar they could find, and had been mentored by an older couple at church. Finally they were able to compromise in key areas and agree on how to raise their children.

Not every couple reaches such a happy ending. Parenting differences can be a major source of division in marriage. Like theological variations, they must be properly managed and resolved lest they form an emotional wedge between spouses.

Let's consider some of the most common issues that arise when mates approach parenting differently—and how you might handle them.

1. *"I'm pretty strict, but she's a total pushover."* This isn't unusual, but it can

be major. The simple solution is to find common ground, a balance between extremes. This is easier said than done, of course.

The Bible tells parents to discipline their children (Proverbs 13:24), but also warns fathers not to be too hard on them (Ephesians 6:4). This implies a balanced approach, not too hard but not too lenient. Couples who have different views on spanking, for instance, should discuss what a balanced approach would look like. Which behaviors should be punished with spanking and which should not be?

Amanda and Aaron, for example, concluded that general disobedience such as failure to pick up toys would be penalized by taking away a privilege. Defiance such as "pitching a fit" would be met with a spanking. In this way Amanda and Aaron were able to provide the discipline their child needed without being inflexible.

Another suggestion is to experiment. Amanda and Aaron could try spanking for two weeks, then switch to other tactics such as time-outs, extra chores, or removing privileges. Some children respond better to spanking than to other methods, and vice versa. At the end of the experiment, the two spouses would discuss the results and use them as a pattern in the future.

2. *"He's overly protective, but I think kids need to experience failure once in a while."* Again, the secret to bringing these two sides together is balance.

It's not healthy to be overprotective—or its opposite. God's parenting style as our Father is a perfect example. He allows us to fall and struggle and learn, but is also there to pick us up and show mercy and compassion. You and your spouse will have to discover when to rescue your child and when to stand at a distance. This balance is achieved through practice and good communication.

Discuss ahead of time which circumstances will require parental involvement and which won't. When will you need to step in—or back off?

Will and Darci, for instance, decided that if their son fell during a soccer game but seemed to be okay, they'd keep their distance. If he seemed to be the victim of bullying at school and couldn't handle the situation himself, though, they'd intervene. In other words, they'd help when the boy couldn't help himself or seemed

Parenting differences can be a major source of division in marriage. They must be properly managed and resolved lest they form an emotional wedge between spouses.

overwhelmed; the rest of the time they'd allow him the space and freedom to fail and to learn to solve problems on his own.

To everything there's a season (Ecclesiastes 3:1). Sometimes you need to kiss a skinned knee; sometimes you need to encourage a child to dust herself off and move on. Most parents have to discover the difference through experience.

3. *"The kids play us against each other."* As great as children are, they're selfish by nature. They'll take advantage of you, learning the contrasts in your parenting styles and the weakest areas in your marital relationship.

If one parent is more "progressive" in what he'll buy the children, they'll learn to approach him when they want something. They'll also use what one parent said—or didn't say—to make their case.

For example, listen to this exchange:

"Barry, why did you go outside without asking me?"

"Well, Mom didn't say I couldn't."

The key to conquering your child's ability to play you and your mate against each other is consistent communication between the two of you. When possible, consult your spouse before making decisions on what your child can or can't do. Don't assume you know what your mate did or didn't say; tell your child to "hold it for one minute" and do a quick check with your spouse.

4. *"Is it okay to disagree in front of the kids?"* Yes. How else will children learn how to discuss and solve problems?

Children raised in homes where spouses never disagreed in the kids' presence often develop the perception that their parents never clashed. To develop the conflict resolution skills they'll need if they marry, children need to know that their parents did struggle—and how those struggles were resolved.

>
> The simple solution is to find common ground, a balance between extremes. This is easier said than done, of course.

Some issues, of course, should be discussed only behind closed doors. These include issues young children can't understand. Adult problems such as sex in marriage, financial trouble, and addictions should be discussed in private. Decide in advance with your spouse which subjects are "off-limits."

Focus on the Family counselor Jim Groesbeck adds this advice: "If your voices remain calm, if there is mutual respect and good listening, and if the subject matter is appropriate for children, then open discussion in front of them may be helpful and serve as a model. But the children must witness a positive outcome, not a negative one."

5. *"Who has the final say on this?"* Ideally, parents should reach agreement on issues related to their children. But this isn't always possible. Sometimes you have to agree to disagree.

This doesn't mean ignoring the issue. It means you and your mate have such diverse experiences and strong opinions that you may always see the topic differently.

The deadlock can be broken when one of you is willing to say something like, "I know we disagree on this issue. But you've had a little more experience with this than I have, because of your upbringing. Why don't you make the decision and I'll back you up?"

This doesn't mean you're giving up your position. It means you realize a decision has to be made, and you're willing to defer on this one. If your spouse takes that approach on other issues, you avoid an impasse and put your child's welfare above and beyond your own desires or opinions.

It's important for one parent not to undermine or override the other when both supposedly have settled an issue. This will only confuse your child, and when children are confused they tend to do as they please.

It's important for one parent not to undermine or override the other when both supposedly have settled an issue. This will only confuse your child, and when children are confused they tend to do as they please or whatever seems to have the fewest repercussions.

Parenting is like learning to dance. You have to learn by watching and doing. And that can't be accomplished without making mistakes and stepping on each other's toes.

As difficult and frustrating as the process may seem, it's a God-ordained thing. The payoff for discussing, negotiating, and compromising on your parenting disagreements will be seeing your children grow into adults who continue the dance into the next generation.

—MITCH TEMPLE

How Can We Get a Break from the Kids?

The sign on the wall of the counseling office read, "How to Know If You Are Ready to Have Children." The rest of the sign went something like this:

- Spread metal cars all over the hardwood floor. Turn out the lights and try to walk across the floor barefooted. If you step on a car, you are not allowed to scream because you will wake the sleeping baby.
- Take four large Labrador retrievers with you to the grocery store as you shop. Remember that you are responsible when they poop on the floor, tear stickers off the racks, chew through candy wrappers, and pock holes in meat packages.
- Rent a hyperactive chimpanzee from the local pet store. Try to dress him in underwear, undershirt, pants, belt, button-down shirt, socks, and lace-up shoes. Then try to get out of the house before he undresses himself.
- Ask your local vet if you can go with him next time he medicates a small calf. Try to hold the calf still long enough to put the medicine in its mouth with a spoon—or (heaven forbid) insert a suppository in the opposite end.
- Program a talking alarm clock to scream in the middle of the night, every hour on the hour, "I am crying for no apparent reason except because I can!" This applies even when you have not had a full night's rest for over six months.
- Have a friend call you every time you and your spouse start to go out for dinner, declaring that you can't go because "the baby is sick." Make sure your friend waits until you both are ready and the babysitter is ringing the front doorbell.
- Smear mashed potatoes on your new suit just before you walk out the door to attend a very important meeting.

The sign concluded, "If you can handle all these challenges and more, you are ready to have a baby."

Having children is one of the most exciting developments in a couple's life, but can be one of the most challenging. The strain and adjustments of child-rearing can cause a great deal of tension in a marriage. In fact, research shows that having children can cause a significant decrease in a couple's satisfaction.[1]

It's no wonder, given the shrinking amount of time most new parents spend alone together. Quiet evenings, candlelight dinners, popcorn and a movie become almost extinct. Time to simply sit down and talk becomes a faint memory. Sex becomes a rare pleasure.

Intimacy no longer grows; it just "hangs on" if you're fortunate. Spending focused time together helps produce intimacy in marriage, and that's the very thing squeezed out by the demands of young children. If you don't make a concerted, constant effort to keep intimacy alive, your relationship will suffer.

> Quiet evenings, candlelight dinners, popcorn and a movie become almost extinct. Time to simply sit down and talk becomes a faint memory.

Many couples realize that making time for each other and getting away from the kids is important—but they never seem to get around to it. Here are some thoughts that often stand in the way, along with suggestions for overcoming them.

1. *"We can't afford a babysitter, and we can't afford to go to dinner once a week."* It's easy to conclude that if you can't go out often, you may as well not go out at all. But once a month is better than never.

Look for creative ways around your tight budget. For instance, choose one night a week to get the kids in bed early, put a pizza in the oven, and enjoy an after-dinner bath together. Ask the church youth director to organize a free babysitting service project for students. Pick up dinner at a fast-food restaurant and head to the local park. Time together doesn't have to be expensive.

2. *"Our relatives don't live around here."* Gone are the days when most couples could rely on extended family for free child care. But there are still opportunities to go out.

Ask trusted friends at work or church to babysit your kids once in a while. Trade child care services with other parents. If faraway relatives ask what you'd like for your birthday, Christmas, or anniversary, request babysitting money. Save money by canceling cable TV or taking your lunch to work, or sell unused items on eBay and put that money in a babysitting fund.

3. *"I can't trust a babysitter with my baby; I'm afraid something will happen while I'm gone."* This is a common concern, especially for first-time mothers. It doesn't mean you're paranoid; it means you feel such a connection with your

new baby that you're uncomfortable leaving him or her with someone else.

One solution is to invite the sitter to come over and watch your baby in another room while you and your husband make dinner and watch a DVD. Or, if you have (or can borrow) a cell phone, take it with you while you go out to dinner; this can go a long way in providing assurance for new parents. If it helps, select a restaurant just down the street rather than across town.

You may feel more comfortable asking an older, experienced mother to watch your baby than you would a teenager. In exchange, you could help the woman with a project or provide some other service while you're home.

> It's easy to conclude that if you can't go out often, you may as well not go out at all. But once a month is better than never.

4. *"Is this really worth the hassle?"* Think about the time you spent with your spouse before the baby arrived. How many hours per week did you spend alone together? Two? Three? Four or more?

Did you enjoy those times? Did they help you grow closer? Wouldn't you like to recapture that closeness and see it increase in the future?

Aim for a similar amount of "together time" in your new schedule. If you can't get anywhere close, take what you can get. The main thing is to keep a conscious, regular lookout for any and all opportunities to be a couple again.

Make sure that both of you take the initiative to plan these intimacy-building moments. Many husbands plead incompetence when it comes to "relationship stuff," but the responsibility shouldn't rest solely on the wife. If both of you are consistent and creative, the team approach will pay off.

Intimacy is the lifeblood of healthy marriages. Don't let another week pass without spending time reconnecting with your spouse. A relationship starved by lack of intimacy will soon create more problems than you know what to do with, but a little planning will reap dividends for a long time.

—MITCH TEMPLE

How Can We Help Our Kids Grow Spiritually?

Picture this: Tonight's football game will be the biggest of the season. Young Michael is excited. After all, he's the star player. His team is about to face its toughest opponent, and all eyes will be on him.

"Wait!" his mom cries as Michael leaves the house. "You don't have any equipment! And your coach is gone!"

"Don't worry, Honey," Michael's dad says. "Michael is a great boy with a good head on his shoulders. I trust him. He'll do fine without a helmet and pads. We don't need to worry. He can figure out the plays without a coach. I have faith in him!"

No parent in his right mind would send his child out to play league football knowing that there would be no coaching or protective equipment. It would be a disaster for the child. At best, he'd learn not to enjoy the sport; at worst, he'd be seriously injured or even killed.

Yet many parents send their children into a hostile world, spiritually unequipped and uncoached—often with disastrous results.

Most Christian parents probably would agree that the spiritual training of their children is important, but feel they don't have the time, energy, or qualifications. They might be surprised to know that spiritual training isn't as hard as they think. Deuteronomy 6:6-9 explains how to work it into family life: "These commandments that I give you today are to be upon your hearts. Impress them on your children. Talk about them when you sit at home and when you walk along the road, when you lie down and when you get up. Tie them as symbols on your hands and bind them on your foreheads. Write them on the doorframes of your houses and on your gates."

Spiritual training isn't just sending children to church, though that's good

> No parent in his right mind would send his child out to play league football knowing that there would be no coaching or protective equipment. Yet many parents send their children into a hostile world, spiritually unequipped and uncoached—often with disastrous results.

and necessary. It's living the principles you believe, letting biblical truths permeate your conversation, using everyday incidents to make a point.

Here are some practical ways to develop your child's spiritual life.

1. *Family devotions or family nights.* Make family devotions brief and age-appropriate. Deal with issues your child might be dealing with. If you have a preschooler, try reading or acting out Bible stories; if you have a teenager, discuss issues like peer pressure and how to wisely choose friends, referring to verses like, "Do not be misled: 'Bad company corrupts good character'" (1 Corinthians 15:33). Help kids see that Scripture is applicable and necessary to daily living.

> Most Christian parents probably would agree that the spiritual training of their children is important, but feel they don't have the time, energy, or qualifications. They might be surprised to know that spiritual training isn't as hard as they think.

Family nights are a less traditional way to accomplish similar goals. These fun times with a spiritual point might feature anything from games to object lessons to watching and discussing a movie. For a more complete explanation of the concept and some ideas to get you started, see *Parents' Guide to the Spiritual Growth of Children* (Focus on the Family/Tyndale, 2000).

2. *Prayer time.* Pray with your child about personal struggles—finding friends, passing a test, performing in a sporting event. When God answers a prayer, call it to your child's attention and thank the Lord for what's He's done. In this way you teach your child to ask God about life decisions because He's interested in your child and wants to be close to him or her.

3. *Teachable moments.* Use everyday events to teach your children biblical principles. Here's one.

Christopher loved his lizard, Lightning. Lightning was the fastest lizard in Christopher's aquarium.

When Lightning escaped, Christopher was devastated. He asked for prayer at family devotions that Lightning would return safely. Two weeks later, Lightning showed up under Christopher's bed.

After two more daring escapes, Lightning met up with Christopher's Rottweiler and lost the battle that ensued. The boy was heartbroken.

His grandmother used this opportunity to remind Christopher that Lightning was just like us. Lightning had an aquarium filled with food, water, play-things, and other lizards. But he wasn't content.

Lightning believed that the aquarium was a place from which to escape. Outside its walls, he thought, was freedom. But in reality, death lurked there.

Grandma explained that, just as Christopher had put Lightning in the aquarium for his own good, our heavenly Father has set rules and boundaries for our benefit. They protect us, just as the aquarium walls protected Lightning.

Teachable moments can come at any time. They needn't be structured; casual is fine. You might tell the story of Noah as you drive through the rain, for example, or talk about revenge when you pass a billboard advertising a violent movie.

4. *Church and youth group.* Spending time with other Christian kids can boost your child's spiritual growth. Worship services and youth group activities should reinforce what your child is being taught at home—and allow your child to develop friendships with peers who share your family's values and beliefs.

5. *Mission trips.* These are opportunities for fellowship and for practicing some of the biblical principles your child is learning at home. They're also a powerful way to show kids how the rest of the world lives.

6. *Parental modeling.* Most important for children's spiritual training is seeing active faith modeled in their parents' lives. If you're not demonstrating the value of a relationship with God, your children won't buy it. No one expects you to be perfect, but your actions truly speak louder than your words.

> Teachable moments can come at any time. You might tell the story of Noah as you drive through the rain, or talk about revenge when you pass a billboard advertising a violent movie.

Letting your children see you read the Bible, for instance, shows them the relevance of Scripture to your life. As one woman says, "I remember getting up early as a kid and every morning seeing my mom on her knees with her Bible open. I knew that Jesus was very important to her. This encouraged me as a young child to want to read about Jesus."

You may be thinking, *But I'm no spiritual giant.* You may be a relatively new believer, or just don't feel like an "expert." One dad, Matt, had recently become a Christian. The idea of spiritual training scared him; he feared not knowing enough to share with his children. He didn't realize that every parent who has a relationship with God is qualified. Matt can impart the little he knows; as he grows, he can share more. He might start by getting some Bible storybooks to read to his kids—thereby learning in the process himself.

What if your spouse won't take an active role in spiritually training your child? This is a problem for many couples.

It's good to encourage each other to train your children. But don't nag your spouse about it or confront him or her in front of the kids. Do the training yourself if needed, praying for your mate to help. If your spouse keeps resisting, just keep living your faith and teaching your children. As one wife told her Mothers of Preschoolers group, "My mom did all the spiritual training in our house. I am so grateful to her for teaching me about the Lord. I feel sad that my dad did not participate, but he was the one who lost out. It was a time for praying together, seeing answered prayer, and getting to know each other. My husband does not help either, but I am determined to teach my children anyway—and I pray that Mike will eventually see the value and join in."

> If you're not demonstrating the value of a relationship with God, your children won't buy it. No one expects you to be perfect, but your actions truly speak louder than your words.

Whether you go it alone or work as a team, giving your child a strong spiritual heritage is the best way to equip him or her to face the challenges ahead.

—SHERYL DEWITT

How Can We Make Sure Our Kids Succeed?

Since the beginning of time, most parents have wanted their kids to succeed. Samson's parents, for example, were concerned about that. Before Samson was born, his father prayed, "O Lord, I beg you, let the man of God you sent to us come again to teach us how to bring up the boy who is to be born" (Judges 13:8). That's not a bad model to follow.

But what does it mean to succeed? To embrace your parents' faith? To be a champion in sports, a prodigy in the arts, or a *wunderkind* in business?

For many parents, it means being the absolute best in school, athletics, language skills, and test scores. That explains why "success centers" have cropped up in so many towns, offering tutoring to propel kids to the tops of their classes. Raising kids who excel seems to be the priority for millions of anxious parents.

This agenda can easily get out of hand, causing parents to try transforming normal kids into "super kids." Some parents do this because they're materialistic, measuring success by career instead of character, and impressive careers usually require top-notch educations. Other parents do it because they want to live out unfulfilled dreams of their childhood through their offspring. Whatever the reason, pressing hard for excessive achievement tends to leave kids tired, stressed out, and angry. Emotional, behavioral, and social problems can result.

>
> What does it mean to succeed? To embrace your parents' faith? To be a champion in sports, a prodigy in the arts, or a *wunderkind* in business?
>

Pushing for "super kids" is unreasonable—and dangerous. It's unreasonable because certain children don't have the natural ability or personality to achieve success in certain areas. It's dangerous because it sends the message that you're more concerned about your dreams than you are about theirs—and creates children who grow up to value the wrong things.

Some anxiety about a child's future success is normal. A moderate dose of it, in fact, can lead parents to take constructive action. But unhealthy, unmanaged anxiety can confuse, discourage, and even paralyze moms and dads.

Some parents become so anxious that they develop a "What's the use?"

mentality. Why even try to get the scholarship when so many are competing? Why aim for a good job when the economy probably will collapse anyway? Children may respond by adopting a fatalistic outlook: "If I can't please my parents, I may as well live like it doesn't matter."

Other parents' fears are driven by simple concern over failure. Their focus is on how others may view and value them if their children aren't successful. This, too, is unhealthy and self-centered.

> Some anxiety about a child's future success is normal. But unhealthy, unmanaged anxiety can confuse, discourage, and even paralyze moms and dads.

Not every couple tries to produce "super kids," of course. Some weren't raised in homes that taught or modeled what success looked like. Children in these homes are often left to figure things out on their own—which can cause problems, too.

So how should you measure success? How much should you expect from your child? Are you just worried about looking good as a parent?

Here are three "benchmark" questions to help you gauge healthy, God-approved success.

1. *Does (or will) my child form and nurture healthy relationships?* Strong relationships are a key to building and maintaining success. Children who don't know how to "connect" will struggle in their careers, marriages, and parenting.

Career experts say one of the skills today's employers look for most is the ability to communicate and build relationships. Even the child who absorbs incredible amounts of knowledge will struggle in the workplace if he or she isn't equipped to get along with others.

The same is true in marriage. Without basic relationship skills, children become adults who have trouble building intimacy and resolving conflict.

2. *Does (or will) my child know and love God and have a relationship with other Christians?* As Hebrews 10:23-25 says, "Let us hold unswervingly to the hope we profess, for he who promised is faithful. And let us consider how we may spur one another on toward love and good deeds. Let us not give up meeting together, as some are in the habit of doing, but let us encourage one another—and all the more as you see the Day approaching."

If you want your child to be successful over the long term, show him or her how to love God and connect with His people. The two are closely linked. God designed us to love Him and to be accountable to Him as part of a community of people who do the same.

3. *Does (or will) my child have the potential to enter the marketplace as an influencer on God's behalf?* In other words, do you want to prepare your child to glorify God in whatever career he or she chooses and in whatever environment he or she lives?

The way you answer this question will help to determine the approach you take in raising your child through each stage of development. Decisions about school, friends, and community involvement will be much clearer. As your child learns Christlike ways to relate to others, his or her behavior will stand in stark contrast to the unhealthy, unproductive habits of the surrounding culture.

> Strong relationships are a key to building and maintaining success. Children who don't know how to "connect" will struggle in their careers, marriages, and parenting.

Maybe you agree with these three goals for your child. But how do you reach them? Here are three suggestions.

1. *Model healthy relationship formation.* Demonstrate how to build productive bonds with other people. The most effective form of teaching is showing, not saying.

As your kids mature, make sure they see how you form friendships with other adults. Allow them to observe how you interact with these adults at social events, at church activities, and especially in difficult times. Let them notice how you serve your friends in their times of need. Most importantly, show how healthy friendships can strengthen your relationship with God as you pray, worship, and serve with others.

2. *Demonstrate what it means to live your faith.* Devotional and teaching times with your children are important, but they should see you praying and reading God's Word for personal benefit, too.

Your kids also need to witness you serving those who need help. "Religion that God our Father accepts as pure and faultless is this: to look after orphans and widows in their distress and to keep oneself from being polluted by the world" (James 1:27). Children might be called the purest forms of God's creation; connect them regularly and creatively to the purest expression of God's love—serving others.

3. *Prepare your children for positions of influence.* Teach your child the why and how of godly virtues like manners, compassion, forgiveness, putting others

first, seeing oneself as God does, and having patience, kindness, and love (see 2 Peter 1:5-9). Most of all, let your child see you living out these virtues as you relate to him or her and to your spouse.

In a world that distorts success, it takes effort to stick with a healthy approach. It takes work to steer yourself away from narcissistic motivations and quests for "super kids." But it's worth discovering what God views as success, and what's best for your individual child.

—MITCH TEMPLE

> Want to prepare your child to glorify God in whatever career he or she chooses? As your child learns Christlike ways to relate to others, his or her behavior will stand in stark contrast to the habits of the surrounding culture.

Should We Put Our Child in Day Care?

Jessica and Tim's first child, Timmy, is five weeks old. While Jessica's been on maternity leave, she and Tim have discussed the idea of her coming home from work to take care of the baby. But so far it doesn't look like that will work financially. Jessica will have to go back to her job while Timmy goes to day care.

But that's not really what Jessica wants. Every day after her husband leaves for work, she cries while holding baby Timmy. It hurts just to think about leaving her little boy in someone else's care.

She doesn't know exactly why she feels this way. Is it unnecessary guilt? Hormones? Or has God wired her to want to raise her baby?

She knows friends who've placed their children in day care. Some of them struggle with it; others seem perfectly content.

Jessica isn't keeping her inner conflict a secret from her husband, but she isn't sharing its intensity with him, either. She feels she must deal with this, get through it, and go back to work.

> The most important question about day care may be the influence other care providers will have on your child. A changing parade of adults won't give your child a stable connection when he or she is away from you.

Are you wondering what to do about the question of day care? Are there moral considerations involved, or is it strictly a matter of preference? Here are some issues to think about.

1. *Which choice gives your child the best caregivers?* The most important question about day care may be the influence other care providers will have on your child.

Your little one needs to "attach" to consistent, loving adults. If you use day care, it's best for your child's emotional well-being that these caregivers be a regular part of your child's life for the first three years. A changing parade of adults won't give your child a stable connection when he or she is away from you.

With that much at stake, you need to evaluate the character and values of alternate caregivers. This is often hard to do. It takes spending time with the facility's administrator, observing the caregivers at work, and talking with other parents.

2. *Which choice allows you to be a good steward?* The Bible says that children are a blessing from God (Psalm 127:3-5). With blessings come responsibilities.

Just as we're to be good managers of time and money, we're responsible for the children God entrusts to us. That includes taking responsibility for the care they receive—whether it's from you, a family member, a day care facility, or a babysitter. Are you confident that the caregivers you're considering will be good stewards of your child?

3. *Which choice lets you spend enough time with your child?* It's been said that the person who teaches your child to speak teaches your child his or her value system. Whether or not that's true, it's clear that the person who spends the most time with your child will have the greatest opportunity to influence his or her development.

A few decades ago, parents were told that they didn't need to spend a lot of time with their kids as long as it was "quality time." That turned out to be wrong. Children need quantity, too. This is one reason why using day care is a difficult and scary decision for many people; they know it's hard to make up for lost time in the few hours before bed or before the day-care day begins.

We're responsible for the children God entrusts to us. Are you confident that the caregivers you're considering will be good stewards of your child?

4. *Which choice can you and your spouse agree on?* Conflict can arise between spouses on this issue— even as it arises between "working moms" and "stay-at-home moms."

Talk with your spouse about your hopes and concerns regarding day care. In the case of Jessica and Tim, the two of them weren't on the same page—even after visiting several highly recommended facilities.

Jessica still felt as if her heart were being torn apart. The night before she was to return to work, Tim could tell she was in turmoil. After she put Timmy to bed, Tim called, "Jess, come here. Tell me what's going on."

Jessica started to sob. "Oh, Tim, this is so hard! I'm trying to be okay with this. But I don't even care about my career now that we have Timmy. I might again one day, I suppose. But I just don't want to leave him."

Tim sighed. "Honey, I'm so sorry. I know you're hurting. I don't want this, either. I wish I made enough money that you could stay home. I just don't see how it's possible right now."

"I know."

"Let's keep talking about it, with each other and with God. Give it a month and let's see how we're doing."

"Okay."

A month later, both of them were struggling with having Timmy in day care. They talked further, and soon shared the goal of bringing Jess and Timmy home within six months. They started considering the pros and cons of selling their second car. As they brainstormed possibilities, they both felt better because they had a goal—and soon might have a plan.

You and your spouse are the ones who'll have to decide prayerfully whether one of you can leave a job in order to stay home with a child. Your decision may change as circumstances do. For example, some women who return to outside-the-home careers after a first child don't go back to work after their second.

It's not possible for some families, including many single-parent households, to have a parent stay home to care for a child. If you determine that your family falls into this category, decide whether your child will be with a family member, in an in-home care placement, or in a day care facility. Many parents feel that having their child with a family member is the next best thing to having the child with Mom or Dad. Other parents don't have this option, and must choose a day care facility.

Conflict can arise between spouses on this issue—even as it arises between "working moms" and "stay-at-home moms."

So how do you assess such a facility?

1. *Security.* Many facilities now have systems requiring parents to type in a code in order to come in and pick up or drop off a child. At the least, doors should be kept locked and visitors monitored.

The center or in-home care provider needs to have a policy on who can pick up each child. An up-to-date authorization list should include first and last names, addresses, and phone numbers of people approved by you. The care provider also needs to know that whoever is picking up your child has a safe way of transporting him or her.

2. *Staff.* How experienced are the workers in providing care? How do they seem to interact with the children? What's the center's ratio of adults to kids? In the U.S., states have different requirements regarding the number of staff caring for children of particular ages.

If in the U.S., does the center require staff background checks from both local police and the FBI? If it doesn't, you should keep looking.

3. *Policies and practices.* Look at the facility itself. Is it clean? Are there enough age-appropriate toys for the children? Are toys disinfected at night? How do workers take care of diapering? Diapers must be changed in a location that's separate from the food preparation area.

What does the center do with a sick child? Is that policy consistently enforced? How are you informed if your child has been exposed to an illness? What are the emergency procedures in case of accident, illness, fire, natural disaster, or attack?

What are the policies regarding discipline of children?

Getting all your questions answered takes time and tenacity. But it's the only way to make an informed choice.

No matter what you decide, always let your child know that you love him or her. If you choose day care, make sure your child knows that being away from him or her is not what you want, but that you aren't able to do otherwise right now.

Spend as much time as you can with your child. Let the dust and the laundry pile up if necessary. Your child will be young for only a short while. You'll never get these days back; do what you can to make sure you don't miss them.

—SANDRA LUNDBERG

No matter what you decide, always let your child know that you love him or her. Spend as much time as you can with your child.

**Part 11:
Sticking with It**

Are We Falling Out of Love?

You remember the sleepless nights and the lightheadedness you experienced after seeing her big, beautiful smile light up a room. You recall when just the thought of him holding your hand caused shortness of breath and a queasy stomach.

In some countries, they call that malaria.

In our culture, we call it romance.

In fact, years ago two doctors actually presented at the Congress of Internal Medicine in Wiesbaden, Germany, the idea that *lieberskimmer*—love sickness— is a definite medical ailment replete with physical symptoms.

At this point in your marriage, are you wondering where the "symptoms" went?

Sustaining the emotional excitement of romance, or "being in love," can be difficult at best—and physically draining at worst. The shimmer of courtship is often replaced with the realities of budget crunches and dirty diapers.

Dorothy Tennov, a clinical psychologist who worked with thousands of couples, said that romantic love, on average, lasts only three years.[1] Does that sound depressing? If there's any truth to what she said, and if marriage is a lifetime commitment, we need to adjust the way we approach romance.

Romance is only one of the types of love important in marriage. If you think of marriage as a house, four kinds of love are like the components that make the house complete.

> Two doctors presented the idea that *lieberskimmer*— love sickness—is a medical ailment replete with physical symptoms. At this point in your marriage, are you wondering where the "symptoms" went?

1. The foundation of the house represents *unconditional love*. When a Realtor writes a house listing, he rarely comments on the quality of its foundation. But that's the first place the home inspector looks when assessing the longevity of the dwelling. This "love in spite of" is encouraged in Ephesians 5:25: "Husbands, love your wives, just as Christ loved the church." This provides the stability for a lasting covenant.

2. The frame of the house signifies *companionship love*. Open communication, shared activities, laughter, and even tears provide the living space for a

couple's love to grow. In fact, being best friends is how happily married couples most often describe their relationship. In Song of Solomon 5:16 the man is described as "my lover . . . my friend."

3. Once the foundation and frame of the house are in place, the roof—or *romantic love*—has something to rest upon. The roof represents romantic love because the latter is a "peak" experience. It's a love generated by the qualities of the loved one, and filled with excitement as Song of Solomon 2:5 attests: "I am faint with love." But basing marriage on romance alone would be like unloading a pile of shingles on an empty lot and thinking you have a house. And when a roof leaks you don't junk the house; you make the necessary repairs.

4. Finally, the furniture brought into the completed house symbolizes *sexual love* after the marriage has occurred. Proverbs 5:19 praises this love: "May her breasts satisfy you always."

All four loves reflect God's design for your marriage. But in Western culture, romantic love has been exalted above the others.

Throughout history, songs, drama, and poems have lauded romance. Today movies and advertising do the same thing. Romance was designed by God, but it pales in comparison to the sacrificial nature of unconditional love. Romantic love looks for what it can get; unconditional love looks for what it can give.

If romance has waned in your marriage, put it in perspective. Work at renewing it. Set aside a regular date night, even if it means paying a babysitter. Write a love letter to your husband. Buy your wife a rose. Be creative in the ways you show affection to each other.

Compile a list of qualities that originally drew you to your spouse. They probably have a little tarnish on them, but you'll likely find them with some polishing. If conflict between the two of you has squeezed out romance, get help to resolve it.

> A psychologist who worked with thousands of couples said that romantic love, on average, lasts only three years. If marriage is a lifetime commitment, we need to adjust the way we approach romance.

A few years into their marriage, Donna and Pete realized that their romance had taken a leave of absence. Work demands, frequent arguments, and the impact of time had dulled the luster that first characterized their relationship.

Instead of bailing out, they took a more realistic look at romance. Then they took steps to "repair the roof." They committed to dating each other twice a month, made time daily for communication, and worked out the in-law problem that had frustrated them for years.

No, the romantic "symptoms" weren't as powerful as they once were. But their love grew deeper as they worked on their marriage.

If you think you've fallen out of love, it may be because marriage requires hard work. Remember: The harder the climb, the better the view!

—GLENN LUTJENS

How Can We Keep Romance Alive?

Romance has been described as "idealized love."

Does that mean it's only an infatuation between high school sweethearts? Is it a short-lived attachment? Is it even *meant* to last?

Megan says she and her husband, Terry, have lost the romance in their marriage. They have two children, and Megan spends every waking hour caring for the needs of her family. At the end of the day she's exhausted, with no energy for candlelight dinners.

What should Megan and Terry do? Is there a list of "rules for romance" they need to follow?

Not exactly. It's actually a deeper issue; the presence of romance reflects the overall quality of a maturing relationship.

> It's actually a deeper issue; the presence of romance reflects the overall quality of a maturing relationship.

A man who was one of four sons tells how, every night, his father would come home and walk right past his boys. He would go directly to his wife and give her a hug and a kiss. Then he would turn to the four little stairsteps who were watching, and say, "I think I am falling in love with your mom."

That man—and his sons—knew something about how romance can survive in a marriage.

So what can you do to help romance survive in yours?

1. *Recall your beginnings.* Remember when you first met and fell in love. What characterized your relationship? Did you listen to every word your intended said?

You probably were considerate and filled with respect. Each of you gave the other your complete, constant attention. You overlooked each other's faults and wanted to be together.

Was your love based on reality? Not the "reality" of annoying habits and thoughtless slights you may have catalogued since the honeymoon. But aren't the qualities that attracted you to each other just as real? Maybe it's time to rediscover them.

2. *Give up the spotlight.* Now that Megan and Terry have children, Megan

can't give all her attention to Terry. Terry can't do that for Megan, either; he may be focusing on his work or a home project to make life better for his family.

Part of maturity is not needing to be the center of attention. Both Megan and Terry can demonstrate love for each other, but in new ways—indirectly as well as directly. As long as each of them views the other's role with respect and consideration, romance—idealized love—doesn't have to elude them.

3. *Live under God's authority.* Keeping romance alive is a lot easier when you're growing the fruit of the Spirit—love, joy, peace, patience, kindness, goodness (love in action), faithfulness, gentleness, and self-control (Galatians 5:22-23). When Megan and Terry submit to God, the spark of romance not only has a chance of being rekindled, but can become a radiant flame.

4. *Honor each other.* Romance certainly involves emotion. But it's also about valuing our spouses.

When Terry and Megan got married, they both felt love for one another. But when Megan was pregnant, she began to feel neglected by Terry, and a wound was opened. Terry sensed the distancing, and soon he felt unappreciated, too.

Aren't the qualities that attracted you to each other just as real? Maybe it's time to rediscover them.

Gary and Norma Smalley offer this advice on honoring your spouse: "When you honor your wife, she will sense that nothing and no one in the world is more important to you. She won't have to wonder if she's number one—she'll know."[1] The same goes for a wife's treatment of her husband.

5. *Be honest.* Feeling guilty, Terry and Megan didn't tell each other about their resentment. This could be the beginning of a downward spiral if they don't start opening up. Resentment is an enemy of romance.

If you and your mate feel you can't be honest with each other, let a Christian counselor or pastor help get the conversation going.

Keeping romance alive requires effort and creativity. It means honoring one another by being honest, kind, and respectful in your responses, showing affection throughout the day without expecting sexual intimacy, having a regular date night, lighting candles or having a sweet fragrance in the bedroom, praying together, sharing feelings, and taking responsibility for your offenses. When these are standard operating procedure in Megan and Terry's home—or yours—romance won't be a thing of the past.

Romance is a living, growing love. Things that grow require "tending to."

No one can do this alone. It takes both marriage partners giving their all; it takes reliance on the Holy Spirit to empower you, especially in the darkest hours.

God designed romance to be an ever-changing treasure. As your marriage progresses, will you allow the rosebud of romance to mature into full bloom?

—BETTY JORDAN

How Can We Avoid Infidelity?

Emily was blown away when she heard that a friend had been caught in an adulterous relationship. "She's in my Bible study on Tuesday mornings!" Emily exclaimed to her mom on the phone that night.

As she absorbed the news over the next few days, Emily began to wonder about her own marriage. Kevin had never given her any reason to question his faithfulness. But her friend's husband had thought the same thing about *his* wife, and now he was devastated.

Should I check his e-mails just to make sure? Emily wondered. Immediately she felt guilty for even thinking such a thing.

Maybe you've noticed that adultery is a huge problem, even in the church. Perhaps you're worried that your marriage might be the next to crumble.

It's no wonder that infidelity is such a threat. Our culture sets us up; television and movies vividly portray sexual desire as an uncontrollable force, unstoppable by moral or spiritual convictions. Dating relationships start younger and younger, with "serial dating" providing a perfect training ground for serial marriage and physical intimacy outside its bonds.

Even our jobs can threaten our marriages. When we're assigned to travel or work long hours with coworkers of the opposite sex, our boundaries—and marriages—can fall.

Not all adultery is physical, of course. Most physical affairs begin as emotional ones. While an infrequent dream about a sexual encounter with someone else is not necessarily something we can control or should feel guilty over, indulging in daydreams about a coworker is dangerous.

Viewing pornography is another form of infidelity. Though there's no contact with another person, it's as adulterous as physically touching a partner (see Matthew 5:27-28). Virtual affairs are becoming commonplace, too, as people visit Internet chat rooms at home and work.

Believing some dangerous myths about adultery

Our culture sets us up; television and movies vividly portray sexual desire as an uncontrollable force, unstoppable by moral or spiritual convictions.

puts us at further risk. Many of us assume unfaithful spouses must have set out to have an affair, and that we would never choose that option ourselves. But most adulterers who are professing Christians never started the process intending to have an affair.

Another misperception is the idea that the husband is usually the unfaithful partner. A moment of reflection will reveal that for every heterosexual man who commits adultery, there's a woman participating, too.

Affairs are not usually with a stranger, as some assume. Most are with someone the unfaithful spouse already knows.

You may wonder whether infidelity always means the end of a marriage. Surprisingly, it doesn't. Most couples don't divorce after adultery. The offended spouse tends to show great emotional stamina after discovering the affair. Sometimes this is due in part to an unhealthy dependency or neediness; but many times there's an ability to forgive that can only be attributed to God's grace.

> Affairs are not usually with a stranger, as some assume. Most are with someone the unfaithful spouse already knows.

Another reason many marriages survive adultery is that God is *for* marriage. While His justice demands we honor Him first, rather than enabling an unrepentant adulterer to continue to sin, He wants to give us a way out of the brokenness.

The best time to deal with infidelity, though, is before it happens. There are ways to protect your marriage.

You can start by becoming informed. Rather than fretting, "If we really trusted each other I wouldn't be concerned about this," you can say, "If I value my marriage I will learn how to protect it."

Basic strategies for guarding your relationship include the following.

1. Don't develop deep friendships with people of the opposite sex. Again, most affairs begin at the emotional level.

2. Bring your marital complaints to your spouse rather than confiding in someone else.

3. Be careful with touch. Dropping physical boundaries is never wise.

4. Don't have private e-mail and phone accounts or keep other significant secrets from your spouse.

5. Avoid business travel or late hours alone with coworkers of the opposite sex. Have a third party present when you work together.

In a larger sense, fending off infidelity means working on the sense of closeness you and your mate share. Adultery is a symptom of intimacy disorder. If your spouse strays, that behavior is only the tip of the iceberg. Under the surface there are damaged thoughts and emotions, and a troubled relationship with God that are the real threats to your ship. If you need the help of a therapist to deal with issues like these, don't hesitate to get it.

"Man, that's awful about your friend," Kevin said when Emily told him about her friend's adultery. "I'm glad we'll never go through that."

"Me, too," Emily nodded. But she was frowning.

"What's in your head?" Kevin prodded.

"Oh, it's silly—nothing, really. It was just such a shock to hear that someone could be going along thinking everything was fine, and had this strong, Christian marriage, and then . . ." Her voice trailed off.

> The best time to deal with infidelity is before it happens. There are ways to protect your marriage.

"You got scared?"

"No, not really. Honestly, I've never felt any reason to worry. It's just . . . neither did he, as far as he knew. Oh, I'm just rattled, that's all."

"Well, how about this, Babe?" Kevin put his arm around her and pulled her close. "Whether it's sharing an e-mail account or anything else you can think of, I want to do whatever it takes to make sure you never have to wonder. That's one thing I can fix."

Kevin had the right idea. A faithful spouse is purposeful, going beyond simply "not meaning to" have an affair. He or she means *not* to, and acts on that intent.

—ROB JACKSON

How Can We Keep from Drifting Apart?

"We just drifted apart."

So many couples cite this as the reason for their divorce that you might think it's inevitable. Is it? If not, how can you prevent it?

Robin admits that she and her husband, Tony, are drifting apart. "We have different interests now. He's immersed in his work, and I'm at home all day with our three sons. I gave up my career to raise a family while Tony gets promotions. When Tony gets home, he has nothing left for me. He doesn't really love me."

Many couples seem to feel marriage is like selecting the right plane—and then putting it on autopilot. That's a good way to ensure that spouses eventually drift apart.

Here's how it often works: One partner is satisfied with the relationship as it is, but the other's needs are overlooked. In the case of Robin and Tony, Tony has been the mostly happy one. He has a beautiful wife, three great kids, a relationship with the Lord, and a job he enjoys. He's seen himself as having made the right choices—so from now on, it's smooth sailing. Autopilot has seemed to work for him.

Robin, on the other hand, is wondering whether she made the right choice of "plane." She needs more of Tony's presence to feel valued.

In a bid for Tony's attention, Robin has started distancing herself from him. His reaction is to feel inadequate, disappointed in himself that he can't make his wife happy, unworthy of her love, and confused. He's thinking, *What am I doing wrong?*

Instead of disclosing her needs, Robin is expecting Tony to do some mind-reading. When he fails, she withdraws her love. He, in turn, feels rejected and helpless to please her. Closeness evaporates, replaced by confusion and disappointment.

The result: Their relationship feels empty. They're drifting apart.

Many couples seem to feel marriage is like selecting the right plane—and then putting it on autopilot. That's a good way to ensure that spouses eventually drift apart.

Robin and Tony need to understand that marriage is a growing, living relationship that needs nurturing. Before nurturing can be accepted, though, both partners have to be willing to take responsibility for their feelings and behaviors.

Using "straight talk" to acknowledge emotions without blaming can lead to resolving conflict. Robin could start the process by saying something like, "Tony, when I've had little adult conversation all day, I really need to talk with you."

Is this statement blaming? No. Is it clear what she needs? Yes. This will prevent defensiveness, contempt, and withdrawal.

Robin also can set the stage for solving the problem by putting the kids on a schedule that allows her "alone time" with Tony. The degree of closeness in a marriage reflects the overall climate in a home, and "climate control" takes spending time together.

Robin needs to know how to handle her resentment, too. When thoughts like *He doesn't really love me* arise, what should she do?

When such a thought strolls into the entryway of her mind, it doesn't belong to her yet; she doesn't have to feel guilty about it. But when she "camps on" this resentful thought instead of analyzing and rejecting it, it takes on a life of its own. She accepts ownership and buys into deception. She allows the thought to keep her from respectfully telling Tony what she's experiencing.

There's hope for Robin and Tony. They're both Christians who take their relationship with God seriously, and have been asking Him what to do about drifting apart. With His leading, they're working on making changes like these:

- becoming better listeners;
- taking responsibility for their actions and feelings;
- avoiding blaming;
- being more affectionate and considerate;
- becoming partners in parenting;
- respecting each other's differences;
- supporting each other in extended family conflicts;
- praying individually and as a couple;
- journaling their feelings individually to their heavenly Father;

> Marriage is a growing, living relationship that needs nurturing. Before nurturing can be accepted, though, both partners have to be willing to take responsibility for their feelings and behaviors.

• placing a priority on time together;
• submitting to God as their authority;
• being proactive by creating a plan.

There are as many reasons for drifting apart as there are marriages. But the way to prevent that drift begins with a single step: taking yourself off autopilot.

—Betty Jordan

> The degree of closeness in a marriage reflects the overall climate in a home, and "climate control" takes spending time together.

How Can We Make It Through a Medical Crisis?

Al, who was in his late twenties, was as healthy as a man could be. He rode his bike about an hour each way to and from his job. When he got there, he delivered heavy oxygen tanks and medical equipment to the homes of very ill patients, frequently up two or three flights of stairs.

He did this with great gusto, seeing it as an opportunity not only to prove his prowess but also to share his faith and occasionally pray for someone who was sick.

Al's wife, Jane, worked part-time at a school cafeteria and took care of their two daughters. It seemed life couldn't have been better.

But then an unexplained pain, running from the lower left side of his back and down his left leg, began to trouble him. He stopped riding his bike. He had to tell his boss about the pain and ask for a helper to get the oxygen tanks delivered.

Jane questioned frequently how long this medical crisis would last. She and Al encouraged their daughters to keep trusting God, but sometimes it seemed impossible to do so themselves.

Soon Al's pain, and the number of over-the-counter medications he was taking for it, compelled him to see the family physician. He and Jane were pale with shock when they came out of the second appointment. Dr. Bracken had just said, "It looks like you may have some sort of tumor." Scans and exploratory surgery were recommended.

By the fourth year of their marriage, with a baby daughter on the way, Al and Jane found their lives turned upside down. It had indeed been a tumor; Al was home all day, attempting to qualify for Social Security disability income. Jane was looking for full-time work.

As Al's condition deteriorated, Jane wondered whether the healthy, strapping man she married would ever return. She tried to empathize when Al couldn't (or wouldn't) fix things around the house as he'd done before. She certainly wasn't feeling good about the changes in their roles.

Now working as a nurse's aide on the night shift, Jane was tired all the time.

She questioned frequently how long this medical crisis would last. She and Al encouraged their daughters to keep trusting God, but sometimes it seemed impossible to do so themselves.

———

Ben and Margaret were in their forties when she was diagnosed with breast cancer. One daughter was in college; the other was a high school sophomore.

> *Mary and Rod didn't have enough time to devote to Kara, much less each other. Rod struggled with his faith, asking how a loving God could allow this to happen.*

Margaret, determined to keep her morale up, made fashion statements with the head coverings she wore following chemotherapy. Ben, though stunned that their family was going through this health crisis, did what he could to support her. He made sure they continued to take their summer vacations and winter ventures to the ski slopes.

This was nothing like Ben's vision of what family life would be like. But it was hardest for the two girls, seeing their vivacious mother wilt before their eyes. Ben and the girls had an unstated policy to make life as normal as possible for the family, but it was sometimes painfully obvious that almost nothing was normal.

———

When Rod and Mary brought their second daughter home from the hospital, it was clear that Baby Becky wasn't going to be like other kids. She'd been born with birth defects including a severely deformed spine; one of her lungs wasn't functioning. Doctors estimated she had only a matter of weeks—at most, a couple of months—to live.

Baby Becky required round-the-clock care. Rod and his five-year-old daughter, Kara, did all they could to help. But Mary was losing weight, had dark circles under her eyes from sleepless nights, and suffered from obvious exhaustion. Rod grew concerned about his wife's health.

Mary and Rod realized that their lives had changed drastically and permanently. They didn't have enough time to devote to Kara, much less each other. Rod struggled with his faith, asking how a loving God could allow this to happen. Rod also felt the loss of his wife, who was consumed with Becky's care.

———

Medical crises easily become emotional and spiritual ones. They're a challenge to any marriage. If you're weathering this kind of crisis, here are five things to consider.

1. *Let go of expectations.* Maybe you had hopes of being a "traditional" family in which the husband is sole provider and the wife and mother is home full-time—only to see a medical crisis change all that. This challenges your faith as well as your marital commitment. Your response as a couple will depend on your willingness to give up your expectations.

When Jane was forced to face the prospect that Al would never return to work, and that she'd have to get a more stressful job to help support their family, she relinquished her dream. She demonstrated not just obedience to her marital vows, but loyalty to the man she'd married.

2. *Count your blessings.* Part of what helps couples get through medical crises is the ability to ask, "In the midst of all that's happened, what can we be truly grateful for?"

Despite Margaret's breast cancer, she and Ben seemed grateful to accept the challenge of continuing to enjoy life and serve others. Mary was thankful for Baby Becky, in spite of the long hours and hard work of caring for her. Al and Jane proved to be a terrific team in their unconventional parenting arrangement, and were grateful to be able to keep their family together.

Part of what helps couples get through medical crises is the ability to ask, "In the midst of all that's happened, what can we be truly grateful for?"

3. *Adapt.* You may have to be very flexible in adjusting to the changes that medical crisis brings. You may have to learn new skills, from using hypodermic needles to trusting God in ways you've never had to before. Jane, for example, had never considered herself a career woman. But, maintaining her faith in God's ability to provide for her family, she accepted the night hospital job and persevered in it.

Rod and Ben had to "go with the flow," too. They modified their expectations of their wives, and of themselves, accepting the fact that a medical crisis requires compromise and sacrifice for the sake of the patient and other family members.

4. *Nurture your faith.* Faith that God is in charge and that He loves you can provide resolve for enduring what you're forced to accept. Ben and Margaret found that prayer and family devotions were a source of strength, as did Al and Jane. The prayers of others for them also made a great and positive difference.

Rod, who struggled with his faith, discovered the value of talking with his pastor. As Rod found, crisis is a good time to reveal and deal with doubts, not to sweep them under the rug.

5. *Get help.* There will be many times during your medical crisis when wise counsel and prayer support from pastors, friends, and therapists may be helpful. Ask and allow others to help bear your burdens, even when those burdens make no sense to you.

Sometimes your need will be as simple as a meal or a listening ear. At other times you may require advice on medical or legal decisions. Ask a friend to help you "network" at church and in your community to locate useful resources.

One of the biggest challenges during and after a medical crisis is to find meaning in it. Philippians 2:12-13 offers wise counsel in this regard: "Continue to work out your salvation with fear and trembling, for it is God who works in you to will and to act according to his good purpose." Even a seeming disaster can be used for God's ultimate good in our lives, and achieving His goals.

> Rod found that crisis is a good time to reveal and deal with doubts, not to sweep them under the rug.

Ben and Margaret found this to be true. Even as cancer caused her to decline, they continued their prayer times. They kept their eyes on the goal of seeking God's presence and wisdom, even in the midst of their struggle to make sense of their changed lives.

Ben and his girls were motivated by Margaret's example of serving others—right up to the moment she went into the hospital for the final time, almost five years after her original diagnosis.

Margaret's earthly life was over. Nothing about that family seemed the same. But Ben and the girls realized God had used Margaret's faith and strength to guide each of them in their relationship with Him.

—LON ADAMS

What If My Spouse Needs Psychological Help?

What leads you to believe that your mate needs help?

Certainly some symptoms are unambiguous. Is he abusing you or your children? Has she quit eating and her loss of weight is possibly life-threatening? Is he hearing voices no one else hears, or seeing things no one else sees? Is she saying she no longer wants to live?

In situations like these, when issues of safety are involved for you or your spouse or your children, arrange immediate intervention. If your children clearly are at risk, it's your responsibility as the rational spouse to take whatever measures are needed to protect them.

Ask a Christian therapist in your area how you can accomplish such intervention quickly and appropriately. You and your children may need to seek a safe refuge and insist that your spouse obtain psychological help. This may include therapy and medication, if indicated, probably over a period of weeks or months, before you return home. If you're in a life-threatening crisis, call 911 and ask law enforcement to act.

Of course, in most cases symptoms of emotional problems are much less dramatic. Sometimes they're so subtle that neither spouse recognizes how serious they're becoming.

Clint, for example, has always been somewhat up and down emotionally—sometimes on a "high" and sometimes subdued—especially compared to Julie, his even-tempered wife. Over the last two or three months, however, it's become increasingly obvious to Julie that her husband is descending into blacker and blacker moods.

Clint denies that he's depressed, believing he's just reacting to things that aren't going well at work. He sees no reason to consider consulting a counselor. He has no idea that he may be suffering from a bipolar disorder that requires medication and therapy if it's not to become even more pronounced.

> When issues of safety are involved for you or your spouse or your children, arrange immediate intervention. If your children clearly are at risk, it's your responsibility as the rational spouse to take whatever measures are needed to protect them.

Then there's Andrea, who's just given birth to her first child. Suddenly she's irrational, in the pits of despair at a time when she's "supposed" to be filled with joy. Ashamed, she tries desperately to hide her feelings—which include the sensation that she's "going crazy."

Andrea has thoughts that the rest of her family might be better off without her. She's seriously considering suicide, even thinking she'll take the new baby with her. Neither she nor her husband knows she's suffering from postpartum depression, which can be successfully treated when properly diagnosed.

You can look for a number of other symptoms which may indicate that your spouse needs psychological help from a professional Christian therapist. These include deviations from that person's normal behaviors—things that are out of character for him or her. If your spouse's personality seems to be changing in a negative way, that can be a red flag.

A string of significant losses also can damage mental health. Death of parents or children, loss of a job, financial reversals, serious medical problems—all can contribute to a major psychological crisis that builds over time.

Sometimes certain stressors, such as marital tensions, resurrect old traumas like the divorce of a husband's parents when he was a boy. This could trigger unrecognized fears of abandonment by a spouse, leading the husband to overreact and obsess over his wife's whereabouts. Anniversary dates marking old wounds or tragedies can also spark reactions that could benefit from therapeutic intervention.

In most cases symptoms of emotional problems aren't dramatic. Sometimes they're so subtle that neither spouse recognizes how serious they're becoming.

But what if your spouse has little or no insight into his or her feelings and behaviors? What if he or she rejects the idea of counseling?

You might begin by suggesting that your spouse see your family physician for a thorough physical and possibly lab tests. This is often less threatening than pushing the notion of therapy, which can result in protests like, "You think I'm crazy!" and "You think I need a shrink!"

Such an approach is also valuable in ruling out other possible causes for some symptoms. Diabetics and those suffering from thyroid disorders may also experience mood swings, for example. Elderly people who seem to be rapidly declining into dementia may be suffering from an undiagnosed urinary tract infection.

In addition, a physician knowledgeable about psychiatric disorders may be able to convince a defensive spouse that he or she does indeed need psychological help. The doctor can then make an appropriate referral.

Finally, it's also important to understand that a spouse with symptoms of emotional distress may have a spiritual problem that hasn't been recognized or addressed.

For example, unconfessed sin with its accompanying guilt can wreak havoc on a person's psychological well-being. Emotional distress due to the need to submit to God's will can be a good thing; it may serve as a siren of spiritual danger.

In such cases, counseling with a pastor or other spiritual mentor as well as a Christian therapist may be useful. It can help the person face himself or herself, to be honest about his or her rebellion and poor choices, and to seek spiritual restoration.

—PHILLIP J. SWIHART

Is It Ever Too Late for a Marriage?

If your relationship with your spouse is in serious trouble, you may be wondering whether your marriage is truly a hopeless case.

What if, for example, your mate has been unfaithful? Dr. James Dobson answered that question this way:

I've seen dozens of families who were in your fix but are now happy and whole. I taught a Sunday school class for young married couples for a number of years, and right there under my nose in a conservative church, infidelity was a surprisingly common event. There was one period of time during which I dealt with nineteen different couples where extramarital affairs had either occurred or were seriously threatened. These families are still known to me, and nine of them are apparently happily married ten years later. Though this percentage may seem low, remember that these were families on the verge of divorce that have now survived intact. Loving toughness played a role in their recovery, although their commitment to the Christian faith was the significant factor. So, yes, hope springs eternal, as well it should.

> The tiniest, flickering ray of hope can give off enough light to encourage your first, hesitant step toward loving and respecting each other.

Let me give you a final word of encouragement. Nothing can seem as fixed but change as rapidly as human emotions. When it comes to romantic endeavors, feelings can turn upside down in a day or two. I've seen husbands or wives who expressed hatred for their spouses, saying, "I never want to see you again," only to fall weeping into the other person's arms some hours later.

Hang tough. God isn't through with you and your husband yet.[1]

But what if you're being abused by your spouse? Isn't ending the marriage the next inevitable step? Here's Dr. Dobson's advice on whether an abused wife should divorce her husband:

No, I think she should separate in an effort to get him to acknowledge and deal with his abusive behavior. Through prayer and a resolute spirit, she may be able to save the marriage and help her husband overcome his violent tendencies. That is easier said than done, of course, and there are no guarantees that the outcome will be as hoped. But I believe it is best to try.[2]

So is it ever too late for a marriage?

Not if God has His way. Not if He's allowed to be an active part of creating healing and peace in the midst of your marital battles and woundedness. Even if there's only a shred of agreement left between you, it can be done.

The tiniest, flickering ray of hope can give off enough light to encourage your first, hesitant step toward loving and respecting each other. True, there can be some last-gasp attempts to vindicate angry motives and behaviors. But faith in God's eagerness to heal can furnish the energy you need to thrust your way past such roadblocks.

If your marriage has reached a painfully crushing state of affairs, though, how can it be rescued and restored?

Perhaps the most insightful and poignant cry for restoration ever penned came from the heart of David, the Israelite king. It's in Psalm 51, which contains core phrases like these:

- "Have mercy" (vs. 1);
- "For I know my transgressions" (vs. 3);
- "You desire truth" (vs. 6);
- "Let me hear joy and gladness" (vs. 8);
- "Create in me a pure heart" (vs. 10);
- "Grant me a willing spirit" (vs. 12);
- "A broken and contrite heart, O God, you will not despise" (vs. 17).

> Restoring your marriage may depend upon your willingness to forgive and honor one another.

That kind of attitude goes a long way toward rebuilding a marriage. David's confession also reminds us of three things:

- God's hand is extended to us.
- He wants us to heal.
- He will honor our cooperation and forgive our delinquencies.

Restoring your marriage may depend upon your willingness to forgive and honor one another. Still, if earnest self-examination and your attempts to make amends fall short, it will be sensible to concede that you could use help.

If your marriage is stressed to the point of collapse, dedicated professionals can save you time and frustration as you try to make a giant leap back into each other's trust and favor. The guidance of an experienced marriage "mender"—a Christian counselor—can shorten your journey appreciably.

Make no mistake: It won't be easy. Reconciliation poses a genuine challenge and demands your God-given best to produce results. Far too often when a marriage teeters on the edge of disaster, a late burst of stubbornness and pride takes hold; jaws lock in denying the need for anyone else's services.

That's not surprising, considering how poorly our culture trains us to pay the price for a committed, healthy relationship. We're hammered with statements like these:

"You're an army of one!"

"Look out for numero uno!"

"Have it your way!"

Small wonder marriages waver and stumble under the weight of such ranting about self-centered superiority.

So the question becomes, "Will you do as well by your marriage as you would by your watch, your car, or your kitchen sink when it requires time, effort, and money?"

Imagine the rewards of mending your relationship. They can be a powerful push, redirecting your thoughts and efforts toward regaining the satisfactions of your lost marital harmony. Just as love's flame flickers from careless inattention, it can be nurtured back to brightness by the decision to take action.

> If your marriage is stressed to the point of collapse, dedicated professionals can save you time and frustration as you try to make a giant leap back into each other's trust and favor.

But what if you're the only partner willing to seek counseling? Should you go anyway?

Yes, yes, yes!

Many marriages have been rescued because one spouse took the initiative toward positive change. Often the partner who stayed home became curious and joined the counseling sessions, leading to a change of heart.

Thousands of couples have discovered the effectiveness of good counseling in rebuilding a marriage—even if they started as skeptics.

Jim and Jolene, for example, weren't the least bit excited about counseling together. But here they finally were, in the therapist's office.

Both spouses were certain of their own rightness and the other's wrongness. They were a bit surprised when, without preliminaries, their counselor asked, "What would you rather do than fight?"

Before they could answer, the counselor instructed them to log the number of times they fought each day and to call him daily with the "score." He'd see them again in one week.

A week later, the counselor gave them another assignment: Log what fights are about. Jim and Jolene soon found that their arguments were too trivial to warrant continuing.

Six months later, they renewed their vows.

Wish you could do the same? Start by refusing to allow self-serving attitudes to snuff out the flame that once lit the rooms of your heart.

For all his fame as a deep spiritual thinker, the apostle Paul could be a surprisingly practical man. Listen to what he had to say about persistence and singleness of purpose: "Let us not become weary in doing good, for at the proper time we will reap a harvest if we do not give up. Therefore, as we have opportunity, let us do good to all people, especially to those who belong to the family of believers" (Galatians 6:9-10).

There it is, in plain language. Were Paul with us today he might say, "Hang in there! Think the best, do the best, by God's grace, and this marriage will come through a winner after all!"

It's yours to experience—if you're willing to work at it.

—SAM KENNEDY

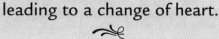

Many marriages have been rescued because one spouse took the initiative toward positive change. Often the partner who stayed home became curious and joined the counseling sessions, leading to a change of heart.

What About Marriage Counseling?

"But if anyone knew we were seeing a counselor, they would think we were getting a divorce or something!" Tamara fretted.

She and Shane were sitting in the office of their pastor, Dan. They'd just had an hour of heated discussion. "We just wanted to see what your opinion was about our situation," Tamara continued. "Why can't you just help us through this little bump in the road?"

"I think you guys are dealing with a lot more than just a disagreement here, Tamara," Dan answered.

Do you or your spouse, like Tamara, get a little queasy at the idea of going to a marriage therapist? Are you afraid that counseling is for "crazies"?

> "But if anyone knew we were seeing a counselor, they would think we were getting a divorce or something!"

While premarital counseling has gained popularity, there is still prejudice against getting help after the wedding. Some churches have counselors on staff, but many Christians still hear, "Just pray about it." Whether voiced or not, the message seems to be that Christians shouldn't need professional counseling unless they are really bad off.

This attitude virtually ensures that people will have bigger problems, because like a sore tooth or raveling thread, early intervention is key to the solution. Every couple has disagreements, and many work through them effectively on their own or with a pastor. But when a pattern of serious conflict starts to emerge, getting help sooner than later can mean big benefits down the road.

Here are five things you need to know about seeing a marriage counselor.

1. *It's not weird.* And it's not like TV.

Many people avoid going to therapy because they fear they'll have to lie on a couch and reveal secrets to someone who just nods a lot. They may also be afraid they'll have tearful and embarrassing "breakthroughs."

Others avoid the counselor's office because they believe it's too expensive or that it will take years to gain any benefit. But most therapy is actually brief—

and, when compared to alternatives like depression, divorce, or chronic anxiety, quite cost effective. For those who need it, counseling is not so much an expense as it is an investment.

Professional counseling is a relationship with safety built in. Professional ethics ensure you will be treated with respect and care. Conversations that occur in the counselor's office could happen as easily at home. The purpose is to affirm, not tear down, and the main task is equipping. As you talk, the counselor tailors his or her professional knowledge to your personal situation.

2. *Christians need Christian therapy.* For one who follows Christ, faith is central to every part of life. For this reason it's rarely wise for people to undergo secular therapy that isolates their emotions, thoughts, or behaviors from their faith. It's like using fertilizer; an all-purpose formula might help any plant a little, but for best results you have to consider whether you're growing tulips or tomatoes.

There is still prejudice against getting help after the wedding. Some churches have counselors on staff, but many Christians still hear, "Just pray about it."

When looking for the right counselor, a good starting place is your local church. Ask for referral to a counselor who's licensed and uses a Christ-centered, biblically sound approach. If your church staff doesn't know of a therapist, Focus on the Family has a referral network of Christian counselors. For information, call (719) 531-3400 and ask for the counseling department.

3. *Be prepared to deal with the whole picture.* Most of us tend to get preoccupied with one or two pieces of our lives. Even therapists run this risk, as they offer communication training to those who actually communicate very well with everyone but their spouse or children. Or a client may request anger management or assertiveness training—instead of addressing the reason he or she is aggressive or timid in the first place.

Often the "big picture" includes the influence of your family of origin. It makes no more sense to ignore that influence on your current conflicts than it would to polish the leaves on a tree suffering from root damage. A good counselor will help you look at your marital issues in context, exploring family systems as well as integrating your relationship with Christ.

4. *It's worth the sacrifice.* At first, the decision to seek counsel may seem to make your life more complicated. Identifying a good therapist, rearranging your

budget, securing child care if needed, and negotiating with a spouse may make sweeping your issues under the rug look appealing. But the longer you put off dealing with the real problems, the more complex they become.

As for cost, you may have a fancier vacation in five years if you put the "counseling money" in the vacation fund. But what good will it do if you aren't together to enjoy it?

5. *Deep wounds need deep treatment.* Some issues, such as abortion, addiction, or sexuality, have deep spiritual ramifications. These topics can cause shame and fear to well up dramatically and unexpectedly. They deserve the intensive care of a professional counselor trained to deal with them.

> Most therapy is actually brief—and, when compared to alternatives like depression, divorce, or chronic anxiety, quite cost effective.

Attending even the best weekend marriage conference to try to address deep wounds is like putting a fresh coat of paint on a house that has a faulty foundation. Marriages with deep, untreated issues can last for years, but collapse unexpectedly when the storm gets bad.

Should you and your spouse see a counselor? Consider the advice Pastor Dan gave Tamara: "Why not just go see this lady and find out what she thinks? You don't have to be crazy or getting a divorce to go to counseling. Sara and I have talked with her ourselves, when we had some tough issues to figure out. It may encourage you and Shane as it did for us to get a better perspective on things."

—Rob Jackson

What Makes a Marriage Last?

Many psychologists believe the greatest predictor of a lasting marriage is a commitment to marriage itself.

A sense of humor on the part of both spouses doesn't hurt, either.

Of course, just knowing this won't necessarily make your marriage last longer. But the right attitude *will* help ensure that your partnership is a lifelong one.

To maintain that attitude, remember that this experience called marriage is a relationship. It's not a possession. Yes, we do say "*my* wife" or "*my* husband," but that simply sets boundaries for others outside your marriage to recognize and respect. It's all yours—to protect and nourish. Look at your marriage as the longest relationship you'll ever experience on purpose.

Then take the measure of your faith. The stronger and livelier it is, the more positively it will influence the way you cherish each other. Faith produces gracious attitudes and kindly behavior. "So I say, live by the Spirit, and you will not gratify the desires of the sinful nature. . . . Since we live by the Spirit, let us keep in step with the Spirit" (Galatians 5:16, 25).

Next, determine that your marriage will last beyond today's sorry statistics. And well it can, by a mile—and more! Take comfort in knowing you're on God's side in the matter. "For this reason a man will leave his father and mother and be united to his wife, and they will become one flesh" (Genesis 2:24).

Naturally, the "how-tos" pop their insistent heads up along the pathway to marital fulfillment. How are you supposed to apply these principles in everyday life?

The following tips have been proven by many couples to be helpful:

1. *Go beyond words.* Smiles and hugs help your spouse know the "I love yous" are genuine. Something about the warmth of a caring embrace generates a sense of acceptance and worth.

> This experience called marriage is a relationship. Look at your marriage as the longest relationship you'll ever experience on purpose.

2. *Lower your weapons.* Emotional traffic flows more smoothly when you honor the "Yield" signs. Remember that no one is everlastingly right.

Jill and Fred told a counselor about their constant disagreements, especially over who started what. The therapist mildly commented that it seemed they were arguing about arguing. After a startled silence they admitted that was correct. The counselor soon was able to show them that their verbal bouts had one goal: to win!

When that happens, the "victor" ignores the wounds of the "loser." The result: increasingly hostile distance.

3. *Don't get smug.* Deny yourself the sour satisfaction of gloating. Without fail it creates festering resentment.

If you do start in that direction, apply the brakes at once and make a U-turn. It will take courage to make amends, but trouble can be opportunity wearing work clothes.

4. *Drop the barbs.* Cleverness is too tempting to be profitable, especially in the thick of a disagreement. It slides all too easily into the hurtfulness of sarcasm, which can be deadly to a healthy marriage.

Speaking of communication, that's an area that deserves special attention. Often counselors hear clients complain, "We just can't communicate!" Actually, that isn't precisely the case. We're all communicators; we can't *not* communicate!

We can be selective, even negative, in the messages we send—but send them we will. Given that fact, you can make strides toward discovering and using helpful signals with your spouse. As lifelong communicators, you can take inventory of the messages you're sending and select the ones which bring happy results. While you're at it, you can demonstrate a bit of wisdom by discarding the unproductive ones.

Give each other the benefit of the doubt as you proceed with caution and tact. Low-key suggestions are usually most helpful. Directness is okay, but sidestep bluntness. And avoid communication styles like the following.

1. *A + B (accuse and blame).* This is an attempt to shift responsibility and a refusal to accept accountability. It's infuriating. A common scenario goes something like this: "Well, if you were the spouse I need you to be, then I wouldn't have to look somewhere else." Another variation plays out as, "If you

> Determine that your marriage will last beyond today's sorry statistics. Take comfort in knowing you're on God's side in the matter.

treated me better, I'd feel more like doing what you ask." Note the consistent use of "If you . . ."

2. *Inanity.* This avoids the subject and leaves your mate as frustrated as if he or she were trying to nail Jell-O to a wall! George Burns' wife, Gracie Allen, had the rare talent to make this sort of behavior humorous. The rest of us don't. Take a typical instance: Doug's exasperated over a flat tire when it's time to leave for work; Vanessa chirps, "Don't the tires on the Browns' new SUV look great?"

3. *I did this for you.* This employs witty but phony justification for actions that are self-serving or uncaring. The bills aren't paid, but Wayne shows up with a snappy sports car and says to his wife, "This red goes just great with your hair!"

> Emotional traffic flows more smoothly when you honor the "Yield" signs. Remember that no one is everlastingly right.

4. *The lockout.* He—and it is more often the husband—either storms from the scene or uses stony silence as punishment and refusal to allow access to himself. Thus he defeats any realistic hope of settling differences.

5. *How could you?* Outraged innocence and super-sensitive righteousness are used to shut down any chance of movement toward resolving issues. The supposed victim's voice might quaver as she wipes away a tear: "How on earth could you ever say such a thing?"

None of this is all that complicated. But husbands and wives who've made a journey of many years together know that theirs is a marriage of more than convenience; it's a commitment. Divorce was never considered an option.

Welcome to the world of the fulfilling partnership called marriage. Your wedding vows will remain bright and buoyant as you understand your goals and relish pursuing them together. And as you do, remember the wisdom of this traditional Irish ditty:

A cup o' kindness
A cup o' cheer
Wears well, wears well
Throughout the year.

—SAM KENNEDY

Recommended Resources

There are many helpful books and other resources to guide you through the first five years of marriage. Check your local bookstore for the following:

Becoming One: Emotionally, Spiritually, Sexually by Joe Beam (Howard Publishing, 2003)

Boundaries in Marriage by Dr. Henry Cloud and Dr. John Townsend (Zondervan, 2002)

The DNA of Relationships by Gary Smalley (Tyndale House Publishers, 2004)

For Women Only by Shaunti Feldhahn (Multnomah, 2004)

The Gift of Sex: A Guide to Sexual Fulfillment by Clifford L. Penner and Joyce J. Penner (W Publishing Group, 2003)

Great Expectations: An Interactive Guide to Your First Year of Marriage by Toben and Joanne Heim (NavPress, 2000)

Healing the Hurt in Your Marriage by Dr. Gary and Barbara Rosberg (Focus on the Family/Tyndale House Publishers, 2004)

Hedges: Loving Your Marriage Enough to Protect It by Jerry B. Jenkins (Crossway Books, 2005)

Hidden Keys of a Loving, Lasting Marriage by Gary Smalley and Norma Smalley (Zondervan, 1993)

His Needs, Her Needs: Building an Affair-Proof Marriage by Willard F. Harley, Jr. (Monarch Books, 1994)

How Do You Say, "I Love You"? by Judson Swihart (InterVarsity Press, 1977)

The Language of Love by Gary Smalley and John Trent, Ph.D. (Focus on the Family/Tyndale House Publishing, 2006)

Love and Respect by Dr. Emerson Eggerichs (Integrity Publishers, 2004)

Love for a Lifetime by Dr. James Dobson (Multnomah, 2004)

Love Must Be Tough: New Hope for Families in Crisis by Dr. James Dobson (Multnomah, 2004)

The Marriage Masterpiece by Al Janssen (Focus on the Family/Tyndale House Publishing, 2001)

The Most Important Year in a Woman's Life/The Most Important Year in a Man's Life by Robert Wolgemuth, Bobbie Wolgemuth, Mark DeVries, and Susan DeVries (Zondervan, 2003)

Sacred Marriage by Gary Thomas (Zondervan, 2002)

Saving Your Marriage Before It Starts by Les and Leslie Parrott (Zondervan, 1995)

Surviving a Spiritual Mismatch in Marriage by Lee and Leslie Strobel (Zondervan, 2002)

The following booklets and recordings are available from Focus on the Family (call 1-800-A-FAMILY):

Accepting Your Mate's Differences by Dr. Kevin Leman (Focus on the Family broadcast CD192)

Building a Marriage That Lasts by Dr. James Dobson (Focus on the Family booklet LF154)

Learning to Communicate by Gary Smalley and John Trent (Focus on the Family broadcast CD111)

Nothing to Hide by Joann Condie (Focus on the Family booklet F00038T)

Notes

Introduction: Why Are the First Five Years So Important?

1. Ted L. Houston, John P. Caughlin, Renate M. Houts, Shanna E. Smith, and Laura J. George, "The Connubial Crucible: Newlywed Years as Predictors of Marital Delight, Distress and Divorce," (*Journal of Personality and Social Psychology*, 2001), pp. 80, 237-252.

Why Isn't My "Blended" Marriage Blending?

1. Ron Deal, *The Smart Step-Family* (Minneapolis: Bethany House Publishers, 2002), p. 64.

Did I Marry the Wrong Person?

1. Erich Fromm, *The Art of Loving* (New York: Harper Perennial, 2000), p. 52.
2. Dr. James Dobson, *Romantic Love* (Ventura, California: Regal Books, 2004), p. 28.

How Much Should We Give?

1. The Barna Group, "Tithing Down 62 Percent in the Past Year" (*The Barna Update*, May 19, 2003), found at www.barna.org.

What If My Spouse Abuses Me?

1. Lisa Brock, "Surviving Abuse," found at www.troubledwith.com.

How Can Faith Keep Us Together?

1. Glenn Stanton, "The Role Faith Plays in Marriage and the Likelihood of Divorce," (Focus on Social Issues, July 8, 2005), found at http://family.org/cforum/fosi/marriage/divorce/a0037068.cfm.
2. W. Bradford Wilcox, "The Cultural Contradictions of Mainline Family Ideology and Practice," publication pending.

When Should We Have Children, and How Many?

1. Dr. David Barad, "Age and Female Fertility," found at the Web site of the American Fertility Association (www.theafa.org).

2. Dr. Richard Scott, Jr., and Pamela Madsen, "What Mother Didn't Tell You about Fertility . . . Because No One Ever Told Her," found at the Web site of the American Fertility Association.
3. Barad, "Age and Female Fertility."

Is It Okay Not to Have Kids?

1. Candice Z. Watters, "Defending 'The Cost of Delaying Marriage,'" *Boundless* webzine (http://www.boundless.org/2005/articles/a0001145.cfm).

What About Adoption?

1. John and Sylvia Van Regenmorter, *When the Cradle Is Empty* (Wheaton, Illinois: Tyndale House Publishers/Focus on the Family, 2004), pp. 141-142.

What Can We Do About Postpartum Depression?

1. Dr. Paul C. Reisser, et al, *Complete Book of Baby and Child Care* (Wheaton, Illinois: Tyndale House Publishers/Focus on the Family, 1997), p. 109.
2. News release, "Postpartum Mood Disorders Can Cause Death and Ruin Lives" (National Depressive and Manic-Depressive Association, May 6, 2002), p. 1.

How Can We Get a Break from the Kids?

1. Sue Shellenbarger, "New Parents Experience More Conflict and Debt," *Wall Street Journal*, December 16, 2004. Found at http://archives.his.com/smartmarriages/2004-December/msg00018.html. Quoting Jean Twenge, San Diego State University, based on a survey of 90 studies of 31,000 married people.

Are We Falling Out of Love?

1. Dorothy Tennov, *Love and Limerence* (Lanham, Maryland: Scarborough House, 1999).

How Can We Keep Romance Alive?

1. Gary and Norma Smalley, *It Takes Two to Tango* (Colorado Springs: Focus on the Family, 1997), p. 25.

Is It Ever Too Late for a Marriage?

1. Dr. James Dobson, *Complete Marriage and Family Home Reference Guide* (Wheaton, Illinois: Tyndale House Publishers, 2000), pp. 351-352.
2. Ibid., p. 362.

Note: Listing of Web sites does not constitute blanket endorsement or complete agreement by Focus on the Family with information or resources offered at or through those sites.

Index

A

abortion 22, 159, 185, 349, 366-367, 416

abortifacient 156

Abraham 52, 280

abstinence 176-177

abuse
>dealing with 275-276, 306, 410
>memories of 21-23, 184-189
>types 306

acceptance
>by in-law 326-327
>by others 382, 384
>of children 367
>of in-law 326
>of spouse 232, 237, 297, 417

accidents 35, 125, 301, 365, 388

Adam and Eve 74-75, 239, 334

addiction 159, 162, 180, 214, 372, 416

adjustment
>to blended family 57-59
>to children 374
>to circumstances 58, 61, 90, 387
>to cultural differences 247
>to in-laws 326
>to marriage 1-2, 17-20, 39-41
>to spouse 17, 65, 81, 96

adoption 22, 336, 339, 347, 350, 351-354

adoptive families 353

adultery
>consequences of 306
>and pornography 162
>preventing 397-399

anger 309, 328, 336, 345, 365
>managing 415

apology 227 (also see forgiveness)

arguing 73, 81, 225, 242, 257, 266, 272, 418

B

babies 85, 89, 221, 298, 323, 345, 348, 360

babysitter 332, 374-375, 386, 392

bankruptcy 129

Barone, Frank and Marie 202-203

Begg, Alistair 4

Bethany Christian Services 346, 353

Bible reading 285-286, 302

birth control 155-157, 298

bitterness 36, 67-68, 209, 234, 263-265, 267, 281

blended family 57-59, 100-103

body image 165, 347

bonding
>between parent and child 352, 360
>between spouses 208, 298, 357

boundaries 78, 253, 309-310, 315, 317, 324, 379, 397-398, 417, 421
Broersma, Margaret 102
budget
    creating 244-246, 342, 375, 391, 416
    reasons for 253, 272, 335-336, 340

C

Calhoun, Dr. Byron 362
Cesarean section 360
changing your spouse 19-20, 35, 84, 238, 313, 355, 396, 408
Chapman, Gary 29
childbirth
    experience of 338, 359
    preparing for 360
child care 85, 324, 332
    challenges of 333, 357, 365, 374
    day care facilities 315, 385-388
    responsibility for 157
children
    childbearing decisions 336, 338-339
    effects on marriage 15, 27
    raising 28, 35, 55, 57, 84-85, 98
    with special needs 352, 365-369
chores 10-11, 73, 80-82, 200, 225, 271, 297, 371
Christ-centered home 288-291

Christian education (see spiritual training)
Christmas 134, 287, 312-314, 323, 375
church
    choice of 4, 244, 247, 282-284
    volunteering in 52, 87, 92, 206-207
    benefits of attending 279-280
Cloninger, Claire 17
college 43, 45, 87-89, 116, 118, 150, 184, 216, 313, 331, 404
commitment
    effect on marriage 10, 15, 20, 44, 55-56, 68, 77, 79, 181, 184, 197, 226, 232, 264, 268, 343, 391, 405, 417, 419
    sources of 60-61, 249, 279, 281, 293, 300, 304-305, 317, 410
communication
    challenges 64, 127, 181, 194, 199-201
    improving 57, 78, 116, 128, 130, 157, 159, 163, 165, 196-197
    types of 12, 193, 195, 202-205, 206-208, 209-211, 212-215, 216-218, 219-221
comparisons
    of spouse with parent or ex-spouse 55, 103
    to other marriages 44

condoms 155-156

conflict

    avoidance 81-82, 84, 126, 132, 209, 212

    inevitability of 59, 114, 199

    overreaction 68, 160, 236

    resolving 12, 36, 102, 111, 133, 162, 183, 210-211, 225-276

confrontation 160

    need for 179

    methods of 9, 227

contraceptives (also see birth control) 155-157, 343

counseling

    genetic 339, 344

    methods of 48, 409

    need for 40, 47, 100-102, 117, 204, 211, 225, 261, 264, 276, 284

    premarital 14, 39, 43, 68, 175, 286, 312

    value of 25, 58, 61, 81, 98, 188, 408, 412-416

courtship 4, 39-41, 43, 45-50, 61, 88, 178, 391

credit cards 123-130, 137, 141

criticism 162, 169, 182, 208, 289

    excessive 25, 75, 273

    responding to 203

Crown Financial Ministries 112

cruelty 32

cultural influences 279

    family background 63, 247-251

    societal 159, 288, 363

    racial 247, 250

cynicism 67, 290

D

dating (also see courtship) 2-4, 28, 32, 39, 45, 48-49, 54, 61, 165, 174, 216, 233, 247, 250, 332, 393, 397

David 52, 205, 411

Deal, Ron L. 102

debt

    avoiding 112-113, 123-126, 132, 137

    overcoming 12, 114, 116, 127-130, 133, 141, 143-144

decisions 11, 39-40, 54, 62, 93-94, 116, 119, 144, 151, 212-213, 244-246, 256, 315-316, 324, 337, 372, 378, 383, 406

De Lamater, John D. 158

denial 40, 240

dependency 398

depression 89, 108, 138, 249, 263, 300-301, 336, 367, 415

    overcoming 301

    postpartum 362-364, 408

devotions

    for couples 405

    for families 244, 292, 378

differences 3, 12, 159, 194, 200, 247-251, 255, 296-298, 304-306, 313, 320, 370, 401, 419

    between sexes 161-163, 164-167, 168-170, 171-173, 174-177, 242

between spouses 2, 27-30,
31-33, 34-36, 43, 45, 56,
63-64, 81, 123, 225, 230,
232, 258, 282-284
disability
of child 365-369
of spouse 87, 403
disagreements 309, 313, 370-373,
414-419
acknowledging 3, 225-228
resolving 108, 229-232,
239-243, 249, 256-262
disappointment 2, 15, 32, 47, 66,
68, 132, 135, 218, 221, 302,
313, 351, 365-369, 400
discipline 27, 101, 113, 121, 124,
126, 147, 231, 247, 275, 371,
388
dishonesty (also see lying) 178
disrespect 179, 310, 317
divorce 2, 9, 20, 31, 63, 100, 161,
226-227, 243, 259, 260, 276,
279, 304-305, 398, 400, 408,
410, 414-416, 419
Dobson, Dr. James 29, 61, 285,
287, 303, 410
Dobson, Shirley 29, 287
doctor 96-97, 144, 155, 301, 343,
346, 348-350, 356-357, 360-
361, 363-364, 365, 409
domination 77, 92
doubt 356, 418
about faith 90, 168, 293, 300
about marrying the "right"
spouse 9, 21-22, 30,
58-59, 178, 193

dreams
during sleep 34, 39, 47,
124, 140
for the future 11-12, 17, 78,
90, 143, 345, 381
"drifting apart" 255, 400-402

E

education
for children 150
for spouses 51, 90, 100,
207, 325
Elijah 300-303
emotions 178, 185-186, 209-211,
225, 332, 399, 410, 415
expressing 45, 58, 178, 194,
351
stifling 205, 300, 363
taking responsibility for
260, 275, 401
employment 84, 90, 174
engagement 9-13, 39-41, 45-50
entertainment 111, 113
Esau 80
ethnicity 247-251
exercise 12, 165, 347
expectations 1, 39-69, 233, 250,
313-314, 363
disappointment of 3-4,
324
expressing 10-13, 83-84,
197, 212, 354, 365
realism 2, 102-103, 157-
159, 176, 182, 208, 258,
286, 310-311, 326, 332,
359, 367, 405

F

faith 87, 143, 147, 220, 230, 381, 383, 403-406, 410-413
  challenges to 247, 282, 299-303, 304-306, 309, 320-322
  role in marriage 10, 15, 60, 90, 92-95, 279-281, 285-287, 414-419
  strengthening 172, 188, 292-295, 366, 377-380
family 12-13, 28, 39, 57-59, 68, 129, 147, 180-181, 232, 289
  extended 3, 10, 43-44, 125, 132-135, 140-145, 151, 187, 207, 225, 230, 247-251, 280, 288, 293, 309-314
  relationships 52, 63, 74-79, 80-82, 87-95, 100-103, 117-119, 136-139, 200, 212, 230, 233, 244-246, 259, 264, 283, 286, 292
  starting a 155-157, 176, 216
Family Center on Technology and Disability 368
fantasy 45, 162, 187
fathers 9, 19, 74, 90, 108, 212, 216, 263-264, 315, 322, 367
  anxieties of 85-86, 200, 209-210, 343
  comparison with 44, 52, 54-56, 77, 80, 184, 194, 204, 273
  influence of 54, 371, 241
fatigue 181, 356

fear 4, 56, 85, 111-112, 117-118, 132, 162, 178-179, 182, 185, 221, 234, 246, 258-259, 261-262, 264, 268, 275, 280, 365-369
  of counseling 187, 414-416
  of having married the wrong spouse 31, 193
  of losing spouse 9, 255
  during pregnancy 359-361
  of pregnancy 176, 340
feelings (also see emotions) 1, 13, 16-18, 22, 43-44, 50, 57, 61, 64, 67-68, 78, 89-90, 101-102, 144, 163, 166, 176, 178, 182, 185, 194
female 16, 54, 80-81
  emotional traits 200, 248
  physical traits 171, 337, 347
fighting 36, 58, 162, 213, 225-228, 256
finances (also see money) 10, 40, 48, 80, 88-89, 107-110, 114-122, 127-130, 138, 212, 218, 230, 233, 244-245, 249, 272, 315, 324, 332, 335, 343-344
forgiveness 280-281
  giving 68, 227, 241, 263-265, 388
  receiving 23, 266-269
freedom 17-20, 31, 35, 58, 65, 75, 94, 107-108, 111-113, 116, 119, 132, 169, 185, 203, 252-254, 259, 265, 271, 316, 335, 343, 366-367, 372, 379
friendship 172, 252-254, 333

Fromm, Erich 61
frustration
    causes of 36, 127-128, 135
    dealing with 1-2, 33, 75, 173, 201, 211, 270, 309, 327, 345, 412
fun 11-12, 29, 39, 82, 101, 131-135, 164, 166, 195, 197, 208, 218, 232-233, 255, 378
future 1, 32, 129, 250, 264, 345
    healthy view of 90, 141, 143-144, 160, 180, 212, 227, 240, 367
    planning for 23, 39, 109, 115-116, 146,151, 261, 276, 289-290, 322, 339, 344, 354, 371, 376, 381

G

gambling 252, 273, 320
giving 16, 22, 25, 30, 33, 44, 85, 111-115, 120-122, 130, 141, 195, 201, 216, 262, 264, 297, 314, 328, 353, 355, 359, 364, 373, 380, 396
goals 317, 378, 406, 419
    for children 383
    financial 108-110, 117-119, 126-130, 148, 149-151, 340
    setting 12, 78, 89-90, 137, 172, 207-208, 256
God 67
    commands for couples 14, 44, 52-53, 62-64, 68, 73-79
    role in marriage 1, 3, 10, 17-20, 23, 25, 31-33, 36, 41
grief 18, 327, 345, 351
growth
    in relationship 2, 35, 68, 133, 142, 168, 239, 249, 264, 366-367
    spiritual 98, 283, 285, 290, 292-295, 378-379
guidance 78, 98, 112, 142, 180, 185, 268, 302, 341, 350, 412
guilt 16, 21, 23, 59, 103, 111, 176, 184-185, 310, 363, 385, 409

H

habits
    establishing healthy 20, 112, 114, 125, 166, 302, 383
    extinguishing unwanted 61, 116, 125, 129, 166, 175, 213, 394
    living with spouse's 34-36, 39, 42, 49, 55, 233, 236-238, 316
Harley, Willard F., Jr. 29
healing
    of relationship 23, 33, 179-180, 185-186, 188, 226, 237, 265-269, 275, 289, 293, 346, 411
health 113, 202, 258-259, 265, 301-302, 349-350, 359, 360
    challenges in marriage 62, 94, 234, 254, 404

mental xiv-xvii, 5, 265, 302, 363, 408

of relationship 11-12, 108-109, 114-115, 159-160

Hegstrom, Paul 273

heritage 339-340, 380

holidays 225, 241, 247, 312-314

Holt International Children's Services 353

Holy Spirit 185, 195, 208, 213-214, 217, 304, 392, 396

home 31, 36, 46, 54, 56, 136-139, 170, 181, 200, 206, 217, 233-234, 237, 249, 253, 264, 266, 272, 283, 286, 298-299, 305-306, 313

    buying 119, 125, 129, 140-146, 245

    establishing 1, 17, 39-40, 77, 79, 83-91, 207, 252, 288-291

    homemaking 24, 127, 174, 214, 248

    maintaining 10-11, 28, 58, 66-67, 73-76, 80-82, 113, 117

    responsibilities 19, 92-99, 172, 292-294

    value of 288-291

honesty 9, 14-16, 22, 294

humor 26, 67, 197, 257, 289, 327-328, 417

husband

    relating to 48-50, 54-56, 168-170

    role of 77-96

Huston, Dr. Ted 1

Hyde, Janet Shibley 158

I

illness

    mental (see psychological problems)

    physical (see medical problems)

immaturity 66

    effects of 16

    overcoming 253, 324

independence

    from parents 315-319, 323-325

    in a marriage 17-20

infatuation 394

infertility 339, 345-351

    causes of 349-350

    effects of 345-346, 351, 354

    treatment 346-347

infidelity

    avoiding 397-399

    consequences of 265-269, 410

in-laws 3, 11

    faith and 320-322

    problems with 247, 250, 280, 312-319, 323-327

    relating to 309-311

insecurity 16, 21-22, 109, 193, 196, 253-254

insensitivity 202-204

Internet 134, 177-180, 397

intimacy
    developing 20, 165-166,
        169, 184-186, 209-210,
        228, 239, 265, 298, 317,
        376, 399
    need for 29, 160, 171-172,
        357, 375
intercourse
    during pregnancy 357
    frequency of 158-160
    pain during 164-167
    satisfaction with 168-173
interest
    earning financial 119, 146-
        151
    in sexual relations 158-160,
        174-177
    paying financial 125, 128,
        141-142, 144
intrauterine device (IUD) 155
investing 129, 133
    benefits of 118
    recommendations for 140-
        148
    timing of 149-151
in vitro fertilization 349-350

J
Jacob 80
Jealousy 16, 230
Jesus Christ 19, 32, 49, 52, 59,
    67, 74, 79, 93-94, 108, 111,
    162, 170, 172, 185, 188,
    203-205, 214, 221, 237, 245,
    252-253, 263, 267, 279, 281,
    283, 285, 288-291, 293-294,
    301-306, 314, 320-321, 357,
    359, 379, 391, 415
Johnson, Barbara 365
journaling 210-211, 401

K
Keller, Helen 350
King Lemuel 53

L
language
    barriers between cultures
        249
    differences between sexes
        194, 199
leadership 57, 74, 78, 92-94, 283
legal issues
    in adoption 352-354
    in cases of abuse 275
    in finances 129, 143
limits 12, 64, 115, 197, 283, 309
loans
    mortgage 125, 140, 141,
        144
loneliness 249, 346
love
    "falling" in and out of 3,
        136, 206, 391
    nature of 19, 53, 61, 78, 179
    types 29, 49, 391-392, 394
lying 14, 16

M
male
    emotional traits 49, 137,
        168-169, 221, 355

physical traits 165, 171-
172, 181, 199, 209
manipulation 64, 242, 310-311
marriage
creation of 417
longevity of 12, 100-101, 391
spiritual symbolism of 10,
17-20, 49
stages of 25, 41, 102, 344
materialism 114, 121, 132
medical problems
of children 249, 298
of spouse 12, 15, 150, 234,
339, 403
medication 349, 359, 363, 407
memories 100, 268
mentors
for children 298
in marriage 98, 245, 286,
302
Miller, Wiley 193
money
attitudes about 10, 87-91,
132, 147
borrowing 115, 123-126, 144
budgeting 111-113
clashes over 107-110
giving 120-122
investing 146-148, 150
saving 109, 111, 117-119
spending 107-110, 111,
114-116
moods
and postpartum depression
362-364, 408
and pregnancy 363

and psychological problems
407-409
morality 36, 155, 162, 279, 385
mothers
anxieties of 359, 363, 375
comparison with 51
influence of 221, 380
Mothers of Preschoolers 380
movies 159, 392, 397
Myers-Briggs Type Indicator 29

N
name-calling 64, 230, 231
National Adoption Information
Clearinghouse 354
National Center on Birth Defects
and Developmental Disabilities
369
Navigators, The 303
needs 29
of husbands 169, 209
of wives 78, 172, 283, 364
newborns 360
Norplant 156
North American Council on
Adoptable Children 354

O
overprotection 326, 371
oversensitivity 31, 203, 236, 327
overwork 77

P
pain 58, 132, 185, 359, 361
parenting
challenges of 3, 29, 331, 372

effects on marriage 332
goals in 371
preparing for 157, 331,
333, 358
past
forgiving 68, 263-265, 267
recovering from 180, 184-
186
revealing 14-16, 21, 23
Paul 4, 33, 64, 74, 133, 234, 241,
245, 253, 263, 296, 304, 305,
412
personality
adjusting to 31-33, 36
role in conflict 98, 247
understanding 29, 195
physician (see doctor)
planning
family 102, 156, 176, 335
financial 111-113, 119,
146, 149
legal 151
Popenoe, David 279
pornography 162, 166, 177-180,
397
postpartum depression (see
depression)
power
and control 162, 268, 273
struggles between spouses
34, 75, 265
prayer 180, 195, 213, 262, 285-
287, 320-321, 357, 378
pregnancy 3, 343, 347, 355-358,
362

premarital counseling (see
counseling)
pride 245, 249, 281, 412
privacy
and personal history 210
and sexual intimacy 159,
181-183
profanity 273
Proverbs 31 woman 3, 53, 80
psychological problems
and getting help for spouse
407-409
and motherhood 362-364

R
racial differences 247-251
reading
with children 378
with spouse 25, 188, 286
reconciliation 226, 271, 412
rejection 23, 203
relationship 4, 10-11, 29, 101,
129, 227, 250, 275, 283, 332,
364, 382, 398
religion
and divorce rates 279
role in marriage 294, 383
remarriage 58-59, 100-101
resentment 256, 265, 395, 418
RESOLVE 346
respect 55, 101, 169, 253, 317,
324
responsibility 85, 87, 92, 157,
253, 283
retirement 147-148, 150

ridicule 218, 274

role models

    and upbringing 51, 54, 194, 298, 373

    for couples 98, 245, 286, 302

    providing 148, 370

roles

    and gender 73, 77, 97

    in child care 83-86

    in domestic tasks 10, 80-82

    in spiritual leadership 92-95

romance 168, 171

    expectations 10, 11, 51, 73, 84, 92, 96, 100

    maintaining 75

Rooney, Mickey 60

Rudner, Rita 17

S

safety

    and abuse 230, 264, 275-276, 318, 407

    in marital relationship 23, 94, 170, 172

salvation

    of children 377-380

    of in-laws 320-322

    of spouse 292-295, 299-306

Samson 381

Sarah 280

saving

    reducing expenses 115, 124-125

setting funds aside 111, 118, 123, 146

school 128, 141, 381, 383

self-control 78, 102, 177, 289, 395

self-esteem 137, 203, 346

selfishness 15, 120, 147, 256, 338, 372

separation 275-276, 323

service 93, 275, 289, 296-297

sex

    and parenting 181-183, 357

    and temptation 170, 178-179, 397-398

    and therapy 162, 180, 185-189

    dissatisfaction with 161-163

    expectations in 3, 11, 158-167

    spiritual significance of 170, 416

sexes, differences between

    in communication 12, 194, 199-201, 304

    in needs 29, 169-173

    in roles 10, 73, 81, 92, 98

sexual abuse (see abuse)

Simpson, Homer 52

sin 93, 179, 187, 228, 234, 294, 398, 409

single parents 68, 214, 387

singleness 17, 40, 48, 93, 252

Smalley, Gary and Norma 395, 421-422

Social Security 121, 149
spending 107-119, 123-127, 131-135
spiritual concerns
    differences between spouses 58, 92-95, 283, 292-294, 304-306
    differences with in-laws 320-322
    regarding children 377-380
spiritual training 377-380
spouse
    confronting 35-36, 108, 212-215, 271
    getting to know 9-13, 26, 161-163, 194
    honoring 231, 253, 395
Spurgeon, Charles 131
Stanley, Scott 279
Stanton, Glenn 279
Stepping Stones 346
stress
    dealing with 81, 138
    effects on marriage 75, 127, 248
    reducing 58, 111, 347
Strobel, Lee 303, 422
Stull, Donald 140
submission 74-75
substance abuse 367
success
    for children 381-384
    in marriage 61, 251, 279
suicide 299, 362, 408
Swihart, Dr. Judson 201, 421

T
Taylor, Hudson 320
Taylor-Johnson Temperament Analysis 29
Tennov, Dorothy 391
Thanksgiving 312-313
therapy (see counseling)
time
    away from children 183, 213, 332, 375-376
    for conversation 24-26, 181, 193-194, 197, 207-208
    to develop intimacy 18-20, 159, 164-166
tithing 120-122
tradition
    and culture 370
    family 10, 80, 310, 312-314
trauma
    adult 185
    childhood 162, 408
trust
    broken 11, 55, 133, 179, 263-264
    establishing 14-15, 102, 267

U
understanding
    your spouse 9-10, 171, 182, 210, 237
    yourself 204
unemployment
    effects of 137
    surviving 118, 136-139

V

values

clashes of 248, 252, 321

shared between spouses 279

teaching to children 290, 352, 379, 385

Van Regenmorter, John and Sylvia 350-351

verbal abuse (see abuse)

violence 229, 261, 273-275, 318

W

Watters, Steve 338

wife

relating to 12, 14, 27, 45-47, 78, 160-161, 171, 201, 234, 355-358

role of 10-12, 73-75, 80-82, 87-88, 92-94, 96-100, 244-245, 283

Wilcox, Brad 279

Wolfe, Glynn DeMoss 60

work 10, 75, 77, 79, 81-91, 136, 254, 297, 385, 387

Y

Yancey, Philip 302

FOCUS ON THE FAMILY®

Welcome to the family!

Whether you purchased this book, borrowed it, or received it as a gift, we're glad you're reading it. It's just one of the many helpful, encouraging, and biblically based resources produced by Focus on the Family for people in all stages of life.

Focus began in 1977 with the vision of one man, Dr. James Dobson, a licensed psychologist and author of numerous best-selling books on marriage, parenting, and family. Alarmed by the societal, political, and economic pressures that were threatening the existence of the American family, Dr. Dobson founded Focus on the Family with one employee and a once-a-week radio broadcast aired on 36 stations.

Now an international organization reaching millions of people daily, Focus on the Family is dedicated to preserving values and strengthening and encouraging families through the life-changing message of Jesus Christ.

- -

Focus on the Family Magazines

These faith-building, character-developing publications address the interests, issues, concerns, and challenges faced by every member of your family from preschool through the senior years.

Focus on the Family
Citizen®
U.S. news issues

Focus on the Family
Clubhouse Jr.™
Ages 4 to 8

Focus on the Family
Clubhouse™
Ages 8 to 12

Breakaway®
Teen guys

Brio®
Teen girls
12 to 16

**Brio &
Beyond**®
Teen girls
16 to 19

Plugged In®
Reviews movies,
music, TV

FOR MORE INFORMATION

Online:
Log on to www.family.org
In Canada, log on to
www.focusonthefamily.ca

Phone:
Call toll free: (800) A-FAMILY
In Canada, call toll free:
(800) 661-9800

More Great Resources
from Focus on the Family®

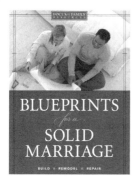

Blueprints for a Solid Marriage
by Dr. Steve Stephens

Light remodeling, minor repair, or major reconstruction? Every marriage could benefit from some fun, extracurricular activities to keep the romance alive. *Blueprints for a Solid Marriage* helps time-strapped couples quickly assess and enhance their relationships with engaging stories and a detailed plan for "marriage improvement projects."

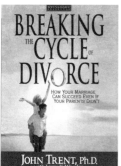

Breaking the Cycle of Divorce
by John Trent, Ph.D. with Larry K. Weeden

In an age when the pressures on marriage are heavier than ever, and divorce is more accepted and easier to obtain, marriages seem to fail as often as they succeed. As an adult child of divorce, Dr. John Trent offers insights into why adult children of divorce tend to repeat their parents' mistakes and provides a plan for a strong, lifelong marriage.

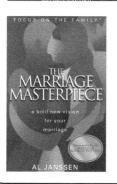

The Marriage Masterpiece
by Al Janssen

Like a long-forgotten work of art, marriage is often undervalued and unappreciated. But beneath the grime, discover the beautiful masterpiece designed for you and your mate by God Himself.

FOR MORE INFORMATION

Online:
Log on to www.family.org
In Canada, log on to
www.focusonthefamily.ca.

Phone:
Call toll free: (800) A-FAMILY
In Canada, call toll free:
(800) 661-9800.

BP06XP1